MUSIC IN THE SEVENTEENTH CENTURY

LORENZO BIANCONI

TRANSLATED BY DAVID BRYANT

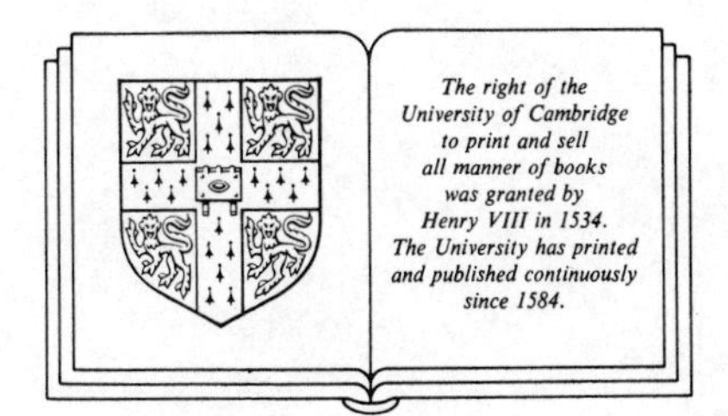

CAMBRIDGE UNIVERSITY PRESS

CAMBRIDGE
NEW YORK NEW ROCHELLE MELBOURNE SYDNEY

Published by the Press Syndicate of the University of Cambridge
The Pitt Building, Trumpington Street, Cambridge CB2 1RP
32 East 57th Street, New York, NY 10022, USA
10 Stamford Road, Oakleigh, Melbourne 3166, Australia

Originally published in Italian as *Il seicento*
by Edizioni di Torino, Turin, 1982 and

First published in English by Cambridge University Press 1987
as *Music in the Seventeenth Century*

Printed in Great Britain at the University Press, Cambridge

British Library cataloguing in publication data

Bianconi, Lorenzo
Music in the seventeenth century.
1. Music – Italy – History – 17th century
I. Title II. Il Seicento. *English*
781.745 ML290.2

Library of Congress cataloguing in publication data

Bianconi, Lorenzo.
Music in the seventeenth century.
Translation of: Il Seicento.
Bibliography.
Includes index.
1. Music – Italy – 17th century – History and criticism.
I. Title.
ML290.2.B513 1987 780′.947 87–11685

ISBN 0 521 26290 9 hard covers
ISBN 0 521 26915 6 paperback

WD

Contents

Author's preface to the English edition

As one British reviewer has rightly observed, the present volume 'unashamedly concentrates on Italian music'. The Seicento, in my opinion, is the final century in the history of European music for which an Italian-oriented approach may not *ipso facto* be defined as misplaced. Italy – and Italy alone – undeniably provides the backcloth for a number of the principal innovations, events and personalities of the period: the 'invention' of opera and the institution of the first public theatres, the beginnings and development of a modern concept of 'concerto', the very name of Monteverdi (himself the most celebrated of a series of major figures who span the century as a whole). In musical terms, seventeenth-century Italy is undoubtedly a centre – or, rather, a whole series of centres – of European significance. This is amply demonstrated by the interest and enthusiasm of northern Europeans – simple tourists or composers of renown (the prime example is Schütz) – for all kinds of musical innovation of Italian derivation, as also by the rate of flow of Italian musicians and musical manuscripts towards the courts and major cities of northern Europe. Seventeenth-century Italy, however, can no longer be described – contrary to the situation in the previous century – as the musical centre of Europe, but rather as one of several centres. Earlier migratory trends are reversed. No longer does the foreign musician settle and rise to fame on Italian soil; rather, Italy is increasingly afflicted by an over-production (albeit excellent in kind) of local manpower and its exportation and 'commercialization' in the north. This is symptomatic not only of the vigour of contemporary Italian musical life but also of an inherent weakness and increasingly peripheral nature which, with the sole exception of opera, finds definitive confirmation in eighteenth- and nineteenth-century developments. Yet the symptoms of this reorganization of European musical geography – a reorganization which, by 1700, can be regarded as all but complete – appear all the more dramatically in cases where the modern historian attempts to preserve that same Italian-oriented outlook which, a mere century before, had been taken for granted by one and all. In other words: as author of the present study, I have pushed my own personal inclinations in this field to the point of consciously embracing an attitude which any seventeenth-century Italian musician would automatically have assumed: a blissful unawareness of musical activities beyond the Alps, matched only by disconcerted surprise on emigration to foreign parts (an event of increasing occurrence as the century wears on) at the artistic vitality of Paris, London, Dresden, Vienna and other northern centres. I can only hope that the adoption of this not altogether traditional – yet historically plausible – perspective will provide some compensation in the eyes of English-speaking readers for the absence from these pages of such figures as the great John Dowland.

Direct discussion of the instrumental repertory, now generally regarded as providing what ranks among the great innovations of seventeenth-century music, has been limited to few pages only. It would, indeed, be difficult to overestimate the importance of the first thoroughgoing attempts – part and parcel of the history of seventeenth-century music – to create a musical structure which might be capable of its own separate existence (independently of all questions of text): a musical discourse which alone provides the laws, logic and, indeed, *raison d'être* for its own intrinsic morphology, phrasing and syntax (laws which themselves can be defined as those of tonal harmony and related rhythmic and metrical organization). Enormous is the benefit for instrumental music. The question, however, is more radical in kind; it involves not just the instrumental repertory but rather the whole complex of contemporary stylistic problems – above all, with regard to vocal music (particularly affected by the very diversity between verbal and musical structures). In 'practical' and statistical terms, the role of seventeenth-century instrumental music is essentially modest and of minority significance – not at all what its relatively profuse cultivation on the part of modern 'baroque' musicians would suggest.

Finally, the reader will not be unduly surprised if, contrary to all expectations and, indeed, scholarly traditions, the term 'baroque' finds no further place in the vocabulary of the present study. In contrast to certain other non-musical terms (e.g., 'classicism') which, if nothing else, can boast a long history of accepted usage in musical literature, the stylistic and historiographical concept of 'baroque' applied originally to the architecture of mid-seventeenth-century Rome and its derivatives, and to these alone can it be applied with any degree of accuracy. It is doubtful whether its extension to music – as, indeed, to the visual arts in general – of the period 1600–1750, though in some respects quite legitimate, can offer any real critical advantage, except (perhaps) as an aid to comparing the dominant characteristics of 'baroque', Gothic, Renaissance or one of the many 'classical' movements in the overall context of some broad, general appraisal of the history of European music. It certainly represents a distinct disadvantage as regards any attempt to understand the irregular and, at times, conflicting interaction and/or co-existence of the many different – indeed, antithetical – currents, traditions and individual phenomena in seventeenth-century musical history. The 'shape of time' – to quote the title of an excellent little book by George Kubler (New Haven, 1972) – has little of the smoothness, consistency and uniformity which the use of such historiographical and stylistic categories as 'baroque' might imply. The 'history of things', i.e., those 'things' produced by man – and this, above all, is the case of the musical work of art – is as discontinuous and many-sided as, indeed, is the history of their destination and use. It is this history which I here attempt to trace.

I am indebted to the translator, David Bryant, for his unfailing attentions in remaining faithful to my original text, to Lucy Carolan for her careful copy-editing, and to Penny Souster for supervising the preparation of the present edition.

The five years since completion of my original Italian text have served only – and in no small degree – to augment my indebtedness and gratitude to its two first dedicatees: my wife Giuseppina and our son Carlo.

Italian versification: a note

According to the standard definition – which has been subjected to some criticism by scholars in recent years – Italian versification is governed by two factors: the *number* of syllables in a line and the *position* of the stressed syllables in the line. Lines may have either an *even* number of syllables (in which case the stress pattern is strictly regulated), or an *odd* number (in which case it is much more flexible). The length or quantity of the individual syllables, however, is not a factor in versification (as it is, for example, in classical Latin).

The most widely used line of Italian verse, whose status may be taken as equivalent to that of the iambic pentameter in English, is the eleven-syllable *endecasillabo* (hendecasyllable); this is the line used in Dante's *Commedia*, Petrarch's sonnets, and other major Italian poetry. The other important 'odd-numbered' lines (*versi imparisillabi*) are the *settenario* (seven syllables) and the *quinario* (five); the *trisillabo* (three) also exists. Less common are the nine-syllable *novenario* and the 'even-numbered' lines (*versi parisillabi*): *decasillabo* (ten syllables), *ottonario* (eight), *senario* (six), and *quaternario* (four). In all these the positioning of stresses is much less variable than in the *endecasillabo* and *settenario*, to which the following remarks chiefly apply.

The majority of Italian words are stressed on the penultimate syllable, and the same is true of 'odd-numbered' lines of verse; thus the *endecasillabo* has what is practically a mandatory stress on the tenth syllable, the *settenario* on the sixth, and so on. Lines with this *penultimate* or paroxytone stress are called *versi piani*. It is possible, however, for the stress to fall on the *final* syllable (*versi tronchi*), or on the *antepenultimate* or proparoxytone (*versi sdruccioli*). Secondary stresses are placed, in the *endecasillabo* and *settenario* at least, with considerable freedom. The most common form of *endecasillabo* will have a stressed syllable in *either* the fourth *or* the sixth position, *and* at least one other stress apart from that on the penultimate; but an eleven-syllable line may contain as many as five stressed syllables, and the number of permissible patterns is very large (though some theorists, such as Petrarch, have tried at times to proscribe certain of them). *Endecasillabi* usually have a metrical pause or *cesura* after the word in which the fourth- or sixth-syllable stress occurs (i.e. after the fifth or seventh syllable, in most cases); the line is thus divided into two unequal *emistichi* (hemistichs). If the longer element comes first, the line is an *endecasillabo a maiore*; if the shorter, an *endecasillabo a minore*.

The major Italian verse forms from the Middle Ages to the early twentieth century were the *canzone*, originally a stanza or group of identically-structured stanzas designed to be set to music, and each divisible into two parts, the *frons* and the *sirma* (of which the former is subdivisible into two equal *pedes*, the latter into two equal *voltae*); the *ballata*, a less complex form of the *canzone*; and the *sonetto*, a fourteen-line structure made up of two four-line *pedes* and two three-line *voltae* (and thus lacking the clinching couplet familiar in English from Shakespeare). The eight-line stanza used in much Renaissance narrative poetry and elsewhere, the *ottava*, gives its name to the stanzaic form *ottava rima*; other regular stanzas are the *sestina* (six lines), the *quartina* (four), and the *terzina* (three). These terms are also used for groups of the requisite number of lines within a more complex structure, such as the *ottava* and *sestina* of a sonnet or the concatenated *terzine* (*terza rima*) which make up the individual *canti* of Dante's *Commedia*. There are, in addition, less common forms such as the *sestina lirica* (or *sestina provenzale*), in which the same six words are used to end the lines of each stanza, in a different order each time, and are all then used in a concluding *terzina*; the *ode*, based on Greek and Roman precedent; and others for which the rules are less clearly defined (*lauda*, *madrigale*, *idillio*, et al.). Blank verse also exists in Italian under the name *versi sciolti*.

Rhyme occurs in Italian verse when the sound of the words involved is identical from and including the vowel of the stressed syllable to the end of the word or line. In most cases the stressed syllable will be the penultimate one of the line (*rima piana*); but it is possible for the rhyming syllable to be a stressed final syllable (*rima tronca*), or a stressed antepenultimate (*rima sdrucciola*). There are several other rarer and more complex varieties of rhyme.

University of California, Berkeley STEVEN BOTTERILL

I

THE EARLY DECADES

1 The seventeenth-century madrigal

To modern eyes, a survey of the musical life of Italy during the first two decades of the Seicento reveals a number of innovations, 'inventions' destined (as a knowledge of later seventeenth-century musical history will show) to fall on fertile ground. There is the rise of the *basso continuo*; the vocal solo with instrumental accompaniment; the birth of opera. As examination of the music of the preceding century will show, these three 'inventions' are in reality the natural outcome of underground practices and experiments that run through much of the earlier period. If they appear so distinctly around the years 1600–02 (not only, indeed, to the eyes of the modern observer, but also to those of contemporaries), this is to be attributed to the fact that only now had their excellence and effectiveness begun to be brought to the attention of a more general public by musical printing. One need think only of the *Cento concerti ecclesiastici . . . con il basso continuo per sonar nell'organo* (1602) of Ludovico da Viadana, the *Nuove musiche* (1602) for vocal solo by Giulio Caccini, the two different settings of *Musiche . . . sopra l'Euridice del sig. Ottavio Rinuccini* (both published in the winter of 1600–01) respectively by Jacopo Peri and Giulio Caccini, and the *Rappresentazione di Anima et di Corpo* (1600) of Emilio de' Cavalieri. All are provided with prefaces of a lengthy and indeed controversial nature – prefaces that provide explicit documentation of their authors' awareness in announcing important innovations, and which, in a short space of time, were to win a permanent place in the annals of musical historiography.

These innovations must have seemed even more remarkable (though perhaps, there and then, less decisive) to contemporaries than they do from our modern point of view – especially if one considers the truly extraordinary nature of such publications in the general context of the music being published in the first years of the Seicento. Now, as in the previous century, this general context was provided in the field of art music by the huge and unvarying repertory, eagerly cultivated and assiduously reworked, of the polyphonic madrigal. From a brief calculation, decade by decade, of the number of surviving editions of polyphonic madrigals for unaccompanied voices, it would appear that no final rupture took place in the level of production after 1600, but only a gradual fall:

Table 1. *Madrigal collections published before 1650*

	First editions[a]	Subsequent editions[b]	Total	Concerted madrigals[a/b]	Overall total
From the beginnings to 1550	82	46	128		
1551–60	70	61	131		
1561–70	139	85	224		
1571–80	125	52	177		
1581–90	271	96	367		
1591–1600	193	68	261		
1601–10	157	107	264	11	275
1611–20	118	57	175	46	221
1621–30	24	21	45	69	114
1631–50	4	9	13	56	69

a the earliest extant edition (not always the true first edition!)
b reprints subsequent to *a*

The total number of madrigal collections published in the first decade of the new century far exceeds the total for each of the decades preceding the boom years of 1581–90. The decline in the number of first editions from 1591 to 1620 is anything but sharp. The combined total of first editions and reprints from the first decade of the century is equal to that of the previous decade (needless to say, reissues of the most famous sixteenth-century madrigalists, such as Luca Marenzio, are well represented). In reality, the true 'collapse' of the madrigal as a genre comes after 1621 – at this point, moreover, it is not to be disguised by the appearance of new collections of many-voiced concerted madrigals with *basso continuo*, with or without solo instruments, nor indeed by the publication of a small number of volumes of single-voiced compositions (respectively, from 1602: some twenty, fifty, sixty and forty). A similar graph, reaching its height during the decade 1591–1600 and falling rapidly only after 1621, plots the editorial fortunes of those secondary madrigal forms (in particular, the canzonetta and villanella) which set texts of a strophic design. Beyond any doubt, the polyphonic madrigal continued overwhelmingly to define the cultural horizons of the musician (be he composer, theorist, singer or listener) well into the new century before finally wearing itself out. It is thus fitting to begin this examination of the musical life of seventeenth-century Europe – a musical life based not on the harmonious progression of musical styles, genres, traditions, languages and practices, but on a co-existence between them that was frequently, indeed gladly, contradictory – with a look at this tenacious, persistent and macroscopic representative of continuity with the sixteenth century.

Abroad, as at home, responsibility for the overall image of Italian music was very much in the hands of the madrigal. In the first place, Venetian music publishers were actively present on the German market (in particular, at the Frankfurt book fairs) with their vast array of madrigal collections. Even more important, however, was the initiative of native publishers at Nuremberg, Munich and Antwerp. They made efforts to exploit the temporary presence of Italian musicians in more northerly climes (in 1608, for example, the young Frescobaldi makes his publishing *début* with a collection of madrigals printed at Antwerp by the firm of Phalèse). Whenever these attempts came to nothing (or whenever, quite simply, such composers were not to be found), they would draw from the most recently issued Italian collections to form madrigal anthologies of their own (christened with such fanciful titles as *Gemma musicalis*, *Musica divina*, *Harmonia celeste*, *Melodia olympica*, *Paradiso musicale*, *Il vago alboreto*, *Ghirlanda di madrigali*, *Nervi d'Orfeo*, *Hortus musicalis*, *Novi frutti musicali*, *Il Parnasso*, *Il Helicone*) or would reprint entire repertories *en bloc*: the 5-part madrigals of Marenzio (Nuremberg, 1601), Benedetto Pallavicino (Antwerp, 1604) and Orazio Vecchi (Nuremberg, 1594), or the 5- and 3-part *Balletti* of Giovan Giacomo Gastoldi. Gastoldi's two volumes, published at Venice in 1591 and 1594, can boast a total of some thirty reprintings in Holland, Germany and France during the period 1596–1664. In these years, the Italian polyphonic madrigal was to become a kind of refined musical language of trans-European, 'supernational' significance, much in demand in the various courts and cities of the North and cultivated not only by Italian musicians but also by their colleagues abroad.

Christian IV of Denmark, with a view to bringing the musical life of his court (at the capital, Copenhagen) up to date, gave orders for the printing of two sumptuous anthologies of recently published madrigals from Italy, the *Giardini novi bellissimi di varii fiori musicali sceltissimi* of 1605–06. Christian was also the dedicatee of that true parlour game in music, the *Veglie di Siena* of Orazio Vecchi. In 1599 and again in 1602, he sent his best Danish musicians to Venice to study with Giovanni Gabrieli; Hans Nielsen (*alias* Fonteiio), Magnus Pedersøn (*alias* Petreo) and Johann Brachrogge were subsequently to publish at least one collection of madrigals each. With them, at the school of Gabrieli, we find the Germans Johann Grabbe, Christoph Clemsee and Heinrich Schütz. It was in Vehice that Schütz, whose sojourn in the city was sponsored by the Landgrave of Hesse-Kassel, was to publish his first printed collection of music, the *Primo libro de' madrigali di Henrico Sagittario allemanno* of 1611. Other northern musicians, whether or not having served their apprenticeship in Italy, published madrigal collections of their own: Hans Leo Haßler (Augsburg, 1596), Jakob Haßler (Nuremberg, 1600), Jan Tollius (Amsterdam, 1597), Cornelis Schuyt (Leiden, 1600, 1611) and Cornelis Verdonck (Antwerp, 1603). On occasion, these madrigals would appear side by side with the various 'national' genres of the countries concerned (such is the case in the *Rimes françaises et italiennes mises en musique* of Jan Pieterszoon Sweelinck, 1612); or composers would even attempt the assimilation of such genres of madrigalian literary style, as in the *Kusjes* (*Kisses*) *a 3*, *4* and *5* by the Dutchman Cornelis Padbrué (1631). In the case of the English madrigal, absorption of the Italian model is so complete as to make possible the word-for-word reproduction, in the *Triumphs of Oriana* (1601), of an Italian anthology (the *Trionfo di Dori*) composed nine years earlier in honour of a Venetian nobleman's bride. Oriana, daughter of the King of Great Britain and beloved by Amadis of Gaul, is an obviously allegorical portrayal of the virgin sovereign, Elizabeth I, herself the dedicatee of this patriotic musical offering.

The madrigal also represented an excellent means of instruction in the art of composition. A collection of madrigals, indeed, would be regarded as a suitable outlet for the budding composer in his first appearance in print (we have already cited the examples of Frescobaldi and Schütz) – and how many composers would leave it at that! Through the contrapuntal style of the polyphonic madrigal, the young musician might acquire a knowledge of theory, mastery of form and respect for the rules on a level with any other type of polyphonic composition (whether mass, psalm or motet). The madrigal, moreover, sets clearly in relief the originality and inventiveness of the various musical motifs it contains; artistic interest, that is, is centred on the musical portrayal of poetic images. This factor is decisive. Departure from the rules of classical counterpoint is legitimate, indeed obligatory, if suggested by the text; audacity, however, must be carefully gauged. Bold dissonance, the lively interplay of the parts, the chromatic alteration of musical subjects and so on must not only be perceived in themselves but must also be perceivable as departures from the normal procedures, not as the arbitrary products of an unfettered will. The breaking of a rule does not involve its abnegation but if anything implies and confirms its validity.

The fact that a number of madrigal classics continued to be reprinted right up to the end of the seventeenth century may itself be interpreted as having a didactic design – from these basic examples, composers could acquire a knowledge of the rudiments of madrigalian polyphony. At least fifty-three reprintings are known of Arcadelt's first book of madrigals *a 4* (1538); of these, nineteen (one edited by Monteverdi himself) appeared between 1601 and 1654. The duets of Jhan Gero (c. 1540) went through a total of thirteen editions between 1609 and 1687. Similar success awaited the *ricercari a 2* of Grammatio Metallo (*ante* 1591–1685) and the 2-part madrigals of Bernardino Lupacchino and Giovan Maria Tasso (*ante* 1559–1688) – the 2-part madrigal, indeed, was the didactic genre *par excellence*. For Domenico Mazzocchi, madrigals (of which he himself published a volume in 1638) are of all 'musical works those most worthy of respect'; in support of this he cites music by Marenzio, Macque, Nenna, Luzzaschi and Gesualdo. In 1652 and 1678, the Papal singer Domenico Dal Pane was to publish two madrigal collections consisting of exercises undertaken by him at the school of his celebrated teacher Antonio Maria Abbatini; in this music, 'the most painstaking care is united with the incomparable beauty of a melody that vividly expresses the sentiments most fitting to the poetry, moving again and again the emotions of the beholder'. These examples are not to be conceived in terms of simple rearguard actions, nor can they be described as reflections of antiquarian taste or the misguided survival of orthodox sixteenth-century counterpoint – the more so when polyphonic madrigals are also included in the output of such reliably modern composers as Giovan Maria Bononcini (1678) and Alessandro Scarlatti.

On the other hand, the madrigals of Carlo Gesualdo continued to circulate throughout the seventeenth century in score; this latter feature was to rescue them from the oblivion that quickly befell almost all the remaining sixteenth- and early seventeenth-century repertory, in which the traditional layout in part-books reigned fully supreme. The edition of 1613 was then to assume a didactic function of its own. Gesualdo's florid and undisciplined counterpoint, his pervading chromaticism and stylistic contrivances became the object of study –

the basis, indeed, for the image of the madrigal in the seventeenth century. Such few editions of madrigals as appeared after 1625 were frequently laid out in score, not in separate part-books. (The market, however, was now lacking, and while the splendid madrigals of Michelangelo Rossi, with their extreme chromaticism, survive only in two unpublished manuscript collections, his no less eccentric toccatas for harpsichord went through a total of four separate printed editions.) Scarlatti (whose own madrigals were never published), in a letter of 1706, confirms that he often took pleasure in singing and studying the madrigals of Gesualdo. Schütz, writing in 1632, asks that copies of madrigals by the Prince of Venosa and his Neapolitan followers be sent him from Italy. Under Frescobaldi, the madrigals of Gesualdo were performed on the viols in the Barberini household in Rome. Gesualdo's madrigals thus figure with all good reason in a history of seventeenth-century music, though there are grounds for believing that even the part of the repertory published only in 1611 had in reality been composed at the end of the preceding century.

A brief examination of a single madrigal by Gesualdo will suffice to demonstrate the peculiarities of compositional technique that differentiate the Seicento repertory from that of the preceding century (the substantial uniformity in kind notwithstanding). In this context, particular importance is assumed by the musical articulation of the text. This is based on a process of segmentation of the various verbal (or poetic) images and their musical individualization. Each musical segment, in turn, is given its individual character through the use of continually varying combinations of a number of polyphonic techniques, themselves reducible to three basic pairs of opposites: homophonic or imitative textures, consonant or dissonant handling of the parts, diatonic or chromatic progression of subjects. The extensive use of the third of these pairs (an exceptional occurrence in sixteenth-century music) increases the number of available combinations from four to eight, thus making possible a differentiated polyphonic treatment of each segment of text. In tabular form:

Beltà, poi che t'assenti, come ne porti il cor }	homophonic	consonant	chromatic
porta i tormenti,	imitatative	consonant	chromatic
che tormentato cor può ben sentire	pseudopolyphonic (falso bordone)	consonant	diatonic
la doglia del morire	imitative	dissonant	(diatonic)
e un'alma senza core	homophonic	consonant	diatonic
non può sentir dolore.	imitative	dissonant	chromatic

Beauty, since on your way you go, / as you bear away your heart, / bear torment too, /

that the tormented heart may well experience / the pangs of death, / and a soul without heart / can feel no pain.

The text, which consists of six seven-syllable and hendecasyllabic (i.e. eleven-syllable) lines, divides naturally into six segments or poetic images. The composer thus requires only six of the eight available stylistic combinations in order to obtain the clear differentiation referred to above (the sharpest contrast, indeed, occurs between lines 5 and 6). He further superimposes on this series of 'opposites' a certain variability of metre and irregularity of rhythm: whereas, in the sixteenth-century *tactus*, the relationship between the metrical units associated with the single syllable (short/long) had generally been expressed in the ratio 1:2 (crotchet/minim or quaver/crotchet), in the hands of Gesualdo this relationship can suddenly arrive at such ratios as 1:4 or even 1:8 (quaver/semibreve). Slow, twisting chromatic or dissonant progressions in long note-values are alternated abruptly with florid melismatic passages in semiquavers or headlong declamation in diatonic and chromatic quaver steps.

The result? The smooth, refined and temperate language of the 'standard' sixteenth-century madrigal is no longer operative. In its place we find scraps of polyphony which, though truly lush and imaginative, are nevertheless discontinuous. The logical thread that runs through this heterogeneous succession of isolated musical units, the subtle 'idea' that links the various poetic and musical images through analogy and antiphrasis, similarity and contradiction: all this is provided by the text. If one omitted the words, as did Stravinsky in his orchestration of this very madrigal, this one formal link would be weakened. The music of Gesualdo, removed from its textual base, would sound modern and fossilized at one and the same time.

2 Giovan Battista Marino and the *poesia per musica*

The text of Gesualdo's *Beltà, poi che t'assenti* is anonymous. Its thoroughly aristocratic and eccentric composer shows a certain contempt for the poets normally preferred by his contemporaries: it is, indeed, quite possible that just as he caused his late madrigal collections to be printed in his own castle at Gesualdo (by the publisher

Giovan Giacomo Carlino, summoned specially for the purpose from Naples), the many hitherto unidentified texts of his madrigals were actually composed within these very same walls for his own personal use. Be this as it may, these texts correspond closely in style to the prevailing madrigalian fashion of the years around 1600. If, as we have said, it is the conceptual relationship between the various logical segments of text that provides the one formal link in the succession of distinct and isolated musical images, it will be necessary to look more closely at the structure of this new madrigal poetry.

Of all poetry collections of the time, none was to achieve more success among the musical community than the *Rime* (Venice, 1602) of the ambitious young Neapolitan, Giovan Battista Marino (1569–1625). Marino was destined to enter the annals as the most celebrated poet of the century. And rarely, indeed, did a collection of poetry rise to such rapid musical acclaim. In 1594 and 1596, the Neapolitan composer Giovan Domenico Montella had already sent two 5-part settings of texts by his young fellow townsman to the press – a sure sign that the poetry of Marino was already circulating in his native city well before 1602. Now, however, composers from Naples and beyond were immediate in their favourable reaction. Settings of Marino appeared later that year in madrigal collections by the Florentines Marco da Gagliano and Giovanni Del Turco and their Sienese contemporary Tommaso Pecci. Hot on their heels, in 1603, were the Mantuans Salomone Rossi and Giovan Bernardo Colombi, the Neapolitan Pomponio Nenna, Alfonso Fontanelli of Modena, Giuseppe Colaianni of Bari, and the Sicilian Antonio Il Verso. These were followed in 1604 by the Neapolitans Ascanio Mayone and Bernardo Bolognini, Pietro Maria Marsolo of Ferrara, Girolamo Ghisuaglio of Rimini, Orazio Vecchi of Modena, and the two Lombard composers Orazio Scaletta and Tiburzio Massaino; in 1605, it is the turn of the Florentine Santi Orlandi; in 1606 come Francesco Bianciardi of Siena, Domenico Brunetti of Bologna, the Neapolitans Giuseppe De Puente and Giovan Vincenzo Macedonio, and Bartolomeo Barbarino of Pesaro; in 1607, the Neapolitans Scipione Dentice, Crescenzio Salzilli and Francesco Lambardi, Bernardo Corsi of Cremona, the Venetian Giovanni Priuli, Giovanni Ceresini from Cesena, and Agostino Agazzari of Siena; in 1608, Antonio Gualtieri, Dattilo Roccia, Vincenzo Liberti, Amante Franzoni, Girolamo Frescobaldi, Marc'Antonio Negri and Severo Bonini; in 1609, Sigismondo d'India, Gabriello Puliti, Domenico Maria Melli, Giovanni Ghizzolo, Johann Grabbe, Johannes Hieronymus Kapsberger; in 1610, Alessandro Scialla, Enrico Radesca, Lodovico Bellanda; in 1611, Heinrich Schütz, Giovan

Francesco Anerio, and so on. Even more striking, however, is the frequency with which certain of Marino's texts were set: madrigals such as *Alma afflitta, che fai?*, *Ch'io mora, ohimè, ch'io mora?*, *Giunto è pur Lidia il mio*, *O chiome erranti, o chiome*, *Pallidetto mio sole*, *Pargoletta è colei*, *Riede la primavera*, *Se la doglia e 'l martire*, *Sospir che dal bel petto*, *Tornate, o cari baci* survive in literally dozens of different musical versions. Few compositions by Petrarch, Tasso or Battista Guarini could boast greater success than the madrigals of Marino. What was it, then, in the poetry of this newcomer that proved so attractive to the composers of his day?

A comparison of a madrigal by Marino (settings, among others, by Sigismondo d'India, Pomponio Nenna and Antonio Il Verso) and another by Tasso (set by d'India and Luca Marenzio) will be sufficient to answer this question:

Tasso

Là dove sono i pargoletti Amori,	There where are the little Cupids,
ed altri ha teso l'arco,	some have drawn the bow,
altri saetta al varco,	others in waiting lie and shoot,
altri polisce le quadrella d'oro,	and others polish the arrows of gold;
voi parete un di loro	you among their number seem,
scherzando in verde colle o 'n riva ombrosa	playing through green hill or shady bank
fra la turba vezzosa;	among the pretty throng;
e se voi non avete auree saette,	and if you golden arrows lack,
le dolci parolette	your little words
e i dolci sguardi son facelle e strali	and glances sweet are flames and darts,
e i bei pensieri in voi son piume ed ali.	and little thoughts in you are wings and plumes.

Marino

Pargoletta è colei	Tiny is she
ch'accende i desir miei,	who lights my desire
e pargoletto Amore	and tiny the Cupid
che mi saetta il core.	who pierces my heart.
Ma ne l'anima io sento	Yet in my soul I feel
e gran foco e gran piaga e gran tormento.	great fire, great pain, great torment.

Common to both is the subject, common to both the subtle poetic invention: the pretty young figure of the beloved is portrayed as a tiny Cupid, armed (as all Cupids are) with arrows and bow. Turning to questions of structure, however, the analogy ends. Tasso delights in describing the setting, not to mention the little Cupids themselves. Taking as his point of departure an implied similarity of subjects ('voi parete'), he then arrives by means of a concessive clause ('e se voi non avete . . . ') at a paradoxical similarity of objects; despite the logical parallelism created by his juxtaposition of 'portrayal' and 'portrayed', he avoids formal symmetry and spins out his verse in an irregular sequence of seven-syllable and hendecasyllable lines whose logical grouping and binary rhyme-scheme have actually very little in common. Marino, on the other hand, organizes his thoughts in six perfectly symmetrical lines of rhymed verse grouped together in twos; the strict parallelism between lines 1–2 and 3–4 (in line 3, the main verb of the first couplet is implied if not actually stated) is answered, again symmetrically, in the final couplet, albeit with one final element of surprise in the unexpectedly 'overweight' conclusion (a three-member hendecasyllable, where a two-member seven-syllable line might have been anticipated for reasons of symmetry). Tasso's tactfully conversational yet reasoned style is replaced by a tersely epigrammatic language. Descriptive analogy between subjects (Cupid – the beloved) gives way to simple identification of the effect (in the present madrigal, the 'pains of love'). Effectiveness of thought is directly proportional to synoptic brevity of style. Of Tasso, there remains nothing but the 'pungent' interplay of well-defined images, 'everything substance and vivacity'.

Wherever 'refinement of the words and facility of expression' are present, 'the concept cannot but suddenly sparkle with immediacy'. The greater the conciseness of style, 'the better and (so to speak) more delicious and alluring the verse becomes'. These are words taken from the *Arte del Verso* (*The art of poetry*; Rome, 1658) of Tommaso Stigliani, erstwhile friend (and later bitter enemy) of Marino: words, indeed, which demonstrate clearly the Neapolitan poet's concern with conciseness in his treatment of the subtle concept of the text. This quality must surely have been regarded by contemporary musicians as providing the perfect conditions for their reduction of the composition as a whole to a series of brief, isolated and well-defined verbal and musical images – images which could then be exploited for the purpose of analogy and contrast. Comparison of Marenzio's setting of Tasso with Nenna's (*viz* Marino's) *Pargoletta è colei* will make clear just how much more musically subtle is the latter in its rapid succession of short-lived repetitions and symmetrical patterns, unexpected rhythmic *volte-faces* and sudden harmonic lacerations instantaneously repaired. The same might equally be said of the other musical interpretations of this text. The overall effect is a little mocking in tone, characterized as it is by a general lack of proportion between the transient, ephemeral style of the poetry on the one hand and the richness and intensity of musical sentiment on the other. Not all composeres, however, display the same degree of conciseness as Nenna and his Neapolitan contemporaries in their settings of texts by

Marino. In the music of the young Heinrich Schütz the isolated and unfettered poetic units, despite their intrinsic brevity, are drawn out to the highest possible degree: the result is a rich and exuberant portrayal of a series of images which, isolated as they are, are nevertheless expanded in every direction with luxurious sonorities and fanciful polyphonic imitations.

Marino quickly secured a reputation as the founder of a new literary movement, defender and greatest exponent of a type of lyric poetry which combined pithiness of style with great subtlety of metaphor. This reputation was in reality the result of what in technical terms might be called a retrospective phenomenon of historical induction. So much did he flaunt his activities as literary protagonist and such was the general stir created by the publication of his colossal masterpiece *L'Adone* in 1623 (a total of 5123 octaves) that he emerged at the end of the day with an image as innovator and originator in every field of his literary output. Ironically, his immense success in the 'poesia per musica' (in particular, the *Rime* of 1602, republished with additional material in 1614 under the title *La lira*) was also the result of the very moderation and temperate 'mediocrity' of his pithy metaphorical language. Others, indeed, were considerably more daring in their unusual and erudite handling of simile. Cesare Rinaldi of Bologna, Tommaso Stigliani from the Kingdom of Naples, Guido Casoni from Treviso near Venice and Angelo Grillo of Genoa were all active well before 1602; Grillo, a Benedictine abbot, was actually of leading importance in the literary and musical development of the *madrigale spirituale* (a form akin to its secular relation in everything but theme). At times, the madrigals of these poets are truly extraordinary in their choice of themes: not only the eyes, hair, breast, hand and voice of the beloved but also her feet, beauty-spots and fan, not to mention the marks on her dress and such apparently extraneous items as bees, puppies, fireflies, dust in the eyes, hour-glasses, etc., are considered worthy of comment. For Stigliani, the life of the lover can become nothing less than a violent storm:

Una tempesta ria	My life
fatta è la vita mia:	is like a hostile tempest made:
poscia ch'a poco a poco	since little by little
divenuto mi sento	I feel myself
e di ghiaccio, e di foco,	like ice and fire,
e di pioggia, e di vento.	like rain and wind become.
Ghiaccio di tema, e foco di desiri,	Ice through fear, fire through my desire,
pioggia di pianto, e vento di sospiri.	rain through tears, wind through sighs.

Here, the relationship between 'lover' and 'tempest' is not entirely without ambiguity: which, it might be asked, is the 'portrayal' and which is the 'portrayed'? This, however, is not the real issue at stake. The fact is that such concepts, while providing the composer with a wealth of tangible images easily imitated in music (rain, fire, sighs, etc.), lie outside the conventional vocabulary of amorous themes that for almost a century had nourished the development of the madrigal. The smoothness and suppleness of madrigal polyphony was undoubtedly such as made room for expansion of the conventional stock of poetic and musical symbols (Pomponio Nenna, for example, shows no hesitation in his simultaneous use of two separate dissonances at the words 'morir di doppia doglia', 'to die of twofold grief'). It did not, however, permit the unlimited renewal of the whole series of symbols in an ever-changing stylistic vocabulary (as, indeed, would have been required by the deliberately eccentric use of metaphor of Marino's 'extremist' contemporaries). In fact, the musical success of Stigliani and the rest of the group went little further than a number, albeit considerable, of isolated cases. In their choice of poetical texts musicians appear to have avoided metaphorical extremes, preferring instead the 'reasonable mediocrity' more characteristic of Marino: a witty and subtle treatment of amorous subjects and metaphors which, in the final analysis, are perfectly conventional. Composers, in short, were happy to operate within the traditional framework of amorous madrigal poetry; despite a notable refinement of polyphonic technique, continuity and consistency prevailed. Almost total, then, was the abandonment of the more complex poetic genres (the sonnet, *ottava rima*, *canzone* and *sestina*) in favour of the epigrammatic madrigal.

Vehicle *par excellence* for the transmission and lasting consolidation of the 'poesia per musica' as a genre was provided by a number of truly gigantic anthologies devoted exclusively to madrigal poetry. In the *Fiori di madrigali di diversi autori illustri* (1598), the *Giardin di rime nel quale si leggono i fiori di nobilissimi pensieri* (1608), *Le muse sacre, scelta di rime spirituali* (1608) and the *Ghirlanda dell'aurora, scelta di madrigali de' più famosi autori di questo secolo* (1609), the contents, which are laid out by author, combine madrigals of recent composition with the lyric poetry of Tasso. The enormous *Gareggiamento poetico* of 1611 is organized according to theme: Pretty young girl, Blond tresses, Dark tresses, Pretty brow, Pretty eyes, Pretty mouth, Pretty breast, Woman at arms, Hands holding flowers, Sweet kisses, Cruel kisses, Singing lady, etc. Similar thematic collections of madrigal poetry were also compiled by musicians: examples are *La rondinella* (1604) by Gabriele Fattorini, *Hymeneo overo madrigali nuptiali* (1611) by Cornelis Schuyt, and *La bocca* and *Gli occhi* (1614–15) by Orazio Brognonico. On the one hand, these literary anthologies reflect the tastes of the musicians of the years around 1600. On the other, they would go on to provide a consolidated repertory of texts to be exploited up to the end of the century by those few composers of madrigals who survived. Giovanni Valentini (1616), Carlo Milanuzzi (1620), Tarquinio Merula (1624), Galeazzo Sabbatini (1625), Francesco Vignali (1640), Giovan Battista Bianchi (1675), Giovan Maria Bononcini (1678): all continue to draw from these same basic anthologies – anthologies, indeed, in which the poetry of Marino has a leading role to play.

The significance of Marino for the history of seventeenth-century music, however, does not rest with his madrigals alone. *Adone*, too, is of singular importance. Mythological, anti-heroic (and as such deliberately at odds with *Orlando furioso* and *Gerusalemme liberata*), enormous – indeed, quite abnormal – in its dimensions and labyrinthine plot, this poem constitutes a document of exceptional richness in the history of mythological and lyric poetry, both ancient and modern – an outstanding compendium of whatever can be set down in verse. Despite its proscription in the Index (a list of books prohibited to Roman Catholics, or to be read only in expurgated versions), *Adone* not only went on to provide a cultural and intellectual framework for the entire subsequent development of seventeenth-century poetry, but also to act, both directly and indirectly, as the literary source for a large number of opera libretti on similar mythological themes beginning with *La catena d' Adone*, produced at Rome in 1626. The poetry of *Adone*, in terms of its remarkable intellectual courage and 'modernity' of content, bears witness to the advance of a new science and philosophy based essentially on the notions of perceptible experience and sensory cognition. In so far as the auditory system is of relevance here, we may cite the remarkably detailed anatomical description of the auricular bones (anvil, hammer and stirrup) and tympanum (the tiny muscle that stands opposite these bones and which, like the stirrup, had only just been discovered) in canto 7, octave 16. In the sceptical, perplexing, many-sided, open-ended world of *Adone*, 'the aim of the poet' is not so much 'to astonish' (a long-held and oversimplified opinion which elevates a purely polemical affirmation of Marino to the rank of poetic manifesto), but rather, if anything, to experience as fully as possible the entire range of sensory cognition – including, of course, the music of his time. In this context, it will be sufficient to cite the names of Virginia Ramponi Andreini and Adriana Basile, the former the original protagonist in Monteverdi's *Arianna*, the latter the leading chamber-music virtuoso of the day. Both are evoked at canto 7, octave 88 in the description of the allegorical character of Flattery. The reference to Basile, indeed, was soon to strike a note of topical concern: in 1624, one year after the appearance of *Adone*, Giulio Strozzi (man of letters and friend of Monteverdi) was to publish his *Venezia edificata*, in which the voice of 'the beautiful Adriana' with her 'charming canzonettas, new arias' and *romanesca* ('Romana ha l'aria, e in otto versi è stretta') is seen to 'quieten, soothe and steal the hearts' of the 'cunning and deceitful' enchantress Irene and her court. Conversely, the rich crop of madrigals in praise of *prime donne* like Basile also provided a point of reference for poetic descriptions of the florid *canto gorgheggiato* – descriptions which were to culminate in the 'nightingale' episode from *Adone* itself (canto 7, octave 33):

Udir musico mostro, o meraviglia,	Melodious prodigy! How marvellous,
che s'ode sì, ma si discerne appena,	that one can hear but scarcely can discern,
come or tronca la voce, or la ripiglia,	as he breaks off his song, and then resumes,
or la ferma, or la torce, or scema, or piena,	now lightly and now full, he holds, he trills,
or la mormora grave, or l'assottiglia,	now murmurs grave, now subtly thinning out,
or fa di dolci groppi ampia catena,	and now he forms a chain of sweet roulades,
e sempre, o se la sparge o se l'accoglie,	and always, whether hushed or shrill the song,
con egual melodia le lega e scioglie.	he blends, dissolves with equal melody.

3 Music for solo voice

The florid and exuberant song of Marino's nightingale is actually featured in a setting of eight '*ottave rime* with *passaggi*' from *Adone*, published eight years before the poem itself in the *Musiche a due voci* (1615) of Sigismondo d'India. The passage in question is the long soliloquy of the enchantress Falsirena ('Ardo, lassa, o non ardo?': canto 12, octaves 198–204, 207) smitten with love for Adone; the musical setting, indeed, is entitled *Pensieri di novelle amante* (*A young lover's thoughts*). Sigismondo d'India, from 1611, was director of chamber music at the court of Savoy, where Marino was also employed in the years between 1608 and 1615. He would thus have had occasion to make the poet's personal acquaintance and obtain these eight stanzas direct from the source – the poem, indeed, was long in preparation. The setting, for two sopranos and *basso continuo*, revolves around a 'strophic' bass: a fixed melodic and harmonic pattern repeated once in the bass for every stanza of text (or in the case of *ottave rime*, as here, every two or four lines). Such is the inexhaustibly florid nature of the two vocal parts that the piece as a whole reaches quite extraordinary proportions. On certain syllables the melismas are some sixty notes long. Taken together, the two voices perform no less than 112 notes of melisma on the final and most important word of the text, 'a*mo*re'. At times, parallel and simultaneous motion is the order of the day. Elsewhere, however, the two voices alternate with each other (a long note in one corresponding to a melisma in the other) – by this, the reader will gain some idea of the degree of expansion undergone by the text in its musical setting. Indeed, the strange fascination of this music derives from the contrast and opposition between the extreme simplicity of the harmonic skeleton in the bass and the melismatic style of the other parts – parts in which the arrival of the cadence is delayed until it can no longer be avoided.

This type of 'solo' song was not the only one in fashion at the time. The 'monody' of the first two decades of the century (the use of the term 'monody', however, is here slightly improper: its first occurrence in contemporary sources dates back only to 1635, with the publications of the somewhat retrospective theoretician Giambattista Doni), like the polyphonic madrigal, reserves a position of fundamental importance for the text – not, however, in terms of the contrived musical reproduction or portrayal of poetic images or a 'fullness and delicacy of harmony', but rather in the manner of delivery and recitation, the 'communication of the poet's every feeling' in a style of 'singing that is both beautiful and graceful'. Thus, while the compositional structure of monody is undoubtedly much weaker and more schematic than that of the polyphonic madrigal, it can boast nevertheless a greater versatility of style and ability to adapt to the different forms of 'musical speech'. This versatility is made possible, above all, by the variety of literary styles characteristic of monody, as opposed to the essential uniformity of the madrigal – a fact that is immediately apparent from a glance at Sigismondo's five books of *Musiche* (1609–23) 'for vocal solo' and duet to the accompaniment 'of clavichord, chitarrone, double harp and other similar instruments'.

Book 1 of the *Musiche a voce sola* (1609) is truly voluminous: a total of forty-seven texts, some of them articulated in several parts, organized more in the style of a poetic anthology in music than a collection of madrigal polyphony (the average contents of which come to no more than twenty-one pieces). The first section (nos. 1–20) would alone be sufficient to fill to the brim any normal collection of monody: the opening invocation of the poet (*Cara mia cetra, andiamne*) is succeeded by an alternating sequence of madrigals and arias (the former to texts by Marino, Guarini and Rinuccini, the latter to the words of Gabriello Chiabrera). The distinction between madrigals and arias dates back to Caccini and the first of his collections of *Nuove musiche* (1602). The madrigal texts are similar or identical to those of their polyphonic namesake; the music is through-composed. The texts of the arias are strophic and the verse frequently 'measured' (four-, five-, six- and eight-syllable lines, strong and rigid in their accentuation, as opposed to the more flexible seven-syllable and hendecasyllable lines of the madrigal). Also to be considered as madrigals are a number of settings of sections of monologue from the *Pastor fido* of Guarini: no. 41, for example, is a series of five madrigals from Mirtillo's soliloquy in Act 3, scene 1; no. 24 is explicitly entitled 'madrigal in recitative style'. More varied is the treatment accorded the *ottave rime* from *Gerusalemme* (Tasso) and *Orlando* (Ariosto). Some are laid out as imaginary monodic recitations on stage: no. 34 (the curse of Armida), for example, bears the heading '*ottava rima* in recitative style'. Others, on the contrary, are not so much recited as 'sung' in florid style above strophic basses of traditional or conventional hue: 'to the *romanesca* bass' (no. 25), 'to the bass of the *aria di Genova*' (no. 42), 'to the bass of the *aria di Ruggiero di Napoli*' (no. 43) (in the latter case, the title bears the imprint not only of the city of origin but also of the name of a character of Ariosto's *Orlando*). One further vehicle for the non-declamatory narrative setting of epic sonnets or *ottave rime* is represented by the 'aria da cantar ottave' (or 'sonetti'): here, not only the bass but also the vocal melody itself is repeated *verbatim* for each octave (no. 33, again featuring Armida) or sonnet (nos. 31 and 32, respectively by Petrarch and Marino). Another source for this poetry, though to a much lesser extent, is provided by the *Arcadia* of Jacopo Sannazaro: from here come the *sdrucciolo* triplets which form the textual basis of nos. 39 and 40.

On balance, these pieces, with their hendecasyllable lines and strophic organization (if only in the bass), might most suitably be classified as 'airs' (as opposed to the declamatory and through-composed style of the madrigals). When, however, these *arie* are set to measured verse in the style popularized by Caccini and much cultivated by the monodists they become different again: different in their regular and accentual rhythm, syllabic declamation, extreme brevity, and use of foreshortened cadences for articulation of the musical phrase. The texts, which represent an attempt to revive the poetic metres of ancient Greek lyrical verse, had begun to come into circulation towards the end of the previous century, thanks above all to the efforts of the poet Gabriello Chiabrera of Savona (1552–1638). They were usually light-hearted in tone – hence the denomination of 'scherzi' ('light' or 'humorous' poems) which frequently headed publications both of literary texts (for example, the anthology *Scherzi de' sig. Academici Trasformati* of 1605) and musical settings (Monteverdi's 3-part *Scherzi musicali* of 1607, with their lively instrumental ritornellos).

Sigismondo, while displaying a preference for the longer declamatory and narrative forms, was also the author of numerous such *arie* and *scherzi*. Sometimes, indeed, the length of his texts is quite minuscule: three or four lines per strophe. In Book 2 of the *Musiche* (1615), entirely *a 2*, these pieces are contrasted with the enormous *ottave rime* of Marino and Tasso and their florid *passaggi*. Book 3 (1618), which consists of music for solo voice, is predominantly in *stile recitativo*: besides the madrigals (one of whose texts is drawn from an earlier chromatic madrigal by Gesualdo, also imitated by d'India in Book 3 of his five-voiced madrigals), it also contains settings of sonnets by Petrarch and Marino, *ottave rime* from *Gerusalemme liberata*, an 'amorous epistle' by Marino (a sorrowful monologue in the tradition of the 'heroic epistles' of Ovid, one of many such imitations in the course of the seventeenth century – see chapter 23), an echo piece (*Ahi, chi fia che consoli il dolor mio? . . . io*), and an excerpt from the *Amaranta* of Giovanni Villifranchi. Book 4 (1621) names the authors of the texts: in this, d'India was possibly following the example of singer-composer-men-of-letters such as Francesco Rasi and Bartolomeo Barbarino. Indeed, just as Rasi and Barbarino occasionally cite themselves as authors of the poetic texts for their own monodic compositions, so too is the author of two declamatory 'laments' (respectively, by Orpheus and Apollo) in Book 4 of the *Musiche* identified as the composer himself. Throughout, the texts chosen for inclusion in this book are of no little weight: the opening invocation (*Piansi e cantai lo strazio e l'aspra guerra*) is a sonnet by Bembo; this is followed by a sonnet by Petrarch, a setting in *stile recitativo* of three octaves from the *Gerusalemme* of Tasso (the baptism and death of Clorinda), a 'nightingale song' from a pastoral drama by Francesco Bracciolini, a 2-part dialogue by Marino and, finally, still by Marino, a second setting of the same 'amorous epistle' of Book 3, musically quite different and textually more complete. Scattered among the various items in *stile recitativo* are a number of strophic airs, which alleviate the sustained literary tone of the whole.

Book 5 (1623) contains a further three 'laments' (those of Jason, Dido and Olympia) to texts by Sigismondo himself. Also included are two pieces of theatrical music performed three years earlier at the court of Turin. The strophic aria *Io che del ciel i sempiterni campi* was sung by a personification of Heroic Virtue in the ballet *Le accoglienze*, performed on 30 January 1620 for the arrival of Christine of France, bride of Crown Prince Vittorio Amedeo (see the description in Source reading 2); the madrigal *Questo dardo, quest'arco* formed part of a festival of dance and allegorical apparitions (where it was sung by the goddess Diana) performed during that same winter in honour of the same illustrious princess. The practice of inserting theatrical material in collections of chamber music for vocal solo may be traced to the founder of the genre, Caccini, whose *Nuove musiche* of 1602 contains a section from the *Rapimento di Cefalo* of Chiabrera, performed two years earlier in Florence during the Medici–Navarra wedding celebrations of 1600. A second volume of *Nuove musiche* (1614) by Caccini includes a 'romanesca' from the *Mascherata di ninfe di Senna* of Ottavio Rinuccini, performed at the Palazzo Pitti, Florence, in 1611. Other composers now followed. Among the *Musiche* (1615) of Marco da Gagliano is a *Ballo di donne turche* (Florence, Palazzo Pitti, 1615). Book 5 (Op. 10) of the *Musiche* of Enrico Radesca (1618) includes songs for Turinese ballets performed in 1608. Monteverdi opens his seventh book of madrigals (1619) with an *introduzione a ballo* entitled *Tempro la cetra*, and closes it with the *dialogo-balletto*, *Tirsi e Clori* (Mantua, 1616); in Book 8 (1638), he concludes the two sections respectively with a complete *balletto* 'in genere rappresentativo' (the *Ballo dell'ingrate*, performed at Mantua in 1608) and a further *introduzione a ballo* (possibly given in Vienna in 1637); even the posthumous madrigals of Monteverdi (1651) include a theatrical canzonetta from the *Proserpina rapita* of Giulio Strozzi (Venice, 1630). In his *Musiche e balli*, d'India himself was to assemble a whole volume of theatrical music performed at Turin for the wedding celebrations of 1619–21.

There is, indeed, nothing surprising in the presence of such pieces in published collections of monody. On the contrary, while the polyphonic madrigal was destined for performance 'at table' for the amusement of the singers themselves (be they courtiers or citizens, amateur or professional), monody was intrinsically dramatic in style. The isolation of the solo voice allows characterization of the individual 'actor'; the technique of vocal ornamentation, moreover, necessitates the employment of professional singers – singers who were practised in the elegant and effective delivery of words and music to a separate audience of listeners and spectators (contemporaries, indeed, frequently pass comment on the bearing most appropriate to the art of the virtuoso, together with the moderate use of both facial and bodily expression). Besides, in the early seventeenth century, monody was the prerogative of a limited number of courts – a much-valued and sought-after novelty to be exhibited in public on only a few great festive and theatrical occasions. The various princes of the Italian peninsula competed with each other for the best virtuosi; displays during banquets and other festive occasions (see Source reading 1) were enriched by the voices of a few great singers whose presence was everywhere much in demand. In Florence there were the Caccini (Giulio, his wives and his daughters, of whom one, Francesca, was to publish a volume of *Musiche* in 1618, followed in 1625 by the theatrical ballet *La liberazione di Ruggiero dall'isola di Alcina* to a theme by Ariosto) and Vittoria Archilei. Particularly prominent at Rome were the singers employed in the household of the passionately musical Cardinal Montalto. Mantua played host to Francesco Rasi of Arezzo (Monteverdi's original Orfeo, subsequently knighted) and the Neapolitan singer Adriana Basile whose voice, beauty, propriety and ability as an instrumental accompanist won her unanimous favour with princes and poets throughout the land (as witness two contemporary publications in her praise: the poetic anthology *Teatro delle glorie* of 1623 and a volume of *Lettere di diversi principi* of 1628); her mantle then passed to her daughter Leonora Baroni, similarly praised in the *Applausi poetici* of 1639. Contemporaries, indeed, were exaggerated in their enthusiasm for these celebrated women and the new vocal style. 'The gentle sighs, discreet accents, moderation in trills, the skilful *portamenti*, daring falls, soaring leaps, interruptions, onward drive, one tone of voice dying out, giving way to another which shoots up to the stars, stopping the spheres in their tracks – celestial wonders indeed': this description of the voice of Adriana Basile is truly worthy of Marino's nightingale. The metaphor of the spheres recurs in the title of an anthology of monody published at Rome in 1629: *Le risonanti sfere da velocissimi ingegni armonicamente raggirate . . . con il primo mobile del* [*basso*] *continuo* (*The resonant spheres, harmonically tricked by the highest intelligence . . . with the* basso continuo *as prime mover*).

The career of Sigismondo d'India is itself indicative of the courtly orientation of the solo song. Despite his three published volumes of concerted motets, this native of Palermo remained noticeably apart from the modest lot of the church musician. Of noble birth, he was present at the Medici court from the early years of the century. He then appears at the courts of Piacenza (1610) and Savoy (where he found stable employment from 1611), before passing (towards 1623) to Rome, where he worked in the service of Cardinal Maurizio of Savoy. He also, however, maintained contacts with the Dukes of Modena, for whom he composed his tragedy *L'isola di Alcina* (1626) to a text by Count Fulvio Testi; also in 1626, he collaborated at Rome in the musical drama *La catena d'Adone* (to a subject inspired by Marino). Two years later, he died. Like all the monodists, d'India was not only a composer but also a singer; in Florence, in fact, his performances were admired by virtuosi in the Caccini circle. Unlike many of his colleagues, however, he not only composed music for solo voice (which he dedicated to members of the Habsburg, Farnese and Este families, together with his Savoyard patrons and the Queen of France) but also eight volumes of madrigals and two of villanellas (dedicated, likewise, to princes and high-ranking diplomats). His music is 'noble' by very definition, spurning (in the words of the composer himself) 'ordinary progressions . . . ordinary modulations . . . and ordinary *passaggi*' in favour of 'the true manner [of composition], using uncommon intervals, and passing in as novel a way as possible from one consonance to another' (that is, through the ostentatious display of irregular sequences of consonances and dissonances).

Some years were still to pass before the solo repertory gained wide circulation in print. Already, however, Sigismondo's Books 4 and 5 contain a significant pointer in this direction: as their very titles announce, the strophic airs interspersed between the items in *stile recitativo* are provided not only with accompaniment for *basso continuo* but also with an elementary letter code which indicates the chords to be played should the piece be accompanied by guitar. This light and ephemeral form of 'scherzo' with guitar accompaniment begins to circulate in the third decade of the century, above all in Venice and Rome where certain musicians actually specialize in the publication of *Scherzi delle ariose vaghezze commode da cantarsi a voce sola*: Carlo Milanuzzi (nine collections with this and similar titles between 1622 and 1643), Giovan Pietro Berti and the blind Martino Pesenti. Great popularity was also achieved by certain collections of canzonettas or villanellas which contained only the text with a figured accompaniment for guitar: particularly famous were the publications of Remigio Romano and Pietro Milioni. This new repertory, at times somewhat vulgar in tone, was designed for the entertainment of a more general public and had nothing in common with the languishing vocalization of the courtly style. For monody – its composers, singers, devotees and, finally, the style itself – the 1620s were to mark the beginning of the end.

4 Claudio Monteverdi before 1620

Towering over the entire musical scene of early seventeenth-century Italy is the figure of Claudio Monteverdi (b. Cremona, 1567; d. Venice, 1643). The nucleus of this remarkable composer's creative output is represented by his eight books of madrigals (of which vols. 1–6 are dedicated exclusively to the 5-part polyphonic repertory) – appropriate, indeed, in an age in which the madrigal production of a composer was regarded as a synthesis of his entire artistic personality (well-known examples are Monte, Wert, Luzzaschi, Marenzio, Macque, Nenna and Gesualdo). Yet the predominance of the madrigal in Monteverdi's compositional activities is also a reflection of his social position in the years up to 1612. From 1590, he was employed at the Mantuan court as a string player, from 1602 as *maestro di cappella* – supplier, in short, of many-voiced settings of literary texts for the private delectation of academies and court. Two collections of church music by Monteverdi also found their way to the press: the *Sanctissimae Vergini missa senis vocibus, ac vesperae pluribus decantandae, cum nonnullis sacris concentibus, ad sacella sive principum cubicula accommodata* of 1610 and the *Selva morale e spirituale* of 1641. In comparison with the regularity of his madrigal production, however, these publications strike a note of exception – almost, indeed, as though conceived as a monumental two-part compendium of their composer's 'public' activities as *maestro di cappella* at Mantua and Venice. Monteverdi's rise to the prestigious rank of *maestro* at the Venetian Ducal Chapel also, nevertheless, affected his relationship with the public as a composer of madrigals. In his new influential and well-paid position, he could now afford the luxury of printing his sixth book of madrigals (1614) without dedication – without, that is, either patronage or subsidy save that of the publisher, himself certain of excellent financial returns. The style, too, of Monteverdi's Venetian madrigals is indicative of a cultural *milieu* that was decidedly more modern in outlook than that of the Mantuan court; they might well, indeed, be described as a breach in the monopoly of the polyphonic madrigal and its esoteric destination. All the more singular, then, is the fact that the principal Venetian publications of Monteverdi all maintain some kind of reference, direct or indirect, to the early years of Gonzaga patronage – years which seem to have left a deep mark on the musician. In the sixth book of madrigals, a 5-part version of the *Lamento d'Arianna* is complemented by a further lament (*Lagrime d'amante al sepolcro dell'amata*, 1610) which bewails the premature death (Mantua, 1608) of the intended protagonist of the opera itself, Caterina Martinelli. Caterina Medici Gonzaga is the name of the illustrious dedicatee of Book 7; Book 8 is inscribed to the Emperor Ferdinand III, stepson of Eleonora Gonzaga who herself is the dedicatee of the *Selva morale e spirituale*. Books 7 and 8, moreover, include pieces of theatrical music for the Mantuan court; the *Selva morale e spirituale* contains a sacred Latin *contrafactum* of the *Lamento d'Arianna* (monodic version) entitled *Pianto della Madonna*.

This retrospective attitude is the outward manifestation of a deep ambivalence which underlines Monteverdi's entire personality. Despite his role as effective destroyer of the absolute stylistic supremacy of the madrigal, he also showed caution and some hesitation with regard to the literary and musical *avant-garde* of his day. Slow, for example, is his adoption of the poetry of Marino, who first appears in Book 6 (1614); here, moreover, the poet is presented in a somewhat anomalous light, represented as he is by four sonnets and a *canzone*, to the total exclusion of the epigrammatic compositions so favoured by others (the four sonnets, indeed, are accompanied by two others by Petrarch). The use of such complex and artificial forms as the sonnet had long been discarded by musicians (Books 1–5 of Monteverdi contain but a single example); their renewed appearance in Book 6 should not, however, be regarded as signalling a literary and musical revival but rather a new interest in the large-scale articulation of musical form. The epigrammatic style of Gesualdo and other madrigalists of the time, founded as it was on the musical transliteration of a concept expressed in the course of a few 'pointed' poetic images, here gives way to extended layers of sound and stark contrasts between solo and *ripieno* episodes (at times, the solo voices are used to portray the characters of an amorous dialogue). Gone is the ideal of a concise musical form deriving from a single poetic concept. Form, instead, is to be based on a pre-established distribution of musical sections, phrases and periods which contrast and correspond to each other; layout and articulation must be broad yet succinct.

In the setting of Petrarch's *Ohimè il bel viso, ohimè 'l soave sguardo*, the two sopranos confine themselves to a sixteen-fold repetition of the single word 'ohimè' ('alas!'), while the other three voices set out the opening lines of the sonnet (these too amply peppered with 'ohimè's) step by step. Of singular effect is the musical construction at lines 5 and 6: the long, languishing interjections of the sopranos on the one hand, the deep-felt articulation of tenor, bass and alto on the other:

S,*S*: et ohimè . . .	*T*: il dolce riso,
S,*S*: et ohimè . . .	*B*: il dolce riso ond'uscì il dardo,
S,*S*: et ohimè . . .	*A*: il dolce riso ond'uscì il dardo,
	di che morte altro ben,
	di che morte altro ben già mai non spero.

and alas . . . the sweet laughter, / and alas . . . the sweet laughter whence sprang the dart of love, / and alas . . . the sweet laughter whence sprang the dart of love, / of which death ne'er worse, / of which death, ne'er worse have I e'er hoped.

Marino's sonnet *Qui rise Tirsi, e qui ver me rivolse* is a nostalgic account of an amorous episode from the past. Monteverdi's setting, concerted with *basso continuo*, is laid out in a series of solo episodes interpolated with *ripieno* interjections of the refrain and central line of the text, 'O memoria felice, o lieto giorno', 'O happy memory, o joyful day':

vv. 1–2	duet (*S*,*S*)
vv. 3–4	duet (*A*,*T*)
v. 14	'O memoria felice . . .' (*a* 5)
vv. 5–6	solo (*S*)
v. 7	trio (*S*,*S*,*A*)
v. 8	duet (*S*,*S*)
v. 14	'O memoria felice . . .' (*a* 5)
vv. 9–11	duet (*S*,*A*)
vv. 12–13	trio (*A*,*T*,*B*)
v. 14	'O memoria felice . . .' (*a* 5)

The formal structure of pieces like this, while partly literary in design, is determined principally by the music itself. And in this it is aided above all by the employment of the *basso continuo*. The latter, which first appears in Book 5 (1605), might indeed be described as the *sine qua non* for the interpolation of any solo episode whatever (as here, at verses 5–6) in an otherwise polyphonic madrigal. While polyphony, by very definition, necessitates the use of two or more parts, only the solo voice is fully capable of character delineation (be this character real or imaginary). Thus, for example, the *basso continuo* provides that second 'voice' which allows a literal rendering of the words 'T'amo, mia vita' by solo soprano in Monteverdi's setting (Book 5) of Battista Guarini's madrigal of that name:

soprano and b. c.	*alto, tenor, bass*
T'amo, mia vita	
	la mia cara vita
	dolcemente mi dice
T'amo, mia vita	
	e in questa sola
	sì soave parola
	par che trasformi lietamente il core
	per farmene signore.
T'amo, mia vita	
	O voce,
T'amo, mia vita	
	voce di dolcezza e di diletto,
	prendila tosto, Amore,
	stampala nel mio petto,
	spiri solo per lei l'anima mia:

a 5

'T'amo, mia vita' la mia vita sia!

I love you, my life, / my dear life / sweetly says to me, / I love you, my life, / and with this sweet word alone / seems happily to transform my heart / that I its master be. / I love you, my life, / O voice, / I love you, my life / voice of sweetness and delight, / take it now, O Love, / forge it in my breast, / that my soul for her alone may live: / 'I love you, my life': may these words my life be!

Already, however, in Book 4 (1603) and the polyphonic madrigals without *basso continuo* of Book 5 (the music of both publications was partly composed prior to 1597), there emerges the need for a musical articulation that is not intensive but broad, coupled with a declamatory-style formal layout – a musical rhetoric, in short, which is capable of graduated change and not confined to the separate illustration of individual poetic images. The frequent occurrence of theatrical texts from the plaintive monologues of *Il pastor fido* is not, in this sense, fortuitous (though this presence could also be interpreted as mere reflection either of the musical fashion of the day or of the lively interest being shown in Guarini's pastoral drama at the Mantuan and Ferrarese courts). The internal organization of Monteverdi's madrigals itself provides the clearest possible indication that an obviously structural dimension has now been added to Gesualdo's 'combinatory' system (see chapter 1, above). *Sì ch'io vorrei morire* (Book 4) consists of alternating episodes in contrasting styles: chords, cadences and tonal stability on the one hand, imitation, chains of dissonant interjections, stepwise harmonic progressions (up to eleven consecutive steps) on the other. In the imitative episodes, one progression answers another in a kind of mirror inversion (ascending or descending motion); the chordal episodes, on the contrary, are organized on a 'circular' basis in which the last line represents an exact poetical and musical repetition of line 1:

homophony/cadences	*imitation/progression*	
┌— Sì ch'io vorrei morire		
ora ch'io bacio, Amore,		
la bella bocca del mio amato core.		
	Ahi, cara e dolce lingua,	↗
datemi tant'umore		
	che di dolcezza in questo sen m'estingua!	↘
Ahi, vita mia, a questo bianco seno		
	Deh stringetemi fin ch'io vengo meno	↘
a questo bianco seno		
	Deh stringetemi fin ch'io vengo meno	↗
a questo bianco seno		
	Deh stringetemi fin ch'io vengo meno!	↘
	Ahi bocca, ahi baci, ahi lingua, torno a dire:	↗
└→ sì ch'io vorrei morire!		

Oh that I should wish to die, / now that I kiss, o Love, / the beautiful mouth of my beloved heart. / *Ah*, tongue sweet and dear, / give me such humour / that I may die of sweetness in this breast. / Ah, my life, to this white breast / *ah* clasp me tight until I die! / *Ah* mouth, ah kisses, ah tongue, I say again: / Oh that I should wish to die!

The all-important innovation in the madrigals of Monteverdi (from Book 4 onwards, at least) is not, then, represented by their harmonic or contrapuntal audacity, but rather by this structural dimension: the declamatory articulation of the musical 'speech', a concept of form that is based on the principles of correspondence, antiphrasis, repetition, alternation and the recapitulation of musically recognizable sections. When, in fact, the Bolognese theorist and cleric Giovan Maria Artusi, guardian of public decency in matters polyphonic, launched his violent attack on the madrigals of Books 4 and 5 (*L'Artusi, overo Delle imperfezioni della moderna musica*, Part 1 1600, Part 2 1603; the *Discorso secondo* of Antonio Braccino da Todi, pseud. Artusi?, 1608) on the grounds of the unlawfulness of certain dissonant contrapuntal procedures which, isolated from their poetic and musical contexts, seemed to him the most terrible blunders, Monteverdi replied with his own manifesto. First published as the preface to the edition of 1605, later annotated by his brother Giulio Cesare in the latter's edition of the *Scherzi musicali* of 1607, it asserts the arrival of a new 'seconda pratica' where 'the words are the mistress of the harmony' (no longer 'the harmony . . . as mistress of the words', as in the 'prima pratica' codified by Zarlino). Justification, however, of contrapuntal licentiousness for the purposes of poetic illustration is in both theoretical and compositional terms as old as the madrigal itself. Monteverdi has no difficulty in tracing an illustrious line of 'heretical' ancestors that goes back to Cipriano de Rore (d. 1565) and which also includes a not inconsiderable number of musicians of noble birth, all of them opposed, like Monteverdi, to the 'mechanical' doctrinairism of Artusi: Gesualdo, Emilio de' Cavalieri, Count Alfonso Fontanelli, Count Girolamo Branciforte, the cavaliere Giovanni Del Turco and the gentleman Tommaso Pecci.

If anything, the true innovation of Monteverdi's 'seconda pratica' lay in the gradual discovery of formal and tonal relationships that transcended the modal horizons of traditional madrigal polyphony and led irrevocably to the demise of its earlier stylistic monopoly. This is true, even if contemporary writers were not yet capable of expressing it in words (as late as 1633 Monteverdi was still to contemplate writing a treatise, though this was never published and perhaps never written). Needless to say, these formal relationships were borrowed (and necessarily so) from those of the literary text – not only, however, from a text perceived as a series of salient poetic images and subtle underlying concept, but also in terms of an overtly rhetorical dimension that was centred on such concepts as oratory, declamation and eloquence. A 'transitional' example ('transitional', too, in terms of its contrapuntal technique) is provided by the remarkable harmonic organization of the *sestina Lagrime d'amante* (Book 6). Characteristic, here, is the persistent syllabic reiteration of a limited number of chords which alternate slowly in extended musical periods – periods which frequently spill over from one hendecasyllable to the next and which constitute, in their harmonic syntax, a musical form which is now tonal in orientation. Nothing could be farther from the isolation of poetic and musical images so typical of the style of Gesualdo.

If Monteverdi was among the first to adopt the *basso continuo* and solo voice in madrigal polyphony, he nevertheless shows a singular reluctance in his attitude towards the new 'monodia da camera' – an attitude all the more surprising in view of his precocious approach to theatrical music in *stile recitativo* (his *Orfeo* was produced at Mantua in 1607, *Arianna* the following year). Chamber monody finally appears in Book 7 (1619), which bears the title *Concerto*. The opening work (also the opening sonnet in Marino's *Lira* of five years before) is the poetic invocation *Tempro la cetra, e per cantar gli onori*; the text is articulated in four distinct sections, each declaimed by solo voice to the accompaniment of a strophic bass and linked by a recurring instrumental ritornello whose final repetition leads into a concluding ballet. A second sonnet by Marino, based on a pastoral theme, receives quite different treatment: *A quest'olmo, a quest'ombre* is a setting for six voices, two violins and two 'flauti o fifara' which alternate with each other in ever varying combinations for the various descriptive episodes of the music. After this twofold introduction, monodic and choral, the bulk of Book 7 is made up of duos (13), trios (4) and quartets (2) with *basso continuo*. The texts – by Guarini, Chiabrera, Marino and Tasso – consist of a random sequence of madrigals and sonnets. Monteverdi, while dismembering the polyphonic madrigal, has also reasserted the independence of the musician in his choice of text – not least from a formal point of view. At this stage in the development of the Monteverdi madrigal, every poetic form is admissible for musical setting; musical style, moreover, is capable at all times of doing justice to the chosen literary configuration.

The final section of Book 7 is unsurpassable in its illustration of the stylistic versatility of its composer. A list of contents will suffice: (1) *Con che soavità, labbra odorate*, a madrigal by Guarini, set as an impassioned monologue and accompanied by three different and alternating groups of instruments (two chitarroni, harpsichord, *spinetta*; three *viole da braccio* and *basso continuo*; three *viole da gamba* and *basso continuo*) which come together only at the points of greatest climax; (2) a *romanesca*, set for two sopranos in the florid style of Sigismondo d'India, to a text (*ottava rima*) by Bernardo Tasso; (3) two theatrical recitatives or 'amorous epistles for vocal solo in *genere rappresentativo*', one to an idyll in blank verse by Claudio Achillini (*L'amorosa ambasciatrice*, 1612), the other to an idyll in rhymed seven-syllable couplets, perhaps by Rinuccini; (4) two canzonettas in measured verse (respectively, four-syllable lines, and five-syllable and '*settenario tronco*'), concerted with two violins and bass and organized in a series of strophic variations (with exact verse-by-verse repetition of the bass) interspersed with ritornellos, themselves varied in accordance with the same strophic principle; (5) to conclude, the ballet *Tirsi e Clori* (Mantua, 1616), the poetry of which is constructed on all possible rhythmic variants of the six-syllable line, not only in the arias and recitatives of the introductory dialogue (invitation to the ball) but also in the ballet itself (*a 5*). The multiplicity of literary genres and musical styles represented in this remarkable publication set it apart from the general run of madrigal collections as then conceived. Generalizing, one might almost describe it as an anthology of everything in contemporary poetry that was capable of expression in music – a sample collection of the enormous resources released by the new oratorical conception of the composer's art.

5 The 'crisis' of the seventeenth century

A work such as the *Concerto* of 1619 must surely have made a positive contribution towards overcoming the limitations imposed by the uniformity and centralizing influence of a polyphonic madrigal repertory whose future as a genre still appeared bright on the horizon. Equally decisive, however, though in a negative sense, must also have been the effect on musical life of the series of political, social and economic catastrophies which were about to overtake seventeenth-century Europe, throwing it into a lasting situation of crisis. We shall not stop to examine the causes – some from the distant past, others of a more immediate nature – of the 'crisis' of the seventeenth century. It will here be sufficient to look briefly at its effects.

Though the economic crisis might initially have appeared transient in nature, it soon revealed itself to be of much more serious proportions. In 1619–22, the European – indeed, world – economy suffered a collapse which severely affected every sphere of financial activity: industry, agriculture, money markets and demographic development. Nor did music and the music publishing business escape: the demise of the polyphonic madrigal in the third decade of the century, in fact, coincides with the collapse of music printing in Italy (see chapters 1 and 12). The fall of the madrigal, however, was more than purely economic in origin. It also reflects the crisis in the social and political life of the time. The remarkable decline in madrigal production and publication is also indicative of the fact that this music was no longer of use. Gone are the sixteenth-century ideals of a social harmony to be imitated in music, of musical harmony as an earthly reflection of the harmony of the spheres and as capable of reproduction at table by the harmonized voices of four or five well-educated gentlemen – themselves in social harmony with each other – in affected performances of madrigals of love, subtle concepts and ingenious musical inventions. In more concrete terms, what we see is the undermining of the sixteenth-century idea of civilized society, centred as it was on the life of the court and academies, the acquisition of awareness on the part of an elitist aristocracy, and the idea of culture and chivalry as symbolic of power and authority. With this, the ideals of courtesy and politeness embodied in the madrigal disappear. In the social and political strife sparked off by the economic crisis of 1620, the exercise of power and authority had necessarily to be seen to be clear, immediate and aggressive, far from the esoteric courteousness of the polyphonic madrigal.

The general standard of living, which had already suffered badly towards the end of the previous century at the hands of a succession of serious famines, now underwent further deterioration. Increased was the power of the minor officials, the inefficiency of the fiscal authorities and, in the south of the Italian peninsula, the greed of a revived feudal authority (of which Gesualdo is a shining example). The struggles between Mantua and Savoy for possession of Monferrato – this despite the many intermarriages which linked their two ruling dynasties and which had also provided the occasion for such outstanding musical entertainments as *Arianna* and *Dafne* (Mantua, 1608) – were finally ended in 1630 by the Imperial invasion of Mantua. This, and the resulting political confusion, were followed by the disastrous plagues of 1630 (northern Italy) and 1656 (in central and southern regions of the country), together with a situation of truly endemic poverty which was far from removed by the charitable work of the great religious and lay institutions. Meanwhile, science and philosophy came under the censorship of the Church, in the guise of the religious orders and inquisitorial practices: the Church itself is now the main supplier of culture in much of Italy. The Catholic orthodoxy of the Counter-Reformation appears fervent and in a state of expansion, but this hides the reality of siege conditions. Though the Thirty Years War (1618–48) was waged north of the Alps, the real participants in the struggle are Catholic *versus* Protestant Europe (as represented on the one hand by Austria and Spain, on the other by Germany, England and Scandinavia); the cultural and idealistic repercussions on Italy are great, as indeed is the bitterness aroused by a growing awareness of the decline of Catholicism. Venice suffers an industrial and commercial collapse, but eagerly continues to cultivate its mythical Republican image, proud opposition to Rome, and freedom of press, opinion and thought; in this way, it is able to conserve its status as a cultural centre of European significance. Pushed irremediably aside, however, by its trading competitors in Holland (the still youthful textile and manufacturing industries) and England (for shipping), reduced to a centre of more touristic than political importance, Venice soon falls once again into battle with the Ottoman Empire – and this, indeed, even before the end of the Thirty Years War. The painful feeling of encirclement which ensued was to last until the end of the century (and the Treaty of Carlowitz, 1699); only the Holy Christian League, agreed between Venice, Rome, the Empire and Poland in 1683, would belatedly revive those lost sentiments of anti-Ottoman Crusade which had made of the Battle of Lepanto (1571) a heroic and memorable episode in the history of Catholicism. If this is Venice – which still remains, in terms of its intellectual, musical and theatrical life, the most extraordinary city in seventeenth-century Italy – still worse are conditions in the remainder of Italy.

For some of the younger European nations (such as, for example, Great Britain), this profound and traumatic crisis was to provide the crucial driving force towards a new capitalist economy and parliamentary democracy; for others (such as France), it was to lead to the equally modern concepts – though modern for other reasons – of the absolute monarchy and State economy; for Italy (as, indeed, for Spain, the Empire and Eastern Europe), it was to assume the negative connotation of stagnation and economic depression and sanction the alienation – or, at any rate, the peripheral role – of political, economic and intellectual life. In England, between 1640 and 1660, the old feudal order is swept aside by the Cromwellian revolution and Commonwealth; of this, the Restoration monarchy is forced to take account. In France, Mazarin emerges from the rebellion of the middle- and upper-class Fronde with complete consolidation of the supremacy of king and country. In both cases, the centralization of the civil and political life of the nation on a great capital city (from 1660, London and Paris become the most heavily populated cities in Europe) leads almost to the creation of a society culture and a public opinion in the modern sense. The Iberian peninsula and Spanish possessions in Italy are also shaken by uprisings and revolutions, though for a single successful insurrection (John IV of Braganza, himself an avid collector and patron of music and musicians, would become the first king of modern Portugal), many were to fail. The Catalan rebellion of 1640 was to last until 1652; the uprisings in Palermo and Naples (1647) would be crushed in a matter of days (despite a timely anti-Spanish intervention on the part of the French): the outcome, however, was essentially the same. Yet the Neapolitan revolution of 1647 and the short-lived Republic which followed were not entirely in vain. After the restoration of an authoritarian yet necessarily populistic Spanish regime, the social order of Naples (largest city in Europe until 1656; largest city in Italy following the plague of that year which reduced its population by half) becomes somewhat more modern in tone. Class conflict quickens and is now more explicit; the conflict between viceroy on the one hand and a feudal and urban aristocracy on the other is mediated by a 'civilian' class of intellectuals and officials who are open to the new ideologies from England and France. It is, indeed, no coincidence that public opera, born in Venice in commercial forms that might virtually be described as capitalistic, subsequently appears in mid-century Naples as a mixture of royal patronage and private enterprise coupled with the support of local charitable institutions (the Hospital of the Incurabili was also proprietor of the public theatre) – a mixture which would act as a model for a large number of opera houses not only elsewhere in Italy but also in Europe at large.

Nations such as England and Holland, whose new-born industry and commerce was sustained by a strong agricultural base, show definite signs of economic, social and political advance; not so in the Mediterranean countries, whose corporate and out-of-date industry was devoted more to the production of luxury items (ever more luxurious, indeed, in proportion to the decline of the market). Culturally and intellectually, things are little different. Bacon, in his *Advancement of learning* (1605), had already put forward the arguments for an approach to the natural sciences that was no longer of purely speculative interest but which could also be applied technologically; this approach, in Restoration England, was to find institutional expression in the shape of the Royal Society. In Italy, not even the humanist Pope Urban VIII is able to spare Galileo from trial for his *Dialogo sui massimi sistemi* (1632); meanwhile, the only scientific academies of any importance – the Accademia dei Lincei (Rome, 1603) and the Accademia del Cimento (Florence, 1657) – are wound up in 1630 and 1667 respectively. Freedom of thought in northern and Scandinavian climes (from 1628 until his death in 1650, Descartes lives and publishes his works not in Catholic Paris but in Amsterdam and later Stockholm) is matched by the libertinism of the Catholic world and the often secret and coded attacks on Church and religion on the part of a highly elitist group of intellectuals. (Religion, however, is justified by the anti-monarchical yet also anti-popular libertines as a useful deceit – an effective means of controlling the superstitious and tumultuous throng.) The freethinking Venetians of the literary Accademia degli Incogniti were also the earliest partisans (if not the true patrons) of Venetian public opera during its first decade of life (see chapter 21). The hermetic and magical conditions of the Golden Age of Elizabethan England turn up also in Germany with the marriage of the daughter of James I to the Elector Palatine (1613); with them come hopes of a new era of peace and religious and intellectual harmony, founded on the study of science and natural magic, and free from the 'political strife' of the Papacy, the grasping fanaticism of the Jesuits and the zealous morality of the Protestants. Music, as mediator between macrocosm and microcosm, the harmony of the world and the harmony of men, would here have displayed its magical powers to the full. The key is provided by the deliberately encyclopaedic *Utriusque cosmi maioris scilicet et minoris metaphysica, physica atque technica historia* of the Englishman Robert Fludd, printed in the Palatinate in 1617. On the title-page, the concept of universal harmony is portrayed as a human being inscribed in a pair of concentric circles representing the cardinal humours and the heavenly bodies; illustrated on an internal frontispiece, moreover, is the wondrous *Templum musicae*, that imaginary building which was said to enshrine all the various attributes of 'practical music'. The Protestant Elector, however, is himself swept away by the Thirty Years War, and the enlightened and mystical ideologies are forced to return into hiding. Open profession of natural magic is replaced by prophetic initiations and underground promotion of philanthropical sects. And while the religious and intellectual movement of Fludd and his associates undoubtedly influenced intellectual life all over Germany, music, in hiding, was reduced to no more than hieroglyphic significance – an obscure, ineffective representative of a universal harmony that patently did not exist. The alchemistic musical symbols of the *Atalanta fugiens* (1617) of Michael Maier remain, in fact, an enigma to this day.

The 'crisis' of the seventeenth century, which opened so tragically with the Thirty Years War and the economic depression of 1619–22, recedes in the second half of the century. Music (as also, indeed, the visual arts) benefits less from the open libertinism of the Incogniti or the occult mystique of Fludd and the Rosicrucian movement than from the great demand for 'authority' brought about all over Europe by the social and political crisis. The royal or wealthy bourgeois portraits by Rubens, Velázquez, Rembrandt and Frans Hals; the didactic or allegorical classicism of Poussin and Pietro da Cortona; the uplifting gesture of the architectural style of Bernini and Borromini; the solemnity and majesty of that of Hardouin-Mansart and Wren: all, from a social and political point of view, are open expressions of intellectual, moral, economic or political authority. This is all the more reason why music, the social art *par excellence* should now have been opened as never before to the public – as the expression, *par excellence*, of political or religious authority (or authoritarianism). In the strife-ridden context of seventeenth-century Europe, the picture of the *dilettante* aristocratic musician and well-read lover of music who performs (or causes the performance of) madrigals of contrived and artificial construction for his own private entertainment gives way to the open utilization of music for ideological ends (see chapter 11), together with the active exploitation of those oratorical qualities of which Monteverdi's Book 7 gives an early testimony. The homogeneity and 'spontaneity' of the market for sixteenth-century polyphony is replaced by the purchase of music on the part of the great organizations of Church and State (cathedrals, basilicas, religious orders, courts, municipalities and guilds) for the purposes of propaganda and representation. For music, in short, the 'crisis' of the seventeenth century assumes truly revolutionary proportions; the disintegration of the old order and the invention of new social procedures.

6 'Concerto'

A quite different set of considerations is suggested by the title of Monteverdi's *Concerto*. The term, indeed, is here used quite categorically. If one considers that not only the noun 'concerto' but also its various derivative forms (the verb 'concertare', the participles 'concertato' and 'concertante') are among those which most frequently recur in the musical terminology of the Seicento, Monteverdi's employment of the term becomes almost 'provocative' in tone.

Contrary to what its history in the eighteenth century would tend to have us believe, the origins of the word 'concerto' are unrelated to musical technique. The Italian 'concerto' is derived from the Latin 'con-certare', meaning 'to compete or struggle together'; in everyday usage, however, this idea of 'militant co-operation' was eventually replaced by that of 'agreement' or 'bringing together' ('concordare'). Needless to say, both 'concertare' and 'concordare' contain strong musico-macrocosmic allusions: the reference to tuning and to the exact intonation of the 'strings' ('corde') or two 'hearts' ('corda') is none other than a microcosmic reflection of the idea of universal harmony, with which man too must necessarily seek to maintain himself in agreement. The idea, indeed, is already implicit in the etymology of the Latin (*con*)-*certare* and derivatives.

From the sixteenth century onwards, 'concerto' was used in music to indicate a harmonious ensemble, any numerous and well-harmonized group of performers or musical parts (be they vocal or instrumental). As we are informed by Ercole Bottrigari in his dialogue treatise *Il Desiderio overo de' concerti di varii strumenti musicali* of 1594, it is also more or less synonymous with 'concento'. Contemporaries speak of 'a *concerto* of musical voices', 'a *concerto* of viols', 'to play in *concerto*', 'a *concerto* instrument' (frequently a continuo instrument with fixed tuning such as harpsichord, organ, chitarrone or lute) and so forth. Musical prints carry titles like *Vespro della Beata Vergine, da concerto, composto sopra canti fermi, sex vocibus, et sex instrumentis* (Monteverdi, 1610). And again Monteverdi, in the score of *Orfeo*, remarks: 'This song was concerted to the sound of all the instruments'.

In the first place, then 'concerto' refers to the practice of group performance, generally with instrumental participation. More specifically, however, the word is also sometimes applied to a group of instruments within a mixed vocal and instrumental ensemble: in this case, 'concerto' implies opposition to 'cappella' (exclusively vocal), as in the *Litanie e motetti da concerto e da capella* (1618) of the Bolognese composer Girolamo Giacobbi. Later, towards the end of the seventeenth century, the term 'concerto grosso' is used less in the context of a definite musical genre than in terms of a large orchestral group which opposes a smaller 'concertino' ensemble of soloists. In fact, the word always refers fundamentally to a union of sounds and distribution of parts, not to a musical form. One need only remember that the terminological combination 'concerto grosso/concertino' occurs most frequently of all in the richly orchestrated cantatas and oratorios of the 1670s, composed by Alessandro Stradella and his Roman contemporaries – not, that is, in instrumental or orchestral compositions.

By obvious extension, 'concerto' was also quickly adopted in reference not only to the vocal/instrumental distribution of the parts in performance but also to the musical composition itself, irrespective of constitution, structure or form. Thus, in the 6–16-part *Concerti di Andrea, e di Gio: Gabrieli* (1587), we find 'sacred music, madrigals and other compositions for voices and instruments': ensemble music of varying character and genre. It is not, in fact, in Italy but rather in Germany that the earliest attempts at a systematic definition of the term 'concerto' occur. Partial responsibility in the formulation of this definition must, however, be shared by the Italian Ludovico da Viadana and his three truly remarkable volumes of *Concerti ecclesiastici* for 1–4 voices and *basso continuo*, whose enormous success north of the Alps was certainly no less considerable than that in their composer's native land. At least eight Italian editions of the first book alone appeared between 1602 and 1612. Four German editions of the three-volume series then appeared between 1609 and 1626, with a fourth volume published in Frankfurt in 1615 – quite sufficient, in short, to fill even the smallest and most provincial of *Kantorien*, Catholic or not.

In his attempt, then, to arrive at a plausible terminological classification of the various musical genres through examination of then current musical denominations, the German theorist and composer Michael Praetorius must reckon with Viadana's *Concerti*. Thus, in his classification (as set out in vol. 3 of his *Syntagma Musicum*, Wolfenbüttel 1619, and subsequently adopted by his German successors), 'concerto' ends up more or less with the meaning of 'few-voiced Latin motet for soloists and *basso continuo*' – exactly, that is, as in the music in question. Praetorius, however, was also aware of the polychoral tradition of Andrea and Giovanni Gabrieli: for this reason, he provides an alternative definition of 'concerto' as a 'polychoral Latin motet'.

Conscious of the flagrant contradiction involved, Praetorius then attempts to impose terminological consistency on a word that was fundamentally generic (and employed as such by Italian musicians); thus, he resorts to the original Latin meaning of the word (*con-certare*), itself far removed from modern Italian reality. Conceptually, this exercise in mediation between two basically different interpretations of musical terminology – the one thoroughly pragmatic (as in Italy), the other just as thoroughly normative (as in Germany) – was bound not to succeed. From it, however, comes the all-too-frequently-cited musicological mis-definition of the '*concertante* principle' as 'struggle': a 'combat' between opposing musical voices, a 'contest' (vocal or instrumental) between one or more soloists on the one hand and one or more groups on the other, a 'competition' between rival stylistic and formal elements. Classical etymology certainly offers Praetorius an excellent means of explaining how 'concerto' has come to be used in the context of few-voiced (solo) and polychoral compositions alike. It also, however, superimposes on the word a competitive, almost bellicose connotation that was totally lacking not only from current Italian usage (based, as this was, on the idea of 'agreement' and 'bringing together') but also from the reality of the music itself.

Having resolved the terminological and etymological tangle in which Praetorius embroils the concept of 'concerto', the fact still remains that the term 'concertare' (in its everyday, non-etymological meaning of 'agreement' and 'bringing together') presupposes an initial heterogeneity, dissimilarity and extraneousness (though without connotations of competitiveness) between the various elements to be 'concerted'. Elements, that is, which would never themselves have been capable of natural or spontaneous harmonization and co-ordination are made to 'concert' with each other: voices with instruments, soloists with *ripieno* ensembles, one choir with another, a large group of instrumentalists with a group of soloists, one style of song with another, a dance-like instrumental style with a madrigal-like episode or a section of recitative, and so on. The union, concord and 'militant' co-operation between disparate yet 'concerted' musical elements represents an agreed compromise – an artificial convergence of tendencies that are naturally divergent. Thus, the concept of 'concerto' presupposes the plurality, multiplicity and diversity of the constituent parts of a composition or performance. In this sense, of course, the use of the word in the title of Monteverdi's Book 7 is highly indicative of the variety, mixture and plurality of the different musical ingredients brought together (or 'concerted') by their composer at will. Or, in a more negative light: the concept of 'concerto' found scanty legitimization in the pervasively polyphonic style of the sixteenth century (despite the high level of formal articulation this style was to reach in the most subtle examples of Seicento madrigal polyphony), with its intentionally compact, balanced and well-blended combination of elements. Rather, this legitimization is to be found in the composite, discontinuous and divided systems and structures of seventeenth-century music, with its plurality of styles and its open and 'breakaway' constitution (see chapter 8). The very ambiguity of the word, however, suspended as it is between a fundamental yet generic significance on the one hand and a terminologically precise but more limited definition of one or more musical genres on the other, is symptomatic of the critical position of the whole seventeenth century.

7 Monteverdi after 1620

After the *Concerto* of 1619, Monteverdi published no further collections of 'madrigals' for almost two decades. The years 1620–22 mark the final reprinting of his 5-part secular works (Books 1–6); after this date, with the advent of the economic and cultural crisis, the interest of publishers and public alike in the madrigal repertory slowly dwindled away. In any case, the interests of the composer himself were subsequently to branch out in a large number of different directions.

Certainly, the years separating Books 7 and 8 (1638) were anything but lacking in activity. *Maestro di cappella* at St Mark's, Monteverdi was also frequently employed as director of the musical entertainments performed in the palaces of the Venetian aristocracy and foreign ambassadors. During these years, a considerable quantity of both sacred and secular music was to flow from his pen, though only a part would be published in his two great collections of later years: the eighth book of madrigals and the *Selva morale e spirituale* (1641). Other compositions were appropriated by Venetian publishers for use either in miscellaneous anthologies or in other somewhat 'opportunist' collections devoted entirely to the music of Monteverdi (the 1- and 2-part *Scherzi musicali cioè arie e madrigali* of 1632; the *Messa a 4 voci e salmi a 1–8 voci concertati, e parte da cappella* of 1650, edited perhaps by the composer's pupil Francesco Cavalli; the 2- and 3-part *Madrigali e canzonette* of 1651). In all these publications, the only 5-part madrigals to preserve even the slightest resemblance to the standard madrigal form are the three *madrigali spirituali* which open the *Selva morale e spirituale*. Only the third of these texts (by Angelo Grillo), however, is a true madrigal. The others – *Voi ch'ascoltate in rime sparse il suono* (the opening sonnet from the *Canzoniere* of Petrarch), and a series of triplet verses from the same poet's *Trionfo della morte* – bear witness once again to the level of freedom attained by their composer in his choice of poetic texts.

Besides music for the palaces and churches of Venice, Monteverdi's output in these years includes a considerable quantity of theatrical music for his earlier employers at the Mantuan court, as also for Parma and Piacenza. Hardly anything of this repertory has been preserved – beyond, that is, the related correspondence, largely consisting of letters addressed by the composer to Alessandro Striggio the younger (secretary to the Gonzaga and librettist of *Orfeo*). Frequently, these letters deal not so much with musical questions as with matters of purely administrative concern: the slowness and reluctance of the Mantuan treasury to see to the payment of long-standing arrears in Monteverdi's pension. Among them, however, is a singularly interesting letter dated 13 March 1620, in which Monteverdi puts forward his reasons for rejecting the entreaties of the Gonzaga to return to court as *maestro di cappella*. In Venice, his services are honoured and rewarded more than those of any of his predecessors (Willaert, Rore, Zarlino), and considerably more so in respect of his previous appointment at Mantua. The composer is also fully aware of a difference in quality between his former and present positions. On the one hand, there is the professionalism of the system of engagement by trial (with obligatory consultation and agreement of the *maestro di cappella*) in use at St Mark's, on the other the arbitrary and all-powerful patronage of a sovereign prince; on the one hand the stability of his highly representative appointment at Venice, on the other the unreliability of the favours of a court that was subject to unpredictable changes within the ruling dynasty, quite apart from abuse of the treasury; on the one hand a city that abounded in patrons of music (not only publishers but also the great diplomatic, religious and lay institutions), on the other a city whose musical life was totally centred within the narrow confines of the court. Monteverdi's awareness of these differences is all the more worthy of note when compared with the 'parallel' analysis – equally disillusioned and by no means less valid – of Galileo Galilei, who finally abandons his public university position at Padua for the peaceful, undiluted dedication to research that only the enlightened authority and protection of the Grand Duke of Tuscany (or his like) had the ability to guarantee. For the experimental scientist and philosopher, the position achieved by the musician means nothing but subjection to the unwritten yet all-powerful law that 'to live from the public exchequer it is necessary to satisfy the public' (Monteverdi, indeed, becomes the musical representative of the dominant culture and authority, purveyor of a service that was destined for public consumption); the 'tranquillity' of the life of the scholar is not to be 'hoped for from any but an absolute prince'.

The letters of Monteverdi, however, are also invaluable for the way in which they present a number of the poetic principles underlying the works of their author. In the absence of the treatise in which Monteverdi had intended to reply to Artusi, letters such as that of 9 December 1616 assume the importance of miniature poetic manifestos. Here, the subject is the text of a series of scenic *intermedi* which the composer feels unable to set. The theme of the entertainment is a 'maritime tale of the marriage of Thetis'; the composer is concerned by the excessive 'depth' of the water, whose realistic representation would require the employment of 'low-sounding' sonorities of poor acoustical effect:

> I shall say then . . . first of all in general that music wishes to be mistress of the air, not only of the water; I mean (in my terminology) that the ensembles described in that fable are all low-pitched and near to the earth, an enormous drawback to beautiful harmony since the said harmony will be placed in the deepest 'air' of the scene – difficult to be heard by everyone, and concerted inside the set . . . because of which defect you will need three *chitarroni* instead of one, and you would want three harps instead of one, and so on and so forth: and instead of a delicate singing voice you would have a forced one. Besides this, in my opinion, the proper imitation of speech should be dependent upon wind instruments rather than upon strings and delicate instruments, for I think that the usic of the Tritons and the other sea-gods should be assigned to trombones and cornetts, not to citterns and harpsichords and harps, since the action (being maritime) properly takes place outside the city; and Plato teaches us that *cithara*

> *debet esse in civitate, et thibia in agris* – so that either the delicate will be unsuitable or the suitable not delicate.

Wind instruments represented the traditional means of portraying the gods of the sea: indeed, they form part of a system of an 'iconography of sound' of sixteenth-century descent, which even now continues to define the horizons of the composer (see chapter 20). Worse again are the problems brought about by the imitation of the speech of the wind:

> In addition, I have noticed that the interlocutors are winds, Cupids, little Zephyrs and Sirens: consequently, many sopranos will be needed, and it might also be added that the winds – that is, the Zephyrs and Boreads – have to sing. How . . . can I imitate the speech of the winds, if they do not speak? And how can I, with their manner [of sound], move the passions? Arianna moved us because she was a woman, and similarly Orfeo because he was a man, not a wind. Music can imitate, without any words, the noise of the winds and the bleating of sheep, the neighing of horses and so on and so forth; but it cannot imitate the speech of the winds, because no such thing exists.

The prosodic and metrical order of the *balli* is not very suitable; above all, however, the composer remains emotionally unconvinced by the drama itself, and consequently asks what the reaction of the audience will be:

> Next, the dances which are scattered throughout the fable do not have dance measures. And as to the story as a whole – as far as my no little ignorance is concerned – I do not feel that it moves me at all (moreover, I find it hard to understand), nor do I feel that it carries me in a natural manner to an end that moves me. *Arianna* led me to a just lament, and *Orfeo* to a righteous prayer, but this fable leads me I don't know to what end. So what does Your Lordship want the music to be able to do?

Scholars have always interpreted these declarations very much to the letter. In reality, their solemnity is tempered with a pinch of irony when Monteverdi, to conclude, advises his Mantuan correspondent that each of the singers (Adriana Basile, Francesco Rasi, among others), whether Sirens or deities, should be asked to compose his own music: 'since this piece, were it to lead (like *Arianna* and *Orfeo*) to a single end, would indeed require a single hand – were its tendency, that is, to speak through singing, and not to sing through speaking as here'. The tone of this closing phrase seems more playful than serious, as indeed is the comment in a letter of 6 January 1617 on the need for a concluding *canzone da ballo*:

> here, we are lacking . . . a canzonetta in praise of the princely bridal pair, the music of which might be heard in the heaven and earth of the stage, and to which noble dancers might nobly dance, since, I believe, such a noble conclusion is fitting and proper for so noble a scene.

More significant evidence of Monteverdi's poetic intent is provided by a letter of 7 May 1627. Here the theme is the somewhat eccentric subject of Giulio Strozzi's drama *La finta pazza Licori*. It is precisely in the figure of the protagonist and his attacks of (simulated) madness that we find the fundamental distinction between imitation of the individual word and the oratorical configuration of musical speech:

> The part of Licoris, because of its variety of moods, must not fall into the hands of a woman who cannot play now a man now a woman, with lively gestures and separate emotions, since the imitation of this feigned madness must only be considered in the present, not in the future or past, and must consequently derive its support not from the sense of the phrase but from the [single] word. Thus, when the words are of war, the singer must imitate war; when of peace, peace; when of death, death; and so on and so forth. And since the transformations take place in the shortest possible time, and the imitations as well – whoever plays this all-important role, which moves us to laughter and compassion, it will be necessary that this woman leave aside all imitations except the immediate one, which the word she utters will suggest to her.

In other words: the vivid musical imitation of the individual word divorced from its context (that is, 'considered only in the present, and not in the future or past') shall provide the most suitable means of portraying a madness which eliminates the rhetorical and syntactical bonds in both music and text (a madness based 'not on the sense of the phrase but on the [single] word') – bonds without which the verbal and musical sense remains incomplete. Conversely, the scenic *intermedi* of Claudio Achillini, performed at Parma in 1628, 'easily' succeed, 'since they consist almost entirely of monologues'; the monologue is the most natural of all forms of sung recitation, and the one most proven by experience (representing, as it does, that condition of musical and oratorical 'normality' already extensively tested in *Arianna*, *Orfeo* and in a host of madrigals which might well be described as none other than miniature monologues). It is hardly by chance that the first of the three would-be chapters of Monteverdi's unwritten treatise would have dealt with the art of 'oration' (the other two chapters were to focus on 'harmony' and 'rhythm') – true basis of the new seventeenth-century style with its ever-present elements (real or potential) of theatre and rhetoric.

More than ever before, it is the concept of oratory (and not the music itself) which provides the point of departure for the preface to Book 8 (the *Madrigali guerrieri et amorosi*). Monteverdi starts off from the premise that music has hitherto offered two equivalents only – those of 'softness' and 'temperance' (*genere molle* and *genere temperato*) – to the trio of stylistic possibilities conceptually recognizable in the affects of wrath, temperance and humility (or supplication). A third musical genre – the *genere concitato*, capable of expressing the affects of anger and war – is lacking. It is, then, in the *Madrigali guerrieri et amorosi* that this missing *genere concitato* first appears. Its oratorical effect is obtained by the rhythmic subdivision of the semibreve into sixteen reiterated semiquavers; this, in the hands of a body of instruments, gives rise to the terrifying effects of extreme agitation which accompany the excitement of battle. The application of this new rhythmic symbolism to the text of the dark and romantic *Combattimento di Tancredi e Clorinda* (a sequence of sixteen *ottave rime* from the *Gerusalemme liberata* of Tasso) is particularly striking: the tenor's declamation of the text (*Testo*) is accompanied by strings and a harpsichord, whose rhythmic reiteration of a few perfect chords is used first in portrayal of the 'motion of the horse', then to evoke the effects of the violent onslaught of the two warriors and their bloody battle (here, the composer also resorts to the occasional use of *pizzicato*). On stage, Tancredi and Clorinda mime the events narrated in the text and add their own few sung interpolations; particularly noteworthy in this context is the lament of the dying Clorinda with her shattered and lacerated declamation of the words 'Amico, – hai vinto; – io ti perdon, – perdona / tu ancora, – al corpo no – che nulla pave . . . ' ('Friend, – you have won; – I forgive you, – forgive / me too, – not this body – which nothing fears'): note the shattering of the two 'gasped' hendecasyllables. The *Combattimento* was first performed during Carnival 1624 at the home of a Venetian patrician: ' . . . an evening's musical entertainment, in the presence of all the nobility, who were so moved by the affect of compassion as almost to cry tears, and who gave their applause for a song never since heard nor seen'. The very novel and exciting effect of the *genere concitato* – in particular, the reiterated semiquaver rhythms – as heard at the Palazzo Mocenigo in 1624 must surely have assumed quite enormous proportions when the work finally appeared in print. Schütz knew it well (he might even have been responsible for a German translation); in the last of his own *Symphoniae sacrae* of 1647, he accompanies the words 'Singet dem Herrn ein neues Lied, macht es gut auf Saitenspiel mit Schalle' ('Sing unto the Lord a new song: let it ring out on the strings') with *tremolo* violins and an agitated syllabic declamation of the text. The tumult and terror of Tasso's two warrior knights is replaced by the awe-inspiring exaltation and Biblical dread of the German psalm.

The *Combattimento* might be described as the fulcrum around which the first half of Book 8 – the *Madrigali guerrieri* – revolves. Parallel is the organization of the *Madrigali amorosi* in the second part of the print (see below); in the index, indeed, the two series of titles are laid out in pairs. In the pieces themselves the mirror images are closely interwoven. The opening text of Part 2 (*Altri canti di Marte . . . Io canto Amor*, which is the opening number in the *Rime* of Marino) is 'opposed' in Part 1 by a sonnet (*Altri canti d'Amor . . . Di Marte io canto*) of corresponding but opposite significance; duos and trios correspond in position (though poetical forms and musical treatments

MADRIGALI GUERRIERI	MADRIGALI AMOROSI
Altri canti d'Amor tenero arciero sonnet (6 voices + insts.)	*Altri canti di Marte e di sua schiera* sonnet: MARINO (6 voices + insts.)
Or che 'l ciel e la terra e 'l vento tace sonnet: PETRARCH (6 voices + insts.)	*Vago augelletto che cantando vai* sonnet: PETRARCH (6–7 voices + insts.)
Gira il nemico insidioso Amore canzonetta: STROZZI (3 voices + b.c.)	*Mentre vaga angioletta* madrigal: GUARINI (2 voices + b.c.)
Se vittorie sì belle madrigal: TESTI (2 voices + b.c.)	*Ardo, e scoprir, ahi lasso, io non ardisco* *ottava rima* (2 voices + b.c.)
Armato il cor d'adamantina fede madrigal (2 voices + b.c.)	*O sia tranquillo il mar, o pien d'orgoglio* sonnet (2 voices + b.c.)
Ogni amante è guerrier; nel suo gran regno elegy: RINUCCINI (after Ovid) (2, 1, 3 voices + b.c.)	*Ninfa che scalza il piede e sciolta il crine* canzonetta (1, 2, 3 voices + b.c.)
Ardo, ardo, avvampo, mi struggo, accorrete sonnet (8 voices + insts.)	*Dolcissimo uscignolo* madrigal: GUARINI (5 voices, *alla francese*) *Chi vuol aver felice e lieto il core* madrigal: GUARINI (5 voices, *alla francese*)
Combattimento di Tancredi e Clorinda *ottave rime*: TASSO (*in genere rappresentativo*)	*Non avea Febo ancora* (Nymph's lament) canzonetta: RINUCCINI (*in genere rappresentativo*)
	Perché ten fuggi, o Fillide canzonetta (3 voices + b.c.)
	Non partir ritrosetta canzonetta (3 voices + b.c.)
	Sù, sù, pastorelli vezzosi canzonetta (3 voices + b.c.)
Introduzione al ballo and *Ballo* sonnets: RINUCCINI (*in genere rappresentativo*)	*Ballo delle ingrate* ballet: RINUCCINI (*in genere rappresentativo*)

are quite dissimilar); theatrical pieces – *da camera* and *da corte* – occur in identical order. Some texts appear in the *Madrigali guerrieri* for no other reason than their incidental use of warlike images and the *genere concitato* (thus, for example, the simile 'war is my state of mind' in the truly agitated musical representation of the anguishes of love in Petrarch's sonnet *Or che 'l ciel*). Sometimes, moreover, the metaphor of the warrior love takes a light-hearted turn, as in the 3-part setting of Giulio Strozzi's canzonetta *Gira il nemico insidioso Amore* with its host of mocking incitements to chivalry and war ('he wants the ramparts of the eyes to assail . . . Come on, quickly . . . All on your horses', or 'on foot, to safety, whoever safety can attain'), or offers the pretext for choral virtuosity and unusual phonetic effects (as, for example, in *Ardo, ardo, avvampo*, with its rapid but stammered reiteration of the cry of 'acqua, acqua, acqua', 'water, water, water . . . ').

Throughout Book 8, Monteverdi demonstrates total freedom of choice in his use of the various formal and creative resources at his disposal, his disregard for 'moderate' means of expression, and his disconcerting and indeed moving exploitation of the contrast between the *genera molle* and the *genere concitato*. At times these two styles are actually employed simultaneously – as in a passage from *Or che 'l ciel*, in which the imploring tone of the tenors in their rendering of the words 'and she who destroys me / is always before me . . . ' is accompanied by the parallel octaves and fifths of the other performers, who literally yell out the text of the previous line ('I keep watch, I think, I burn, I cry'). The stylistic and formal links in the poetry, of fundamental importance in the structure of the polyphonic madrigal, are now much less restricting. Rinuccini's *Non avea Febo ancora*, for example, is a strophic *arietta* comprised of a series of seven- and eight-syllable lines; Monteverdi's monologue setting, however, could easily do service as a perfect operatic aria, so removed is the musical form from the original strophic organization of the text (see chapter 23).

The formal principles of the music, while heterogeneous, are always perceptible and clear (not merely implied, as in the polyphonic madrigal). In the setting of Guarini's madrigal *Mentre vaga angioletta*, originally penned in 1581 in praise of a certain singer named Laura, the wondrous effects of virtuoso singing are illustrated word by word in the two tenor voices: fluttering vocalizations (to the words: 'fluttering harmony'), chromatic folds ('pliant' or 'supple voice'), soaring progressions ('and she pushes it [high]'), broken sighs ('with broken tones': 'con rot-ti ac-centi'), twists ('with twisted turns'), delays and headlong rushes ('here slow – and there she rushes on'), and so forth, in a free succession of episodes held together by nothing more than the opening passage for unaccompanied voice and a *cantabile* conclusion in ternary rhythm ('singing, then, and singing'). At times, the strophic texts are treated as true canzonettas (with a repetition of the same music for each strophe); on other occasions, the form is essentially cyclic (with a different yet related musical setting for each strophe); yet again, the setting can take the form of a through-composed cycle (with a fundamentally different musical section for each strophe); a fourth possibility is represented by a 'monologue' setting for several voices (without but a trace of the original strophic form of the text: a case in point is the canzonetta *Perché ten fuggi*, transformed by the music to an affectedly touching lament). Two formal characteristics mark the light and chatty manner *alla francese* of a number of the *madrigali amorosi*: the responsorial layout of the whole (each phrase is announced by a solo voice with *basso continuo*, then repeated by the other voices together) and the melodiously regular articulation of the syllables (two slurred quavers per syllable). In this, these pieces stand clearly apart from the grand opening sonnets and their spectacular musical gesticulation.

Monteverdi's Book 8 is a perfect example of that multiplicity and variety of styles which typifies the Seicento as a whole. All are enjoyable; all, from the emotional heights of the monologue to the plain and simple style of the canzonetta, co-exist side by side on an equal footing, without regard to stylistic hierarchies. There is nothing, however, undignified in their indiscriminate juxtaposition: the laws of stylistic propriety which govern their correct distribution are, if anything, reformulated case by case in relation to the particular aims and intentions of each text. Each time, the language chosen is that which offers the composer the most effective (though not necessarily the most obvious) means of obtaining a vivid musical representation of the affects – exploiting, indeed, the still novel resources of emphasis and wonder – and consequently of moving the emotions of the listener (see chapters 8 and 9). The form itself is always the result of an interplay of analogies, proportions and repetitions, the result of a musical syntax (a distribution of musical phrases and periods) that strengthens, enhances or opposes the syntactic articulation of the poetry without ever allowing the latter to dominate. Two types of formal articulation – one poetic, the other musical – meet together in harmony and battle: hand in hand with the multiplicity of styles goes the full maturation of a musical phraseology now capable of assuming a form of its own.

II

PROBLEMS OF SEVENTEENTH-CENTURY MUSIC

8 The classification of styles

The multiplicity of musical styles brought together so perfectly in Monteverdi's Book 8 is indicative of an aesthetic and poetic problem of which the seventeenth century itself – in Italy, as indeed throughout Europe – was fully aware. This awareness was above all empirical: the musician who had lived through the decades surrounding the turn of the century and witnessed the disintegration of vocal polyphony as the dominant musical force of the day had every reason to raise the issue of the proliferation of styles. On the surface, it was a question of pronouncing either for or against 'modern' music. Thus, the *Della musica dell'età nostra, che non è punto inferiore, anzi è migliore di quella dell'età passata* (1640) of the Roman patrician Pietro Della Valle is a controversial attack on a defender of the music of the past; for its author, the fundamental distinction is between a concept of music as counterpoint *tout court*, and another in which it is seen as a harmony of three identifiable components or requisites: 'counterpoint', 'song' and 'sound'. In other words: within the framework of a contrapuntal theory and art handed down from the previous century, different manners of singing and playing now imbue contemporary music with a variety of qualities – all quite separate and distinct. These qualities derive not only from different manners of performance but also from different compositional styles: each musical genre is attributed with specific, variable 'song' and 'sound' characteristics. This, undeniably, is progress – an enrichment of the music of the Seicento compared with that of the previous century.

Della Valle (1586–1652), man of letters, experimenter, antiquarian, traveller to the East, was himself a composer: his output, indeed, includes one of the first true oratorios, the *Dialogo per la festa della Purificazione* (composed in 1640 though never performed), in which a certain 'triharmonic' harpsichord, tuned in 'ancient' style, is used in a somewhat *avant-garde* attempt to imitate the early Greek modes. The marchese Vicenzo Giustiniani (1564–1638), Papal banker and avid collector of art (one of the earliest patrons, indeed, of the highly controversial art of Caravaggio and his disciples), was in musical terms a mere cultivated amateur – a status reflected in his own rather unsophisticated classification of the various genres of which he was aware. His list reads as follows: (1) the madrigals of Arcadelt, Lassus, Striggio, Rore and Monte, and the villanellas current in the days of his youth; (2) the music of Marenzio, Giovanelli and Palestrina, 'delectable' polyphonists and notably more advanced, compared with Group 1; (3) the vogue for virtuoso singing which flourished in Rome after 1575 and later spread to the courts of Ferrara and Mantua; (4) the 'great artifice' of the madrigals of the Prince of Venosa and his Neapolitan circle; (5) Caccini and the other great singers of monody, much favoured by Cardinals Ferdinando de' Medici of Florence (later Grand Duke of Tuscany) and Michele Montalto of Rome; (6) sacred music for *cori spezzati*, much appreciated in Spain (as elsewhere) by the sovereign Philip IV. Not without reason, Giustiniani concludes that 'the variety of tastes of the great nobles and princes who delight in music' are such as 'from time to time . . . ' will lead to change ' . . . in the style and manner of singing'. This, indeed, finds parallel in contemporary 'fashions of clothing, which change continuously in accordance with the styles introduced in courtly circles'. So charming is the inconstancy of musical fashion that even the most tradition-bound repertory of all – that of the sacred vocal music of Rome – now pays more heed to the need for 'great variety and diversity' than to 'solidity and artfulness of counterpoint'. And since variety and diversity are favoured more by 'great skill and liveliness of invention' than by 'great maturity and refinement in the science of counterpoint', the average age of the *maestri di cappella* of the various basilicas of the Papal city falls sharply – to such an extent, indeed, that the most senior among them, Vincenzo Ugolini, is already ex-*maestro di cappella* of St Peter's at the tender age of forty.

Such pictures as Giustiniani's vivid sketch of the co-existence and alternation of the various musical styles (each different in origin, age, function, structure and effect) provide the seed which subsequently gives birth, in seventeenth-century musical theory, to the notion of 'style'. This concept was well known in sixteenth-century literature, as also – by extension – in the most literary of all musical styles: the madrigal. Marenzio, in 1587, speaks of madrigals composed 'in a manner very different to that of the past . . . by virtue of a style that aims at . . . mournful seriousness'; indeed, the concept of changing style is embodied in his very choice of texts (by Petrarch and Jacopo Sannazaro), in particular in such verses as 'where'er my am'rous style is brought / to speak of anger and of death', ' . . . and you, Fortune, change this barb'rous style'. For music, however, the question is more one of literary metaphor than of any clearly defined terminological concept. Of literary origin, too, is the notion of the distinction between styles and their respective 'decorum' (their appropriateness and suitability for a clearly defined sphere of topics and themes): one need go no further than the chapter *Che si debbono usar vari stili, sì come varia è la materia del discorso* ('The necessity of using different styles in accordance with the various topics of discourse') from what was possibly the most read treatise on literary precepts of the entire seventeenth century, Daniello Bartoli's *Uomo di lettere difeso ed emendato* (1645).

For musicians, these notions were to arouse particular controversy in the field of Catholic church music, dominated as it was by the traditional stylistic criteria of Counter-Reformation polyphony (see chapter 15), itself hallowed by use and thus tending to reject compositional innovations (which are viewed as stylistic incongruities and breaches of 'decorum'). In 1643, for example, Marco Scacchi (Roman by origin and education, now *maestro di cappella* to the king of Poland) publishes his *Cribrum musicum ad triticum Syferticum*, an attack on certain psalms of Paul Siefert of Danzig (who subsequently replies with a pamphlet of his own, the *Anticribratio musica ad avenam Scacchianam*). In these psalms, Scacchi criticizes a number of modern licences of style: in particular, the use of the *basso continuo* and certain chromatic figurations incompatible with the *a cappella* style traditionally associated with polyphonic settings of the psalms. The versatile Scacchi, whose output embraces not only a number of concerted madrigals but also the earliest theatrical compositions performed in Poland, was certainly anything but a hater of innovation: the point of departure for his treatise is not the out-of-hand rejection of modern music but rather an insistence on the clear-cut distinction between *stylus antiquus* and *stylus modernus* (categorizations, these, which themselves reflect the grouping of the classical authors into ancients and moderns). Object of the controversy is the 'differentia styli in arte musica diversi' (to use a phrase coined by Schütz with reference to the same stylistic distinctions). The two styles, ancient and modern, have equal dignity but differing functions. Each is governed by its own laws and constitution; mixing them together would compromise not only their effectiveness but also, above all, their grammatical correctness. The 'classicism' of Scacchi defines, codifies and consolidates the position of the 'ancient' *a cappella* style of Counter-Reformation polyphony in a way that sets it apart from all notion of historical change; it can, indeed, appear alongside – though not together with – other more modern styles when required by the text, occasion or destination of the work in question.

Over and above the formal and structural distinctions between *stylus antiquus* and *stylus modernus* (which Scacchi, not unforgetful of the Artusi–Monteverdi controversy of some four decades earlier, refers to also as 'prima' and 'seconda pratica': see chapter 4), the function and social destination of the music gives rise to a further, threefold classification of style: *stylus ecclesiasticus* (for church), *stylus cubicularis* (chamber music) and *stylus theatralis* (for theatrical use). This system, as laid out by Scacchi in the *Cribrum* and *Breve discorso sopra la musica moderna* (1649), is further expounded by his pupil Angelo Berardi in the *Ragionamenti musicali* (1681) and *Miscellanea musicale* (1689). In the following summary the authors cited in square brackets are those given by Berardi; they thus represent the stylistic horizons not of the 1640s but of forty years later:

stylus ecclesiasticus

1. masses, motets, etc. in 4–8 parts without organ
   [Morales, Josquin, Willaert, Palestrina]
2. *idem* with organ, including music for *cori spezzati*
   [Bernardino Nanino, Paolo Agostini, Francesco Foggia, Graziani, etc.]
3. *idem*, concerted with various instruments
   [Giovan Vincenzo Sarti, Scacchi, Cossoni]
4. motets and *concerti* in modern style (Scacchi's *stile imbastardito* or 'corrupted style', mixed with arias and recitative)
   [Carissimi, Bicilli, Alessandro Melani, Giuseppe Corsi Celano]

stylus cubicularis

1. *a capella* madrigals 'da tavolino' ('to be sung around a table')
   [Marenzio, Nenna, Abbatini]
2. vocal music with *basso continuo*
   [Monteverdi, Domenico Mazzocchi, Scacchi, Savioni]
3. vocal music with solo instruments
   [Caprioli, Carissimi, Tenaglia, Luigi Rossi, etc.]

stylus theatralis

1. simple recitative style (the only style of theatrical music known to Scacchi, who cites the examples of Caccini and Gagliano; references to the mixed style of arias and recitative are reserved exclusively for the *stylus ecclesiasticus* (4))
   [Peri, Monteverdi, Cesti, Pasquini, Cavalli, Pier Simone Agostini]

Scacchi's classification of styles, while originating in a specific accusation of 'impropriety' with respect to the traditional church music of the Counter-Reformation, also reveals its author's thorough awareness of the many different functions which contemporary music was called upon to perform. As a model it enjoyed considerable success, gaining currency on a European scale. Besides Berardi in Italy, it is also adopted in the unpublished *Tractatus compositionis augmentatus* of Christoph Bernhard (1628–92), colleague of Schütz at the court of Dresden; from here, it subsequently finds its way into Johann Mattheson's *Der vollkommene Capellmeister* (1739). Inherent in the classification itself, however, is a certain disparity between the two sets of criteria, used and interpreted by each author in his own way without ever achieving full 'integration' or reconciliation: on the one hand, a formal-structural classification, based on the compositional and/or expressive qualities of the work in question (*antiquus/modernus*, *a cappella/concertato*, *gravis/luxurians*); on the other, a functional and 'sociological' division in accordance with questions of use and destination (*da chiesa*, *da camera*, *da teatro*). Here, indeed, it is also worth noting how the co-existence of terms such as *grave*, *a cappella*, *antico*, *osservato*, *alla Palestrina* reflects an implicitly 'heterogeneous' view of musical style; the terms in question, though used as synonyms, refer to distinct particulars of one and the same style: respectively, strict and solemn handling of parts, manner of performance, antiquity of style, 'rigorousness' of compositional technique, illustrious master and object of imitation and emulation.

The impossibility of perfect reconciliation between functional and formal classifications is even more apparent in the pages of the immense and labyrinthine *Musurgia universalis* (Rome, 1650) of the Jesuit priest Athanasius Kircher. Though Kircher is anything but systematic in his approach, his classification nevertheless takes account of other relevant aspects of seventeenth-century style which merit consideration. In the first place, his distinction between *stylus impressus* and *stylus expressus* does justice to the dual definition – 'anthropological' and artistic – of the musical styles, their contexts and effects. An identical style or, indeed, composition will have different effects on two different individuals or societies (*stylus impressus*). This difference is determined by the emotional constitution (*constitutio temperamenti*) of the individuals or societies concerned, together with the conditioning of climate and race (*constitutio regionis*): thus, the melancholic will prefer a serious style of composition, the choleric a more martial disposition, the German (colder northern climes) a slow, heavy, serious and elaborate music, the Italian (temperate climate) a florid, melodious and joyful orientation. The *stylus expressus*, for its part, defines the 'particular kind of calculation and method' (i.e., intentional structure) and poetic characteristics of the composition. Kircher lists eight such *styli*, illustrating each with the names of a number of specialist composers (mostly Romans, well known to the author) and, at times, musical examples:

stylus ecclesiasticus (for church), *ligatus* or *solutus* (i.e., with or without *cantus firmus*):

'full of majesty, miraculously transporting the heart to contemplation of the solemn and grave, imprinting on the heart its own motion'. Examples: Palestrina, Lassus, Gregorio Allegri, etc. The *stylus motecticus* is 'a more varied and florid' variant of the *stylus ecclesiasticus*.

stylus canonicus (in canon):

'here, the musical ability of a composer is shown at its most skilful'. Examples: the Romans Pier Francesco Valentini and Romano Micheli (canons in 36 voices divided in nine different choirs). In this context, Kircher might also have cited his own solution to a puzzle canon by Valentini: the *Nodus Salomonis*, a perpetual canon to the notes G–B–D, articulated in no less than 96 voices (24 choirs) – or 512 voices (128 choirs), 128,000 voices (32,000 choirs), 256,000 voices (64,000 choirs), 12,800,000 voices (3,200,000 choirs), something in excess of 232 days of continuous singing, akin to the 144,000 voices of the blessed souls which intone the *canticum novum* at the Apocalypse . . .

stylus phantasticus (using freely invented musical subjects):

'an extremely free and uninhibited method of composition particularly suitable for instrumental music' (in so far as unrestricted by text). Examples: toccatas, ricercars, fantasias and sonatas for keyboard (Kircher cites the works of the German organist and composer Johann Jakob Froberger, pupil of Frescobaldi).

stylus madrigalescus:

'Italian style *par excellence*, joyful, lively, full of sweetness and grace, lending itself easily to vocal diminutions, and eschewing slowness of movement (unless specifically required by the text)'. This style is suitable for the portrayal of love, affection and pain. Distinguished examples: Lassus, Monteverdi, Marenzio, Gesualdo.

stylus melismaticus (measured):

'particularly appropriate for measured verses and metres': strophic texts, ariettas and villanellas (solo or polyphonic), sung sweetly without agitation or affected dissonance. Examples: Giovan Battista Ferrini della Spinetta (today remembered only as a composer of keyboard music).

stylus hyporchematicus (for feasts and festivities) or *choraicus* (for dances and ballets):

this style has the effect of 'exciting emotions of joy, exaltation, wantonness and licentiousness'. Examples: on the one hand, galliards, sarabands, courantes, *passamezzi* and allemandes in the style of Johannes Hieronymus Kapsberger (lutenist at the Papal court); on the other, stage music for ballets and other festivities.

stylus symphoniacus (for instrumental ensemble):

characterized by its use of combinations of instruments. Examples again chosen from Kapsberger.

stylus dramaticus or *stylus recitativus* (recitative style):

suitable for the representation of any of the so-called affections (as also for abrupt changes of affection through sudden alterations in tonality: the so-called *stylus metabolicus*). Examples: Caccini's *Euridice*, Monteverdi's *Arianna*, Landi's *Sant'Alessio*.

Kircher's criteria for the classification and definition of styles are even more heterogeneous than those of Scacchi: social function, indeed, alternates somewhat confusedly with compositional structure and manner of performance as ostensible yardsticks. One homogeneous means of classification does, however, emerge: the ability of each of the various styles to portray the different affections and to excite different emotions – in differing ways and to differing ends – in the listener. In other words: the *styli expressi* are defined by virtue of their 'expressive' qualities, the *styli impressi* by means of the varying 'impressions' they exert on different individuals and peoples. Yet, even here, there remains a flagrant contradiction: the *stylus dramaticus*, which, by very definition, is capable of portraying and exciting not one or few but all the different affections. Here, Kircher reverts to implicitly sociological criteria of distinction – criteria in open contradiction to his exclusively psychological definition of the *stylus ecclesiasticus* or practical description of the *stylus symphoniacus*.

9 Scientific thought and musical theory

Behind Kircher's classification of musical style there lies the psychological theory of the affections, legacy of the natural magic of the sixteenth century, in particular, of the *musicae vis mirifica* (the wondrous power of music), itself based on a supposed harmony and affinity between numerical proportion in music and the passions of the human heart. Of the doctrine of the affections, the Seicento attempted a systematic rationalization. Descartes, in his treatise *Les passions de l'âme* (1649), distinguishes between six basic affections, six simple and fundamental states of mind: admiration (wonder), love, hate, desire, joy and sadness. Christian Wolff, in his *Psychologia empirica* of 1732, was to arrange them in two general categories, *affecti jucundi* and *affecti molesti*. According to ancient physiology, the affections are derived from the various combinations of the four cardinal humours of the body (blood, phlegm, bile, black bile), which themselves correspond to the four temperaments (sanguine, phlegmatic, choleric, melancholic), the four elements (air, water, fire, earth), the four primary qualities (hot and moist, cold and moist, hot and dry, cold and dry) and so on. In the human body, a balanced relationship between the four cardinal humours favours a condition of salubrious harmony; imbalance tends to produce a state of morbid discord. Through the diffusion of the *esprits animaux* in the body, it is possible for the particular melodic, rhythmic and harmonic characteristics of a musical composition to influence, when perceived by the ear, the humoral balance of the individual, in whose heart they provoke 'perturbations' (transitory and gratifying): feelings and sensations that correspond to given emotions.

In providing, then, an effective scientific rationale for the doctrine of *musica pathetica* – a rationale which the sixteenth century had perceived in terms of analogy and affinity – the chief task of seventeenth-century musical theory was to differentiate precisely the relationships between the various individual elements of musical form and technique and individual affections. Kircher (Book 7, chapter 6: 'on the rational organization that must be accorded a melody in order to move a given affection') combines, as usual, unsystematic argumentation with an abundance of contemporary musical examples. Music, he says, may express eight different affections: love, grief/pain, joy/exultancy, rage/indignation, compassion/tears, fear/distress, presumption/audacity, admiration/astonishment. (Elsewhere, however, he groups them into three fundamental affections: joy, calmness and sadness). He accompanies his musical illustrations of each of the affections with truly analytical descriptions (as rudimentary as one could wish) of their effective qualities. Thus, in a madrigal of Gesualdo (*paradigma affectus amoris*), we are told 'how the intervals languish, how the sweet syncopation of the voices is as if to express the syncope of the languishing heart'. No less generic in nature is his famous description of the deeply moving lament of Jephtha's daughter in Carissimi's oratorio of that name (*paradigma affectus dolorosi*). The effect of the music is heightened by an unexpected change of mode:

> . . . after the recitative with which he ingeniously and subtly expresses the jubilant welcome accorded Jephtha by his daughter (who celebrates the victories and triumphs of her father in a joyous dance, accompanied by all sorts of musical instruments), Carissimi depicts, by means of a sudden change of mode, the dismay into which Jephtha has been plunged by this unexpected meeting with his only begotten daughter, against whom he has taken an irrevocable vow, and whom he despairs of being able to save. Joy thus gives way to the opposing affections of sorrow and grief. This is followed by the six-voice lament of the daughter's virgin companions, which Carissimi composes with such skill that you would swear you could hear their sobbings and lamentations. Having, in fact, begun with a festive dialogue, cast in the dance-like tone 8, Carissimi sets this lament in a very different mode, in this case tone 4 intermingled with tone

3. Given this tragic story to portray – a story in which joy is dispelled by the distress and intense sorrow of the heart – the composer suitably chose a mode that is as distant from tone 8 as are the extremes of the heavens from each other, that he might better express, through this opposition, the differences between the affections. And nothing is more capable than this of portraying such unhappy events, such tragic happenings interwoven with affections of a different kind.

Often less suggestive and more rational in tone are the copious speculative writings of other seventeenth-century musical theorists, mathematicians and men of learning, who describe the expressive effect of particular intervals, tonalities, consonances and dissonances. At this point, however, our terms of reference widen. The fundamental problem is less, if anything, the doctrine of the affections than the scientific investigation (both speculative and empirical) of the precise physical definitions of consonances and dissonances, of intervallic relationships and of the temperament of the octave. The solutions offered by the Seicento to these problems show just how much – in music as elsewhere – the systematic and experimental investigation of the age was emancipating itself, in a modern sense, from a slavish and aprioristic respect for the ancients. They undermine the myths and literary *topoi* that surround the wondrous and mysterious power of music, the *ethos* implicit in the ancient Greek modes, and the harmony of the spheres and its effect on the human heart. Nevertheless, the traditional stock of conceptual analogies was certainly widely diffused in the culture of the seventeenth century. Three examples will be sufficient to show this. (1) The second of Marino's three *Dicerie sacre* – imaginary sermons or 'spiritual discourses' – of 1614, entitled *La musica*, spins a lengthy analogy around the themes of the Seven Last Words of Christ on the Cross, the Seven Sorrows of the Virgin Mary, the seven reeds of the syrinx of Pan, Christ/Orpheus, *musica humana/mundana/instrumentalis*, and so on, without even a single reference to the music of his time. (2) In the *Muse napolitane* (1635) of Giambattista Basile (brother of the celebrated Adriana), the section devoted to *Museca* contains the following passage in which the author ironically refers to the tradition of analogy (the original is written in Neapolitan dialect): 'I remember having once heard / from some scholars . . . / that this world is music, / music is man and everything is music, / that heaven is upturned with music, / that beauty is music, and the effects / are musical harmonies, / and music is wholesomeness'. (3) In 1647, Nicholas Poussin proposes the adoption in painting of a system of pictorial 'modes', similar in concept to the musical modes of the Greeks, whose respective ethical qualities would correspond to the various subjects to be depicted. (Indeed, at the end of the century, by which time the superiority of modern tonality had been well established, the *Règles de composition* of Marc-Antoine Charpentier actually define the specific characteristics of seventeen different tonalities – C major martial and gay, C minor gloomy and sad, and so forth. In this tonal variant, the *topos* of the affective qualities of the modes and tones was to continue to find lasting popularity.)

The seventeenth-century mind seeks not to predict and interpret relationships of general analogy and affinity, but rather to investigate measurable relationships of identity and diversity. In the field of musical theory, indeed, this 'modernity' can at times assume forms that to us appear strange. However, the ground between musical and scientific speculation is fertile, and its fruits are decidedly rational and systematic in direction. Thus the imperial astronomer Kepler, in his attempt to explain the structure of the universe (*Harmonices mundi libri V*, 1619), has recourse to modern music: celestial harmony, he says, is not metaphorical but real, though silent nevertheless. (Tommaso Campanella, on the contrary, believed that just as the telescope had revealed the existence of previously invisible worlds, so also the invention of an acoustical aid would one day make possible the perception of the music of the spheres.) Kepler's assertion, apparently absurd, is actually daring in concept. For him, celestial harmony is polyphonic (not merely scalar) and is formed from the interaction of modern consonances (thirds and sixths, which intervals the Pythagorean tradition considered imperfect) that are determined geometrically (a prerequisite for the justification of the tempered thirds and sixths that differed from the arithmetically determined intervals of the Pythagorean model) and are centred on and audible on the sun (not the earth). For Kepler, in other words, modern polyphonic music does not merely imitate, but actually 'reveals', the archetypal structure of the heavens. This would never have been possible in the monodic music of the ancients. Modern music, in its greater affinity with celestial harmony, is therefore more 'beautiful' than that of the ancients, and is also the bearer of an inherent meaning, even when lacking the conceptual aid of a text. (Compare the antiquarian and backward-looking Giovan Battista Doni, whose theories are quite the reverse. His strenuous attempt to demonstrate the polyphonic nature of ancient Greek music – prerequisite for his attempt to legitimize and dignify modern music with the *auctoritas* of the ancient world, thence a revival, highly unlikely in the event, of the *effectus musicae* – is not, however, very productive.)

In the speculative and experimental attempts to determine scientifically the precise intervallic ratios from which consonances are formed, major and minor thirds and sixths – precisely those intervals that from a theoretical and mathematical standpoint are most fragile and unstable – now assume a predominant role. 'Arithmeticians' (from Zarlino to Padre Martini: consonances defined by elementary numerical ratios, 1/1, 1/2, 1/3, 1/4 . . .), 'geometricians' (from Kepler to Tartini: ratios between the area of polygons inscribed in a circle) and 'physicists' (Galileo Galilei and Christian Huygens, both of them sons of musicians: coincidence between the vibrations of two sound-waves), all cannot but recognize the everyday reality of a polyphony based on the preponderance of these intervals. Once the scale had been tempered in a way that gave rise to the largest possible number of just thirds and sixths (the solutions put forward are manifold, the tendency unambiguous), speculation on the ethical significance of each of the ancient modes became meaningless. Instead, theorists turn to consider the specific expressive content of individual intervals (both melodic and harmonic) irrespective of their overall tonal context, the expressive power of modulations, and the function of the dissonances (in their capacity as carriers of transitory perturbations, immediately reabsorbed in the sequence of consonances) as effective means of moving the affections.

The expressive functions of the major and minor thirds form the basis of a bipartite division between the different affective qualities of the major and minor tonalities. (Exemplary is the duet, cited as ever by Kircher, in which Carissimi contrasts the mirth of Democritus, in the major, with Heraclitus' lament, in the minor.) This bipartite division, already operational in polyphonic music at the end of the sixteenth century, is still apparent in nineteenth-century music, though there are now some significant variations in the distribution of the affections. These variations, for the sake of brevity, may be summarized as follows:

	major 3rd		*minor 3rd*	
	softness		harshness	
	sweetness	18th–19th c.	bitterness	
	joy		anger	18th–19th c.
	vigour		sadness	
16th–17th c.	harshness	16th–17th c.	weakness	
	bitterness		softness	
	anger		sweetness	

In the marriage of the doctrine of the affections with the theory of intervals and tonalities, one can detect the possible beginnings of a modern poetic and analytical theory of musical composition. Extremely rare and fortuitous in occurrence, however, is the idea that the expressive power of an interval is determined, or at least conditioned, not merely by its physical extent but also by its harmonic, tonal and rhythmic context. One of the few cases in point is provided by Descartes, in a letter of 4 March 1630 to Marin Mersenne:

> . . . it is one thing to say that a consonance is sweeter than another, another thing to say it is more pleasing. Everyone knows that honey is sweeter than olives, yet many would prefer to eat olives, not honey. Thus, everyone knows that the fifth is sweeter than the fourth, the fourth sweeter than the major third, this in turn sweeter than the minor third. Yet there are places in which the minor third is more pleasing than the fifth, others, indeed, where a dissonance is more pleasing that a consonance.

Meanwhile, Mersenne – whose encyclopaedic compendium of systematic musicology, *Harmonie universelle* (Paris, 1636–37), was the inspiration of a great deal of correspondence between scholars and music theorists from all over Europe – had announced contests in musical composition, involving the Frenchman Antoine Boësset and his Dutch contemporary Joan Albert Ban. This allowed him and his friends and correspondents to speculate comparatively on the expressive qualities of the various musical settings of a given text. Here, as before – thanks, possibly, to the rational method – the most discerning attempt at an analysis is provided by Descartes, whose interest in the metric and rhythmic structure of text and music sets him apart from all the other theorists, concerned exclusively as they are with matters of intonation, harmony, melody, consonance and dissonance. (All in all, the metric and rhythmic theory of the seventeenth century – as indeed, of later periods – is far behind musical reality. Agostino Pisa, whose *Battuta della musica* was published in 1611, confines himself to an untidy summary of sixteenth-century notions and *topoi*. Descartes' observations on musical time, contained in his *Musicae compendium* of 1650 – written, however, in 1618 – do not, as some would say, foreshadow late eighteenth-century theories of musical periodicity, but represent but a sketch of a theory on the rational perception of temporal structures. Of greater importance – though less for his contemporaries than for theorists of the early eighteenth century – is the *De poematum cantu et viribus rhythmi* of Isaac Voss (1673), in which the expressive and symbolic characteristics of the Greek poetic metres are classified and applied to musical rhythm. Voss' erudite theories are symptomatic of the quite singular fact that a concept of rhythm which was based, as in mensural music, on the subdivision of given units of duration, had given way to a radically different system that was based on accentuation and on an essentially temporal concept of motion.)

10 Theory and practice

Rhythm and metre are not the only elements of compositional technique to suffer neglect in the hands of contemporary theorists. In general, seventeenth-century musical theory is little concerned with updating its outlook in line with the precepts of modern 'practical' music. Equally, however, little of the speculative and experimental work of the great theoretical writers of the period finds its way into musical practice. This is more than a question of time-lag: the division between practical and theoretical traditions is profound. Symptomatic of this radical divergence of perspective is the fact that the Franciscan Minim Mersenne, in his strenuous attempt at reconciliation between the conflicting demands of theology and modern science, reserves a full thirty pages for discussion of the unison – three pages more than the space set aside for the various dissonances. It is in the concept of 'unity' – itself unattainable in the limited and finite world of human imperfection, diversity, variety, multiplicity and plurality – that the divine principle behind each and every thing is to be found. Thus, polyphony (*alias* modern music) is viewed by Mersenne as a worthy yet imperfect reflection of music for solo voice (i.e., 'true' music).

Composers – for whom the unison is of little real importance – are well aware of the gap between theory and practice. Marco Scacchi, in his *Breve discorso sopra la musica moderna*, asserts the existence of a 'seconda pratica' but no 'seconda teoria'. In fact, the theory of composition remains quite unaffected by changing musical styles: a single theory is considered sufficient for both *stylus antiquus* and *stylus modernus* ('first' and 'second practices'). Only the applications have changed; the principles remain.

Seventeenth-century compositional theory is essentially the theory of vocal counterpoint. In this sense, complete continuity with the previous century is maintained: in particular, with the great theoretical and practical treatises of Gioseffo Zarlino (*Le istitutioni harmoniche*: Venice, 1558), Lodovico Zacconi (*Prattica di musica*: Venice, 1592 and 1622) and Pedro Cerone (*El melopeo y maestro*: Naples, 1613), themselves subsequently popularized in the many *Specchi di musica*, *Arcani musicali*, *Primi albori musicali*, *Regole di contrapunto*, *Regole di musica*, etc., eagerly compiled throughout the century by modest ecclesiastics for the use of even more modest ecclesiastical musicians. Even the best of the theoretical treatises reflect little of the formal and stylistic innovations of the age: at most, the classification of genres and styles (see chapter 8), the naming and definition of instruments, and the illustration of idiomatic instrumental figuration as an aspect of contemporary performance practice. Twin leaders here, though for different reasons, are the *Syntagma musicum* of Michael Praetorius (Wittenberg–Wolfenbüttel, 1615–20) and *Il Transilvano* of Girolamo Diruta (Venice, 1593–1610). Systematic training in composition, however, is – and remains – synonymous with systematic training in counterpoint. With one significant difference; seventeenth-century counterpoint no longer does justice to that great triumvirate of 'counterpoint', 'song' and 'sound' described by Della Valle as the constituent parts of modern music (see chapter 8).

Contrapuntal theory – i.e., the systematic classification of the intervals (melodic and harmonic) and their various possible combinations and progressions – might be said to constitute the sole terms of reference for all types of sixteenth- and seventeenth-century musical composition. Though certain obsolete rules gradually lose currency, the contrapuntal system as such remains. Perfectly legitimate, moreover, is the extension of permitted margins of licence, in accordance with the genre involved and its degree of adherence to the concept of *musica osservata*. Obviously, however, the system itself is unable to take in those aspects of musical and compositional practice which lie outside its bounds. Seventeenth-century contrapuntal theory, necessarily restricted to a system of fundamentally modal – not tonal – interrelationships, is essentially incapable of formulating a theory of modulation: mid-seventeenth-century theorists, indeed, resort to a motley collection of metaphors (Kircher to modal 'metabolism', Giovanni d'Avella to transitory modal 'eclipses') to explain the chromatic alteration of the modes. Contrapuntal theory, moreover, is unable to explain the typically short-lived phrasing of instrumental music, with its ever-present propensity (in the absence of the conceptual or literary support of a text) for articulation in a veritable frenzy of cadences (at times, one cadence per bar, continued for tens or even hundreds of bars); on the contrary, the golden precept of vocal counterpoint might, if anything, be identified in the notion of the artful forestalment of the end of the musical period and phrase. Worse still, vocal music too (examples may be found in many of the madrigals in Monteverdi's Books 7 and 8) indulges wantonly in this 'madness', freely heaping cadence upon cadence, progression upon progression, repetition upon repetition. This is not 'heresy'; counterpoint, on the contrary, emerges fundamentally unscathed. Undoubtedly, however, the links in the system are too loose to give adequate expression to the many peculiarities of contemporary performance and compositional practice; too uniform, moreover, to offer any acceptable justification for the proliferation of musical genres and styles. Viewed alongside the monodic compositions of Sigismondo d'India, contrapuntal theory loses less in terms of its validity than it does in sheer authority – powerless as it is to explain the reasons for such exuberant efflorescence on the basis of the poverty and rudimentary nature of a 2-part polyphonic skeleton. Counterpoint, moreover, is incapable of offering sufficient theoretical justification for the development of cyclic or repetitive structures such as those of the *scherzo*, strophic aria (with or without *da capo* repetition), chaconne or passacaglia, courante or gigue; it is unable to explain the oscillations or sudden changes of 'affection' of a Frescobaldi toccata, the freakish progressions and scales of a fantasia by Sweelinck or the contrapuntal 'inertia' of recitative (theatrical or *da camera*). In other words, there is an ever-increasing area in the field of compositional practice which, though not directly contradicting the tenets of contrapuntal theory, no longer comes under its control and is thus 'neglected in contemporary theoretical writings.

Some degree of compensation for this deficiency is represented by contemporary handbooks on the art of *basso continuo*. The latter, indeed, might well be defined less as a matter of performance than of true compositional technique, regulated by its own set of internal rules and requirements. These rules are by no means incompatible with the law of contrapuntal technique; on the contrary, their purpose is that of ensuring the contrapuntal validity of the inner parts of the composition: parts left unwritten by the composer of the music but, at most, figured and assigned to the improvisatory abilities of the performer. Adoption of the *basso continuo* is not uniform throughout Europe. In France, for example, its earliest appearances in print – the *Pathodia sacra et profana* of the Dutchman Constantijn Huygens (1647) and *Cantica sacra* of Henry Du Mont (1652) – postdate their Italian equivalents by some fifty years. Treatises on the principles and rudiments of the *basso continuo* circulate in Italy from the first decade of the century. One such example is the *Del sonare sopra 'l basso con tutti li stromenti e dell'uso loro nel conserto* (Siena, 1607) of Agostino Agazzari; the re-publication of this brief text in the *basso continuo* part-book of a collection of Agazzari's own motets (1609) is indicative of its basic orientation as a hand-book for performers (not composers). The same might be said of the *Breve regola per imparar a sonare sopra il basso* (Siena, 1607) of Francesco Bianciardi. Gradually, however, in the course of the century, treatises on the *basso continuo* assume the character of elementary guide-lines for compositional practice; eloquent testimony to this development is provided by the very title of Johann David Heinichen's *Der General-Bass in der Composition* ('The *basso continuo* in composition'), published at Dresden in 1728. Clearly, however, there exists a notable difference between the conceptual framework of a complex and all-inclusive theoretical system of counterpoint such as that of Zarlino and the rudimentary nature of these little treatises on *basso continuo*. The latter, indeed, serve only as aids to practical study and offer nothing by way of theoretical explanation.

Under such conditions, practical training in musical composition is increasingly assigned to the role of imitation: formal study of counterpoint and exercise in the practice of *basso continuo* is now flanked by the (non-codified) emulation of the different musical styles and genres in modern use. From time immemorial, imitation of the 'classics' has provided a touchstone for instruction in music; particular justification for such practices is, indeed, provided in the humanistic orientation of the training of sixteenth-century musicians. If anything, the 'peculiarity' of the seventeenth century resides in the fact that large areas of contemporary musical practice (everything, in short, which eschews definition as 'stile antico' or 'polifonia osservata') lack the support of any kind of poetic and/or theoretical canon and body of recognized 'classic' examples: direct imitation of practical music-making thus provides the only realistic means of study and reproduction. In other words: the compositional procedures described by Zarlino are both necessary and sufficient for madrigals and motets, yet insufficient – albeit equally necessary – for cantatas, toccatas, chaconnes, arias, oratorios, etc. Compensation for this deficiency is provided only by the daily practice of direct imitation. In institutional terms, the result is a strengthening in the concept of 'school' (as reflected in the absence of any generalized, all-embracing theoretical canon and the increased personal importance of the *maestro*); in terms of 'poetics' the effect is a greater propensity for imitation of fashion and an ephemeral musical 'taste'.

Between these two poles – on the one hand, the illustrious genealogy of the great musical schools; on the other, the fickleness of the public market for singers and composers – lies the destiny of 'a profession which', in seventeenth-century Italy, 'is all opinion, with no certainties . . . since the practice of music differs in accordance with the diversity of the schools', 'always *quoad praxim*, not *quoad scientiam*': these are the not insignificant comments of the Roman contrapuntist

Antimo Liberati (himself of direct 'Palestrinian' descent) when asked, in 1684, for his judgment of the works of the various candidates – all non-'Roman' – for the post of *maestro di cappella* at the Duomo of Milan. A picturesque account of the mixture of 'imitative' and formalized methods in musical didactics is provided by the *castrato* Giovanni Andrea Angelini Bontempi in his *Historia musica* (Perugia, 1695). Bontempi, with the hindsight of some fifty years of practical experience in Europe at large, looks back at the great Roman school of the 1640s:

> The schools of Rome obliged their pupils to dedicate a total of one hour per day to the singing of difficult things; this served for the acquisition of experience. One hour on the trill, another on *passaggi*, a third on the study of letters, a fourth on training and other exercises – in the presence of the master and/or in front of the mirror – with the purpose of eliminating all unseemly movement of body, face, brows and mouth. These were the morning activities. After noon, pupils underwent half an hour of theoretical training, half an hour of counterpoint above a *cantus firmus*, an hour of instruction and practice in counterpoint in open score and a further hour in the study of letters; the remainder of the day was spent at the harpsichord or in the composition of some psalm, motet, canzonetta or other form of song, in accordance with individual flair and ability. These were the normal exercises for days on which pupils remained indoors. 'Outdoor' exercises consisted of frequent trips to sing and listen to the echo outside Porta Angelica (towards Monte Mario), with the aim of increasing self-criticism of the scholar's tone of voice; participation in almost all the music of the various churches of Rome; observation of the manners of performance of the many illustrious singers who flourished under Urban VIII; later, at home, practice in these manners of singing and description thereof to the *maestro*: who himself, in his efforts to impress them more firmly upon the minds of his pupils, added all necessary warnings and other remarks. These exercises and general training in the art of music are those given us in Rome by Virgilio Mazzocchi, illustrious professor and *maestro di cappella* of St Peter's.

The deep schism between theory and practice in seventeenth-century music (a schism which, for Italy at least, is laden with far-reaching consequences) brings widespread 'loss of musical competence', a perceptible gap between critical reflection and musical experience. Competent judgments on contemporary music are conspicuously absent throughout the seventeenth century; not before Mattheson and Rameau is there any significant 'improvement' of attitudes. 'The music was excellent', 'truly miraculous music', 'music perfect in its every refinement': these are the typical comments of seventeenth-century poets, singers, composers and cultured observers. A cult of 'ineffability' ('it would be impossible to express the pleasure and enjoyment aroused by this new entertainment in the hearts of the listeners'): the seventeenth century is literally without words to describe the specific qualities of a musical composition. Gone – or no longer sufficient – are the critical and analytical tools as used by Zarlino, Zacconi, Artusi, Pontio and their various contemporaries for the description of sixteenth-century madrigals, masses, motets and other contrapuntal compositions; in the hands of later theorists, these methods are adopted only with reference to vocal polyphony (a case in point is the *Esemplare o sia Saggio fondamentale pratico di contrappunto* of Giovanni Battista Martini, published in Bologna in 1774–76). For the seventeenth-century singer, *maestro di cappella* or amateur madrigal lover, competent analytical reading and reception of music is replaced by ecstatic admiration, sensual or enraptured 'experience', generic and/or emphatic judgment. Attention is shifted entirely away from matters of compositional artifice – which must remain hidden to all persons except 'those who are skilled in their profession and thus capable of particular reflection' (Giustiniani) – to the wondrously evocative allegorical, affective or representative effects of the composition in question. It may even happen that music serves merely as ceremonial accompaniment for some extra-musical event or social entertainment: musical experience is relegated to simple 'atmosphere' or distraction.

The general loss of competence in the production and consumption of music is equally evident in the attitudes and orientations of composers, who lose not only in terms of specifically cultural and musical awareness but also – with the passing of time – in intellectual autonomy and social prestige (see chapter 13). Conversely, there is a notable upsurge of competence in the reproduction of music: an increase in the abilities of singers and other virtuoso performers, who themselves gain enormously in fame, esteem, reputation and social standing.

It might here be objected that the development of a specifically musical rhetoric – a lexical and hermeneutic code of symbolic 'figurae' by which the musical setting reflects the inherent 'rhetoric' of the text – dates precisely from the period in question. The traditional affinities – superficial and generic – between music and rhetoric serve only to accentuate the highly limited nature of the specific phenomenon. More than as an organic project of musical poetics, the seventeenth-century development – itself essentially limited to the activities of a handful of German theorists: Joachim Burmeister, author of a *Musica poetica* (1606); Christoph Bernhard, pupil of Schütz and author of an unpublished *Tractatus compositionis augmentatus*; etc. – may be seen as an attempt to provide a rational explanation, based on the traditional concepts of classical rhetoric and what might best be described as a kind of borrowed rhetorical terminology, for the various contrapuntal licences typical of contemporary Italian musical expression but unjustifiable in terms of the traditional theory of counterpoint. In this sense, the phenomenon – though short-lived – is of true historical significance: the result is an extension of earlier contrapuntal theory to incorporate and legitimize – hence, neutralize and exorcize – licences which would otherwise be regarded as totally irrational. Rhetoric, in short, is used not in the service of oratory and the affections but as simple legitimization of lexical and syntactic irregularities. It is quite impossible to speak of any effective consolidation of the 'system' in the form of a coherent poetic or hermeneutic code. 'I call *figura* a certain pleasing and artful manner of employing dissonances', are the words of Bernhard; since, however, the term 'dissonance' is used by Bernhard himself to describe even an ascending or descending chromatic line – a 'symbol' frequently encountered in the portrayal of affections of notable pain or delight but for which contrapuntal theory offers no explanation save that of a series of consecutive false relations in a single voice – it proves necessary to coin a new 'rhetorical' term: *passus duriusculus*. Indeed, the essentially non-contrapuntal, 'harmonic' nature of this and many other contemporary 'figurae' escapes the notice of the German rhetoricians.

The extent and gravity of the schism between seventeenth-century theory and practice, the prevalence of 'imitative' over formalized training, the importance and significance of the 'non-competent', 'non-analytical' musical experience: all these factors are open to differences of opinion as regards their precise quantification. Clearly, however, the phenomenon as a whole is of massive dimensions, and conditions our own understanding of the music no less than it must have conditioned contemporary means of production and consumption. One reality merits further investigation: the decreasingly 'individual' and humanistic nature of seventeenth-century musical instruction, and its increasingly standardized and functional orientation. As in the previous century, the *maestro di cappella* is responsible for the training of a number of choirboys, for whose board and lodging he receives extra compensation: this ensures – albeit on a minimal basis – a constant turnover in the personnel of the institution concerned and the continuity of the school. Typical, however, of the seventeenth century is the organization of musical education around the great metropolitan hospice-conservatories. Although founded in the sixteenth century, in the course of the Seicento, the orphanages and other benevolent institutions of Venice (the Ospedali of the Pietà, the Mendicanti and the Ospedaletto), Naples (S. Maria di Loreto, S.

Onofrio, S. Maria della Pietà dei Turchini, Poveri di Gesù Cristo) and Palermo (the Casa degli Spersi) introduce regular musical tuision as part of their curriculum of studies. Musical performances or other services organized or otherwise facilitated by the Ospedali bring abundant economic reward. In Venice, offerings for performances by the 'putte' during liturgical functions suffice for the dowries of the girls themselves. Whereas, however, the musical activities of the various Venetian Ospedali are exclusively internal (once married, the 'putte' are required to abstain from all professional musical activity; aristocratic boarders at the Pietà are in any case subsequently restricted to domestic, non-public music-making), their late seventeenth-century Neapolitan equivalents have already become abundant suppliers of singers, virtuosi, *maestri di musica*, *maestri di cappella* and other personnel – manpower for which they will become justly famous in the course of the eighteenth century. Admission of 'external' students – boarders, whose sole purpose is that of acquiring a comprehensive training in music – is encouraged on the grounds that their fees provide a sound economic basis for the more strictly charitable activities of the institutions. The principle of mass production is evident not only in the high number of pupils (an average of some 100 scholars) but also in the type of instruction effectively received: efficient but essentially summary, sometimes provided by a total of no more than three 'all-purpose' teachers (one for winds, one for strings, one for voice, counterpoint and harpsichord). Yet the high-class musical talent supplied by the Neapolitan conservatories is sufficient to satisfy a public demand far exceeding that of previous centuries.

Meanwhile, in Rome, the Jesuit German College is instrumental in creating a musical elite which subsequently serves not only at the various courts of the Italian peninsula but also for the propagation of Catholicism in Protestant lands: the result is a unique combination of prestigious demand, vast geographical coverage, high pedagogical standards and a didactic structure of notable dimensions. Non-ecclesiastical pupils at the College are lavishly sponsored by a wide variety of princes, themselves only too willing to invest heavily in the training of their court singers and composers in Rome. In this way, the organization of musical education in Italy falls increasingly to the Church, which is well aware of the value of music as religious and cultural propaganda. By the late seventeenth century, even the education of the Italian aristocracy and ruling classes – inclusive not only of letters, dancing and fencing but also of the rudiments of music – has passed from the aristocratic management of the literary academies to the much more efficient control of the Jesuit Collegi dei Nobili.

11 Musical publicity

Attribute of authority, pedagogical requisite of the ruling classes, instrument of propaganda and persuasion: these are the three central features of seventeenth-century music as an agent of 'publicity'. To the modern observer, the term 'publicity' – a word which owes its first appearance in Italy to the mid-seventeenth-century Jesuit polemics on the moral lawfulness of theatre – implies several different meanings. 'Public' is the abundant use of music for demonstrative purposes – on a scale, indeed, hitherto unknown – in the various cities and courts of seventeenth-century Europe (festivals, tournaments, processions, ballets, theatrical productions, religious rites, solemn feasts, commemorative odes, etc.). No less 'public', though quite different in kind, is the late seventeenth-century market – particularly expansive in the northern capitals of London, Paris and Amsterdam – for instrumental chamber music: music, this, for private consumption, yet necessarily sustained by a socially conditioned collective taste. In contemporary usage, the concept of 'public' (whichever its grammatical function) is applied in a number of different ways. First, it can be used to describe the intrinsically 'representable' quality of an artistic patrimony which belongs to society as a whole; public authority, the public good, public institutions and their guarantors, etc. It also, however, refers to the collective fruition – effective or potential – of any artistic event or 'product' for the use and/or consumption of a restricted or generalized 'public': a particular assembly of spectators, or music lovers in general. Finally, it alludes – in its modern sense of 'publicity' – to the propagandistic function of a music which incorporates a multitude of cultural and ideological messages and symbols, effectively exploited as a means of 'public' persuasion. These three different forms of musical 'publicity' can frequently co-exist side by side in a single 'cultural' event: the celebration of solemn Mass with music in one or other of the Roman basilicas, for example, serves also as the public 'representation' of a clearly defined social grouping (itself ideally embracing the ecclesiastical hierarchies of both heaven and earth) and an alluring occasion for collective ceremonial and spectacle. Pietro Della Valle openly confesses his 'much more frequent' attendance 'at churches where the singing is good' and where his soul is more easily moved to a 'spirit of devotion, repentance and elevated desire for heaven and the other life'. However, the various definitions of 'public' do not always coincide with each other. It is necessary to proceed case by case.

The notions of 'public' and 'publicity' vary widely in accordance with social structure, forms of government and modes of artistic production and consumption. No less variable is the extent – both quantitative and qualitative – of the definition in question. Public 'musical' events, with participation of the populace as a whole, are by no means uncommon: one such example is the ceremony for the laying of the first stone of the church of S. Maria della Salute, Venice, at the conclusion of the plague of 1631 (with solemn Mass expressly composed for the occasion by Monteverdi). More frequently, however, the event is addressed to a limited number of persons of more or less homogeneous social standing and derivation: a 'public', then, in so far only as representative of a particular community (and on condition that the event in question be intended as a manifestation of the authority of its promoters). In this sense, much of the ceremonial and – consequently – musical life of a court is essentially 'public' in nature (in so far as it is an 'action of State'), even in cases where the audience is restricted to sovereign, courtiers and, at most, the political representatives of the populace. Particularly instructive in this respect are the many contemporary court *balli*, *ballets de cour* and masques (see Source reading 2) – forms, these, of ceremonial exaltation of sovereign power. Not surprisingly, in fact, this represents the dominant conception of 'publicity' in seventeenth-century Europe: a 'publicity' directed towards – and emanating from – what, in social terms, might be described as a highly select form of audience (albeit formally delegated to represent society as a whole). Only in the complex social dynamic of the larger cities – Venice, Naples, Paris, London, Amsterdam – is it possible to speak of more generalized and pervasive forms of musical 'publicity'.

In terms both of musical didactics (a sector of no small importance for the social employment of music) and the professional organization of musicians, a glance at the situation in northern Europe – where the Church is no longer the greatest promoter and organizer of contemporary culture – reveals a number of significant variants in the notion of musical 'publicity'. In Paris, for example, professional instruction in music takes place not against a background of Italian-style pedagogical structures but on an essentially individual basis; teaching activities, however, are regulated by the corporation of musicians – the confraternity of Saint-Julien-des-Ménétriers – on the basis of royal patent and monopoly. Under Louis XIV, the monopoly becomes the property of the Académie royale de musique (see chapter 25). The latter, however, is principally engaged in the field of operatic production and contemplates only such teaching as necessary to guarantee the 'turnover' and replacement of singers and other musicians. In any case, the corporate management of musical instruction provides a strong incentive for the hereditary transmission of the profession: entire dynasties of musicians will dominate the Parisian market for decades to come. The State monopoly, moreover, exerts a highly centralizing influence: musicians tend to congregate around the institutions of sovereign, court and capital. In short: the monopoly, though preventing any widespread diffusion of the profession, ensures the constant availability of an efficient team of musicians in the service of the State and its forms of 'public' representation.

'Public' musical requirements are, in fact, of notable dimensions. The 'musique' of the Roi Soleil – organized in three distinct institutions: the Chapelle (for sacred music), Écurie (for military needs and parades) and Chambre (a 'chamber' institution which includes the *Vingt-quatre violons du roi*, a permanent orchestra established at the time of Louis XIII) – provides employment for some 150–200 musicians, of which half (the so-called *musiciens officiers*) are registered as permanent court officials, the remainder (the *musiciens ordinaires*) as employees on an indeterminate basis. Occasions for musical performances range from the commemoration of great historical events (as, for example, a triumphal *Te Deum* in thanksgiving for some military victory) to the day-to-day etiquette of court life (the spectacular *petit lever du roi* or *souper du roi*, celebrated in fact only twice monthly in music). The favour bestowed by the sovereign upon the *tragédie lyrique*, together with the managerial initiative of its creator Jean-Baptiste Lully, succeed in establishing the remarkably active Académie royale de musique as the effective standard for musical and theatrical custom and taste in Parisian 'public' life (see chapter 25). Such fervid and continuous deployment of 'regal' music and musicians has an openly propagandistic significance: in short, the musical portrayal of the excellence of government and the glorious future of the nation. As such, it presupposes the existence of musical institutions of suitable lushness and exuberance, as also the creation of a well-organized system of musical functionaries and other professionals. The absolute monarchy of Louis XIV brings further consolidation of the ceremonial and, above all, demonstrative functions of music in France; in this respect, music does nothing but follow the other sciences and arts, themselves enshrined by the King's minister Colbert in a series of

Académies whose aim was the prosperous development of the disciplines concerned for the benefit of 'all': economy, technology, industry, the art of war, the 'public' good, the nation as a whole. Further consolidated, too, is the intrinsically 'public' position of music: court and city look on in wonder at musical exhibitions which, as agents of 'publicity', are directed towards – and, so to speak, belong to – the entire nation. In comparison with the esoteric and encyclopaedic projects and programmes of the Académie de poésie et de musique (founded in 1570 under the auspices of Charles IX), the contrast could hardly be more acute: typical of this latter Academy is the almost secret cultivation, in the course of a series of private Sunday meetings, of the natural sciences, languages, geography, mathematics and art of war, together with the training of a few selected poets and musicians in the exercise of 'measured' music in the ancient style (an attempt, this, to procure for the members of the organization those identical effects of moral regeneration attributed by the ancients to the virtues of music). The Académie, indeed, would eventually come under attack from both parliament and Sorbonne, jealous of the royal privileges and favour enjoyed by this exclusive circle of non-'public' intellectuals.

In London, where the position of the monarchy is undeniably less stable, the patent and monopoly for the teaching and public performance of music is the subject of bitter competition between city and court. All attempts to institute a 'public' school of theoretical music (such as that of the composer and organist John Bull, from 1596 to 1606) end in early failure. By the early sixteenth century, music degrees are obtainable at the universities of Oxford and Cambridge: one of the many graduates is the lutenist and composer John Dowland, himself little appreciated at court but highly acclaimed in noble *dilettante* circles by virtue of the intensely pervading melancholy – most private, least 'public' of the affections – which inspires his four books of *Airs* (1597–1612) and the seven mournful pavans of his *Lachrimae* (1604) for consort of viols. England, throughout the seventeenth century, boasts nothing of similar structure and intent to the Académie royale de musique. The enormity of the difference between England and France emerges no less plainly from a reading of two highly successful tutors: the *Plaine and easie introduction to practicall musicke* (1597) of Thomas Morley and the *Introduction to the skill of musick* (1654) of John Playford. Collaborator for the twelfth edition of the latter (1694) is Henry Purcell. These rapid 'do-it-yourself' tutors are promoted by two local publishers, themselves only too aware of the advantages of rapid dissemination of the rudiments of music in terms of domestic consumption and increased sales potential. Morley's editorial initiative is undoubtedly responsible in part for the ephemeral yet flourishing success of the English madrigal 'school' (a total of some fifty publications, spanning the years 1588–1627 and containing some 1,000 different madrigals). That of Playford lays the basis (in the aftermath of the Civil War) for the relaunching of a modern English musical press – a notable contributor to the diffusion of the contemporary vocal and instrumetal chamber repertory. Fundamental, in both cases, is the expansion of a lively 'private' sector.

'Private', however, is perhaps something of a misnomer in the light of other contemporary innovations. In the second half of the century, the domestic market for bourgeois/*dilettante* consumption leads to the development of a variety of entrepreneurial forms and occasions which clearly prefigure modern patterns of 'public' musical consumption. In 1672, the first series of regular, commercially-orientated public concerts takes place in London; performances are organized in taverns, and quickly come to be accepted as part of the normal civic life of the capital (along, indeed, with tea, coffee and other 'sociable' tavern drinks). In 1683, Henry Purcell – writing in the *London Gazette* – invites subscriptions for an edition (of which he himself is both editor and distributor) of his own trio sonatas; in the following decade, theatrical airs by Purcell begin to appear now and then in the pages of the *Gentleman's Journal*. In short: the composer addresses himself directly to what is an essentially bourgeois public, without necessity for aristocratic patronage or royal privilege and monopoly (in open contrast with Italy and France). Public concert and domestic consumption are two complementary aspects of a musical life based largely on a bourgeois notion of 'publicity' – a notion which owes its very origins to contemporary developments in English and Dutch society. This is a 'dynamic' publicity, enshrined in a 'public opinion' which finds its ideal means of expression in the press and the cultural circles of the elite – a publicity quite out of keeping with contemporary forms of public representation of royal power. The Restoration monarchy, in fact, resorts to blatant imitation of the most openly absolutist models of musical publicity available from continental Europe: those of Lully and the Roi Soleil. Purcell himself, arbiter of the musical tastes of his fellow countrymen, is also the leading musical functionary at court.

Meanwhile, in France, the musical 'publicity' of the sovereign – dominant in court and city alike – overshadows but by no means eliminates the domestic consumption of music. The glories of the

French lute tradition – glories epitomized in the title (*La rhétorique des dieux*) of an illuminated manuscript of works by the greatest of all French lutenists, Denis Gaultier – decline notably as a consequence of the decreasing political and cultural autonomy of the French aristocracy (themselves the natural patrons of the repertory in question) under the absolutist policies of the Roi Soleil (himself an exponent of the somewhat less 'noble' guitar). Original lute characteristics do feature, however, in the small and highly 'private' repertory of French keyboard suites (of which the earliest important collections are those published by Jacques Champion de Chambonnières in 1670, together with a notably limited number of later seventeenth-century publications by Jean-Henri d'Anglebert and Nicolas-Antoine Lebègue): in particular, the so-called *style luthé* (or *brisé*), with keyboard imitation of the typically lute-inspired refraction of arpeggiated chords. The French keyboard repertory is based in its entirety on the artificial stylization of what might best be described as 'society music'. Every *homme de qualité* – like Monsieur Jourdain, the 'bourgeois gentilhomme' of the celebrated *comédie-ballet* by Molière and Lully – maintains his own *maître de musique* and *maître à danser*. In a centralized, conformist society such as that of the French capital, 'chamber' concerts in the various palaces of the nobility come to be seen as something of a fashion. These concerts, while essentially 'private', are openly flaunted to society in general – information on performances is published in the *Mercure galant* (general chronicle and gazette of political, social and cultural happenings in the fashionable life of both city and court) – and contribute enormously to the formation and consolidation of a standardized and highly selective 'goût' (to which society as a whole must conform). A further effect is the increasing importation of vocal and instrumental music from Italy, and, with this, the highly controversial and fiery debate on the superiority of French or Italian musical style (a debate, this, set in an 'intellectual' atmosphere which, in the spheres of literature, theatre and music, literally 'creates' public opinion: a public opinion at times openly in conflict – though invariably conditioned by a relationship of action and reaction – with official court culture).

Not only Paris and London (the former with its heavily centralized social and cultural models, the latter with its fervent mercantile and parliamentary activities) but also many other cities are characterized by the almost total 'involvement' of music in public life. 'Public' musical consumption is a growing feature of a number of centres on the Italian peninsula: in the contemporary 'guide-books' to the monuments of Ferrara, Genoa, Venice and Rome, 'tourists' are informed in precisely which churches they will find the most excellent choirs, organs, organists and singing nuns. In cases where power is divided between different institutions, music serves as a means of individualization and differentiation. Conflicts can arise: at Naples, competition between the musical establishments of the Viceroy and Tesoro di S. Gennaro (respectively, the court music and city music) can sometimes erupt in open conflict, even on occasions when political and ecclesiastical powers are seen to converge. The *cappella vicereale* does all in its power to prevent the employment of 'outside' theatrical singers in its midst – a development, for example, favoured by the young Alessandro Scarlatti. These singers, representatives of a new and undoubtedly fascinating – but ill-famed – form of 'publicity', are viewed as undue intrusions in the traditional 'sacredness' of the ecclesiastical repertory. In Bologna, even in cases where the personnel of the various local institutions – the Concerto Palatino, the *cappella* of the Basilica di S. Petronio, the Oratorians, the Accademia Filarmonica – coincide, their functions remain quite distinct. When, however, civil, political and ecclesiastical powers are but one, the fundamental contest for musical 'publicity' is waged between State and private sectors: the prime example is Venice, where State and semi-State institutions (the Ducal Basilica di S. Marco, the Scuole Grandi and Piccole, the 'Ospedali') are flanked by a truly massive array of 'extra-institutional' structures (above all, operatic: see chapter 21) equipped for the 'public' performance of music. During Christmastide – in the immediate run-up to the operatic season – the great virtuoso *castrati* of the late seventeenth century (Francesco Antonio Pistocchi, Domenico Cecchi, Matteo Sassano, etc.), themselves under contract to one or other of the city's theatres, can be heard in the performance of solo motets during Office and Mass in St Mark's; this 'occasional' osmosis of theatrical and ecclesiastical modes is by no means considered unseemly or 'corrupt'.

What, then, of Rome, capital city of world Catholicism? The jurist Grazioso Uberti, in his *Contrasto musico* of 1630, names seven different types of venue where music is performed: 'schools', 'private houses where concerts are given', 'palaces of princes', 'churches', 'oratories', 'open-air settings', 'the houses of composers'. Not many years later, an eighth venue – the theatre – might legitimately have been added. At Rome, though theatres are located in the private palaces, they are not without obviously 'public' connotations: a theatre such as that of the Barberini family of Pope Urban VIII – with its capacity for literally thousands of spectators (see chapter 20) – can hardly be considered as 'private'. In the Colleges – themselves centres of education for the future leadership (both civic and religious) of Rome – musical activities culminate in end-of-year 'displays' and Carnival-tide cantatas. Concert life is centred on those palaces which set the tone of Roman artistic life as a whole (in particular, the residences of the Papal families, cardinals, fashionable men-of-letters and foreign ambassadors). In church not only the normal liturgical year but also the forty hours' devotion, adorations, triumphs, funerals, canonizations and anniversaries are celebrated in music; during Advent and Lent, piety and devotion are fuelled by musical performances at the Oratories. 'Open-air' spectacles range from masquerades to triumphal carnival chariots, serenades, illuminations, tournaments, jousts and processions – always, however, with music. Of all Uberti's categories, only the houses of composers (as, for example, the Abbatini household: see Source reading 3) can be regarded as truly 'private'.

In short: the development of an essentially dynamic concept of 'public' and 'publicity' – a culturally and socially defined concept which eschews all question of a rigid, 'legal' distinction between private and 'public' – necessarily requires both flexibility and fluidity of environment; the result is the growth of the enormous variety of forms of collective musical consumption effectively available for seventeenth-century musicians. The dynamic role of 'publicity' is apparent in every form of contemporary musical life – in ways and to degrees quite unknown in the previous century (itself dominated almost exclusively by the tradition of vocal polyphony), yet rationalized and institutionally organized only in the course of subsequent generations of patrons, composers and society. Related – if not, indeed, subordinated – to the predominantly 'public' role of seventeenth-century musical performance is the veritable schism (itself rich in consequences for the future) which comes to divide the functions of performer and listener. Gone is the earlier 'circularity' of relationship between musical production and consumption, as epitomized by the 'inside' knowledge of compositional procedures presupposed from the listener and implicit in the poetics and theory of sixteenth-century vocal polyphony (it should not, however, be forgotten that the late seventeenth century sees the widespread growth of domestic music-making on the part of amateur instrumentalists, and that this phenomenon will eventually form the nucleus of eighteenth-century bourgeois musical culture). Source of glory and prestige, sonorous device of an institution, collective entertainment for a community, adornment for ceremonial occasions, instrument of worship, demonstration of power: these are the ideologically orientated functions which dominate the horizons of seventeenth-century musical consumption; knowledgeable appreciation of music, while still undoubtedly a feature of seventeenth-century cultural life, is relegated to the sphere of the private and elite. Likewise, music is increasingly absent from the list of the traditional sciences. Frequently, indeed, it assumes the somewhat servile characteristics of a functional and essentially disposable commodity; Mersenne's desire to resurrect the 'encyclopaedic' attitude of the late sixteenth-century Académie de poésie et de musique runs contrary to reality. Private and public performance, the autonomous cultivation and heteronomous purposes of music are now divided in a problematic yet fruitful opposition which culminates with the integration of the art of music in the processes and conflicts of modern dynamic society.

12 Music publishing and music collecting

If, as it would appear, the seventeenth century brings a gradually increasing awareness of the value of music as 'publicity', the repercussions for the music publishing trade will not be difficult to envisage. Business, in fact, declines: a few good manuscript copies in the hands of the right musicians are now sufficient to reach the particular public in question. At the same time, manuscript circulation facilitates the preselection of audiences to a degree quite inconceivable in the case of printed editions.

Certainly, the publishing trade can act as official 'guarantee' of adequate circulation when required. A case in point is the sumptuous folio choir-book edition of Palestrina's 4-part hymns (Antwerp, 1644), itself an effective musical 'ratification' of Urban VIII's reform of the Catholic hymnal. Such, indeed, is the weight of this gesture of authority on the part of the Holy Catholic Church that neither composer nor revisers are named in the print. On a somewhat more modest plane, certain Roman publishers and editors of anthologies of few-voiced motets and psalms (with *basso continuo*) by contemporary Roman musicians provide an effective means of distribution for a modern ecclesiastical genre of sufficient accessibility to ensure the availability of a sober and respectable musical repertory for even the smallest and least distinguished of musical establishments: examples are provided by the prints of Fabio Costantini, *maestro di cappella* at Orvieto (eleven anthologies between 1614 and 1639), Don Florido de Silvestris da Barbarano, canon at the Church of Santo Spirito (sixteen anthologies between 1643 and 1672) and the publisher Giovan Battista Caifabri (four anthologies between 1665 and 1683). In France, the concession of a royal printing privilege and monopoly to the firm of Ballard ensures maximum prestige for official editions of royally patronized music (examples are the *tragédies lyriques* of Lully, and the fifty *grands motets* of 1684–86). These 'monumental' documents of French State culture – destined more for the admiration of the nation than for any practical consumption – are thus set apart from all questions of market competition (itself effectively eliminated). The beginning of the century saw the publication of the complete score of several Italian court operas (for example the two Florentine settings of *Euridice* of 1600, the Mantuan *Orfeo* and *Dafne* of 1607–08, the Roman *La catena d'Adone* of 1626 and the Roman *Sant'Alessio* of 1631). These publications serve less as the basis of future performances (i.e., the musical 'reproduction' of what, in reality, is a unique and unrepeatable theatrical event) than as simple souvenirs: retrospective testimony to the splendour of some politically and/or artistically important 'happening', the self-glorification of a court in the eyes of its peers both in Italy and abroad – as represented by the copious network of ambassadors, residents, legates, orators, etc. (On occasion, however, these scores can indeed serve the purposes of some enterprising provincial impresario or singer, who thus attempts to save the costs involved in new operatic commissions: *La catena d'Adone* and *Sant'Alessio*, for example, are the subject of a few scattered northern Italian revivals in the 1640s; *Sant'Alessio* is revived as far afield as Poland.) Sovereigns, in fact, are quick to take advantage of the greater effect of engraving not the music but the fabulous set designs of their operas; collectors of these documents, after all, are not musicians but princes, courtiers and men of letters. After the fourth decade of the century, publication of operatic scores all but ceases to exist and the repertory circulates almost exclusively in manuscript form.

The *Symphonies pour le souper du Roi* of De La Lande, in common with other ceremonial works of exclusive yet 'repetitive' destination, long continue to be performed from manuscript copies but are never published. Likewise, the specific musical repertories of the great basilicas and congregations survive in manuscript form; these repertories are frequently linked to particular local traditions and performance practices, not easily transferable to other situations and contexts. Examples are the polychoral compositions of Virgilio Mazzocchi and Orazio Benevoli for the Cappella Giulia of St Peter's, the instrumental music and motets with solo trumpet(s) for the Basilica di S. Petronio of Bologna, the state requiems and masses for the Venetian ducal chapel of St Mark's, the polychoral masses, motets and psalms (two choirs, two organs) for S. Maria Maggiore of Bergamo, the evening lessons, Passions and Christmas pastorals for the Oratory of Naples. Other reasons can also lead to the effective 'limitation' of a repertory to a particular church. Alexander VIII, it would appear, objects to the publication of the Latin dialogues and motets of Giacomo Carissimi on grounds of the less than strictly liturgical nature of their texts: in one Christmas motet, for example, a metrical Latin text (in hendecasyllables) is combined with a *strambotto*-like musical setting in a concluding imitation of bagpipes ('piva si placet'). The prohibition, however, applies only in Rome, and a certain number of Carissimi's compositions are eventually published in German editions (the composer himself is employed as *maestro di musica* at the Jesuit-run German College of Rome, itself dedicated to the defence and propagation of the Catholic faith in German-speaking lands). After Carissimi's death, provisions in his will and a Papal brief (issued by Clement X) protect the integrity and inalienability of the manuscripts concerned, which remain the property of the Jesuit College (a sole Roman publication of Carissimi's music – a selection of *Sacri concerti* – is printed posthumously by Caifabri for Holy Year, 1675): as in many other cases, however, the result is a general 'squandering' of repertory potential once immediate need and topical interest has subsided.

The free circulation of manuscript copies brings a high degree of early 'selection' and, ultimately, dispersion of the repertory in accordance with 'taste' (itself a phenomenon whose history may be said to begin in the century under consideration). Accurate and authoritative copies have been conserved of the various Latin *historiae* composed by Carissimi for the German College and Oratory of the SS. Crocifisso at Rome: these, however, are now housed in Paris, where they were brought by Carissimi's pupil Marc-Antoine Charpentier (who copied several of the manuscripts in question). Manuscript collections of cantatas and operatic arias are compiled by teams of copyists for the courts of the various Papal families and Roman aristocracy in general (prominent are the Ottoboni, Pamphili, Chigi, Barberini, Ruspoli, Colonna); these manuscripts are produced at the expense and for the private consumption of the families concerned. Other manuscripts circulate in the 'baggage' of individual singers; still more are produced on an occasional basis for the needs of 'tourists' from northern Europe (young gentlemen from England, Germany and France, engaged on the grand tour of Europe). No local Dutch manuscripts of the music composed and performed by Sweelinck for the Reformed Church of Amsterdam have survived (though the music itself was provided at the

Table 2. *Anthologies and selected individual publications, 1591–1700*

	1591–1600	1601–10	1611–20	1621–30	1631–40	1641–50	1651–60	1661–70	1671–80	1681–90	1691–1700
Venice (anth.)	95	90	52	41	9	14	6	4	1	3	—
Venice (indiv.)	220	162	151	117	39	15	10	9	8	6	15
Milan (anth.)	10	16	13	6	1	4	2	—	1	1	1
Bologna (anth.)	—	—	3	—	—	1	—	4	2	2	4
Bologna (indiv.)	—	—	2	—	—	2	2	8	26	29	34
Rome (anth.)	12	3	13	18	8	16	9	11	4	2	—
Naples (anth.)	3	8	15	9	—	2	2	—	—	—	—
Germany (anth.)	24	56	47	34	10	23	25	11	6	4	4
Germany (indiv.)	33	50	61	33	9	7	43	44	38	13	15
Low Countries (anth.)	25	19	16	17	5	13	6	4	1	1	17

Data for both anthologies and individual publications have been taken from the listings in *Répertoire international des sources musicales*. The latter, however, contains only editions of which one or more part-books have survived (with omission of those publications documented exclusively in the non-musical sources), and fails to distinguish between true anthologies and single-author prints containing a limited number of pieces by additional composers. Data must thus be regarded as approximate. Individual publications have been considered on the basis of a very limited sample: only those composers whose names begin with B or G.

city council's expense: the employment of musicians and production of 'cultivated' music was forbidden by the Calvinist Church as such); only the manuscript copies compiled by and for the composer's various German pupils (Heinrich Scheidemann, Samuel Scheidt, Paul Siefert, Andreas Düben, etc.) have prevented the total destruction of the repertory. As for England, the colossal Fitzwilliam Virginal Book – principal source of the contemporary English virginal repertory – would never have existed had its copyist, the persecuted Catholic Francis Tregian, not set himself the unenviable task of relieving the boredom of a ten-year spell (1609 until his death in 1619) in the Fleet prison in London.

The decline of publishing activities throughout Europe (and, in particular, in Italy) may also be attributed directly or indirectly to the effects of the grave economic crisis of 1619–22. The cost of wood – and, consequently, of paper – rises steeply; by mid-century, Venetian publishers have universally come to prefer rough and fragile paper made from rags. The increase in production costs and retail prices serves only to add to the general pattern of market contraction. The crisis is particularly evident in the case of anthologies; these require greatest financial investment on the part of the printer and thus most directly react to market sluggishness. Individual publications are more slowly affected (the composer or dedicatee can usually be expected to cover a significant percentage of printing costs and/or to purchase not inconsiderable numbers of copies). A limited survey of prints by musicians whose surnames commence with the letters 'B' or 'G', however, provides eloquent comment on the fortunes of printing at Venice. In Table 2, individual ('B' and 'G') and anthological data from the Low Countries, Germany and the principal cities of the Italian peninsula (Venice, Milan, Bologna, Rome, Naples) are compared decade by decade. More striking than the disappearance of 'anthological' printing at Milan (second only to Venice in the period prior to 1620) and Naples (after a period of moderate activity at the time of Gesualdo and Montella) is the remarkable decline of music publishing in Venice – a city which, throughout the sixteenth and opening decades of the seventeenth centuries, had attracted the overwhelming majority of the Italian publishing business, with regular diffusion of works not only on the Italian peninsula but also in German-speaking lands. German printing activities – which, with the exception of the few great publishing houses and distributors of Nuremberg, Frankfurt and Cologne, exude an air of all-pervading provincialism – are largely confined to the re-issue of earlier Venetian editions and the production of new sacred and secular anthologies; here, too, contraction is a necessary consequence of decline at the source. The albeit short-lived revival of German publishing after decades of depression (decades which coincide, above all, with the Thirty Years War) is based on the 'provincial' distribution of Protestant church music for local consumption. Something similar occurs in the two 'Papal' cities of Rome and Bologna. Roman publications include not only the aforementioned anthologies but also a series of 'model' prints of music for mass consumption: the twenty-five collections of motets or *sacri concerti*, psalms, hymns, litanies and masses, published (largely posthumously) between 1650 and 1678 by Bonifacio Graziani (d. 1664), *maestro di cappella* at the Church of the Gesù and Roman Seminary; the eighteen analogous publications (1645–81) of Francesco Foggia, *maestro di cappella* at St John Lateran and S. Maria Maggiore. At Bologna, towards 1660, the booksellers Antonio Pisarri, Marino Silvani and Giacomo Monti succeed in creating – practically from nothing – a flourishing business and market for printed music. Activities, however, are essentially limited to a 'pool' of local – albeit prolific – *maestri di cappella*: a predominantly sacred repertory includes a total of over forty publications (1659–77) by Maurizio Cazzati (*maestro di cappella* at S. Petronio), twelve (1681–94) by his successor Giovanni Paolo Colonna, eleven (1667–75) by Carlo Donato Cossoni (organist at S. Petronio), twenty-two (1677–1710) by Giovan Battista Bassani (organist and *maestro di cappella* at the cathedral of Ferrara). More interesting than this 'militant' Catholic sector is the increased role of instrumental music in the catalogues of late seventeenth-century Bolognese publishers: five such collections (1666–69) by Giovan Battista Vitali (instrumentalist at S. Petronio, subsequently *vicemaestro di cappella* at the court of Modena), five (1668–89) by Giuseppe Colombi (director of instrumental music to the Duke of Modena), six (1669–78) by Giovanni Maria Bononcini (*maestro di cappella* at Modena Cathedral). Neither Rome nor Bologna, however, is of sufficient importance to offset the general decline in music printing on the Italian peninsula.

A further reason for this decline is the changing nature of musical 'consumption': the 'consumer', in fact, is increasingly synonymous with 'listener', less and less frequently with 'performer'. *Concertato* music replaces the sixteenth-century idea of vocal polyphony as the dominant form of expression. Yet the musical press is insufficiently flexible in respect of the contemporary proliferation of styles, forms and functions. The average publication of 5-part madrigals contains some twenty-one compositions: one madrigal per page (divided between each of the five part-books) with three 'supplementary' pages (title-page, dedication, index), for a total of 24 pages (or six sheets) per part-book. In contrast, Monteverdi's Book 8 comprises eight vocal part-books (small format), respectively of 35, 43, 28, 91, 51, 28, 44 and 28 pages, and a folio score (for the *basso continuo*) of 81 pages. Dimensions, in general, are highly variable; each new volume presents its own particular problems of pagination, typography and publishing techniques. In Italy, instrumental music (solo and ensemble) alone can be said to 'print' well. This sector, in common with the sixteenth- and early seventeenth-century madrigal, is destined essentially for private consumption; a total of under forty editions published in the fourth decade of the century increases to almost seventy in the 1670s and over 110 in the 1690s.

In the competition for control of this expanding market, modern printing techniques prevail. In Italy, movable type – one piece of lead per musical symbol – reigns supreme. The process, however, is costly and the results of no particular elegance (the stave-lines are invariably broken between consecutive symbols); movable type, moreover, does little to facilitate the connection of groups of quavers and semiquavers (themselves increasingly common – and, hence, increasingly illegible – in the course of the seventeenth century) – in other words, it soon proves incapable of meeting the various demands of contemporary notation. In 1700, in his efforts to reproduce the double stopping of certain passages in Corelli's sonatas for solo violin, a Bolognese printer introduces a number of brief passages of musical engraving between the various movable characters (themselves, as noted, incapable of supplying combinations of symbols). Elsewhere, however, musical engraving had already been adopted on a regular basis for some decades; in particular Holland and England, both noted centres of capitalist enterprise and commercial liberty, quickly conquer the European market and monopolize the publication of instrumental music in Europe as a whole (Italy included). Musical engraving, however, was not entirely unknown on the Italian peninsula. At Rome, in the late sixteenth century, the procedure had been adopted by the Flemish publisher Simone Verovio for his scores and harpsichord and lute intabulations. Rome, in 1615 and 1627, sees the publication of two veritable masterpieces of musical engraving: the two volumes of *Toccate* by Girolamo Frescobaldi; here, a notation of hitherto unknown expressive subtlety both suggests the most suitable phrasing and organizes the four intersecting voices in a way which illustrates their inherent musical and 'manual' logic. These, however, are luxury editions of exceptional technical refinement: their lack of any real 'industrial' sequel confirms the increasingly marginal importance of

Italian printing and printers in the context of Europe as a whole. Insignificant for the development of printing techniques is the contemporary Italian production of 'poor-man's' or popular prints: songbooks for current devotional or liturgical use; canzonetta publications, frequently lacking the melodies (themselves taken as known by readers) and accompanied only by the symbols of Spanish guitar notation. In France, on the contrary, a series of (largely anonymous) collections of *chansons* and *airs à boire*, published annually from 1658 (monthly from 1694) proves a notable source of income for their printer Ballard.

What, then, are the artistic repercussions of this depression in the fortunes of seventeenth-century publishing? The principal effect is a loss of what might best be described as 'historical horizon'. Every seventeenth-century musician is familiar with one or other of the various published editions of Arcadelt, Gesualdo and the masterpieces of the sixteenth-century madrigal (see chapter 1), as also with the grandiose editions of the works of Palestrina (see chapter 15) and Frescobaldi (themselves known even to J. S. Bach). This knowledge, however, does not extend to the sacred and secular vocal repertory (*da camera*) of composers of the previous generation, nor to the music of composers employed in other cities (near and far). The 'universality' of the polyphonic style, as propagated through the multitude of sixteenth-century printed editions, now gives way to a series of individual mentors and models, a provincial circuit of local colleagues, short-lived acquaintances and collaborations with 'itinerant' singers and musicians (themselves procurers of manuscript copies).

Nor is this situation significantly altered (were such, indeed, the original intention) by the widespread seventeenth-century phenomenon of musical 'collectionism'. Collectors, as a rule, are members of the cultural and erudite classes of society: music 'cabinets' are thus created in the same way as 'cabinets' of prints, drawings or works on the natural sciences. Essentially, the phenomenon is one of wholesale removal of 'consumer goods' from the open market; the importance and monetary value of the collection is, indeed, inextricably linked to its non-functional role, the abstract 'representativeness' of its contents as market-alienated goods. Thus, the collection of instruments, portraits of musicians, musical manuscripts and prints assembled by the Ferrarese musician Antonio Goretti and extolled in the various early seventeenth-century guide-books of Ferrara remains quite unaffected by questions of practical use even after its transference to the court of Innsbruck (itself endowed with a *cappella* of notable stature and dimensions). All that remains of the fashionably 'modern' musical library of John IV of Portugal (destroyed in the earthquake of 1755) is the catalogue, printed in 1649; in the sovereign's *Defensa de la música moderna* (1649, Italian edition, 1666), however, overall attention is focussed on the sixteenth-century debate – itself anything but 'modern' – on the legitimacy of contrapuntal polyphony in the Catholic liturgy! The dukes of Modena – who, rivalled only by the Medici of Florence, can lay claim to the most committed and coherent cultural policy on a European scale of all Italian princes – assemble, towards 1662, an eminent collection of cantatas by Roman composers; more surprisingly, towards 1688, they also give rise to the collection of dozens of manuscripts of operatic arias (reflecting performances all over northern Italy) and entire operas (themselves Roman by extraction, and never actually performed in the duchy of Modena), almost as though in an attempt to create some abstract anthology of contemporary theatrical life (including, for example, practically the entire theatrical production – posthumously assembled – of Alessandro Stradella). In 1679, the Venetian patrician Marco Contarini inaugurates a sumptuous court theatre at Piazzola sul Brenta: almost by way of historical legitimization of this personal initiative, he also inaugurates his own private collection of Venetian and non-Venetian operatic scores (comprising everything on which he succeeds in laying his hands). Among these is a manuscript copy of Monteverdi's *Incoronazione di Poppea*, which, by then 'out of use' for thirty years, has 're-surfaced' only in recent times. (Only in the nineteenth century do the Contarini manuscripts return to their original home of Vehice, where they can now be consulted at the Biblioteca Marciana.)

In reality, the impact of these collections on contemporary musical life and historical awareness is practically negligible. From a modern viewpoint, indeed, their principal function can be seen as the physical conservation of the objects in question, removing them from what would otherwise have been their natural destiny of rapid, 'voracious' and irregular consumption. In artistic terms the absence of all trace of 'contemporary' critical interest for the operas – as, indeed, for other compositions – of the recent past results in their total oblivion.

13 Social condition of the musician

Responsible in no small degree for the particular physiognomy and, indeed, very existence of the Contarini collection is the last will and testament of Francesco Cavalli (1602–76), in which provision is made for the conservation of the composer's personal manuscripts of *drammi per musica*. These manuscripts form the nucleus of Contarini's collection. Cavalli, as the first 'producer' of operatic music on an impresarial basis, is responsible – almost uninterruptedly from 1639 to 1666 – for the music of one or two operas per year for the theatres of Venice. His is the typical case of the artist 'created' by the institution (and not vice versa). In 1637, on the opening of the first Venetian public theatre, the thirty-five-year-old Cavalli is already firmly embarked on the quiet and somewhat bureaucratic career of a church musician: singer and (subsequently) organist at St Mark's under Monteverdi, active also as organist at other Venetian churches and, from 1668, successor to Monteverdi's successor as *maestro di cappella* at the Ducal Basilica. Only at the age of thirty-seven does the now fully mature composer embark on a notably more glorious and arduously competitive theatrical career: a career which, until only a few years before, would have seemed quite inconceivable, and which establishes Cavalli as the first in a long line of truly 'operatic' composers. Cavalli, on his late and almost accidental approach to theatrical music (to which, however, he dedicates practically the entire second half of his notably extended career), must surely have perceived the sheer novelty of his position as operatic composer (in contrast to the day-to-day routine of the average church musician). His determined conservation of his own theatrical scores for posterity (despite his undoubted awareness of contemporary market conditions, which require not revivals but a regular turnover of new operas) is indicative of a level of 'self-consciousness' quite absent in the next generation of operatic composers in Italy: a generation for whom the operatic theatre and itsmethods of production and consumption have already come to represent the 'natural', most obvious means of practical employment.

Opera, indeed, is responsible for the creation of a new type of musician. For the composer, participation in a venture of essentially capitalist structure (albeit rudimentary and somewhat ambiguous in form: see chapter 21) brings a hitherto unknown degree of exposure to the risks of economic failure and artistic success, the inconstancy of public taste and competition with rivals – this despite the fact that the musician rarely has any direct financial involvement in the operatic initiative as such but works to contract (in the same way as the singers or costume designer): the composer, indeed, is a mere 'supplier' of music, paid on a basis inferior to the celebrated virtuoso protagonists of his operas and frequently unnamed in contemporary libretti and scores. This position of subordination is further underlined by the fact that the composer, on termination of his contract, surrenders his score – and, consequently, all right to financial remuneration for subsequent performances of the opera in other theatres and cities – to the theatre impresario or proprietor; in contrast, singers in the various 'repertory' productions on the Italian operatic circuit (see chapter 22) are well rewarded with generous 'lump-sum' payments for the season as a whole, regardless of the 'novelty' and success (i.e., number of performances) of the opera(s) concerned. The composer, deprived of his original creation, is thus also subjected – in the course of this early phase of development towards modern forms and structures of production – to a heavy loss of social and artistic prestige. It should, however, be noted that even before the opening of the first public theatres, glory and riches are more the prerogative of singers than of professional composers – confirmation, this, of the pre-eminence of performance over compositional practice in seventeenth-century musical experience. In the writings of contemporary poets, moreover, singers are much more enthusiastically praised than composers or, indeed, the poets themselves (laudatory sonnets in praise of the virtuoso performers are, in fact, printed and distributed in the auditoriums of public theatres): thus, for example, the cavaliere Loreto Vittori, author of comedies and a mock-heroic poem, is more highly extolled for his abilities as a virtuoso *castrato*. Two further signs of distinction: besides their agreed financial remuneration, singers at the Venetian public theatres are also provided with free lodging for the season in some nobleman's palace; in non-impresarial theatres, the virtuoso performers are paid not in money but with gifts and silverware.

Notably independent from 'impresarial' models is the position of the court theatrical composer. The twenty-eight-year-old Antonio Cesti (1623–69), Franciscan friar and obscure *maestro di cappella* at Volterra (armed, indeed, with nothing but the 'occasional' experience of theatrical initiatives at the Florentine court), is launched by his Medici patrons in 1651 as singer and composer on the Venetian public stage. He is then engaged to fill the specially created position of *maestro di cappella della camera* to the Archduke of Innsbruck (himself brother-in-law to the Grand Duke of Tuscany): here, in practice, he serves as director of the 'musici di camera' (themselves almost exclusively Italian) of the prince, composer of chamber cantatas for the entertainment of his noble patron, and *maestro di cappella* of the court theatre. In accepting this new and somewhat unexpected vocation, however, Cesti must first come to terms with the obstacles presented by his membership of the Franciscan Order, itself little given to collaboration and familiarity with *prime donne*, not to mention the other, more secular aspects of theatrical life. Only the successive interventions of Pope, Papal nephew, Archduke, Grand Duke of Tuscany and, finally, the Emperor himself will succeed in procuring the unconditional release of the composer from religious constraints: *sine qua non* for continuation of the programme of operatic productions at the court of Innsbruck. On his subsequent arrival at the Imperial court of Vienna, the ex-friar (now cavaliere) is made chaplain of honour and director of theatrical music; a similar title, external to the institutional structure of the court *cappella*, awaits him on his return to Florence shortly prior to his death in 1669. Throughout his career, Cesti is much in demand as producer of court entertainments (fundamental in the creation of an appropriately princely image of magnificence); his life, indeed, is one of constant interaction with sovereign princes, singers and librettists. His scores are conserved in the private libraries of his patrons and protectors at Rome (the Chigi) and Vienna (the Emperor). Only, however, those works which subsequently enter the frequently anonymous, routine circuit of the Italian public theatres (in a way much more typical of the operas of Cavalli) enjoy widespread diffusion and any real significance for the formation of an 'average' seventeenth-century musical taste and horizon of expectations (see chapter 22). The great theatrical spectaculars of the Viennese court – culminating in the immensely sumptuous *Il pomo d'oro*, performed in 1668 as climax to the two-year-long Imperial wedding celebrations (and itself widely celebrated in Europe as a whole) – are one-off events: memorable souvenirs of dynastic splendour and majesty (see chapter 24).

The parallel yet highly differentiated biographies of Cavalli and Cesti provide clear illustration of the fact that composers' careers are forged less out of personal initiative than through contact with particular artistic institutions and social structures. The thirteen-year-old Jean-Baptiste Lully (1632–87) exchanges his humble Florentine beginnings for residence in Paris, soon gaining a position as the favourite dancer and musician of the young Roi Soleil and attaining the rank of veritable functionary of State: what might today be described as an all-powerful 'minister for musical affairs'. He is subsequently appointed *Surintendant et compositeur de la musique de la chambre du roi*, acquires French nationality, gains the title of *Maître de musique* to the royal family and, finally, that of *Secrétaire royal* (in practice: subscriber to the royal debt). Composer, organizer, beneficiary (by virtue of exclusive royal privilege gained in 1672) of the profits from the printing and performance of all *tragédies lyriques* at Paris and Versailles, Lully is also the instigator and creator of a radical propaganda operation: the institutionalization of a national 'operatic' taste which eschews all foreign influence and which 'officially' establishes the forms and style of French musical theatre for at least a century to come (see chapter 25). This operation, unique in the history of seventeenth-century music, is conducted with a zeal rivalled only by the vanity and ambition of Lully himself, quickly rewarded for his labours by fame, riches, honours, aristocratic rank and real estate. Nor does the composer fail to attract the envious admiration of his contemporaries: on his death, one poetic apotheosis – itself couched in language poised uneasily between reverence and facetiousness – envisages his appointment by Jove as *Surintendant de la musique* to the Gods. In more general terms, however, the 'Lully operation' may be seen as a tool and result of the absolutist policies and overall political expansion of Louis XIV, as also of the large-scale 'academic' project of the prime minister, Colbert – inconceivable, in short, if not in the context of the centralist policies of the Roi Soleil and his attempt to raise the French nation to the level of arbiter of Europe. Needless to say, there is scope for one Lully only in this authoritarian design: many other musicians will eke out a living in some lesser court position (awarded, not infrequently, on the basis of three-month rotation) or in the service of some private patron whose feudal *train de vie* has resisted the centralizing pull of State-sponsored culture.

Notably at variance with this picture is the situation of the musician in a 'multiform' city such as Rome, itself characterized by a myriad of small-scale centres of power and initiative and fragmentation of public and political life. The Papal system of elective, non-dynastic monarchy (or 'gerontocracy') encourages the proliferation of courts: each cardinal, as a potential heir to the throne, maintains a private household proportionate less to his resources than to his pretensions in the ecclesiastical hierarchy. Under these conditions, few musicians indeed earn their living from a single job or occupation: the organist of one ecclesiastical establishment is singer in another and *maestro di musica* to the sons of some local prince or other dignitary. The jurist

Uberti affirms that the maximum position to which any 'virtuoso' (i.e., professional singer) may aspire in the courts of the various cardinals and princes is that of 'household adjutant' (with all its incumbent duties). Composers, at most, may aspire to gentlemanly status: examples, however, are rather rare in the mid and late century. The race for church livings – often minimal but always guaranteed – is widespread: tacit yet fierce competition exists between colleagues (themselves of invariably mediocre social and economic condition) for the patronage and protection of prelates and nobles in the sponsorship of musical prints or the 'placing' of some pupil in the choir of one or other of the Roman churches and basilicas. Favours are granted on an occasional and/or on-going basis as to other categories of clients – always, however, on an essentially limited scale. In 1664, the Congregazione di S. Cecilia (established in 1585) can lay claim to an effective membership of some fifty musicians; twenty years later, on Papal approval of the new congregational statute – regulating all musicians active in Rome, with the exception of the singers of the Cappella Sistina (Sistine Chapel) – the total has increased fivefold. This, in relation to an overall population of some 100,000, is quite remarkable in size: equivalent, in terms of modern Rome, to a total of some 8,000 active professional musicians. How different is the situation in Venice (with its 150,000 inhabitants), where 'assistance to the musicians of St Cecilia' is limited to a maximum of 100 effective members (singers, instrumentalists and composers included); the number of locally-active 'sonadori' is at all times contained within a figure of some 200. Surprising, in the context of these statistics, is the fact that an average of only twelve Roman churches and ecclesiastical institutions possess their own permanent *cappella musicale* (St Peter's, St John Lateran, S. Maria Maggiore, SS. Lorenzo e Damaso, S. Maria in Trastevere, S. Luigi dei Francesi, S. Giovanni dei Fiorentini, S. Spirito in Saxia, SS. Apostoli, the Church of the Gesù and the Roman Seminary, S. Apollinare); many more offer permanent employment to nont bue a *maestro di cappella* and organist, plus four singers, often employed at two different churches. Thus, though there is certainly no shortage of demand for the services of musicians, this is by no means sufficient to satisfy supply in any stable and comprehensive way. Instructive is the case of Antonio Maria Abbatini – prominent member of the Congregazione di S. Cecilia, *maestro di cappella* in many of the principal Roman churches and basilicas, teacher of several generations of musicians, composer of music for a couple of Rospigliosi's *drammi per musica* (see chapter 22), founder and host to a learned musical academy (for discussion of themes of theoretical and practical interest) – whose somewhat depressing autobiographical poem (addressed to the poet and literary scholar Sebastiano Baldini, influential friend of the family of Pope Alexander VII) appears in the present volume as Source reading 3.

Rome, however, offers certain notable advantages. The musical 'schools' of the Jesuits, as also of such great contemporary teachers as Abbatini, Virgilio Mazzocchi and Giacomo Carissimi, provide many of the greatest singers of successive generations in Italy and abroad; European-based careers find a fruitful point of departure in the service of foreign cardinals and ambassadors; sovereigns in voluntary exile – Queen Christina of Sweden (resident in Rome from 1656 until her death in 1689) or Maria Casimira of Poland (likewise in Rome from 1699 to 1714) – compensate for lost political authority with patronage of operatic and other cultural activities. When required, musical forces of extraordinary dimensions are available for use (this, at least, is the impression to be gained from a reading of contemporary descriptions). In the Chiesa Nuova, for the ordination of the Papal *castrato* Loreto Vittori in 1643, a total of 150 singers (grouped in six different choirs) engage in performances of music by the greatest *maestri di cappella*; in February 1687, the coronation of the Catholic James II of England is celebrated by Christina of Sweden in a new *Accademia per musica*, in which the music by Pasquini, scored for five solo voices, 150 instrumentalists and a 100-strong choir, is conducted by Arcangelo Corelli; in August of that year, for the name-day of the Queen, a *serenata* (music, again by Pasquini, for five voices and eighty instruments) is staged by the Spanish ambassador near his residence in the Piazza di Spagna. This, in turn, is nothing but a 'national' response to a previous festivity: that of April 1687, when, at Trinità dei Monti, the French community celebrates the recovery to health of the Roi Soleil with illuminations and fireworks, a 'magnificent serenata accompanied by timpani, trumpets and cornetts' and a 'most beautiful instrumental *sinfonia*, composed by the celebrated Arcangelo [Corelli, under whose direction were] united the best *violoni* [i.e., strings] of Rome'.

In the 'day-to-day' musical life of the capital, the necessarily minuscule dimensions of the various private courts bring a notable degree of interaction – otherwise rare in seventeenth-century culture – between musicians, men of letters and intellectuals. In musical terms, the peculiarly Roman offshoot of this interaction is the *cantata da camera*: a musical and poetic composition of limited dimensions and structure (a short sequence of arias interspersed with recitative, performed by one or two voices with *basso continuo* and, at times, two violins) but highly ingenious and spirited inventiveness – destined, as it is, for a restricted audience of connoisseurs. All the major composers of cantatas – Giacomo Carissimi, Mario Savioni, Luigi Rossi, Antonio Cesti, Alessandro Stradella, Pier Simone Agostini, Alessandro Melani, Marco Marazzoli, Alessandro Scarlatti – are Roman by birth or adoption. The typically Roman interaction between musicians and intellectuals, moreover, would also explain the presence of three 'Roman' musicians from the court of Christina of Sweden – Arcangelo Corelli, Bernardo Pasquini, Alessandro Scarlatti – among the early members of the Arcadian Academy: a literary grouping founded in 1690 as an organic attempt – in effect, *the* most organic attempt – to re-organize Italian culture on a national basis under the banner of renewed Roman supremacy. This presence, however, was perhaps more symbolic than effective. Later composer-members of the Arcadian Academy are few indeed – confirmation, this, of the lasting intellectual subordination of the musician.

In seventeenth-century Italy, the status of the musician is essentially that of artisan-supplier of highly qualified services; never or seldom is he regarded as an artist in the modern sense of the word. Exceptions are Cavalli, Corelli, Pasquini and Scarlatti. At court, the professional musician is generally treated on a level with cup-bearers and cooks; among his various duties, indeed, is that of supplier of the music at the table of the prince. In church, he is treated as an equal to the minor clerics. Other, more 'existential' solutions seem less rooted in fact than in fiction. Alessandro Stradella (*c.* 1639–82), for example, provides the archetypal image of the wild, adventurous and turbulent life of a musician surrounded by women and intrigue, participant no less as Eros than Orpheus in the pastimes of the elite. Imprisoned, in danger of his very life, he flees from Rome, Venice and Turin; at Genoa, he finally falls victim to a patrician vendetta (here, indeed, begins the all-too-easy 'mythology' of the *effectus musicae*: in church, the knives of his would-be assassins fall limply to the ground on the sound of his truly angelic voice . . .). This, however, should not be taken as representative of any attitude of extremist rebellion, transgression or even cynicism on the part of certain composers. Nothing in the cantatas and operas of Stradella suggests the existence of similar tendencies to those which, in the hands of certain men of letters and painters (as exemplified, in both fields, by the figure of Salvator Rosa), would at times assume passionate, almost overbearing dimensions.

Social organization and nominal protection are salient features of the work of the various representative 'companies' of musicians. Abbatini (see Source reading 3) openly envies the regularity of employment of the Roman *pifferi*, with their dual role at Castel Sant'Angelo and the Capitol. Certain feudal customs survive. Best paid of all the instrumentalists, for example, are the buglers; this accords with their (albeit symbolic) martial prestige. In general, however, salaries are low and frequently made up in kind. Thanks only to his rations of cereals and wine does Alessandro Grandi – *maestro di cappella* at S. Maria Maggiore of Bergamo – succeed in maintaining a respectable standard of living; in Bologna, the cornettists and trombonists of the Concerto Palatino (the band of the city magistrature) acquire the right – by dint of quality or quantity of service – to one loaf of wholemeal bread per day. The various companies, confraternities and congregations of musicians which, beginning in the late sixteenth century, spring up in Italy under the aegis of St Cecilia are nothing but 'self-help' societies, which also regulate the activities of a city's musicians in matters of teaching and public performance: in practice, they govern the distribution of the limited work supply and offer protection – by virtue of their rights of corporate monopoly – against itinerant and other non-recognized musicians. Through company organization, moreover, the musicians of each individual locality provide for the medical assistance and common burial of their poorest brethren; one particularly illustrious – albeit exceptional – example of this phenomenon is the common grave for the singers of the Cappella Sistina, erected in 1639 in the Chiesa Nuova of Rome. On occasion, in default of legitimate heirs, the company itself will inherit the possessions of its members. Particularly profitable in this respect are 'clerical' musicians (for the lower classes, ecclesiastical vows represent the sole possibility for any kind of cultural education and/or access to benefices and other incomes) and *castrati*. 'Matrimony or patrimony', one might almost say, is the rule by which a somewhat rigid seventeenth-century society concedes, if ever, social advancement and accumulation of wealth to its musicians. Instructive – if exceptional – is the case of the bell-ringer Domenico Melani of Pistoia: seven sons, all musicians, all but one intended for the priesthood, holy orders or castration. The sole exception is destined to continue a family succession which, in the course of two generations (thanks, above all, to the remarkable success of certain singer and composer members of the family), will accumulate not inconsiderable wealth and a place in the nobility.

Further eloquent testimony of the interaction between seventeenth-century musicians, their patrons and contemporary society is provided by the various ways in which they are remembered after their deaths. Corelli is commemorated in a monument at the Pantheon in

Rome, Pasquini in a splendid tombstone with bust in high relief at S. Lorenzo in Lucina; yet of Monteverdi and Cavalli, 'Republican' *maestri di cappella* (and, as such, holders of the most elevated social position available to musicians in seventeenth-century Venice), all trace is now lost. Cavalli – a widower, childless, well-to-do – leaves testamentary provision for a requiem Mass to be sung twice yearly in his memory by the *cappella* of St Mark's. In certain cases, the *castrati* – richest of all categories of musician – establish charitable foundations for welfare or didactic purposes: Loreto Vittori in Rome, Domenico Melani (former singer and diplomat of the Landgrave of Saxony) in his native city of Florence. Lully is perhaps the only musician of the entire century who can comfortably permit himself the luxury of constructing a number of houses (for himself and his family) and a family tomb. Schütz and Purcell are the subjects of posthumous poetic and musical tributes (see chapter 17 and Source reading 5) which demonstrate not only the 'intellectual' reverence of their authors for recognized artistic supremacy but also the relative ideological importance of music in non-Catholic cultures.

The phenomenon of the unsung genius is alien to the culture of a century which perpetrates no injustice against individual artists and thus leaves little scope for posthumous re-evaluation: equally, however, there is no attempt to 'deify' musicians (in contrast to a Rubens, Bernini or Marino). Memory is short. Even such musicians as are accorded particular funeral honours (in relation, always, to the varying customs of different localities and social structures) are considered by sovereigns and subjects as nothing but worthy representatives of their 'art' – an art which, though of undoubted importance and uncommon public utility, is fleeting and transitory by very definition and destined to enjoy a limited memory in the consciousness of listeners. How different is the 'memory' of sixteenth-century polyphony! The relatively subordinate social position of the seventeenth-century musician is a consequence of his new-found role as supplier of musical 'services' to a 'modern' consumer audience. His overall relationship to society and authority, however, is now more functional and organic; in social terms, his art is potentially more varied, 'articulated' and effective. Indeed, behind the somewhat deceptive façade of apparent ideological homogeneity, the vastly more 'articulated' and many-sided nature of seventeenth-century music betrays analogous tendencies in the civic structure of seventeenth-century European society as a whole.

14 Instrumental and dance music

Most ambivalent and problematic of all seventeenth-century musical figures is the composer of music for instruments and dance. The emancipation of sixteenth-century music from its vocal models and its elevation to a truly classical dignity in the early years of the eighteenth century – an 'ennoblement' based principally upon the six great instrumental publications of Corelli – are the two extremities of a tortuous yet plainly visible path of development. Yet the very nature of the instrumental composer is an object of some fluctuation: invariably himself a performer, he oscillates between the varying demands of technical virtuosity and compositional ingenuity and conceit. Between these two poles lies an enormous range of possibilities, themselves little susceptible to present-day analysis – possibilities which might best be described under the overall heading of extemporized improvisation: 'additions' made to the composer's original score in the course of performance. The effects of this practice are readily discernible in the very nature of the scores: certain sources (above all, the manuscripts) show definite traces of one-off improvisatory interventions, others (in particular, the printed editions) make allowance for some degree of indeterminacy and freedom. 'Abstract' notation, such as the 'score' (in which each melodic line is set out on a separate stave) and 'prescriptive' notation, such as the 'intabulation' (for harpsichord, organ, lute or guitar, figured or unfigured, in all its national variants, in which the music, regardless of the number of voices, is laid out in the most convenient form: on two staves for keyboard instruments, in tablature for lute and guitar, and so on), exist side by side. Whereas the score is by definition a 'composition' for two, three, four or more melodic lines conceived as virtually autonomous, the intabulation tells the performer how and when to extract particular sounds from his instrument. In the former, the performer's task is that of reading, reproducing and 'recomposing' the basic musical text (which itself exists quite independently from the act of performance); in the latter, he responds to a series of precise operational instructions, of which the musical work is the final, transient result.

The instrumental 'composer' is thus suspended between two

apparently contradictory orientations: on the one hand the production of a definitive *opus*, on the other the exercise of what might best be described as an 'activity' (or, in practical terms, a 'pastime': music as a 'machine à supprimer le temps'). The highly concentrated and complex intertwining of parts in Giovanni Maria Trabaci's *Ricercate* ('ricercars') or 1603 and 1615, themselves published in 4-part score, would appear to scorn all question of performability on keyboard; yet Sweelinck, no less devoted than Trabaci to experimentation with the mysterious effects of the strictly contrapuntal style, entertains his friends until midnight (according to one eye-witness account) with extemporized variations on popular themes. These two attitudes – apparently antithetical yet by no means incompatible – set the terms of reference for what we might describe as the 'modes of expression' in seventeenth-century instrumental music. Their presence, indeed, may be felt in the very designations of the repertory. In the early decades of the seventeenth century, the distinction between the instrumental canzona and sonata – two denominations for instrumental compositions of largely similar formal, stylistic and 'executive' configurations – is, above all, sociological: a majority of the canzonas are composed by organists (who, as such, vaunt a comprehensive theoretical training and keyboard experience), a majority of the sonatas by instrumentalists (above all, violinists: exponents, that is, of the emergent monophonic instrument of seventeenth-century music). The composer-organist excels in the clarity and complexity of his contrapuntal web, itself less fully developed in the sonatas of his violinist colleagues. The latter, in contrast, show a greater propensity for idiomatic effects, the exploitation of the specific technical resources of the instrument and a more clearly defined utilization of timbre. As the century wears on, sonata production clearly outweighs that of the 'rival' canzona: publications of idiomatically defined compositions gain numerical ascendancy over collections of neutral, 'analytical' scores for unspecified timbres. At the same time, there is an increase of *dilettante* interest in instrumental performance, *sine qua non* for the expansion of the sonata market. Indicative in this sense is the very title of the following publication (by Gasparo Zanetti): *Il scolaro . . . per imparar a suonare di violino et altri stromenti . . . ove si contengono gli veri principii dell'arie, passi e mezzi, saltarelli, gagliarde, zoppe, balletti, alemane et correnti . . . con una nuova aggiunta d'intavolatura de numeri . . . dalla quale intavolatura qual si voglia persona da se stesso potrà imparare di musica con facilità* (*The scholar . . . how to learn to play the violin and other instruments . . . wherein are contained the true principles of arias, passamezzi, saltarelli, galliards, zoppe, balletti, alemane and correnti . . . with a new addition of tablature by numbers . . . from which tablature anyone who wishes can learn music easily by himself*) (Milan, 1645). Zanetti's new tablature is an elementary system of numbers and letters by which an inexpert violinist is shown which finger to place on which string and instructed as to the direction of the bow; the method is illustrated in a series of short and simple dances.

The instrumental musician, caught in this somewhat ambiguous situation between composition and performance, is faced with different problems and obstacles to those encountered by the composer of vocal music. Without text, instrumental music is deprived not only of any pre-existing structural support (of a kind, indeed, which largely determines the stylistic configuration of the music itself: see chapter 8) but also of a clearly defined expressive or 'representational' pretext. True, compensation for this latter deficiency is provided by the fashion for instrumental compositions on figurative, pictorial, imitative or affectively determinate themes (as, for example, the plaintive 'laments' of Froberger, or the many toccatas and capriccios on 'cuckoo' themes by Frescobaldi and later composers); the necessarily exceptional nature of such pretexts, however, severely limits their range of practical application. Instrumental music, more than any other category of contemporary musical production, is dynamic in formal conception: the musical form of a fantasia, toccata, *capriccio*, etc. is developed in the course of the composition itself. Symmetry, correspondence, equivalence and balance between the various sections of a composition (features, these, more readily apparent to the eye than to the ear) are subordinated to matters of musical discourse: the organization of musical 'time' in a series of sections of variable density and tension, the orientation of 'motion' around a succession of phases of acceleration, slowing down, stability and inertia. To this end, a variety of musical resources are used. The frequency, rapidity, complexity and direction of 'ornamental' figurations – a term which is appropriate only if one recognizes the decisive structural role of the ornament in instrumental music – produces different forms of temporal organization. The stepwise scales and 'garlands' of semiquaver motion in the fantasias of Jan Pieterszoon Sweelinck (1562–1621) have a smoothness and agility which a shower of arpeggiated chords (still in semiquavers), can suddenly transform into agglomerations or precipitations of sound. Augmentation and diminution of a given melodic subject serves less as a means of 'proportional' (hence, 'static') imitation than as tools of deflection, acceleration and/or intensification of the temporal structure. In Sweelinck's 'Chromatic Fantasia' – itself famous from earliest days – the descending chromatic subject (D–D–D–C♯–C♮–B–B♭–A) is first stated in minims, accompanied by the diatonic countersubject in crotchets. Both themes then undergo a graduated process of absolute/relative acceleration and deceleration; the result is a series of constantly shifting relationships and combinations of velocity:

chromatic subject	*countersubject/figurations*
minims	crotchets
minims	quavers
semibreves	minims/semiquavers
semibreves	minims
semibreves	semiquavers
crotchets	semiquavers
crotchets	quavers/semiquavers
crotchets	semiquaver sextuplets
crotchets	quavers
quavers	crotchets

Observe how the overall effect of acceleration is achieved not least by means of certain 'decelerations' and 'composite accelerations' (i.e., deceleration of the subject and parallel acceleration of the countersubject). The conclusion is marked by a reversal in the unitary relationship between the two themes: for the first time, the subject proceeds in faster note values than the other voices.

In Sweelinck's 'echo' fantasias, the temporal structure is further complicated by a sort of 'spatial' dimension: an effect of proximity/remoteness, caused by the *forte/piano* (or high/low) repetition of identical passages. The resulting sensation of momentary, almost 'stupefied' suspension and motionlessness might be described as a deliberate perturbation of the regular flow of 'time'. The echo itself is somewhat artificially contrived: it patiently awaits the conclusion of the phrase before adding its reply (rapidly or slowly in accordance with the brevity or length of the phrase in question). All in all, the effect is one of intermittent flow on two parallel planes. The quest for *varietas* – an aesthetic principle, this, valid for every form of contemporary artistic production (and applied, in the field of instrumental music, not just to cyclic variations but to every form of current compositional practice) – is to be observed in the sheer mobility of the varied, momentaneous and imaginative structural organization.

The discursive nature of seventeenth-century instrumental music – a music invented 'there and then' by the composer-performer; a music which, in the absence of any text or figurative image, itself contains the justification for its own rhetorical configuration – derives not only from the imaginative inventiveness of its creators and its particular temporal structure but also from its ability for representation of the affections. Instrumental music, indeed, 'speaks' – or, rather, 'sings' – on a level with its vocal counterpart. Though necessarily limited to the portrayal of generic affections (in so far as it is devoid of all textual support), the overall result is by no means inferior in intensity. Instructive is the preface of Girolamo Frescobaldi (1583–1643) to his two monumental collections of *Toccate*, published respectively in 1615 and 1627 (with repeated re-issues up to and including 1637). The composer here provides a point-by-point illustration of 'the manner of playing with singable affections and a variety of passages', i.e. the adaptation of performance to the innate elocution of the musical text:

> 1. . . . this manner of playing must not be subject to [the dictates of] beat, of a kind which is observed in modern madrigals; these, however difficult, are facilitated [in performance] by means of the beat, now languid now fast, likewise sustained in mid-air in accordance with the affections [of the said madrigals] or the sense of the words.
>
> 2. In the toccatas, I have taken care not only that they be abundantly provided with different passages and affections but also that each one of the said passages can be played separately; the performer is thus under no obligation to finish them all but can end wherever he thinks best.
>
> 3. The beginnings of the toccatas should be played *adagio* and with arpeggios; and in the *ligature* and *durezze*, as also in the middle sections of the composition, [the notes] will be played together, that the instrument not remain empty; these notes shall be re-played at will by the performer [Frescobaldi is concerned that the sound of a dissonance or other chord may not be allowed to fade away too quickly, and invites performers to use arpeggios or repeated notes].
>
> 4. It is necessary to stop on the final note of both trills and *passaggi*, stepwise or by leap, even if the said note is a quaver or demisemiquaver, or different to the note which follows it: this pause will avoid confusion between one *passaggio* and another [i.e., each *passaggio* must be given its own distinct physiognomy].
>
> 5. Cadences, though written [as though to be performed] fast, must be greatly sustained [i.e., played more slowly]; and drawing near to the conclusion of a *passaggio* or cadence, the tempo must become more *adagio*. The separation and conclusion of a passage shall occur when both hands together shall produce a consonance, written in minims.
>
> 6. When a trill is to be played in the left or right hand, with a *passaggio* placed simultaneously in the other hand, [these] must not be distributed note for note; the performer must merely see that the trill be rapidly played, and the *passaggio* tenderly and less rapidly: this would otherwise lead to confusion [i.e., though trills are indeed notated fully in semiquavers, this is to be regarded as a merely 'conventional' notation which lacks the structural value of the semiquavers adopted for a melodic *passaggio* in the other hand].
>
> 7. On finding a passage of quavers and semiquavers together in both hands, [the performer] must not play too quickly; and that [hand] which has the semiquavers must play them somewhat 'dotted' [i.e., one short, the other long.]
>
> 8. Before playing a double passage with both hands in semiquavers [the per-

former] must stop on the previous note, even if [this is] black [i.e., short in value]: [he] will then resolutely play the *passaggio*, that the agility of the hand seem much greater [a sigh and 'colon', before proceeding to the tender and virtuosic *passaggio*].

9. In *partite* [i.e., series of variations], on finding *passaggi* and affections, it will be well to adopt a broad *tempo*; this should also be observed in toccatas. Works without *passaggi* can be played at a rather fast beat, entrusting control of the *tempo* – in which consists the spirit and perfection of this manner and style of playing – to the good taste and fine judgment of the performer.

Of Frescobaldi's instrumental publications the *Toccate* alone are notated in keyboard intabulation; the others – the twelve 4-part *Fantasie* of 1608; the ten plus five *Ricercari et canzoni franzese* of 1615; the twelve *Capricci fatti sopra diversi soggetti et arie* of 1624; the *Canzoni* of 1628 (designated, in contrast to the other volumes, not for keyboard but 'per ogni sorte di stromenti'); the *Fiori musicali di diverse compo-sizioni* of 1635 (for ecclesiastical use); the eleven posthumous *Canzoni alla francese* of 1645 – were all published in score or in partbooks. More, too, than the other instrumental works, the toccatas – some two dozen in all – reveal a subtle quest for 'affective' elocution. Melodic line, distribution of dissonances, the jagged yet flexible profile of the various graces and *passaggi* (turns, trills, arpeggio figurations, etc.): all show a definite orientation in this respect. The various sections of these pieces – in reality, much less easily separable than the words of the composer might suggest (see above: no. 2) – range in style from the splendid solemnity of the opening bars to the dance-like motion of certain ternary episodes, the tormented Gesualdo-like writhing of the so-called 'durezze e ligature' ('dissonances and suspensions', on occasion – see, for example, the eighth toccata of Book 2 – prevalent to the point of total domination of the piece as a whole), jubilant or ecstatic melismatic figuration, emphatic recitative and brisk imitation of contrapuntal subjects. By no means out of place is comparison with the seventeenth-century madrigal – a comparison, indeed, fully justified by the opening rubric of the preface quoted above, which paradoxically draws on the practice of madrigal performance 'in accordance with the sense of the words' as a model for the more recent instrumental tradition.

Frescobaldi's toccatas are designated without distinction for harpsichord or organ. The latter instrument, indeed, is specified only in the case of four pieces from Book 2. Yet the prefatory nature of the toccata and its original function as prelude renders it eminently suitable for performance on organ in a specifically liturgical context (see chapter 15). A similar ambivalence of function is also characteristic of the six canzonas of Book 2. In contrast, the hymns and Magnificat of Book 2, designed to be performed *alternatim* with plainchant, are necessarily destined for organ (an orientation, this, clearly reflected in their broad, temperate and sonorous structure). Decidedly *da camera* and harpsichord-like in style is the final section of each of the two volumes of toccatas. The partitas of Book 1 (variations upon a given melody or air, generally of vocal origin: the *aria della romanesca*, *aria della Monica*, *aria del Ruggiero*, etc.) are imbued with an inventive melodic vocalization of notable affinity with that of the contemporary repertory for solo voice (see chapter 3), but without limitations of text; the absence of words, indeed, permits a virtually inexhaustible variety of metrical and rhythmic constructions in those very situations where the composer of vocal music is faced with a pre-existing 'metrical' syntax and phraseology and given number of syllables and accents. Both books, moreover, contain a not insignificant amount of dance music, presented sometimes individually (the five galliards and ten *correnti*), sometimes grouped together in brief and elementary suites: 'balletto, corrente e passacagli', 'corrente e ciaccona', or a galliard and *corrente* interspersed with three further variations (for a total of five variations in all) on a given theme. This is the case with the variations on the so-called 'aria detta la Frescobalda' – a name which betrays not only the particular fame of the composition in question but also the vastness (though, as such, not easily demonstrable) of contemporary recourse (especially in the field of the dance) to works by other composers or of public domain.

Dance music plays a role of enormous historical importance in the development of seventeenth-century instrumental music – decidedly greater, indeed, than its purely numerical presence in seventeenth-century editions for harpsichord, violin or other instruments would lead one to believe. Clearly, in the two great Frescobaldi collections, the sheer sublimity of the toccatas takes precedence over the rhythmic vitality of the galliards and *correnti*; here too, however, in common with all contemporary instrumental forms and genres, the influence of the dance repertory is apparent in the periodic and accentual organization of the musical phrase – an organization which reveals a wealth of hitherto unexplored possibilities. The ideally continuous flow of imitative polyphony characteristic of the fantasias and ricercars (with its tendency to delay termination of the periods and camouflage the various divisions and articulations), the industrious contrapuntal and figurative elaboration of the capriccios (on given themes) and canzonas, the inspired and/or bizarre recitation of the toccatas: all, in the dance, are replaced by a somewhat 'rough-and-ready' texture, a brevity of phrase (with cadences every eight, six, four or even two bars) and a parallel increase in tonal energy and conciseness. The physical, bodily nature of the choreographical movements gives rise to a certain periodicity of melodic, rhythmic and harmonic motion and gesture: a kind of gravitational force, which itself leads to the creation of a series of rudimentary yet tenacious tonal connections between the various basic levels of the scale (I–IV–V), and whose irresistible accentual force reverberates throughout the melodic phraseology. The characteristic approach by which the various metric, melodic and harmonic models provided by contemporary dance are adapted by the virtuoso instrumentalist to exclusively sonorous, non-choreographical ends is, however, only too open to the temptation of artful elaboration, subtle dissimulation of the original model and its sublimation in the interplay of idiomatic figures and passages. In this way, the instrumental composer-performer takes possession of the tradition of dance music, reproducing it on his instrument and subjecting it to further compositional and/or 'practical' elaboration – which itself becomes the centre of artistic interest in the new composition. Complications and refinements tend to attenuate the physiognomy of the original model. The process appears at its most evident in dance suites by late seventeenth-century French harpsichordists. Already, however, by the period around 1650, clear precedents for these developments are provided by the diffusely arpeggiated suites of Johann Jakob Froberger (himself a pupil of Frescobaldi); typical, here, is the stylization of the original dance movement as a diffuse and evocative melodic and sonorous gesture, a distant image of the innate 'bodily' gestures of a whole range of dances (allemande, courante, sarabande, gigue, etc.) which, by 1650, have effectively ceased for at least two generations to exhibit all form of dance-like behaviour. And yet, even in conditions such as these, the process of appropriation of the dance on the part of instrumental *musica da camera* goes beyond the mere defunctionalization and sublimation of the original model: the model itself, with its propulsively periodic structure, accentual rhythm and clear and simple tonal articulation, is present in the various compositional and 'executive' procedures – and, indeed, in the very structure – of the instrumental repertory. This osmosis of instrumental music and dance – in common with the other general phenomena already discussed in relation to the instrumental repertory – is by no means exclusive to the music of the seventeenth century; it is, however, in these very years that it leads to a general re-evaluation and re-organization of the principles of composition and the very concept of musical 'time' (increasingly dynamic and accentual in orientation) and space (increasingly anchored to the fundamental cornerstones of tonality).

The ample degree of contact and coincidence between instrumental music and dance music provides excellent ground for a profitable exchange between 'artistic' and popular musical traditions. Here, as in other areas of seventeenth-century music, this interchange is undoubtedly of greater intensity than revealed by modern musicological research (itself, both by custom and convenience, somewhat myopic in its attitudes towards popular musical traditions). Both directions are involved. An excellent example of high-, middle- and low-class divulgation of an originally aristocratic dance – itself, more precisely, a ceremonial ballet of representational hue – is provided by the concluding epithalamial dance of the Florentine *intermedi* of 1589, commonly denominated 'ballo del granduca' or 'aria di Firenze'. This piece remains highly popular throughout the first half of the seventeenth century. The original music, by Emilio de' Cavalieri, is a choral-scenic ballet, set to a text of strongly metric disposition; the six seven-syllable *sdruccioli* ('Oh che nuovo miracolo, / ecco ch'in terra scendono, / celeste alto spettacolo, / gli dèi ch'il mondo accendono . . . ') are mirrored in the music by six four-bar phrases of notably cadential orientation. Published in 1591 in conjunction with the other music for the *intermedi*, the 'ballo del granduca' quickly becomes something of a model and supplier of melodic and harmonic material for an infinity of compositions of every kind and genre. It appears among the various pieces of the celebrated dance treatise *La nobiltà di dame* by Fabrizio Caroso (1600). It also occurs in various intabulations for lute or *chitarrone* (Santino Garsi, *ante* 1603; Johannes Hieronymus Kapsberger, 1604; Pier Paolo Melli, 1614; Jean-Baptiste Besard, 1617), compositions for solo harpsichord (Floriano Canale, c.1600; Sweelinck; Frescobaldi; Scipione Giovanni, 1652; Giovan Battista Ferrini, c.1661) and instrumental ensemble (didactic or otherwise: Ludovico Viadana, 1610; Peter Philips, *ante* 1619; Adriano Banchieri, 1620; Giovanni Battista Buonamente, 1626; Gasparo Zanetti, 16454; Gioseffo Giamberti, 1657), vocal music for *da camera* consumption (Banchieri, 1626) and even masses and motets (Banchieri, 1613 and 1620; Frescobaldi, c.1630). The list is incomplete. A further vehicle of notable importance for the popular diffusion of this and other compositions is represented by intabulations for Spanish guitar, an instrument whose faicility of performance is proportional only to its restrictedness of melodic resources and chordal fullness of sound. Chords, indeed, are easily produced by a single movement of the hand on the five strings of the instrument (nine strings with doublings); it is thus not difficult to see why the Spanish guitar comes practically to supersede the lute as a means of accompaniment for song and dance alike. Girolamo Montesardo (1606), Foriano Pico (1608), Giovanni Ambrogio Colonna (1620), Benedetto Sanseverino (1620), Carlo Milanuzzi (1622), Pietro Milioni (1627), Giovanni Battista Abbatessa (1627), Fabrizio Costanzo (1627), Giovanni Paolo Foscarini (1629), Francesco Corbetta (1639), Agostino Trombetti (1639), Antonio Carbonchi (1643), Giovanni Battista Granata (1646), Stefano Pesori (1648), Tommaso Marchetti (1648), Antonino Di Micheli (1680): these are but some of the authors whose editions of dance music and/or 'model' accompaniments for Spanish guitar include settings of the 'ballo del granduca'.

The enormous diffusion of the 'ballo del granduca' is equalled only by its capacity for penetration of the most disparate environments. In Naples, for example, it appears alongside other airs in fashionable Neapolitan use for the entertainment of the 'prince' of Giambattista Basile's collection of fairy-tales in Neapolitan dialect, *Pentamerone*:

> The prince, irritated by all these games and pastimes, ordered that some few instruments be brought and that there be singing. And, immediately, a handful of servants capable of playing appeared, with lutes, drums, zithers, harps, castanets, *vottafuoche*, *crò crò*, Jew's harps and *zuche zuche*. A beautiful *sinfonia* was performed. The tenor [i.e., melody] of the *Abbate*, *Zefero*, *cuccara giammartino* and *ballo de Schiorenza* [= 'ballo di Firenze' or 'ballo del granduca'] were played. A handful of songs of that good old time were also sung – songs now more easily regretted than rewritten.

In Bologna, the 'ballo del granduca' is cited alongside twelve further dances of varying nature and provenance in the burlesque sonnet *La sua donna per cavargli denari fa tutti i balli usati in Bologna* (*His mistress, to pick his pocket, does all the dances danced in Bologna*) by Zan Muzzina:

Fa la mia cruda ogn'or la *Bergamasca*,	Continually my mistress does the *Bergamasca*,
e nel susiego un *Spagnoletto* imita,	and haughtily the *Spagnoletto* imitates,
forma *Chiacone* in dimenar la vita,	wiggling her waist an excellent *Chiacone* does form,
ma con inchini in *Pavaniglia* casca.	but with curtseys in the *Pavaniglia* falls.
Si move a la *Gagliarda*, e ben che frasca,	To the *Gagliarda* like a scatter-brain does move,
e di *Tor di Leon* [= tordiglione] forse più ardita,	and in the *Tor di Leon* [= tordiglione] perhaps more daring still;
meco finge la *Zoppa*, e poi scaltrita,	with me a *Zoppa* does she feign and then (shrewd as she is),
a un *Passo e mezzo* mi ha la mano in tasca.	at nothing but a *Pass'e mezzo* her hand into my pocket delves.

Ma da *Ruggiero* appassionato pesca,	But from passionate *Ruggiero* does she fish,
e perché il *Bal del duca* in me non trova,	and since, in me, not e'en a *Bal del duca* finds,
con un sonaglio sol fa la *Moresca*.	she dances the *Moresca* with a single bell,
sì che adirata il bel *Pianton* rinova,	that, in anger, she renews the old *Pianton*,
la *Corrente* ribatte, e mi rinfresca	the *Corrente* does she trace again,
la vecchia frenesia con fuga nova.	and refreshes my old frenzy with new flight.

The 'ballo del granduca' is one of the very few pieces of the contemporary dance repertory whose authorship, place and date of composition are known with precision. This is undoubtedly a consequence of its aristocratic origins. In general, the line of descent passes not from the aristocratic ballet to more popular forms of diffusion but, on the contrary, from 'low-class' dance to 'higher' and more artistically orientated forms of instrumental music. A case in point is the chaconne (third of Zan Muzzina's twelve dance types). This strongly ethnic and erotic form of dance (as such, not unlike the earlier *sarabande*) is Latin American in origin. Its first literary appearance may be traced to a satire of 1598 on contemporary Peruvian life. A year later, it re-surfaces in the text of a burlesque *intermezzo* composed on the occasion of the wedding of Philip III of Spain: here, a highly novel and somewhat reckless 'chacona' is danced by a band of thieves as an artful ploy to rob an unsuspecting Indian of his silver. Still in 1599, a greatly alarmed Friar Juan de la Cerda warns all upright ladies against obscene corporeal gestures in such dances as the sarabande and chaconne. In 1615, the chaconne is prohibited from use in theatrical entertainments on grounds of its irredeemably infectious lasciviousness. In Cervantes' *La ilustre fregona*, the collective 'baile de la chacona' – itself 'vaster than the ocean' – is performed to words such as these:

. . . Requieran las castañetas	. . . To the castanets they lay their hands,
y bájense á refregar	lowering themselves until they touch
las manos por esa arena,	these arenas with their hands,
o terra del muladar.	earth to fertilize.
Todos lo han hecho muy bien	All have well performed,
no tengo que les retar:	there's nothing more to be said
Santigüense, y dén al diablo	Now cross yourselves, and to the devil offer
dos higas de su higueral.	the figs of his fig-orchard.
Escupan al hideputa,	Spit at the son of a bitch,
porque nos deje holgar,	that he trouble us not,
puesto que de la chacona	since he is ever-present

nunca se suele apartar.
El baile de la chacona
encierra la vida bona.
¡Que de veces ha intentado
a questa noble señora
con la alegre zarabanda,
el pésame, y perra mora,

entrarse por los requicios
de las casas religiosas,
a inquietar la honestidad
que en las santas celdas mora!
El baile de la chacona
encierra la vida bona.

in the dance of the chaconne . . .
In the dance of the chaconne
lies the secret of *vie bonne*.
. . . How often
has this noble lady tried,
with gay sarabande,
with *pesame* and with *perra mora* [other popular dances],
to enter through the cracks and clefts
into the convents of the nuns,
their virtue to disturb,
which is those cells doth always reign! . . .
In the dance of the chaconne
lies the secret of *vie bonne*.

The 'noble señora' finally reveals herself in her true guise as a sacrilegious 'indiana amulatada', whose function is that of tempting the company as a whole to the frenzy of the dance. Likewise, in the comedies of Lope de Vega (in particular those composed in the second decade of the seventeenth century), the 'hymn' to the chaconne is personified in the figure of a sensual and dissolute old woman: 'Vida bona, vida bona, / esta vieja es la chacona!'. The frenzied melody and rhythm of the chaconne find a picturesque echo in many other Spanish literary works of the early decades of the century – and tones of indignant disapproval in contemporary treatises on morality. The obscurely transatlantic origins and shameful, shameless reputation of the chaconne (itself quite absent from the pages of fashionable treatises on ballet) find further confirmation in the writings of contemporary Italian poets; the Italians however have a more limited propensity for realistic portrayal of lower-class life (rural and/or urban). In the final canto of *Adone* (canto 20, octave 84) – itself constructed around the various dances invoked by Venus in memory of Adonis (florid *moresche*, *contredanses*, galliards, country-dances, round dances, etc.) – Marino speaks with (feigned?, ironic?) indignation:

Compito il primo ballo, ecco s'appresta
la coppia lieta a variar mutanza,
e prende ad agitar, poco modesta,
con mill'atti difformi oscena danza.

Pera il sozzo inventor che tra noi questa

introdusse primier barbara usanza.
Chiama questo suo giuoco empio e profano
saravanda e ciaccona il novo ispano.

The first dance over, the happy couple
now prepares to change the tune,
and starts to move with little restraint
in a thousand deformed actions to an obscene dance.

Perish the foul inventor who first amongst us

introduced this barbaric custom.
The new Spaniard (i.e. the American) calls this impious profane game of his
saravanda and *ciaccona*.

(As reward, Venus then invites the two excited – and indeed, exhausted – dancers to 'finish the game' in that very bed which has earlier played host to the loves of Cupid and Psyche!) The chaconne attracts the censure of Angelico Aprosio (1645), a member of the Accademia degli Incogniti, as responsible for the corruption of young ladies: no morality is capable of resisting the seductive charms of this suggestively swaying dance. In 1643, the *Tacito abburattato* of Anton Giulio Brignole Sale refers to certain indecent scenic representations performed to the sound of the chaconne.

The chaconne, indeed, arrives in Italy not many years after its first recorded appearance in South America; channels of transmission are those sáme intabulations for Spanish guitar which, in general, act as 'clearing house' for enormous quantities of dance music of different types and origins. The earliest known reference is found in the *Nuova invenzione d'intavolatura per sonare li balletti sopra la chitarra spagniuola* (1606) of Girolamo Montesardo, himself active in what was possibly his native city of Naples (capital of the Spanish possessions on the Italian peninsula). Side by side with the 'ballo della ciaccona', the collections of intabulations for Spanish guitar contain a series of ritornellos (or 'passacagli'): brief instrumental formulas of Iberian descent, used as introductions to – or interludes between – the various stanzas of a song. In contrast to the sarabande (which quickly sheds its original cloak of impetuous lasciviousness, sublimating its ethnic origins in the severely measured rhythms of a slow instrumental dance, which itself finds a permanent place in the seventeenth- and eighteenth-century instrumental suite), the 'ballo della ciaccona' and 'ritornello del passacaglio' never entirely discard their characteristically frank, rudimentary and 'popular' nature; in guitar intabulations both dance and ritornello are reduced to the level of mere harmonic and rhythmic formulas: cadential figurations of strongly accentual orientation. Two such formulae, commonly observable in conjunction with chaconnes and passacaglias (see, for example, Monteverdi), are: G–D–E–B–C–D[– G] and respectively A–G–F–E[–A]. These and other similar formulas can be repeated *ad libitum* for the accompaniment of dances and songs. Perhaps the most remarkable example of perpetual variation technique is provided by the truly obsessive repetitions of Frescobaldi's *Cento partie sopra passacagli* (comprising, in reality, also a whole series of chaconnes), published in the 1637 edition of the *Toccate*: a variation cycle, this, which passes somewhat bizarrely from one musical gesture and affection to another, without once interrupting the hypnotic swirl of the basic cadential formulas (themselves reiterated at regular, two-bar intervals). This truly inimitable composition was frequently imitated in the hands of Frescobaldi's successors. The harmonic fixity of the basic musical cell, however, inevitably produces a uniformity of motion by which even the laudable compositions of such worthy harpsichordists as Bernardo Storace (1664) and the Neapolitan Gregorio Strozzi (1687) are rendered monotonous; only, indeed, in its (non-Italian) theatrical applications of the final decades of the century – the enormous *passacailles* and *chaconnes* of Lully and Purcell (see chapters 25 and 26) – does this uniformity find a truly pertinent application as the basis of the great choral and ceremonial dances. This function, we might add, has little in common with the earlier erotic connotations of this originally 'popular' dance; nor, indeed, is it linked to the realism of the earliest scenic applications – themselves surely of decidedly 'low-class' orientation – of the passacaglia/chaconne on the Italian peninsula. 'Low-class' is the coarse and burlesquely plaintive dialogue between Madama Lucia and Cola Napoletano in what can only be described as a true miniature scene of *commedia dell'arte* descent, set to music by Francesco Manelli (known as 'Il Fasolo') 'sopra la ciaccona'. Madama Lucia's mocking 'lament' is accompanied not by the traditional chaconne but by a lament-style passacaglia for Spanish guitar (the frequent confusion between the names of dance (chaconne) and ritornello (passacaglia) – both Iberian in origin – is indicative of the strong functional and structural affinities of their 'modular' versions in Italian guitar intabulation). Nucleus of the earliest version (1628) is a descending minor tetrachord (G–F–E♭–E), altered to the major (F–E–C–D) in a later drafting (1636). The amorous and rustic ballet at the end is set on the same passacaglia tetrachords.

III

SACRED VOCAL MUSIC

15 Music in the Catholic liturgy

Musicologists, in some future attempt to reconstruct the history not only of musical style and composition but also of what the listener actually heard, would not be unjustified in asking, paradoxically indeed, whether the composer of greatest significance for seventeenth-century liturgical music were not, in reality, Giovanni Pierluigi da Palestrina (d. 1594). There are no easy answers to this question. The editorial appeal of Palestrina endures, roughly speaking, to the second decade of the new century; latest of all to be reprinted are his hymns (1625, again in 1644 after the textual reforms of Pope Urban VIII – see chapter 12), most frequently published are his settings from the Song of Songs (the most highly impassioned and least severe of all his motet compositions, possibly destined for a function that was more devotional than strictly liturgical) with six editions between 1601 and 1613. But the various sixteenth-century editions of his masses were already well represented in *cappelle musicali* up and down the Italian peninsula, where they continued to represent a permanent *corpus* of performable music (surviving copies, indeed, bear every sign of wear and tear). The seventeenth century also gives rise to the myth of Palestrina *princeps musicae*, 'restorer and benefactor of music', as also to the legend which tells how his *Missa Papae Marcelli* (first published in 1567) was responsible, at the eleventh hour, for convincing delegates to the Council of Trent to desist from the proposal that polyphonic music be banned from liturgical use. The story first appears in Agostino Agazzari's *Del sonare sopra 'l basso* (1607), where it serves merely to highlight the difference in style between the *Missa Papae Marcelli* and that type of sacred polyphony which, characterized as it was by an excess of 'counterpoint and fugue' with resulting 'confusion of the words', no longer found favour with 'judicious connoisseurs' any more than with the Holy Fathers of the Council; in reality, the Palestrina style *par excellence* is counterpoint and fugue, now tempered (as in the *Missa Papae Marcelli*), now carried to insuperable heights of complexity and artifice.

The *Missa Papae Marcelli* is present in more than just name in the musical experience of the Seicento. In 1609, Palestrina's six-part original appeared with a further two voices by Francesco Soriano; ten years later, a simplified version *a 4* was prepared by Giovanni Francesco Anerio in a highly successful arrangement which was reprinted as late as 1662. Both Soriano and Anerio were Roman by birth and profession, direct descendants of the Palestrina tradition (itself mostly Roman). In Rome, indeed, one of the principal musical establishments of the city – the Cappella Sistina, private *cappella* of the Pope – was actually geared to the continued cultivation of Palestrina and the perpetuation of *a cappella* polyphony (a manner of performance based exclusively on unaccompanied voices, with male *castrati* and falsettists respectively as sopranos and altos), itself obliquely yet eloquently designated 'alla Palestrina' (see chapter 8). In 1616 (one of the very few years for which an accurate reconstruction of the Papal repertory is possible), no less than twenty-nine of the thirty-three festive or solemn Masses sung with polyphonic music by the Cappella Sistina (in the Apostolic Palace, St Peter's, S. Maria Maggiore and other churches of the Holy City) were by Palestrina (other composers represented were Animuccia, Victoria, Soriano and Crivelli); on twenty-four of these occasions, Palestrina's music also formed the Offertory motet.

Is it, then, the case that the hegemony of Palestrina continued undisputed in Italian – or, at any rate, Roman – church music of the seventeenth century? Not necessarily so. Certainly, Palestrina represented an authoritative model, authoritatively sanctioned by no lesser figure than the head of the Church. It will not nevertheless go unnoticed that the music of Palestrina, to singers and listeners alike, was certainly less predominant beyond the confines of Rome; indeed, the drive of the Counter-Reformation Church towards unity in matters of rite, liturgy and ceremonial was inevitably forced to come to terms with a multiplicity of local prerogatives and liturgical traditions. And even in Rome, not everyone was unreserved in their praise of the *Missa Papae Marcelli*; Pietro Della Valle qualifies his admiration with the statement that 'today such things are valued not for practical use but rather as museum pieces, to be conserved as beautiful curiosities and antiques'. In general, Palestrina is venerated more by the theorists as the ultimate musico-liturgical ideal than as author of a rigid stylistic code (a code, nevertheless, which comes high in the classified table of musical styles as given in chapter 8, though its limited functional validity is explicitly recognized, with specific reference to the composition of the Ordinary of the Mass; if anything, it is in the hands of the eighteenth-century theorists – Fux, Martini, etc. – that it becomes a definite musical 'canon'). In reality, the exclusive cultivation of Palestrina by the Cappella Sistina forms part of a system of institutional 'delimitations' in which the *cappelle musicali* of St Peter's (the so-called Cappella Giulia) and the other Roman basilicas are given priority in the cultivation of more modern, 'monumental' forms of sacred polyphony; it is, indeed, the very immensity of the architecture of St Peter's (itself finished only in the course of the seventeenth century) that leads to the phonic and spatial 'expansion' of the Palestrina style through an increase in the number of voices and use of polychoral divisions (famous, in the words of Della Valle, is 'the grand enormity of music' composed by Virgilio Mazzocchi, *maestro di cappella* of St Peter's, sung by 'twelve or sixteen choirs – I know not – with a *coro di eco* right from the top of the dome'). Finally, it should be noted that the levels of tolerance, flexibility and, indeed, vagueness of the Catholic liturgy in matters of liturgical music are by no means negligible, and that these can be discerned in the practices of the Cappella Sistina itself; in 1616, on no less an occasion than Christmas Day, and in what can only be described as the supreme bastion of the Church of Rome, the mass performed by the singers of the Papal Chapel was actually one of those originally commissioned from Palestrina by Duke Guglielmo Gonzaga in accordance with the particular rite and *cantus firmi* in use at S. Barbara of Mantua (whose liturgy still differed from that of Rome). During Vespers, moreover, Palestrina was abandoned in favour of a medley of four-choir psalms with 'admirably concerted' antiphons for solo voice and a 12-part *Magnificat*: all freshly composed by the various members of the Cappella Sistina and other fashionable musicians of non-Papal – indeed, non-Vatican – extraction.

In short, Palestrina is undoubtedly the Catholic composer *par excellence*, his music a model for the 'perfect' ecclesiastical style, an exemplary yard-stick (with Papal recognition as such) for the music of the Catholic Church; Palestrinian polyphony, however, by no means accounts for the totality of the Italian sacred repertory, nor is it capable of resolving all the various problems and conflicts which in the aftermath of the Council of Trent (as, indeed, in the preceding period) continue to characterize relations between artistic and liturgical necessities. The *Editto sopra le musiche* (*Edict on music*) of 1665, inspired by the singers of the Papal Chapel and promulgated by the congregation of the Holy Apostolic Visitation (the competent body in matters of ecclesiastical discipline) in enforcement of an earlier bull (1657) of Alexander VII aimed at the diocese of Rome, provides eloquent documentation of the nature of these problems and conflicts:

> The Holy Apostolic Visitation, in order that the Constitution of His Holiness regarding music be given full and due execution, with the oracle of the living voice of His Holiness, orders and commands that in future, in the churches and oratories of Rome, when concerted music with organ is performed during the celebration of the divine offices or when the Blessed sacrament is exposed, the following things be strictly observed:
>
> First, that the style or the music to be observed for masses, psalms, antiphons, motets, hymns, canticles, etc., as also in *sinfonie*, be grave, ecclesiastical and devout.
>
> Second, with regard to the Mass, that only those words prescribed by the Roman Missal for the offices proper to the feasts of each day and the solemnities of the saints may be sung; and, in particular, that only the Gradual or Tract may be sung after the Epistle, that only the Offertory may follow the Creed, and that after the Sanctus the Benedictus or a motet shall be sung, but only with those words laid down by the Church in the Breviary or Missal in honour of the Blessed Sacrament.
>
> Third, in Vespers, that nothing be sung but the psalms and the hymn, if not also the current antiphons as prescribed by the Breviary; and the same at Compline.
>
> Fourth, that when the Blessed Sacrament is exposed, only those words laid down in the Roman Breviary or Missal in honour of the Blessed Sacrament may be sung; if it is wished to sing words from Holy Scripture or of some Holy Father, the special approval of the Holy Congregation of Rites must first be granted, as prescribed by the Constitution; the said approval is necessary in this case, though not when the words are those prescribed by the Breviary or Missal; words taken from the Holy Fathers must be of one Father only, and not of many Holy Fathers together.
>
> Fifth, that it not be permissible that all or a considerable part of a psalm, hymn or motet be sung by solo voice, high or low; but, if this is not sung by the full choir, that it be sung continually varying the manner of performance, alternating between high choral voices and low.
>
> Sixth, that the words of the Breviary, Missal, Holy Scripture and Holy Fathers be set *ut jacent* in such a way as they are not inverted, no alterations are made and extraneous words are not interposed.
>
> Seventh, that in Passiontide the music be sung without organ, in accordance with the prescriptions of rubrics and Church.
>
> Eighth, that within a period of twenty days from the publication of the present edict by the Fathers Superior and others whose duty it is, that shutters or narrow grilles be placed in the choirs, be the latter temporary or permanent, and that the said shutters be of such a height as the singers will not be seen, under pain of privation of office and other penalties at the discretion of the Holy Visitation.
>
> Ninth, that no *maestro di cappella* or other person entrusted with ordering the music or giving the beat contravene the aforesaid prescriptions (or any one thereof) under pain of privation of office and perpetual disqualification from the exercise of this office and the right to make music; and, moreover, that he be punished with a fine of 100 *scudi*, of which one quarter be given the denouncer

(whose name will be held secret), three quarters to the holy places at the discretion of the Holy Visitation, and with other penalties – including corporal punishment – at the discretion of the said Holy Visitation.

Tenth, that no *maestro di cappella* or other individual can in future make music in the churches and oratories as above, if he have not first sworn on the hand of the Vicar Cardinal of Rome or his viceregent, under pain of the aforesaid penalties, that he will observe everything contained in the present edict; and, having taken this oath (which must be given once only, but registered), if he contravene the aforesaid prescriptions in any way, he shall be punished as an oath-breaker in accordance with the Constitution of His Holiness.
Rome, 30 July 1665.

(The reader will have noticed of what little importance is the perceptibility and intelligibility of the text: in the context of a non-spoken language such as Latin, the integrity of the liturgical text matters more than its comprehension on the part of the faithful.)

The edict of 1665 cannot have achieved the desired effect if both Innocent XI and Innocent XII (respectively, in 1678 and 1692) were compelled to reconfirm the Papal bull of 1657. Meanwhile, the steady stream of Roman publications of motets for solo voice with *basso continuo* accompaniment (see chapter 12) illustrates the reasons for such measures – as, indeed, their inefficacy.

Indeed, the above directives were aimed at curbing a dual reality. From a moral point of view, they represented an attempt to bring under control the worrying degree of exploitation of the various compositional, vocal and instrumental resources as required by contemporary taste (and accepted by musicians, prelates and faithful alike); this represented a form of sensuous enticement suspected of contravening the officially sanctioned decorum, sobriety and, indeed, compunction of the Church. In general terms, the suspicion was that of the pervading secularization of sacred music; in reality, however, liturgical secularization was nothing but an obvious manifestation of the creeping secularization now enveloping the Church (as, indeed, society) as a whole, which may be perceived behind even the most evident displays of religious piety. Equally symptomatic of this process is the origin of the term 'sacred music', whose first appearance may be traced only to the years around 1600. Before this date (or, at all events, prior to the Council of Trent), any terminological distinction between the 'sacred' and 'secular' in music would have been fairly pointless; at this stage, the fields of *musica da chiesa* and *musica da camera* are adjacent even to the point of ambiguity, and are defined less in terms of any distinctive structural characteristics as with reference to their function and use. It is, indeed, the very distinction between 'sacred' and 'secular' as defined by the Counter-Reformation

Church which forms the basis for all future references to mutual contamination (whether casual or pre-meditated) – a mutual contamination which comes to be viewed with particular concern in relation to the liturgical use of the arts.

From a liturgical point of view, the edict of 1665 reflects a clear preoccupation with the widespread employment – common, indeed, from the earliest years of the seventeenth century – of texts of convenience (texts, that is, derived not from the Scriptures but from modern devotional writings, and thus not always fully irreproachable in theological terms) as substitute formulae for texts from the Proper of the Mass (Graduals and Offertories, for example) and Vespers (antiphons and hymns) – a practice dictated by the obviously impossible task of continually updating a (motet) repertory which, in its efforts to account for every single Proper (Mass and Vespers) of the liturgical year, would necessarily have involved the musical setting of thousands of different texts, each destined for nothing but the most occasional use. (Obviously, however, the contradiction cannot be eliminated once the premise is accepted – itself by no means obvious – that liturgical music, too, must keep abreast of developments in musical style.) Thus, the seventeenth century sees the almost total demise of the great systematic collections of offertories (e.g. Palestrina, 1593), antiphons (Giovanni Francesco Anerio, 1613) and other texts from the Proper – collections of hundreds of pieces which had at least succeeded in satisfying the current requirements of the liturgical calendar. Composers continue in their production of all kinds and formations of music for the Ordinary of the Mass (Kyrie, Gloria, Credo, Sanctus, Agnus), as also for a dozen or so of the most frequently used psalms (*Dixit Dominus*, *Beatus vir*, *Laudate pueri*, *Nisi Dominus*, etc.); beyond this, however, they limit themselves to collections of liturgically miscellaneous motets on a variety of essentially generic texts (Marian, Christological, eucharistic, hagiographic), from which substitute texts for the Proper can be drawn in accordance with the particular circumstances in hand.

Open to question, in the eyes of the Church, is the spiritual value of such procedures as edification for the faithful. Before God, however, the validity of the rite is unimpaired: the recitation of the holy texts remains the exclusive prerogative of the celebrant and his ministers, by whom the texts of the Proper are murmured during the performance of the substitute motet. Thus, music does not 'replace' the celebration of the rite, but functions as glorification and adornment: liturgy and music co-exist in a relationship not of identity but of pure simultaneity. Similarly, the participation of the organ in the liturgy (both *alternatim* with Gregorian chant and in 'substitution' for the texts of the Proper) is willingly tolerated – indeed, prescribed – by the Church. The use of the organ is regulated by the *Caeremoniale episcoporum* of 1600 (significantly, the appearance of the French equivalent of this volume – the *Caeremoniale parisiense* – in 1662 led almost immediately to a sudden and lasting rise in the publication of French liturgical music for organ; such music, which until this time had prospered only in the semi-secrecy of particular local traditions, now revealed itself in the guise of a tenacious national idiom with peculiar characteristics). Its practical application quickly finds illustration in such manuals as the *Arte organica* (Brescia, 1608) of Costanzo Antegnati (member of the illustrious Brescian family of organ builders) and *L'organo suonarino* (Venice, 1605, reprinted in various revised editions as late as 1638) of Adriano Banchieri. The musical repertory itself embraces various types of publication. These include such all-purpose collections as the *Annuale che contiene tutto quello che deve far un organista per risponder al coro tutto l'anno, cioè tutti gl'inni delli vesperi, tutte le messe, cioè doppia, che serve ad ambe le classi, della Domenica, e della Beatissima Vergine Madre di Dio; sono regolate sotto l'ordine de' toni ecclesiastici; otto magnificat . . . otto ricercate, otto canzoni francese, quattro fughe . . . la Salve regina ed il Te Deum laudamus* (*Annual containing all that an organist needs do to respond to the chorus throughout the year; that is, all the hymns of vespers, all the masses, 'in duplicibus diebus' both for Sunday and for the Blessed Virgin; classed in the order of ecclesiastical tones; eight magnificats . . . eight ricercars, eight canzoni francesi, four fugues . . . the Salve regina and the Te Deum laudamus*) of the friar Giovanni Battista Fasolo of Monreale (1645), or the *livre d'orgue contenant cent pièces de tous les tons de l'Église* of Guillaume-Gabriel Nivers (1665); there are also, however, the various specialized collections of ricercars, canzonas, capriccios or toccatas, from which the organist is invited to draw the various 'substitute' items for the Gradual, Offertory, antiphons or – climactic moment of the Mass – Elevation. (Indicative, in this sense, is the frequent occurrence of instrumental canzonas and ricercars in collections of otherwise sacred vocal music: these pieces, where local tradition allowed, may well have been performed not by organ but by *ad lib.* instrumental ensembles. In the second half of the century, particularly in northern Italy, the organ gladly makes way for the trio *sonata da chiesa* – in its standard formation of two violins and bass – itself specifically designed for the instrumental 'substitution' of the Proper.) Finally, there are collections of organ masses. These volumes, which represent a more liturgically integrated and artistically sophisticated form of publication than the two preceding groups, combine (partially, at least) the two functions of Proper 'substitution' and, in the Ordinary, *alternatim* performance with Gregorian chant; notable examples are the *Pièces d'orgue, consistant en deux messes* 'for current parish use, as also for monasteries and convents' of François Couperin (composed in 1690 but never published), as also the three organ masses (*della Domenica*, *degli Apostoli* and *della Madonna*) of the *Fiori musicali* (Venice, 1635) of Girolamo Frescobaldi, himself organist of St Peter's, Rome. Here, it will be sufficient to illustrate just one of the various possible distributions of pieces in the *Messa della Madonna* (a slight excess of numbers allows for some freedom of choice on the part of the performer); note, in the Ordinary, how each of the pieces for organ is composed – or, in the case of the Gloria and subsequent items, improvised or drawn from some other handbook for organ – upon the relevant Gregorian *cantus firmus*, sung *alternatim* with the chorus.

Proper	Ordinary	Organ	Gregorian chant
		Toccata before the Mass	
Introit			
	Kyrie	*Kyrie* [I]	
			[Kyrie II]
		Kyrie [III]	
			[Christe I]
		Christe [II]	
			[Christe III]
		Kyrie [I]	
			[Kyrie II]
		Kyrie [III]	
	Gloria	[*alternatim*]	
Gradual		*Canzona after the Epistle*	
	Credo	[*alternatim*]	
Offertory		*Ricercar after the Credo*	
Prayers after the Offertory		*Toccata before the ricercar*	
		Ricercar	
	Sanctus	[*alternatim*]	
	(Elevation)	*Toccata for the Elevation*	
	Agnus	[*alternatim*]	
Communion		*Bergamasca*	
	(Deo gratias)	*Capriccio sopra la Girolmeta*	

The same 'problem' as was given such drastic formulation in the Roman edict of 1665 is also clearly present in other, non-Roman jurisdictions and liturgical traditions. In 1639, for example, the Procurators of St Mark's, Venice (jealous guardians – in music as in all other matters – of their autonomy from Rome) complain of 'abuses not only in the dress of the musicians but also in the use of musical instruments; and in the words that are sung one discerns greater care for the enjoyment of the listeners than for matters of devotion'. Indeed, the Procurators decree that:

> in musical solemnities, the use of instruments other than those normally used in church is not allowed; in particular, [it is necessary to] refrain from the use of warlike instruments such as trumpets, drums and the like, more suitable for armies than for the house of God . . . and that all the musicians, secular and ecclesiastical alike, while serving their musical functions, must come dressed in surplices ([which constitute] the appropriate clothing for church); and, finally, that the transposition of words or the singing of newly-invented words not contained in the holy books [must not be] permitted except at the Offertory, Elevation and after the Agnus Dei, and, likewise, at Vespers, that motets may be sung between the psalms, but [only] to devout words obtained from the holy books and from ecclesiastical authors; on this particular, [all] those with insufficient knowledge can and must receive instruction from the Reverend parish priests or other intelligent persons or priests of the churches, under pain of a 25 ducat fine and other penalties for each offence.

From this excerpt, however, it emerges that the levels of tolerance and margins for individual judgment at Venice were relatively wide. In the light of this and similar documents, all of which – in comparison with Rome – betray a consistently greater (though variable) level of permissiveness in local liturgical usage, the seemingly arbitrary choices of text and musical style in the motets 'between the psalms' of Monteverdi's *Vespro della Beata Vergine* (1610: published three years before Monteverdi's appointment as *maestro di cappella* of St Mark's) can be more easily explained: a monologue (*Nigra sum*) and duet (*Pulchra es*), both in pure *stile recitativo* and based on 'amorous' texts from the Song of Songs, whose reference to the cult of the Blessed Virgin is at most allegorical; a (necessarily 3-part) setting of a Trinitarian text (*Duo Seraphim clamabant alter ad alterum*), organized as a contest of vocal virtuosity between angels; there is also a devotional trope to the *Salve regina* (*Audi coelum verba mea plena desiderio et perfusa gaudio / audio*), this too with echo effects from the skies, and, finally, what is in reality an instrumental sonata with viols, cornetts and trombones, built around the eleven-fold repetition (by soprano solo) of the *cantus firmus* 'Sancta Maria ora pro nobis'.

Despite, however, the apparent liturgical anomaly in the texts of the motets, and their unrestrained application of a *stile recitativo* of thoroughly non-ecclesiastical derivation (more appropriate, if anything, for contemporary *musica da corte*: see chapter 3), it is the music of the five psalms and two concerted Magnificats (one of which, a more modest 6-part setting, is for use on the vigil; the other, quite similar in terms of its musical invention, but more sonorous and grand – scored as it is for seven voices and instruments – is for the feast-day itself) of the 1610 collection which, all things considered, merits greatest attention. It is, in fact, precisely in the psalms and Magnificat (the very 'pillars' of the Vespers rite, corresponding in function to the Ordinary of the Mass) that reconciliation between Monteverdi's capacity for affective and oratorical elocution (see chapters 4 and 7) and the liturgical requirements of musical dignity and respectability become more problematic. The composer's solution is complex. Psalms and Magnificats are set for five, six or seven voices, or for double choir, above the liturgically appropriate *cantus firmus* (which appear in long notes in one of the voices). The verse-by-verse repetition of the *cantus firmus* automatically produces as many musical sections as verses themselves and also gives an overall sense of unity: this notably segmented yet coherent structure, moreover, provides a framework within which the solo and choral counterpoint of the other voices and instruments can combine in a series of highly differentiated episodes of florid polyphony. *Jubilus* effects are frequent; the pure vocal ecstasy of the exhaustingly lengthy divisions (frequently with echo replies), while gravitating around the fixed structure of the *cantus firmus*, itself reaches celestial heights. In the second (and larger) Magnificat, cornetts and violins rejoice alongside the voices. At the opposite extreme, Monteverdi sometimes resorts to the use of *falso bordone*, a type of pseudo-polyphony for ferial use, in which the psalm verses are recited chorally to a single chord, punctuated cadentially at the mid-point and end of each verse. The programmed, reiterated discontinuity of heterogeneous compositional techniques produces divergent sonorities and leads to agitated, 'open' effects; the whole, however, is articulated by a clearly perceptible formal organization, based on the principle of alternation. Thus, the first psalm of the series may be represented as in the diagram on p. 115.

Historically speaking, however, the Monteverdi *Vespers* is a work of quite exceptional nature; for the remainder of the seventeenth century, the concerted *cantus firmus* mass and vespers is something of a rarity. There are, in fact, three commonly adopted solutions to the problem of musico-liturgical coherence (and Monteverdi, in his post-1610 compositions, illustrates them all). The first involves a full-

v. 1	*Dixit Dominus . . .*	*a 6*
		on *cantus firmus*
	Donec ponam inimicos . . .	*falso bordone*
		final cadence of *falso bordone* repeated *instrumentaliter*
v. 2	*Virgam virtutis tuae . . .*	soprano duet
		cantus firmus in bass
v. 3	*Tecum principium*	*falso bordone*
		final cadence of *falso bordone* repeated *instrumentaliter*
v. 4	*Juravit Dominus . . .*	tenor duet
		cantus firmus in bass
v. 5	*Dominus a dextris . . .*	*falso bordone*
		final cadence of *falso bordone* repeated *instrumentaliter*
v. 6	*Judicabat in nationibus . . .*	vocal quintet
		cantus firmus in bass
v. 7	*De torrente in via . . .*	*false bordone*

[this is followed by a six-part setting of the Doxology (*Gloria Patri*); the *cantus firmus*, while still fully present, is now shifted in mode]

voiced, syllabic, choral (at times, double-choir) declamation, without pretensions to artistic elegance; the verses are reeled off, none of them being accorded any special emphasis. A second solution envisages an openly 'madrigalian' style (few-voiced pieces with *basso continuo*, as in some of the more emotional madrigals from Monteverdi's Books 7 and 8): the psalms, however, are anything but monologues. Finally, there is the *stile concertato* – chorus, soloists, instrumentalists – in which each verse receives its own individual treatment; the result is an innumerable series of miniature arias, a chain of solo and choral episodes whose very distinctiveness produces a tiresome effect of unmotivated confusion. This, for example – despite an undoubted melodic perfection and beauty of sound – is the effect of the psalms of Cavalli (upright but modest heir to Monteverdi as a composer of sacred music) and his colleagues at St Mark's, who, in rejecting the liturgically orthodox but compositionally obsolete and cumbersome element of the *cantus firmus*, confer on their psalms and Magnificats the overall appearance of a blithely and openly multisectional progression of links in a chain. Monteverdi himself, in his Venetian psalm compositions without *cantus firmus*, sometimes obviates the problem by means of certain formal expedients which, on first sight, might create the impression of hybrid 'contaminations' of secular orientation; on the contrary, these expedients provide that very stylistic seal which the liturgy (alien as it is to discontinuous expressions of an affective nature) requires.

Two examples will suffice. In *Beatus vir* (1641), for six voices, instruments and *basso continuo*, the succession of verses is rendered coherent by means of a double recurring element. The first is also the motif which opens the work ('Beatus, beatus vir'), where it is enunciated in the joyful manner of a canzonetta (first by the first soprano, then by the full choir); this appears (complete or incomplete, but always identical) no less than five times in the course of verses 1–4, only to re-emerge triumphant (after a ternary episode in minor mode) at the end of verses 9 and 10 (before the Doxology). Placed in correlation with this motif – precisely in the same way as the strophic canzonettas of Book 7 – is a dance-like ritornello for two violins; this, too, makes some half a dozen appearances, both independently and in conjunction with the aforesaid vocal motto. Each verse or half-verse of the psalm is thus accompanied by at least one of these two musical symbols of the joy of him who fears the Lord; the result is a cyclical effect of expectation–surprise, which sustains the interior 'life' of the composition.

Besides unification of the verses, the composer of the psalms is presented with one other formal difficulty: the integration of that extraneous body – the Doxology – which brings up the rear of each text. In his *Laetatus sum* for six voices, instruments and *basso continuo*, published posthumously in 1650, Monteverdi offers a radical solution to both problems. Here, the verses are based upon a series of vocal and instrumental duets (two sopranos and two violins; two tenors and two trombones; two basses and a bassoon), delivered above a rudimentary four-note *basso ostinato* (G–G–C–D) whose total of 138 bar-by-bar reiterations continue for the entire duration of the psalm text itself. The incantatory effect of this circular motion derives essentially from the fixed tonal feeling (G) of the four notes in question; the exaltation of the final 'Gloria', proclaimed by a 'full-voiced' choir, is all the greater for its introduction of sequences of notes which point outwards towards opposite corners of the tonal horizon (E, A, D, etc.). In the end, however, the original *basso continuo* re-emerges intact to the sound of 'semper, semper', thus effecting – both formally and conceptually – a retrospective connection with the music of the psalm. Only the final 'Amen' puts an end to the quite literal continuation of this music 'in saecula saeculorum'.

Such formal procedures – effective by virtue of their very visibility (it is thus that they are also easily described in words) – are badly suited to frequent imitation. And, indeed, the sacred music of Monteverdi (none of which was ever reprinted) is solemn and exceptional by its very nature, destined for use by only those *cappelle musicali* of the very highest standing, in churches and cities which – like the *Serenissima Repubblica* – tolerated the extensive liturgical use of musical instruments and extra-liturgical styles. Other specifically local liturgical traditions are to be found in the great basilicas and churches of Bologna, Naples, Rome, etc. (as, indeed, already mentioned in chapter 12), and this fact undoubtedly impeded the free circulation of the repertory. On the contrary, statistically much more widespread and (hence) significant is the middle- to low-range performance bracket, as represented by provincial musical establishments, as also by the choirs of minor churches in the larger cities: the restricted vocal resources of these *cappelle musicali* find succour in an essentially consumer repertory of limited technical demands and wide circulation, frequently linked to the peregrinations of a variety of religious and clerical *maestri di cappella*, expert or not. Exemplary in this respect is the career of the Augustinian monk Stefano Filippini (known as l'Argentina) of Rimini, himself author of twelve volumes of sacred vocal music: *maestro di cappella* in 1620 at the church of S. Stefano in Venice, Filippini was subsequently to serve at the time of Urban VIII at S. Agostino in Rome and, from 1648, at the church of S. Giovanni Evangelista in Rimini – punctuated, moreover, by shorter spells at Forlì, Ravenna (the Duomo), Genoa (the Jesuit church), Montefiascone, San Marino, *et al.* He died at Rimini in 1690.

A far more distinguished representative of this type of church musician is Alessandro Grandi, whose music, indeed, may usefully be compared with that of the sublime Monteverdi. Born around 1585, musician and subsequently *maestro* at two Ferrarese religious academies (the Accademia della Morte and Accademia dello Spirito Santo), as well as at the Cathedral, Grandi left Ferrara in 1617 to join the musical establishment of St Mark's as *vicemaestro* to Monteverdi; finally, in 1627, he moved to Bergamo (where he died three years later of plague), as *maestro di cappella* at S. Maria Maggiore. Though probably northern Italian in origin, he is erroneously given as Sicilian by one eighteenth-century lexicographer, who bases his remarks on the existence of a Sicilian reprint of volumes 1–5 of Grandi's motets *a 2, 3, 4* (Venice, 1610–19; Palermo, 1620). The oversight is revealing; Grandi's success in the deep south of the Italian peninsula (copies of his works can be found as far afield as the Cathedral of Malta) provides unequivocal evidence of the functionality of his motets, which were several times reprinted in Venice and also enjoyed considerable popularity in northern Europe (where, for some half a century after their composer's death, they continue to appear by their dozens in German anthologies). The texts are part liturgical, part devotional, and form a repertory from which appropriate or other compatible texts may easily be drawn for use in the Proper. In contrast to Monteverdi, Grandi's style is somewhat 'middle of the road'; gone is the vocal and compositional virtuosity, the madrigal- and recitative-like affectation, the imitative severity of the *a cappella* 'stile osservato', the sonority of Monteverdi's great *cantus firmus* constructions. Instead, the various rhythmic, harmonic and melodic configurations of a simple counterpoint of voices – frequently solo, sometimes presented in dialogue form – are used to give suitable relief to crucial images alone. As stated in the dedication to Grandi's five-part motets of 1614:

> here, the clarity of the words is not impaired by the fugues of the composer, nor is the art of speaking rendered any less excellent through the art of song; on the contrary, the latter is elevated and humbled, runs, rests and cries with the former; in whatever way the former is arranged, the latter gives rise to a more effective portrayal of the affections therein: thus, in short, Your Highness will see how the art of this composer is characterized by a judicious light, an animated strength and a thoroughly lively spirit of oration; how, indeed, almost in the way of the chisel of the harmonious sculptor, it brings out the words for the hearers, which function is as appropriate to song as it is little understood by many professors of the latter, whose untimely and excessively frequent breaks in the notes both darken and disturb the serene progress of the oration, whose excessive greed for wide-roaming melody lacerates the words and destroys their clarity, and whose various series of inanimate *passaggi* are nothing but monsters and fancy ideas to the listeners. The valorous composer will indeed interrupt the current of the oration with song, but in the same way as the passage of the water of a pleasant stream is broken by tiny stones; certainly, its waters will not be rendered obscure by such perturbations, which, on the contrary, intensify the clarity of the waves and produce the sweetest babbling for the pleasure of the ears.

The sixteenth-century idea of music in the service of rhetoric (see chapter 4) is now seen less as a justification for licence and daring than as an obvious incitement to clarity and care over diction.

Grandi, on his arrival in Venice, applies these identical 'virtues' to a totally different genre: the devotional motet for solo voice (with or without violins). As *vicemaestro* to Monteverdi, his duties did not include the production of liturgical music for the Basilica; his solo motets, however, are among the earliest examples of a modern – and abidingly successful – musical genre which, whether or not deemed appropriate for performance by the great virtuosi of St Mark's, found an easy market in the *cappelle* of the fashionable monasteries and convents, private oratories and lay confraternities (in the case of one strophic setting, the reference is specific: ' . . . Defende Virgo confraternitatem istam et Venetos populos tibi devotos'). Indicative of the non-ecclesiastical function of these motets is their very designation: 'per cantar e sonar col chitarrone' ('to be sung and played with chitarrone'). Composed as they are to non-liturgical texts of generically Marian or laudatory orientation, the style of these compositions is not dissimilar to that of the concerted madrigal, though less openly affective and generally alien to sentiments of ecstasy and exaltation (never, for example, do we find the pulsating tones of suffering and sheer physical lament of Monteverdi's 2-part *Salve regina* of 1641, itself the product of a spiritual *pathos* of superbly indecorous complexion). At most, in cases where the text represents a compilation of Scriptural prose and metrical verse, the result – in formal terms – will resemble those secular cantatas of which Grandi is one of the earliest Venetian representatives: recitative, *ariette*, strophic verse, ritornellos. Only towards the end of his life – as head of the illustrious musical establishment of Bergamo – does Grandi (without, however, abandoning the production of motets) turn to the great compositional forms of the Ordinary: three masses, three Magnificats, thirty-four psalms are the published results of his final three years of activity. To the texts of the Ordinary, too, he applies the identical approach of a moderately 'oratorical' musical interpretation – which, indeed, will continue throughout the seventeenth century to represent the highest threshold for everyday church music in Italy.

16 Catholic devotional music

The use of music by the Catholic Church is by no means restricted to the liturgy – any more, indeed, than is the very manifestation of collective religious piety. Over and above liturgical ritual, the Church has always promoted a variety of forms of lay and religious community devotion, in which music has frequently been called upon to provide stimulus and enlivenment. To cite but one example: in the fifteenth and sixteenth centuries, beginning in Florence, then in the Roman circle of the Florentine priest Filippo Neri (founder, in 1575, of the Congregazione dell'Oratorio), the community singing of devotional *laudi spirituali* was exploited as a powerful means of lay edification. These polyphonic 'praises' are particularly significant in the context of Italian musical history, not only in terms of the richness of the repertory itself, but also by virtue of its collective diffusion through the various monasteries subsequently founded by the Oratorians in Naples (1586), Bologna (1616), Florence (1632) and (in the course of the seventeenth century) other centres up and down the Italian peninsula. Of fundamental importance, too, in the spread of the repertory is the musical press: the period 1563–1600 sees the appearance of a dozen different editions of polyphonic *laudi* by friends and companions of Filippo Neri (e.g., Animuccia) and Oratorian musician priests. An example is Giovenale Ancina, architect of the monumental anthology *Tempio armonico della Beatissima Vergine* of 1599. These prints were joined by numerous sixteenth- and seventeenth-century publications of non-Oratorian devotional *laudi* (in the seventeenth century, as before, Florence remains the most important centre of production), together with even more numerous editions of the texts alone in which the melodies, frequently identical to those of popular secular song, are regarded as common property.

The spiritual parody of popular urban song (discarding, that is, the original texts of erotic and/or aphoristic complexion) was widely used in every period of *laudi* production; it is, indeed, nothing but the most obvious musical expression of a more general process of 'taming' and exploitation of popular culture (itself the insidious bearer of hidden magical significations, though as such no less potent as a tool of missionary penetration), a process of appropriation-expropriation which, zealously cultivated by the Church from the Counter-Reformation onwards (as, indeed, by society in general) as a means of propaganda, was at its height in the period between the sixteenth and eighteenth centuries. The defunctionalization of popular music in its new context of devotional recreation and religious edification played a determining role in this process. The phenomenon may be seen in all its glory in the missionary activities of the period. Here, we may cite two exemplary cases. In 1578, on the occasion of the arrival in Mexico City of some holy relics sent from Rome, the festivities – organized by the Jesuit missionaries – included not only European-style liturgical polyphony but also indigenous dancing by 'indios niños' in plumes, with 'canto de organo' (i.e., polyphonic singing) 'concerted in Spanish style' but accompanied by indigenous instruments (e.g., the *teponaztli*, a kind of two-pitched 'sacred' drum); this was followed by a hymn to St Hippolytus (patron saint of Mexico City), sung in the local language (*náhuatl*) to indigenous ritual music. And again, towards the end of the seventeenth century, the Jesuit priest Giovanni Maria Salvaterra (himself of noble birth and educated in the art of dance and music), though desirous of a mission to China ('While at the

Collegio de' Nobili of Parma, I studied lute for four years; and to the aforesaid instrument I applied myself with even greater zeal when I learned . . . that a certain member of the Society, by means of this art, had deeply ingratiated himself with the kings of China'), was sent instead to the desolate Mexican peninsula of Lower California, where he made a personal acquaintance with the ritual dances of the Indios (of which he leaves mention of upwards of thirty) and propagated the Gospel through song (both his own, and that of the indigenous children).

Thus, the Church of Rome sought with every possible means to combat not only the latent paganism inherent in the religious beliefs of the less privileged at home but also the open paganism of the missionary territories abroad, the creeping expansion of Christian heresy and the sinful pleasures of contemporary society. In the main, the 'field of battle' lay outside the strictly ecclesiastical realms of liturgy and theology; of central importance, instead, was the mobilization – both individually and *en masse* – of interested parties from both lay and religious communities. The tools of this mobilization: the institution of militant religious orders, whose twin aims are conversion and instruction (the Jesuits, Oratorians, Capuchins and Barnabites, while all begin life in the course of the previous century, enjoy their greatest period of expansion during the period in question); the pastoral re-organization of all levels of society (Carlo Borromeo's mule-back missions to the parishes; the re-organization of the seminaries; the institution of centres for higher cultural learning, as, for example, in 1609, when the doors of the Biblioteca Ambrosiana of Milan – at the instigation of Cardinal Federico Borromeo – were opened to the public); the propagandistic and demonstrative effects of the canonization of latter-day saints, e.g. St Carlo Borromeo (1610) and the fivefold canonization (1622) of Sts Ignatius of Loyola (founder of the Jesuit movement) and Francis Xavier (promoter of the Jesuit missions to the Far East), the humble peasant St Isidor of Madrid, St Filippo Neri and the Carmelite mystic St Teresa of Ávila; the re-awakening of a spirit of inspired, mystic devotionalism (as, indeed, epitomized in the life of St Teresa of Ávila, immortalized, in her pose of painful ecstasy, in the marble of Gian Lorenzo Bernini); the promotion of a literally 'spectacular' hagiographical literature (culminating, indeed, 'operatically' in such works as Andrea Salvadori's *La regina sant'Orsola*, or the *Sant'Alessio*, *San Bonifacio* and *Santa Genoinda* of Mgr Giulio Rospigliosi – see chapter 20); the institution, in 1622, of a centralized body for missionary work (the Congregation *de propaganda fide*, which enjoyed as its centre a magnificent building designed by Borromini);

the ever more solemn and spectacular celebration of Jubilees (once every twenty-five years), and the urban transformation of the modest Papal city of the previous century, which now provided a sensational setting for the reception of a constant stream of pilgrims; the propagation of collective devotional forms with active participation of the faithful (e.g., the adoration of the Sacrament during the forty hours' devotion).

The degree to which sensory pleasure – and 'secular' incursions in general – was responsible for the successful outcome of such devotional practices is discreetly revealed in the following letter, in which Baccio del Bianco (a Florentine architect at the court of Spain) describes to a member of the Medici family the celebration of the forty hours' devotion for the birth of the Infanta in 1651:

> The Most Holy Sacrament . . . is exposed with a wealth of lights and silver, truly with the utmost majesty and decorum. At the foot of the altar is an enclosure of benches; sitting here are all the musicians of the Chapel Royal, with harp, trombone, cornett and regal, with the long held notes of the *cornamusa*: these continually sing hymns and *laudi*, but in Spanish, this being the greatest language in the world; I have asked for and await these *ariette*, which, immediately on receipt, I wish to send to Signor Atto Melani, who, with his company of musicians, will perform them for Your Highness: in my opinion, however, it will be quite impossible to hear them sung with the same spirit as here. Here, in short, a visit to the forty hours' devotion is like entering the music school of Giovanni Battista Gagliano of Florence; and they sing all the louder when a greater number of young ladies are present – who, kneeling on the ground, winking from behind their cloaks, give rise to the most beautiful chatter (with the friars, confessor and young men) that ever was heard . . .

In all probability, the 'ariette' described by Baccio del Bianco were *villancicos*. These, essentially, were the Spanish equivalent of the Italian *laudi spirituali*: popular strophic songs, based on a variety of themes (but frequently provided with devotional texts), which circulated widely in Portugal and Spain and which, beginning in the sixteenth century, assumed the characteristics of an independent 'sacred' genre – liable, indeed, to no small degree of artistic elaboration (though never beyond the limits of a charmingly 'popular' metre, rhythm and melody – itself sing-song and dance-like in style – which made these pieces the favourite vehicle for Christmas devotion). Their use in church was prohibited only in 1765. Meanwhile, however, for the churches of Latin America, the *villancico* had become the preferred genre of 'sacred' music; emigrant Spanish *maestri di cappella* were, indeed, given every encouragement to increase production of the repertory. Beginning in 1591, for example, the *maestro di cappella* of

Mexico City Cathedral was granted eighty days' annual leave, during which time he was to procure the new poetic texts to be performed as *villancicos* on the feasts of *Corpus Christi* and Christmas. Pride and joy of seventeenth-century Mexican literature is Sister Juana Inés de la Cruz, herself the author of considerable numbers of *villancicos*; the heterogeneous and extremely noisy assortment of instruments described in one of her texts – an ensemble by no means unsuitable as accompaniment for the frequently onomatopoeic refrains of surviving *villancicos* (nor for the dance-like ardour revealed in the surviving pieces) – is not totally beyond the bounds of imagination, though quite within the limits of poetic verisimilitude: clarino, trumpet, trombone, cornett, organ, bassoon, violin, shawm, tromba marina, cittern, violone, vielle, rebec, pandora, harp . . .

While liturgical music in general is characterized by a clearly perceptible dialectic between the tendency towards canonical uniformity and the application of a wide variety of artistic resources (see chapter 15), the much less definable area of devotional worship gives rise to a number of types of musical production which resist easy characterization by a few constant features. Indeed, in an age of great religious mobility and propagandistic activity in which the Church attempts to embrace and impose unity upon an increasingly fragmentary social reality, music for devotional purposes has a tendency to proliferate in a variety of forms and occasions, which rarely come together in an autonomous artistic tradition. If anything, local traditions preponderate – traditions peculiar to and exclusively cultivated by a particular city or institution, but little suited to any wider diffusion. Typical is the case of the 'Easter sepulchres' of Vienna: immobile, contemplative scenes which, beginning in the seventh decade of the century, were performed (in Italian) on Holy Thursday and Good Friday on a temporary stage specially erected in the Hofburg chapel or in the private chapel of the Empress Mother: this illustrious genre remained the exclusive prerogative of the Imperial court.

The oratorio – statistically the most important of all seventeenth-century devotional genres – presents a very heterogeneous picture. Varied in institutional setting, discontinuous and multiform by artistic tradition, even the very definition of the term 'oratorio' is somewhat unclear. Moreover, an albeit ample musicological literature on the seventeenth-century oratorio has not infrequently suffered from a teleological perspective which seeks to trace the prehistory and precursors of the golden age of the genre – as represented by Handel and Bach – and has thus tended to impose the idea of an historical continuity in oratorio production which links the distant Catholic origins of the 'form' to the culminating masterpieces of the two Protestant giants. In reality, this 'continuity' is nothing but a multitude of different musical and devotional practices. 'Oratorio', in the seventeenth century, has an extremely limited terminological consistency; more than a musical genre, it may be said to designate a type of 'sacred' building, together with its function as a place of prayer. Contemporary terminology for the *oratorio in musica* is extremely varied and/or generic: terms such as *historia*, *melodrama*, cantata, dialogue, *drama rhythmometrum* are superseded only at the end of the century by *oratorio*. This enormous breadth – indeed, arbitrariness – of terminological usage, as also variety of definition, can be illustrated in brief through comparison of three separate episodes from the presumed 'history' of the seventeenth-century oratorio: early in the century in the Oratory of Rome; at mid-century in the Oratory of the SS. Crocifisso (Most Holy Cross); in the last years throughout all Italy.

Undoubtedly prominent are the spiritual activities of the Oratorians at Rome. The early generations of the followers of St Filippo Neri continued in their promotion of highly frequented spiritual and devotional activities in association with religious festivities; in summer these 'meetings' were held in the open, in winter in the Oratory of the Chiesa Nuova (the present building, humble in its materials – brick and plaster – but splendid in architectural design, was erected by Borromini in 1640). Music invariably played an important part in these devotional practices, not only through the community singing of *laudi spirituali* but also by virtue of 'guest' appearances of outside musicians hired by the Congregation (a lasting tradition of affection for the Oratory on the part of the Papal singers may be traced back to the very outset of the movement, culminating in 1639 with the erection in the Oratory of a private tomb for the singers of the Cappella Sistina). Emilio de' Cavalieri's *Rappresentazione di Anima e di Corpo* ('per recitar cantando'), staged by the Oratorians in February 1600 (Holy Year), must certainly have represented an anomaly with respect to this practice of sacred and devotional song: in reality, the occasion was a great society event, graced by the presence of dozens of cardinals among the spectators. This allegorical drama (the two antagonists of the title are joined in the course of the libretto by various other personifications: Time, Intellect, the World, Counsel, Pleasure, the Damned Souls, etc.) is based throughout on recitatives in very simple rhymed couplets, interpolated with strophic episodes in a variety of metres (for the choruses and dialogues). One of these strophic sections – which recounts the initial disagreement between Body and Soul (Act 1, scene 4): 'Anima mia, che pensi? / perché dogliosa stai, / sempre traendo guai? – Vorrei riposo e pace, / vorrei diletto e gioia, / e trovo affanno e noia . . . ' corresponds exactly to the text of a polyphonic *laude spirituale* of 1577; it is, moreover, quite within the bounds of probability that many of the generically devotional strophes in the choruses of the *Rappresentazione* were drawn from *laudi* in Oratorian use. This circumstance has led some scholars to detect in the *laudi* of the Oratorian movement the original germ for the oratorio as drama and music; by a similar token, the *Rappresentazione* of Cavalieri is taken as the first fully-fledged example of the new genre. It would be wiser to take the *Rappresentazione* for what it really was: a theatrical event of outstanding artistic significance (as testified by the very luxuriousness of the musical edition), which, given the edifying nature of the occasion, availed itself of that very type of devotional poetry – the Oratorian *laudi* – whose use was already quite customary on the part of both promoters and 'recipients' of the entertainment: in short, nothing but the 'one-off' adoption of spiritual texts for artistic ends (in much the same way as Palestrina, some twenty years before, had turned to *laudi* texts for his *madrigali spirituali* of 1581; conversely, in 1613, Giovanni de Macque uses the text of a chorus from Cavalieri's *Rappresentazione* as the material for two further *madrigali spirituali*). It is, indeed, true that the incorporation of devotional *laudi* in 'theatrical'-ritualistic contexts was far from unknown in cities other than Rome – and, moreover, in the years prior to 1600. For example: a *Trionfo della verginità* (an '*operina*, performed by the Virgins of the Compagnia di Sant'Orsola, in which the excellence of the virgin state is briefly described'), printed at Cremona in 1595, portrays the 'clothing' of a nun, with a chorus of angels and holy virgins who sing devotional *laudi* and octaves between the acts of the investiture rite. *Laudi spirituali* and *rappresentazioni* on sacred themes were cultivated both before and after 1600 in Florence – at the Confraternity of the Archangel Raphael – by Bardi, Peri, Rinuccini, Caccini, Gagliano, etc. The oratorio as music and dialogue thus derived not from the *laudi* themselves but rather from the devotional practices of which the *laudi*, at most, represented a favourite ingredient.

Much more than the inimitable *Rappresentazione* of 1600, it is the *Teatro armonico spirituale* (1619) of Giovanni Francesco Anerio which gives an idea of the contribution of the Roman Oratorians to the development of the new genre as both music and dialogue. In this collection, the *madrigali spirituali* and dialogues in *stile recitativo* make up a kind of 'winter theatre of the Gospels and Holy Scriptures, with the *laudi* of all the saints' – words, these, from the dedication to the collection, addressed to the memory of Filippo Neri and St Jerome (this latter the patron saint of the first Oratorian church in Rome, S. Girolamo della Carità). The relationship between the madrigals and dialogues of the *Teatro* and the winter feasts of the liturgical calendar is clear: for each feast, the Latin reading from the Scriptures is paralleled in the Vespers 'oratorio' of the Fathers of Filippo Neri by the singing of an Italian poetic paraphrase of the reading concerned. In short, an attractive way of propagating the Lessons, in much the same way as the sermon could be used as a means of providing critical commentary.

The textual sources for the Italian dialogues of the *Teatro armonico* are, then, the Scriptures (and, for commemorations of the saints, the Lives); thus, the devotional and edifying nature of these pieces resides not in the texts themselves (as is true of the extra-liturgical community singing of *laudi spirituali*, no less than the sacred-allegorical *rappresentazioni*) but rather in their function as mediators between the liturgical text in its original Latin configuration – inaccessible to all but the few – and the multitude of the faithful. An interesting basis, in fact, for the development of the various types of *oratorio in musica* is provided by the inherently narrative and dialogue-orientated nature of many of the Old and New Testament passages in the Proper of the Mass. A powerful incentive for cultivation of the genre, however, must also have been provided by the caution and diffidence with which the Church of Rome has always viewed direct access to Biblical texts on the part of the faithful. The oratorio – a fascinating musical recitation of adroitly paraphrased scenes from the Bible and Gospels – acted as both vehicle and filter for the controlled divulgation and popularization of the Scriptures in a way that was undoubtedly more attractive – and innocuous – than anything offered by direct reading of the original sacred texts (whose perusal was not to be abandoned to the initiative of private individuals). The Bible and the Lives of the Saints, in fact, are the sources for the overwhelming majority of seventeenth-century oratorios; contemplative and allegorical subjects are in a clear minority.

Official Church diffidence towards the Scriptures is further increased at the time of the Counter-Reformation by the anti-evangelical controversy. While, for Protestants, the Holy Scriptures are the only source of revelation, the Catholic Church – which has always tended to emphasize the preponderance of its own theological and ecclesiastical tradition over the Bible as source of revelation – prefers to submit the Holy Scriptures to non-historical, non-moral, 'symbolic' interpretation. The Old Testament thus comes to be viewed as a prefiguration of the New, the history of the Chosen People as a symbol of future Redemption. In Catholic theology, the sacrifice of Isaac – which, in its original Old Testament context, is a Jewish myth held up as an historical example of total obedience and devotion to God (and, as such, worthy of imitation) – is the prefiguration, or 'symbol', of the sacrifice of the Son of God: thus, the Crucifixion provides a symbolic explanation of the Old Testament story of Abraham and Isaac, while the sacrificial lamb of the latter is symbolic of the mystic New Testament Lamb. The New Testament represents the fulfilment and realization of everything explicitly foretold by the Old Testament prophets or implicit in the acts of such 'figures' – or 'symbols' – as Isaac. This kind of figurative interpretation does not detract from the historical reality of either Testament, which is merely subordinated to the idea of a symbolic inter-relationship of mirror images within an overall context of the inscrutable designs of Providence – in favour, that is, of the unambiguous significance acquired by these images in the general perspective of redemption through Christ. In the hands of the seventeenth-century Church, the *oratorio in musica* comes to be exploited as a highly effective means of promoting this 'allegorical' interpretation of the Bible; self-evident, in this respect, are such titles as *Il sacrificio del Verbo umanato figurato in quello della figlia di Jefte* (*The sacrifice of the Word made Flesh prefigured in that of the daughter of Jephtha*), *Abel figura dell'Agnello mistico eucaristico* (*Abel, figure of the mystic eucharistic Lamb*) and *Giona simbolo della sacrosanta Eucaristia* (*Jonah symbol of the Most Holy Eucharist*). Likewise, Latin oratorios (or *historiae*), though necessarily based on Biblical narrative prose (and not on a system of Italian poetic paraphrase, with its tendencies towards free interpretation), were also performed in a devotional context which enhanced their figurative interpretation. This clearly emerges from an eye-witness account of 1639, in which the French musician André Maugars describes the audiences held every Friday in Lent at the Roman Oratory of the SS. Crocifisso (at the expense of the noble Archconfraternity of that name): after an opening psalm or motet and instrumental *sinfonia* there followed an Old Testament story, sung in *musica recitativa* 'in the form of a *commedia spirituale*' (i.e., one voice per character); after the sermon, the Gospel for the day was 'performed' in similar style.

Undoubtedly most interesting of all to the author of this brief description was the extraordinary quality of Italian *musica recitativa* (unknown, as it was, to his readers at home) – not, certainly, the Scriptural derivations of the texts. The choice of these latter, however, cannot have been totally at random if, among the Old Testament stories cited by Maugars, is the bath of Susanna, paralleled in the New Testament examples by the episode of the Samaritan woman at the well. Both passages are present in the Proper of the Mass, where they occupy adjacent positions in the liturgies for the third Saturday and third Friday of Lent; in his Oratory sermon, it would thus have been the task of the preacher to establish – by way of explanation – a figurative relationship between the stories in question. Musical oratorio and ecclesiastical rhetoric, though separate genres, are closely concurrent in their area of uplifting the faithful through charm and persuasion: indeed, the triumph of the *oratorio in musica* coincides with the definitive establishment – thanks to such outstanding preachers as the Capuchin friar Emanuele Orchi (whose *Quaresimale* was posthumously published in 1650) and the Jesuit Paolo Segneri (whose own *Quaresimale* appeared in 1679) – of sacred oratory as a literary genre. Latin oratorio – in which there is a general predominance of Biblical texts from the liturgy – is articulated in a single part only; two such oratorios could thus suitably have combined as figurative mirror images around a centrally-placed sermon (as in the aforementioned paraliturgical meetings, held during Lent at the Oratory of the SS. Crocifisso). On the contrary, Italian-language oratorio (based as it is on the poetic paraphrase of the Scriptures, and as such clearly extra-liturgical) is generally articulated as a two-part dramatic dialogue with intervening sermon. In both cases, the proximity in relation to the sermon is of fundamental importance.

Indeed, the differences between Latin and vernacular oratorio are less to be sought in divergences of form – or, for that matter, in their respective degrees of adherence to Biblical sources – as in their different functions and fruitions. The practice of oratorio in Latin was extremely circumscribed. Its regular and systematic cultivation remained in fact the prerogative of a single institution: the aforementioned Archconfraternity of the SS. Crocifisso. Throughout the Seicento (it is only in the early eighteenth century that the practice begins to lose ground), the five Latin oratorios performed on the Fridays of Lent before this exclusive club of Roman aristocrats represented what might almost be described as an 'oratorial' afterview – and counterbalance – to the operatic season of Carnival. The Biblical *historiae* of Giacomo Carissimi (1605–74), highly praised in the annals of foreign visitors to Rome, were mostly destined for performance at the Oratory of the SS. Crocifisso. The 'representational' force of this music – still immediately perceptible to the modern ear – exploits to considerable advantage the particular structure of the chosen texts, which, though essentially derived from Biblical prose, are not without that touch of amplification and paraphrase which greatly enhances the 'vividness' of the Scriptural text and offers considerable potential for musical imitation (thus, in the trials of Jonah, the original three-line Biblical description of the storm at sea is transformed – both poetically and musically – in Carissimi's *historia*, which provides an extensive account of the tempest in all its meteorological splendour). Frequent, too, are the metrical (verse) interpolations, which – in musical terms – give rise to those moments of greatest pictorial charm or intensity. Thus, in the *Historia divitis*, St Luke's Biblical account of the parable of the Rich Man and Lazarus (which appears in the liturgy as the Gospel for the second Thursday of Lent) is only moderately paraphrased in the recitative of the *Historicus* (or Narrator), the Rich Man and Abraham (these latter two direct protagonists in the drama); within this basic framework, however, the work is literally crammed from beginning to end with 'interpolations' of a highly picturesque orientation: the horrid, pandemoniac scenes of devils who ravish the wicked man's soul ('Iam satis edisti, / iam satis bibisti, / iam satis plausisti, iam satis lusisti . . . '), the contrast between the devils and the soul ('Quas gustabo epulas? / Serpentes et viperas. / Quae bibam vina? / Picem et sulphura. / Quali recubam lectulo? / Ferreo et candenti. / . . . / Quibus fruar spectaculis? / Teterrimorum daemonum . . . '). The two moving scenes which led to the immense celebrity of the *historia* of *Jephte* are both interpolations in the original Biblical prose (itself from the Book of Judges): the exultation ('Incipite in tympanis, / et psallite in cymbalis, / hymnum cantemus Domino, / et modulemur canticum . . . ') and desperation ('Plorate, colles; dolete, montes; et in afflictione cordis mei ululate') of the Daughter and Virgins.

The fame of *Jephte*, however, is essentially a creation of 'musicologists' (see, for example, the comments of Kircher – chapter 9) and collectors (see chapter 12 for an account of the fortunes of the Carissimi manuscripts). As already mentioned, the performance of Latin oratorios was reserved for a few highly exclusive audiences, such as those at the SS. Crocifisso and German College (where Carissimi was *maestro di musica*); the music of these works was never printed, nor did it circulate beyond the confines of those institutions for which it was originally composed. (Atypical, retrospective and devoid of all practical function are the seven double-choir Latin dialogues in Domenico Mazzocchi's *Sacrae concertationes . . . pro oratoriis* of 1664: these works, presumably destined for use at the Oratory of the SS. Crocifisso, were composed in the fourth decade of the century.) Carissimi, noted north of the Alps for his sacred liturgical music (through the disseminating influence of the Jesuits), in Rome (to music-loving tourists, at least) for his Latin oratorios, was celebrated elsewhere in Italy for his secular cantatas (whose use, unlike the Biblical *historiae*, was not restricted to a handful of institutions in the Papal city). In France, a similar form of cultural isolation – accentuated by the general disinterest of French courtly circles for devotional music – befell the *historiae* and Latin *cantica* of Marc-Antoine Charpentier, himself a pupil of Carissimi at Rome; a total of some thirty 'oratorios', composed by Charpentier for the Jesuit churches and *hôtels particuliers* of Paris in the late seventeenth and early eighteenth centuries, nevertheless failed to produce any lasting tradition. In the main, these works are based on Biblical subjects of the type also used by Carissimi; a *Judicium Salomonis* was the highly appropriate music for the inaugural session of the French parliament in 1702. Exceptional, in this general context, is the recourse to modern hagiography in the oratorio *Pestis mediolanensis* (in honour of St Carlo Borromeo), with its suggestive representation of the Milanese plague of 1576.

Notably different is the case of the vernacular oratorio, which, in the second half of the century, spreads rapidly outwards from Rome to establish itself throughout the Italian peninsula (grafting itself onto a variety of pre-existing local institutions and traditions or creating them anew), with a functional effectiveness that was quite unknown to its Latin counterpart. Together with contemporary opera – perhaps, indeed, to an even greater degree than the latter – (see chapter 22), the Italian oratorio was responsible for the levelling of the musical outlook of the 'nation' and the creation of an 'average' musical taste. Vehicles for the spread and proliferation of the *oratorio in musica* were the aristocratic lay confraternities and religious orders. In the second half of the century, the Jesuits – initially, in Rome, little dedicated to the production of public oratorio, and, if anything, assiduous cultivators of the scholastic Latin drama, in which, at best, music has a limited role – compete on an equal footing with the Oratorians themselves. Their activities as musical patrons are particularly evident in Sicily (Palermo and Messina) and southern Italy in general (the phenomenon, however, still awaits adequate investigation). Remunerative, at most, in terms of civil approval and spiritual edification (the financial burden of each production lay entirely with the organizers), the oratorio nevertheless assumed the irrepressible and periodic character of a customary civic tradition. A few examples only will be sufficient to demonstrate the importance of a phenomenon which asserts itself in practically every city in Italy.

At Rome, in the final decade of the century, the normal liturgical calendar is paralleled by what can only be described as a veritable calendar of oratorios. Together with the scores of the music performed during the winter meetings held every Sunday in the Oratory of S. Filippo Neri (the texts of these works were never published), the printed librettos relating to other performances tive a representative (though undoubtedly incomplete) picture of the oratorios of greatest appeal: the five Latin oratorios performed annually for the five Fridays of Lent at the Oratory of the SS. Crocifisso; simultaneously, at least one 'Oratorian' oratorio at S. Girolamo della Carità; one or more oratorios at the Cancelleria; occasional oratorios at the Chiesa Nuova and S. Giacomo degli Spagnoli; during Carnival, oratorios or sacred dramas at the Nazarene and Clementine Colleges; for St Teresa, in October, an oratorio in the Oratory (itself dedicated to St Teresa) at S. Maria della Scala; on the night of 24 December, a Christmas oratorio in the Apostolic Palace; for Holy Year, 1700 (as also in 1675), a special series of Lenten oratorios in the Oratory of the Fiorentini; finally, for the aristocratic circles of the cardinals in Rome, a series of privately commissioned oratorios . . . At Ferrara, no longer the seat of the Este dynasty but only of a modest Papal legation, and greatly declined from its earlier position as a musical capital, the local musicians – organized in two Academies (the Accademia della Morte and Accademia dello Spirito Santo) – still manage to produce six new Italian oratorios in 1675 (two further oratorios, one imported from Rome, were privately performed in the castle of the Cardinal Legate), ten in 1677, twelve in 1678, fifteen in 1679, etc.; from time to time, the names of local Ferrarese composers (Bassani, Mazzaferrata, Cherici, Legrenzi) are joined by the Romans Alessandro Melani, Giuseppe Peranda and Bernardo Pasquini. This latter is particularly ubiquitous (in the 1680s, first performances of his oratorios occur in such disparate centres as Messina, Modena, Palermo and Florence); indeed, his career provides an excellent example of a composer on the Italian oratorio circuit (itself parallel in every respect to the contemporary opera circuit, though centred not on Venice but on Rome – see chapter 22), with its network of exchange and circulation of musicians and scores. At Perugia, beginning in the 1680s, the annual feast of St Cecilia (22 November) – patron saint of musicians – is celebrated with an oratorio performed in the church of the Oratorians (further oratorios are promoted at Perugia by the Jesuits). In Florence, no fewer than thirty-five 'Oratorian' oratorio libretti are published in the course of 1693 alone; this is the high point in what was a consistently rich tradition of oratorio production (one oratorio per Sunday was the winter season norm); Roman works predominate, some of recent composition (Alessandro Scarlatti, Pasquini, etc.), others of ten or twenty years before (Stradella, Melani, etc.). At Modena, in the 1680s, the oratorio is cultivated by Francesco II d'Este (with something under ten productions a year), whose patronage takes the form of Ducal commissions to the best composers in Italy, coupled with a system of 'drainage' from the 'central' repertory at Rome; the manuscript scores – some 100 in all – of these works are conserved in the Estense library of Modena, where they form what is probably the most representative collection in Europe – numerically tiny, however, in comparison with the almost 400 oratorios – largely Roman in origin – possessed by the Oratorians of Bologna in 1682.

In this latter phase of oratorio production, the texts – composed by amateur poets (frequently high-ranking ecclesiastical dignitaries, e.g. the Cardinals Pietro Ottoboni and Benedetto Pamphili) and professional theatre librettists alike – are based, as before, on Biblical or hagiographical themes, but now with all the features of miniature operas: sacred 'azioni', often dramatically weak or merely contemplative in tone, interwoven with monologues, dialogues, recitatives and arias (themselves sometimes lifted *en bloc* from successful operatic productions). The elimination of Scriptural prose leads inevitably to the almost complete disappearance of the figure of the *historicus* or narrator, whose epic recitation of the story, in mid-seventeenth-century oratorio (both Latin and Italian), had acted as a framework for the direct interventions of the various protagonists. When, in 1706, Arcangelo Spagna – himself author of a number of oratorio texts – addresses himself to a theoretical rationalization of the dialogue oratorio (or 'perfect spiritual opera'), his remarks are nothing but a retrospective codification of a type of oratorio now sanctioned by over three decades of practical use; in reality, his detested *historicus* is a merely imaginary foe. Closer examination, indeed, suggests that only with this late seventeenth-century dramatic oratorio – spiritual, non-scenic substitute for opera – is it possible to speak of any truly continuous and institutionally consolidated oratorio tradition (a tradition which now invades the length and breadth of the Italian peninsula, prospering well into the eighteenth century). Hardly fortuitous is the publication in these very same years (1695) of the earliest set of summary rules for the poetic composition of oratorio texts – this despite the fact that their author (the singer and opera composer Giovanni Andrea Angelini Bontempi) still makes provision for the presence of a narrator.

In other words the oratorio as a musical and literary genre is less the result of the expansive and many-sided devotional fervour of the early seventeenth century than the institutionalized expression of the pervasively secularized religious devotion of the 1680s and 90s. It is, indeed, within these boundaries – geographically widespread but culturally restrictive – that it runs its course.

17 The music of the Lutheran Church: Heinrich Schütz

The distinction between liturgical and devotional forms, fundamental for the music of the Catholic Church, is much less apparent in the Lutheran tradition. Firstly, the relative value of 'liturgy' is substantially reduced in the context of a confession which rejects the doctrine of transubstantiation (the nucleus of the Catholic Mass). Equally reduced – in the absence of any formalized sacramental rite – is the degree of definiteness and standardization of a Mass which is celebrated with a high number of local variants in many different vernacular translations. Radically different, moreover, are the roles of the celebrant and faithful; Lutheranism rejects the pre-eminence of the clergy, as also the very distinction between clerics and laity: all Christians are priests, and the pastor – himself devoid of any sacramental ordination – is appointed by the community of the faithful. His function is that of illustrating and expounding the word of God: i.e., the Holy Scriptures, one and only Bible of the Faith. Each believer, however, has independent access to the word of God through direct intercession of the Holy Spirit. A profound inclination towards individual and community devotion is thus inherent in the very concept of the Lutheran service, whose principal aim may be defined as the theological and spiritual exposition of the Word: in this way, doctrinal orthodoxy and mystic piety are inextricably linked. Despite this, however, the Lutheran service is similar in formal organization to its Catholic counterpart; similar, too, is the Lutheran liturgical calendar, though bereft of the cult of the saints (with its many occasions – in the Catholic tradition – for liturgical and devotional worship) and based exclusively on Scripture.

Sacred, however, is the Word, not the rite itself; this basic point of difference with the Church of Rome would help explain the initial absence of any specifically Lutheran repertory of liturgical music (beyond, that is, simple community singing). Given the high degree of formal and textual compatibility with large parts of the Catholic liturgy, the Lutheran Church has frequent recourse to the Latin motet: this process of osmosis is further encouraged by the cosmopolitan style and European-based reputation of such composers as Orlando di Lasso. The period around 1600 is characterized by a broadly inter-confessional area in the field of Latin music as cultivated by the German theological colleges (where the teaching of rhetoric and languages is invariably accompanied by the study of music). Small-scale evidence for this phenomenon is provided by the enormous popularity in Germany of Ludovico da Viadana's three handy volumes of *Concerti ecclesiastici* (see chapter 6); on a larger scale, these are accompanied by a number of exceptionally copious (and lastingly popular) anthologies of motets, which – in their tenacious resistance to the rapid changes of modern taste – will continue to set the polyphonic horizons for the average German church musician until the time of Bach: 8-part (double-choir) motets are particularly well represented in the *Florilegium Portense* (1603, reprinted in 1618; and 1621) of Erhard Bodenschatz (ed.), singer at the Gymnasium of Schulpforta (hence the title of the print), and the *Promptuarium musicum* (1611, 1612, 1613, 1617) of Abraham Schadaeus, rector of Speyer; a further *Promptuarium* (with editions in 1622, 1623, 1627), this time compiled by a Catholic (Johannes Donfried), contains motets for two, three and four voices with *basso continuo*. Characteristic of all these collections is a certain predilection for motets of the Venetian school, with a corresponding lack of interest in Palestrina and other Roman composers. A demarcation, then, based more on style and ideology than on any confessional principles.

Even, however, in this somewhat 'inter-confessional' context, there comes a critical moment when Lutheran and Catholic repertories divide. The crucial point concerns the presence in the German tradition (in varying degrees of intensity) of community singing: a heritage of strophic melodies and texts (based on spiritual themes), fostered by Luther himself, which greatly contributed to the development of evangelical piety in its collective manifestations. This poetic and musical heritage was itself rejected by the more 'strictly' orientated of the Reformed Churches (the Calvinists and Zwinglians of Switzerland, Holland and North America), with the sole authorization of monodic singing of the psalms and the total exclusion of art music from divine worship. In short: the Catholic, in church, listens without singing; the Calvinist sings without listening; the Lutheran both listens and sings – simultaneously! The Lutheran chorale melodies, however, were not without a certain influence in Calvinist circles: of the thirteen authentic sets of chorale variations for organ by

Jan Pieterszoon Sweelinck, four only are based on melodies from the Genevan Psalter, eight on the Lutheran chorales (these pieces, performed in their appropriate position before or after the sermon, or at the beginning and end of the services, thus punctuated the latter without ever becoming an integral part of religious worship). In view of this fact, it is hardly surprising that the Sweelinck tradition was more readily accepted in Lutheran Germany than in Dutch Reformed circles. In Germany the principle of keyboard elaboration of chorale melodies (in various forms: free verses, alternating strophe-by-strophe with congregational singing; autonomous chains of variations; fantasias with *cantus firmus*) finds a legitimate use in the context of the divine service and leads to the appearance of such compendious publications as the three-volume *Tabulatura nova* (Hamburg, 1624) of Samuel Scheidt, himself a pupil of Sweelinck.

The original chorale may be used in a variety of ways. Of these, the first – and simplest – involves a four-part harmonization of the melody (*Kantionalsatz*); this practice, from its earliest beginnings in the final years of the sixteenth century, gradually comes to replace monodic singing as the only form of community participation in the chorale. Alternatively, the chorale melody can be used as a *cantus firmus* for polyphonic elaboration (in much the same way as Gregorian or secular *cantus firmi* in the sixteenth-century Latin motet). Several examples of this style are provided by the motets of Michael Praetorius (c. 1571–1621), *Kapellmeister* at the court of Wolfenbüttel, whose immense musical output – upwards of 1,200 liturgical compositions, published in a nine-volume series of *Musae Sionae* of 1605–10 (characteristic is the use of erudite Latin titles) – provides illustration of a truly universal range of styles and genres: Latin, German, with or without chorale melody, few- or many-voiced.

A third and somewhat ingenious procedure soon evolved, in the application to the chorale melody of techniques derived from the few-voiced concerted (Latin) motet. In particular, this style of composition was developed by Johann Hermann Schein (1586–1630), cantor at the Thomaskirche, Leipzig, and notably receptive to the most recent innovations in Italian musical style. In his two volumes of *Opella nova* (spiritual *concerti*, 'in the Italian style', for 2–5 voices and *basso continuo*), published respectively in 1618 and 1626, Schein refers explicitly to the model of the *Concerti ecclesiastici* of Viadana: his own motets, however, make use of both melody and text from the first strophe of each of the various chorales. Different melodic (Lutheran) and compositional (Italian) practices thus confront each other in the rhythmic and contrapuntal adaptation of the chorale (itself, however, invariably recognizable) to the requirements of a setting for high-voiced imitative duet: the diffraction is particularly attractive at points where the vocal duet – with its paraphrase of the original chorale – is interrupted by the entry of the basic melody, stated verse by verse in the tenor. This type of vocal *concerto* subsequently finds abundant use – indeed, abuse – in the works of Scheidt; with Schein, however, it represents but one of a large number of musical genres of Italian inspiration. At the opposite extreme – on the secular front – are a number of collections of convivial, indeed erotic, compositions ('auf Madrigal-Manier', 'auf Italian-Villanellische Invention'), published under the banner of such spirited titles as *Venus Kräntzlein* ('Garland of Venus', 1609), *Musica boscareccia* ('Sylvan' or 'pastoral music', 1621–28), *Diletti pastorali* ('Pastoral pleasures', 1624), *Studentenschmaus* ('a student bellyful of the excellent company of wine and beer', 1626). No translation of the following text will be necessary for the reader to grasp – in the reiteration of its endearing diminutives – the sonorous, Italianate playfulness of its metrical, canzonetta-like style: 'O Sternen Äugelein! / O Seiden Härelein! / O Rosen Wängelein! / Corallen Lippelein! / O Honig Züngelein! / O Perlemutter Öhrelein! / O Elffenbeinen Hälselein! / O Pomerantzen Brüstelein! / Bisher an euch ist alles fein: / Abr O du steinern Hertzelein, / Wie daß du tödst das Leben mein?'

One final means of utilization of the original chorale involves the employment of the words alone (without music), as a parallel textual source to Holy Scripture. This procedure is statistically significant. In the period after c. 1620, new vocal compositions are characterized by a marked decline in the combined use of original melody and text; seventeenth-century Lutheran music, moreover, while somewhat removed from the process of secularization now affecting the Catholic Church (a senseless concept if, with Luther, one accepts the idea of 'all music – secular music included! – as dedicated to the service of its Creator and Donor'), nevertheless witnesses the development of a profound division between traditional community singing and a musical culture which, for the first time, is becoming aware of its own advancement and progress. In Lutheran music, it is misleading to speak of any historical continuity based on community singing of the chorale and its artistic applications. Bach's dedication to the chorale is undoubtedly equal (though quite different in kind) to that of Praetorius and Schein, but this should not be construed as implying any direct or indirect descent. Not only is the work – itself of truly monumental significance – of the supreme Lutheran musician of the century, Heinrich Schütz (Köstritz, Thuringia, 1585 – Dresden,

1672), noticeably removed from the world of the chorale; it is also doubtful that Bach had ever heard a note of music by either Schütz or Schein. The 'interruption' could hardly be more complete. Schütz, clearly, is somewhat extraneous to that Bach-orientated teleological perspective by which both composer and works have traditionally been viewed as a function of later developments.

Schütz, too, leaves one conspicuous example of the employment of a chorale melody: the truly anomalous character of this work, however, does nothing but confirm the almost total extraneousness of the music of Schütz to traditional community singing of the chorale. By its very artistic exceptionality, it nevertheless merits our attention. The work in question – the *Musicalische Exequien* (or 'funeral music') – was composed for the solemn funeral of Heinrich Posthumus, Count of Reuß (Gera, 4 February 1636), where it was performed before and after the oration. It consists of three distinct compositions: a ceremonial form, indeed, meticulously pre-ordained by the Count, who, in accordance with contemporary German use, also selected the theme of the funeral oration, the holy texts and even the date of the ceremony (the commemoration of St Simeon). The second of the three pieces – a double-choir motet – is, in fact, based on the theme of the sermon (the psalm verse 'Lord, who have I in heaven besides thee?') that it was destined to follow. The concluding piece (*a 5*), a setting of the Canticle of Simeon (or *Nunc dimittis*), was performed prior to burial (here the composer himself, with ingenious invention, has added the words of the Apocalypse: 'Blessed are they who die in the Lord', which, sung as they are by a distant trio of voices – two Seraphim and the Blessed Spirit – provide what might almost be described as a luminous rent in the skies, opening up the gravity and austerity of the musical lament to the infinite beatitude of the heavens). The opening work (performed before the oration) is a broad vocal *concerto* 'or German Requiem Mass' (Kyrie and Gloria) for six voices and *basso continuo*. In reality, however, the entire text is made up from those very same Biblical verses and chorale strophes which, by order of the deceased, were also inscribed on his funeral bier. In much the same way as each Biblical verse (penitential or soteriological in theme) on the lid or walls of the coffin is paralleled by a chorale strophe of similar argument, so too, in the pseudo-Gloria of Schütz's Mass, the solo singing of the Biblical verses is interspersed with a full choral rendition of the texts and melodies of the respective chorales. On closer inspection, the binary layout of this composition (Bible/chorale) is nothing but the musical expression of a more general system of symbolic parallels between Scripture and devotional song which presides over the entire funeral ceremony, and which is permeated throughout by a profound sense of the helpless mortality of human flesh: on the coffin, those texts which expound the themes of earthly sin and divine punishment are located around the legs of the corpse; clemency and redemption are the themes of the texts around the head. Not entirely dissimilar in terms of its symbolism and emphasis on mortality is the *Membra Jesu nostri* of Dietrich Buxtehude (composed in 1680 for the court of Sweden): seven Latin 'meditations' on the Passion, each of which contemplates a different part of the body of Christ on the Cross (feet, knees, hands, ribs, chest, heart, face). Each section consists of an introductory instrumental sonata, an Old Testament passage (sung by the choir) in which the part in question is mentioned, and three half-strophes (three solo arias) from the hymn *Rhythmica oratio ad unum quodlibet membrorum Christi patientis* (attributed to St Bernard). In this context, indeed, it should be noted that all seventeenth-century devotional and liturgical music of the Protestant Church, even when characterized by tendentially pietistic forms of spiritual contemplation (as in the *Membra Jesu nostri*), is based – as here – on the principle of textual compilation, without the addition of any newly-composed religious lyrics (of the kind typical of the cantatas of Bach).

With the exception of the quite extraordinary *Musicalische Exequien* (which, though printed, was presumably never performed – or capable of performance – outside its original ceremonial context), the use of chorale melodies in Schütz is extremely rare indeed: only slightly more frequent, moreover, is the use of texts derived from the strophes of the chorales. The music of Schütz – written not for any normal ecclesiastical establishment but for a court chapel – is little concerned with community devotion; the composer, in Lutheran terms, is 'liturgist' only in so far as he is a preacher in music, individual expounder of the word of God. In the majority of cases, his textual source is the Bible; nevertheless, the unity of this nucleus is treated in a variety of highly differentiated musical settings, as a rapid glance at the printed output of the composer will show. Op. 1, the Italian madrigals of 1611 (see chapters 1 and 2), would hardly merit inclusion in the present context had it not represented what must surely have acted as inspiration and model for one of the unique masterpieces of Lutheran music: the 5-part *Israelsbrünnlein* of Johann Hermann Schein. In this work, composed in 1623 and dedicated to the Burgomasters and town council of Leipzig (hence probably intended more for a civic, devotional use than as accompaniment for the divine service), German spiritual texts from Proverbs, Prophets, Ecclesiastes and Revelation are set 'in a strange and charming Italian madrigal style'. Schein's madrigals, in fact, share with those of Schütz their length and expansiveness of individual episodes and expressive boldness of polyphony. In this 'fountain of Israel', the overripe musical language of the Italian madrigal combines with the richly metaphoric, affective prose of the Biblical text and its unusual poetic images – with fascinating results.

Schütz's Op. 2 – the *Psalmen Davids*: 'German psalms in the Italian style' in two-, three- and four-choir settings for eight or more voices and instruments – was dedicated in 1619 to the Elector of Saxony, at whose court (situated at Dresden) the composer was to serve as *Kapellmeister* for over half a century (from 1617 to his death in 1672). Its contents bear witness to the Venetian origins of Schütz's style (in particular, to his period of study with Giovanni Gabrieli): this is apparent in the sonorous splendour of the music and excited declamation of the text (an excitedness, indeed, enhanced by the consonant-based richness of the German language). In the preface (which faithfully echoes Viadana's instructions for the performance of polychoral music), Schütz justifies his choice of the *stylus recitativus* (i.e., rapidly flowing recitation in the modern madrigal style) as most suitable for the psalms in so far as this permits 'the prolonged recitation of a large number of words without lengthy repetitions'. He then warns against excessive speed of delivery, that the words will be clearly perceived without risk of a 'battle of flies'.

Op. 3, the *Historia der . . . Auferstehung* of 1623, recounts the Easter Resurrection Gospel in accordance with a pre-existing textual compilation in use at Dresden: the test is recited by the Evangelist, a tenor, in *falso bordone* with four *viole da gamba*; other significant roles (those, for example, of Mary Magdalene and Christ) are set for two voices and *basso continuo*. Op. 4, the Latin *Cantiones sacrae* of 1625, bears the composer's own designation 'opus ecclesiasticum primum'; however, the liturgical destination (Protestant or Catholic) of this collection – most of whose contents are settings of mystical texts attributed to Sts Augustine (the *Meditationes* and *Manuale*) and Bernard – remains open to question. The florid, madrigal-like tone of the polyphony (not dissimilar to that of the *Israelsbrünnlein* of Schein) exalts the penitential and contemplative *pàthos* of the words: a good example is the sense of passionate self-accusation conveyed by the coloratura and dissonances on the personal pronoun *Ego* in the sequence 'Ego sum tui plaga doloris . . . Ego enim inique egi . . . ', as also on the various verbal images of suffering, penitence and supplication. Op. 5 (1628) is a four-part *Kantionalsatz* setting of the German psalter. Its 150 psalms were reprinted in 1661; Schütz's newly-composed chorale melodies, however, were never accepted into regular community use, and the composer's most orthodox contribution to the Lutheran rite was thus to end in historical oblivion.

The *Symphoniae sacrae* of Op. 6 (the second of Schütz's 'ecclesiastical' or Latin collections) was published at Venice in 1629, during the composer's second period in Italy. In all probability, these compositions (settings of texts from the psalms, Gospels and Song of Songs, scored for 1–3 voices, 2–4 *obbligato* instruments and *basso continuo*) passed quite unnoticed in southern countries; no copies, in fact, are known to have survived in Italy, nor are they mentioned in the writings of any Italian musicians. The point of departure, however, is still provided by the music of Giovanni Gabrieli (cited by Schütz in the dedication to the volume, and reflected in the music itself by the wide range of instrumental timbres employed: violins, 'flauti', fifes, cornetts, trumpet, trombones, bassoons). The melodies linger on the salient images of the Biblical prose in the manner of musical sermons; the overall form of these motets (lengthy as they are, but articulated in a myriad of rhythmically and melodically differentiated segments) is, in fact, borrowed from the 'discourse' of the text.

Fundamental, given this approach, is the influence of Monteverdi and his style of musical rhetoric – the result of Schütz's inevitable contacts (direct or indirect) with the *maestro di cappella* during his second trip to Venice in 1629. This influence is clearly visible in all subsequent publications: after Op. 7, the already-mentioned *Musicalische Exequien* of 1636, there are the two volumes of *Kleine geistliche Konzerte* (Op. 8 and Op. 9, respectively 1636 and 1639) and two collections of German *Symphoniae sacrae* (Op. 10 and Op. 12, respectively 1647 and 1650). The fifty-five *Konzerte* for 1–5 voices and *basso continuo* are based predominantly on Old Testament texts (in German) for the Gradual of the Mass (these texts, sung in proximity to the New Testament readings, would have provided an 'idealized' figurative commentary on the latter); also featured, however, are excerpts from the Gospels, the Epistles of St Paul, mystical texts (in Latin or German translation) from Sts Augustine and Bernard (it is these, indeed, which give rise to the most impassioned of the pieces in recitative), Vespers hymns, and even the occasional Lutheran chorale (with melody). Of the latter, one is set in full (to music already published in 1625 under the title *De vitae fugacitate*): a total of eighteen funeral strophes, laid out as a series of 5-part strophic variations.

In these few-voiced *concerti* without *obbligato* instruments, Schütz sets out to cater for the needs of the average musician; the 'smallness' of these pieces (to quote from the dedication) reflects the impoverished state to which German church choirs had been reduced in the course of the Thirty Years War. (Schütz, indeed, was all too aware of the problems concerned, and his sorrowful petitions to the Elector of Saxony reveal the enormous decline of the Dresden court chapel during these years; it is, moreover, in the fourth and fifth decades of the century that the composer accepts an interim appointment as *Kapellmeister* at the much more sumptuous musical establishment of the king of Denmark.) Dimensions apart, however, the rhetorical and musical structure of the *Kleine geistliche Konzerte* is identical – and equally Italianate – to that of the more sonorous *Symphoniae sacrae*. In the *Symphoniae* for 1–3 voices and two violins, dedicated to the king of Denmark in 1647 (though it also contains compositions from the previous decade), the presence of Monteverdi is evident not only in Schütz's adoption of the *genere concitato* (see chapter 7; in his own preface to the volume, Schütz actually alludes to the preface of the *Madrigali guerrieri* of 1638, and remarks on the limited familiarity of German composers with the rhythmic and other idiomatic peculiarities of modern Italian writing for strings) but also in the wholesale musical borrowing of a duet from the *Madrigali guerrieri* and an amorous chaconne for two tenors (now set to the German text of a triumphal psalm). The original text, 'Armato il cor d'adamantina fede, / nell'amoroso regno / a militar ne vegno' ('My heart is girded with a determined faith / in the Kingdom of Love / I come to do battle') is thus recast in the image of a warlike God, ever ready to do battle with his foes; echoes of this are also to be found in the exultant dance of the righteous, set to the music of 'Zefiro torna e di soavi accenti / l'aer fa grato . . . e . . . fa danzar . . . Fillide e Clori' ('Zephyrus turns and with ethereal tones / beautifies the air . . . and . . . makes Phyllis and Cloris dance'). The substitution of the 'symbolized' (i.e., the images of the text) serves only to strengthen and exalt – without altering – the 'symbol' itself (i.e., the musical 'images' of Monteverdi): in this way, the Biblical word acquires a gestural significance of previously unknown dimensions (this, indeed, is a dominant characteristic of all Schütz's *concerti* from the 1630s and 40s). The *Symphoniae* for 3–6 solo voices with two violins and *ad libitum* chorus (published in 1650, but datable in part up to thirty years earlier) are less remarkable, if anything, for their German paraphrase of a Marian motet by Alessandro Grandi than for their many-voiced 'concerto' settings of texts from the Gospel: here, the web of Scriptural similes is intersected and mirrored by the interplay of musical images in a spectacular theatre of sound. (In the long-drawn-out parable of the sower and his seed, set for four solo voices, the admonishment of Christ – 'Whosoever has ears let him hear' – is extrapolated from its original Biblical context and proclaimed as a double-choir ritornello, insistently repeated in the course of the tale: this epic procedure, while reducing the integrity of the holy text, fully renders the provocatory nature of the words.)

Quite different from these 'concerti' are the compositions of Op. 11 – the *Musicalia ad chorum sacrum* or *Geistliche Chor-Music* ('sacred choral music') – of 1648 (though it also contains a funeral motet composed as early as 1630 for the death of Schein), dedicated (like the *Israelsbrünnlein* of Schein, with which it has a number of characteristics in common) to the city of Leipzig. The texts are drawn from Old and New Testaments alike; the settings are for 5–7 voices *a cappella* (the *basso continuo* is optional; *obbligato* instruments are prescribed in a few cases only). More than any other collection, the *Musicalia ad chorum sacrum* demonstrates the sheer vastness of its composer's musical horizons: Schütz, German champion of modern Italian compositional practice, here bears witness to the unimpaired validity and effectiveness of the *a capella* style (it is not by chance that the composer alludes in his lengthy preface to the volume – here reproduced as Source reading 4; see also chapter 8 – to the classification of musical styles as defined by his younger contemporary Marco Scacchi); the emphatic use of dissonance is reminiscent of the series of rich Neapolitan madrigals and motets which Schütz caused to be sent from Naples in 1632; in one of the few chorale-based motets, the Lutheran melody is treated imitatively in the manner of a *cantus firmus*; finally, another motet has been lifted, virtually without alteration, from the posthumous *Concerti* of Andrea Gabrieli (1587), with a German translation of the original Latin text.

Op. 13, the *Zwölf geistliche Gesänge* ('twelve 4-part spiritual songs for small choirs', including a German Mass and Vespers), was published in 1657 by a pupil of the composer. This is the only collection specifically designated by Schütz for liturgical – Lutheran – use: the *stile antico* here finds its most sober and rigorous application, quite removed from the madrigal-like affectiveness of Op. 4 (from which, nevertheless, a part of the musical material of the prayers 'for the table' has been derived) and Op. 11. The German litanies, however, are couched entirely in black notation, in an attempt – the words are those of the composer himself – to counter the slowness and tedium of the litanies as normally sung in Germany.

Of the *Historia der . . . Geburt . . . Christi* (the story of the Nativity and the flight into Egypt), only the part of the Evangelist was printed (at the composer's instigation) in 1664. This is a tenor role in *stile recitativo* with *basso continuo* accompaniment (a total novelty for

Germany, says the composer): in contrast, the passages in direct speech are carried by a similar number of few-voiced 'concerti', with specific timbres and instruments for each individual role (two 'violette' and violone for the Angel; recorders and bassoon for the shepherds; trombones for the priests; cornetts or clarino trumpets for King Herod). A year before his death, Schütz prepared one further work for publication: a setting of Psalm 119 (118), *Divinae legis encomium*, articulated in a series of eleven double-choir motets with German Magnificat. Contained in this psalm is the very same verse – 'Thy statutes have been my songs in the house of my pilgrimage' – prescribed by the composer as the theme for his funeral oration, which also served – again, at Schütz's own request – as the text of his funeral motet, composed 'in the style of Palestrina' by his favourite pupil Christoph Bernhard (this, at least, on the basis of one later testimony). The choice of this particular Scriptural verse is emblematic of the extraordinarily long and productive career of the composer, dedicated with single-minded intensity – though with astonishing formal and stylistic variety – to a sole artistic aim: that of the musical expression and interpretation of the Biblical word.

Christoph Bernhard, younger colleague of Schütz at the Dresden chapel, has already been mentioned (see chapter 10) as codifier of a rhetorical and mysical system which takes as its point of departure the music of his master. As noted, Bernhard's *figurae* mostly designate contrapuntal licences or anomalies of an intentional nature: licences and anomalies which enrich the musical counterpoint in much the same way as the *ornatus* (verbal estrangements and embellishments) with which the orator raises his speech above the level of neutral communication in his efforts to charm (*delectare*), move (*movere*) and thus better instruct (*docere*) his listeners. In a much wider sense, there is a natural affinity between the 'discursive' structure of music and the art of rhetoric; nothing, in fact, could be more true of the seventeenth century (in Germany as elsewhere) than the statement that 'in such agreeable licences consists every secret of the art of music, endowed as this is with its own *figurae* (on a par with rhetoric) by which the listener is imperceptibly charmed and seduced' (these are the words of the Frenchman, André Maugars, in his description of Italian music of 1639). A clearly oratorical intent underlies all the music of Schütz (with its enormous variety of styles): in the *Kleine geistliche Konzerte* of 1639, the voice of the Lord is fully seen to 'shake the roots of the cedars of Lebanon like suckling calves' and 'flicker in flames of fire'; in the *Musicalia ad chorum sacrum* of 1648, the Jews banished from the kingdom are fully heard to 'cry and gnash their teeth', the voice of John the

Baptist truly cries out in the desert, and the sowers truly bathe their seeds with tears; in the *Symphoniae* of 1650, the girder of the Biblical parable assumes truly fearful dimensions, inexorable is the fall of the blind man led by the blind; etc. Schütz himself describes the process of musical composition as the art of 'translating the text into music'. And, for Schütz, this text – the Biblical prose of the various musical settings – is spoken and/or recited, not written. In short, an objective textual basis (the word of God) is, however, entrusted to a fervently individual style of declamation, flagrantly suggestive in its melodic, rhythmic and harmonic accentuation. (Highly appropriate, indeed, in this context is the very nature of German accentuation, which, unlike Italian and Latin – 'oráre, óro, oratiónis' – is non-tonic and non-grammatical, but fundamentally semantic in orientation and linked to the etymological root of the word in question – 'béten, ich béte, des Gebéts'. In comparison with the Italian versification of Monteverdi, the metrically indistinct prosaic structure of the Biblical texts also allows the composer, as both musician and orator, a wider margin of interpretation in his use of recitation.)

It would, however, be something of an over-simplification to attribute the predicatory and 'explanatory' power of the Biblical music of Schütz solely to Bernhard's contrapuntal *figurae*. These *figurae*, in fact, while permitting identification of the various contrapuntal licences (*superjectio*, *anticipatio*, *subsumtio*, *variatio*, *multiplicatio*, *syncopatio catachrestica*, *inchoatio imperfecta*, *ellipsis*, *abruptio*, *heterolepsis*, etc.), are less useful as a means of perceiving the reasons behind their successful expressive application. There are at least two such reasons – one particular, the other general. The first regards the depth of 'historical memory' and vastness of personal artistic experience at Schütz's disposition: the composer demonstrates a total theoretical and practical mastery of a wealth of styles from various eras and cultures (everything from sacred vocal music to the madrigal and musical theatre: Andrea and Giovanni Gabrieli, Palestrina, Monteverdi, Viadana, Gesualdo, Luther, Praetorius and Schein); all interaction and 'contamination' of styles, moreover, is admitted only after due consideration, as a means of emphasizing some aspect of image or text. The second reason, quite different from the first, regards the tonally oriented – and tonally defined – context of Schütz's rhetorical figures. Contrapuntal licence – which, in earlier modal polyphony, had been limited to the presence of fleeting grammatical perturbations, themselves immediately re-absorbed in the regular flow of intervallic chains – now reverberates with magnified force over the entire length of a musical phrase itself invested with a particular tonal function. The music of Schütz (like, indeed, the music of Monteverdi's Venetian period) exploits the various expressive and descriptive/symbolic possibilities inherent in the ambivalence between the contrapuntal determination of intervals and the tonal function of sonorities; the musical language, though still closely linked to traditional contrapuntal models, now assumes the concise syntax more typical of a fundamentally tonal organization, transforming the whole into a language of rhetorical gesture (in relation, that is, to the text). The poetic function of tonality is clearly of greater importance than that of the rhetorical/musical *figurae* (which can even at times be dispensed with altogether) in its ability to give meaningful form to the music in terms of an articulated whole (and not, that is, as a mere series of details) – its capacity, in short, to assume a rhetorical form of its own. The following examples, which represent a variety of styles and dates of publication, provide ample illustration of this fact. For the sake of simplicity, the original texts are cited in English translation.

Psalm 136 – a psalm of praise and jubilation – has an unusual poetic configuration; its twenty-six verses, which enumerate the various deeds of the Lord, each end with identical words ('for His mercy will endure for ever'). The resulting binary structure (A*x*B*x*C*x*D*x* . . .) is particularly suited to the antiphonal procedure adopted by Schütz in the *Psalmen Davids* of 1619: of the three vocal groups, one is devoted to the delivery of the verses, while the other two (supported by a fourth choir of martial trumpets and drums) reply with never-ceasing proclamation of God's eternal love. While, moreover, the music of the verses is characterized by widely-ranging modulation, the military din of the choral/instrumental ritornello is firmly anchored to a truly 'eternal' C major, which thus tangibly represents the unswerving mercy of the Divine. All the more striking, then, is the final, one-off appearance of the ritornello in D major, with no preparatory modulation: the listener is disconcerted by his clear perception of the fact that the fixed tonal point of reference established in earlier ritornellos is quite literally to be found 'in every place'.

David's lament on the death of Absalom – the motet *Fili mi, Absalon!*, from the *Symphoniae sacrae* of 1629 – takes the form of a long, sorrowful monologue. The opening invocation of the bass, supported by a quartet of trombones, outlines the principal degrees of the scale of G minor through a series of ascending and descending triads. The unusual augmented (ascending) and diminished (descending) intervals which result from this procedure are nothing but a chain of *saltus duriusculi* (to cite the terminology of Bernhard), and as such excite feelings of melancholy. It is, however, their tonally defined context (the reference to the fundamental notes of the harmony) which unifies and lends meaning to a melodic figuration which, if read contrapuntally, would amount to nothing but a string of 'nonsensical' solecisms.

At the centre of the pseudo-Gloria of the *Musicalische Exequien* is the same verse that runs around the edge of the entire funeral bier of Heinrich Posthumus; the words, from the Book of Wisdom, are as follows: 'The souls of the righteous are in the hands of the Lord, untouched by the torment of death. To the foolish, they seem to die, and their death is regarded an affliction: but they rest in peace.' This antithesis between the error of the foolish and the blessedness of the souls of the righteous finds its musical counterpart in the simultaneous opposition of a bass and two soprano voices. The bass, with its slow, stepwise, upwards chromatic progression, sings of death and affliction; from above, the sopranos sing constantly of peace, without changes of tone. In contrapuntal terms, this means that the accented syllable of the word 'Frieden' ('peace') falls first on a dissonance (diminished fifth), then – the bass having moved – on a consonance (minor third). However, it is from the ambivalence between tonality and counterpoint that this section – conceptual climax of the entire composition – derives its fundamental logic. Only a change in the tonal context (the deceptive 'affliction' of the bass) is capable of changing the tonal significance of the phrase of the soprano duet (in its movement towards the 'peace' of a consonance); the phrase itself, however, remains constant – or, in the words of the text, 'rests in peace'.

One last celebrated composition by Schütz is from the *Symphoniae sacrae* of 1650: 'Saul, why persecutest thou me? It is hard for thee to kick against the pricks'. Of the original text from the Acts of the Apostles, Schütz sets only the section in direct speech, i.e., the words of God (of which his music thus attempts to provide a sonorous representation or image). Three pairs of solo voices (respectively, basses, tenors and sopranos), followed at the end by two solo violins, engage in a fourfold repetition of the opening phrase (with overall upwards movement of some three and a half octaves): on each occasion, the fourfold apostrophe of the name is made to resound through the space of an octave, with God's indignant question as cadence. The overall scheme is rudimentary (mirroring, indeed, the awesome conciseness of the question) but versatile: the phrase reappears in various tonalities, encircling and persecuting the persecutor – Saul – from every side; 'Saul' is tossed ferociously to and fro (seven times, over unchanging harmony, in the space of a bar and a half) by the two halves of the double choir; the question itself – massive tonic–

dominant–tonic cadence – is thrice stated in double echo (*forte–mezzopiano–pianissimo*). The music reaches its awesome climax when the second tenor detaches itself from the remaining thirteen voices (with their never-ceasing repetition of the words 'why persecutest thou me?') and simultaneously, in long-held notes, shouts out the name of Saul; three times over, while the (choral) question resounds in double echo (*mezzopiano–pianissimo*), the name of Saul is made to reverberate ever more strongly, each time a tone higher in pitch. The technique itself might be described as the non-theatrical – yet rhetorical – *mise en scène* of a simple progression (the repetition of the same music in three different tonalities in stepwise succession): but the result, in affective terms, is nothing short of a representation of the horror of such awe-inspiring divinity. Apparent, here, with the same dazzling brightness and clarity responsible for the blinding of Saul, is the force of tonality as an organizational tool – a force, indeed, whose web of perceptible syntactical links lend articulation to a musical 'discourse' which, despite its discontinuity of mood (magniloquent, allusive, moved, sorrowful, terrified, joyful), thus achieves its own inner coherence.

18 Sacred music as music of State: France and England

Schütz himself viewed his role less in terms of a traditional ecclesiastical *Kapellmeister* than as a musical functionary in the service of the court. The practical utilization of his music in this context is indirectly but eloquently summarized in the following proposal for archival classification drawn up by the composer for the court of Zeitz in the years around 1670:

> 1. Large psalms, large spiritual *concerti*, *Te Deums* and other similar full-voiced pieces, with their vocal and instrumental parts, to be used at any moment as the need might occur.
> 2. Few-voiced psalms and *concerti*, to be used at the beginning of a princely table service.
> 3. *Concerti* for the eight major feasts of Christmas, Easter and Pentecost.
> 4. *Concerti* for the lesser feasts: New Year, Epiphany, Purification, Ascension, Holy Trinity, etc.
> 5. *Concerti* for the Sunday Gospels.
> 6. Secular and moral songs for the princely table.

Categories 2 and 6 provide evidence for the frequent employment of both sacred and spiritual texts in non-ecclesiastical contexts – following, indeed, a courtly tradition which pre-dates the 'schism' between sacred and secular music (a 'schism' which, in any case, had little meaning in the context of Lutheran worship – see chapter 17).

The principle of *cuius regio, eius religio* is valid for seventeenth-century Germany as for no other century or country in European civilization. The case of Dresden well illustrates the religious discontinuity and 'promiscuity' of German, court circles. Beginning in the time of Schütz (and in direct parallel to the court chapel under Schütz's direction), the crown prince establishes a separate musical chapel of his own, Italian in origin and virtually Catholic in orientation; on his accession to the throne, the contrast between this Italianate *cappella* and the 'German' court chapel becomes somewhat acute. Even before the death of Schütz, the 'Italian' establishment with its virtuoso *castrati* has clearly come to predominate; at the first change of sovereign, however, the Italians are discharged without notice. Finally, in 1697, Duke Friedrich August is crowned king of Poland and is consequently converted to Catholicism; he formally establishes a Catholic Chapel Royal in direct parallel to the Protestant *cappella* of the Ducal court (for the successor of Friedrich August, Johann Sebastian Bach – himself a Protestant – was to compose a Catholic *missa solemnis*). Ups and downs of this kind are little conducive to the lasting conservation of a musical repertory: at Dresden, in fact, the legacy of Schütz disappears even more quickly than elsewhere in Germany.

Quite different are the conditions surrounding the production of sacred 'courtly' music in France and England, each – in its own way – highly centralized upon a stable and absolute monarchy. Differences of cult and confession – predominantly Catholic in France, Protestant in England – are insignificant in comparison with certain affinities of social and political structure (also apparent in the roles of their respective churches). The affinity is evident, too, from the legal and doctrinal point of view: the Anglican Church, established in the sixteenth century as the English version of the Reformation, was subject to the direct jurisdiction of the Crown; the Gallican Church, too, enjoyed a relative autonomy from the Papacy, and arrogated to the 'Most Christian King' a number of extremely far-reaching prerogatives in matters of ecclesiastical authority. From a musical standpoint, a clear affinity exists (though in differing degrees) with regard to at least three different aspects: the noticeable impermeability of French and English sacred music to foreign styles (compare the process of osmosis by which the music of the Lutheran Church receives sustenance from Italy); the stylistic gap between sacred music at court (moulded by the dictatorial tastes of the sovereign and the various requirements of ceremonial, but quite impervious – unlike the music of the Papal court – to the dictates of the *stile antico* as ratified by the respective ecclesiastical traditions) and the sacred music of the great urban cathedrals (themselves jealous and tenacious guardians of the ancient polyphonic tradition); the eloquent, declamatory, emphatic gestures and attitudes characteristic of a sacred 'music of State' which – in the hands of the greatest musicians of the nation: Lully in France, Purcell in England – apostrophizes the sovereign of the skies on a level with the prestige accorded only a monarch or pontiff on earth.

The so-called *Declaration of the Gallican clergy regarding power in the Church* (1682) is but one of the many authoritarian gestures which emanated from the absolute sovereignty of Louis XIV (whose authoritarianism, however, degenerates into nothing short of intolerance with the revocation of the Edict of Nantes in 1685). Hardly fortuitous, just at this time (in 1684 and 1686), is the publication – under royal patronage – of three exemplary collections of *grands motets* 'for the Chapel Royal'; these represented less an attempt to assist in the popular diffusion of a style of sacred music considered, above all, a prerogative of court, than an effort to sanction the supremacy of the Gallican Church and the use of a peculiarly French style of musical composition. This 'demonstrative' intention is also apparent on what might be defined as a more strictly 'internal' level: the publication, in 1684 and 1686, of these *grands motets* by Pierre Robert and Henry Du Mont – both distinguished choirmasters at the Chapel Royal prior to their retirement in 1683 – meant the imposition upon their successors and consequent perpetuation of a model and style of sacred music which enjoyed royal approval. The competition held in 1683 to decide the successors of Robert and Du Mont might itself be described as a further demonstration of the political and cultural supremacy of the monarch. Participants in the contest were a total of thirty-five choirmasters, sent – at the request of the King – by the various bishops of the Gallican Church; the four winners were given the task of furnishing and directing the music of the French Chapel Royal, on the basis of a system of quarterly rotation. Most eminent of the winners on this occasion was Michel-Richard de La Lande (1657–1726); most eminent of the losers (ill during the final stages of the competition) was Marc-Antoine Charpentier (d. 1704). The disappointment of the latter, however, was in some way compensated by the patronage – both direct and indirect – of the French court for his many-sided activities at Paris. As choirmaster at the Saint-Chapelle and the Jesuit

Church of St Louis, Charpentier is less to be regarded as the unfortunate rival of de La Lande as his metropolitan equivalent; an albeit perceptible difference of personal style between the two composers is clearly outweighed, in these sacred *grands motets*, by the essential unity of a national style which, 'invented' as it was in the opening decades of the long reign of Louis XIV, was destined to last through several generations of composers. Here, it will be sufficient to cite the example of the aforementioned de La Lande, whose twenty volumes of *grands motets*, though published posthumously in 1729, date in part from the composer's earliest years at the helm of the Chapel Royal; these early motets were subsequently revised by the composer himself, who 'updated' them in accordance with modern ideas of harmonic colour and instrumentation. Having taken their place in the public tradition of the Parisian *Concerts spirituels* (concerts of vocal and instrumental music, which customarily began with the performance of a *grand motet*), these pieces continued in use for the remainder of the century. Indeed, their disappearance from the repertory is closely linked to the demise of that very *ancien régime* whose 'ancienneté' they so magnificently expressed (paralleled, in this role, by the *tragédies lyriques* of the Lully tradition – see chapter 25).

This extra-liturgical use of the *grand motet* is not anomalous, nor is it an eighteenth-century corruption of the original tradition. The texts of the *grands motets*, though generally drawn from the psalms (e.g., the *Miserere*), sequences (*Dies irae*), canticles (*Magnificat*) and hymns (*Te Deum*), can also embrace newly-composed Latin poetry such as that published in 1665 by the enterprising Abbé Perrin (also noted for his subsequent involvement in the earliest Parisian operatic productions) under the title of *Cantica pro capella regis latine composita*. Strictly liturgical derivation was thus not a prerequisite for the *grand motet*, whose opulent orchestration was in any case openly at variance with the stipulations of the Council of Trent (in this latter respect, the sovereign was obliged to procure a licence for Du Mont from the Archbishop of Paris, himself responsible for the strict enforcement of the Tridentine decrees at Notre-Dame until the final decade of the century, by which time the various provincial cathedrals had long since updated their musical repertories in accordance with modern dictates of style and employment of instruments). Liturgically inappropriate, above all, was the natural function of the *grand motet* as used at court: sung as it was at the beginning of the 'solemn low Mass' for the King, it might easily last from the Introit right through to the Elevation; it would be followed at the Elevation itself by a solo *petit motet*, whose contemplative and devotional character was well suited for use at this particular point in the Mass (frequently, the piece in question was Italian in origin: a sacred *concerto* by Carissimi or Francesco Foggia); then came the concluding psalm motet *Domine, salvum fac regem*, a customary feature of the royal Mass. The designation 'low' thus refers exclusively to the liturgical aspects of the Mass (which itself was spoken); 'solemn' (and as such quite clearly differentiated from the liturgy itself) are the musical and ceremonial aspects: the glorification of the heavenly King by his terrestial 'namesake' thus dominates the celebration of a sacred rite which verges on a kind of aesthetic commemoration of regal power. In short: the *grand motet*, in its guise of a sacred musical genre, is devoid of all liturgical justification. Its style must be understood more in relation to its ceremonial function than in terms of the liturgy itself.

This 'defunctionalization' of sacred music at court – or, more precisely, its functionalization in terms of a somewhat 'alien' liturgy based essentially on the celebration of royal power – leads to a certain dissociation of the repertory from that of traditional sacred music and the creation of a new, parallel tradition. At no time did Louis XIV show any predilection for the sung polyphonic mass – perhaps, indeed, by reason of its typically serious *stile osservato*. Thus, of all the various composers associated directly or indirectly with courtly circles, it is hardly surprising that only the 'Parisian' Charpentier produced any masses whatever of the types current in France before or after the accession of Louis XIV to the throne (a total of some twelve compositions, never published). All types, however, are represented: music for solo voice with *basso continuo* (for monastic use), *a cappella* and polychoral masses, the concerted mass for voices and instruments, *alternatim* masses for instruments alone (with, indeed, 'a variety of instruments in place of the organ'), the *cantus firmus* mass, a mass for Christmas Night replete with popular 'noëls'. Elsewhere, however, in the so-called *maîtrises* (the musical establishments of the various cathedrals), the polyphonic routine continued without interruption. Vivid testimony of this fact is provided by the *Entretien des musiciens* (1643) of Annibal Gantez (himself director, at various stages in his career, of the *scholae cantorum* at Aigues-Mortes, Aix-en-Provence, Annecy, Arles, Aurillac, Auxerre, Avignon, Carpentras, Grenoble, La Châtre, Le Havre, Marseilles, Montauban, Nancy, Nevers, Rouen, Toulouse, Valence and various churches in the capital itself), with its series of jovial considerations on the day-to-day conditions of contemporary church musicians (more given to the tankard and – wherever possible – good eating than to the art of singing). Among other things, Gantez complains of the printing monopoly accorded the publisher Ballard and its deadening effect on the output of contemporary sacred music. In the early years of the eighteenth century, in fact, the sales catalogues of Parisian publishers still list a not inconsiderable number of masses by Orlando di Lasso: stock on hand, no doubt, but as such no less valid as models for provincial French musicians of the seventeenth century. French monarchs, for their part, would come to attribute a specifically ceremonial significance to the ancient *stile osservato* – a style reserved exclusively for requiem Masses at royal funerals (at most, enlivened during performance by instrumental doublings and insertions). The *Missa pro defunctis* of Eustache Du Caurroy (d. 1609) – who himself, with reference to the outdated style of his musical compositions, admitted to 'having slept for forty years' – was posthumously performed at the funeral service for Henri IV; published in 1636, it subsequently came to be regarded as something of a State Requiem Mass, and as such remained in use right into the following century. Charles d'Helfer's severe 4-part requiem of 1656 was sung in 1726 at the funeral service of de La Lande (who himself wrote no masses whatever) and again, as late as 1774, for the repose of the soul of Louis XV. Louis, however, like Jean-Philippe Rameau before him, had at least been interred to the somewhat less austere sound of the *Messe des morts* of Jean Gilles (d. 1705); this concerted requiem, re-exhumed by the *Concert spirituel* in 1750, came – and, indeed, continues – to represent a permanent feature of that repertory of ancient and immortal glories as offered by 'classical' national culture for the admiration of posterity.

Beginning in the 1660s with the music of Robert and the versatile Du Mont, the overbearing influence of Jean-Baptiste Lully is noticeable in the stylistic development of sacred music at the French Chapel Royal. Lully, while eschewing all direct involvement in French ecclesiastical institutions, nevertheless offers the musical interpretation *par excellence* of the royal 'image'; his *Miserere* of 1664, together with his *Te Deum* of 1677 and his few other contributions to the motet repertory, came – even before their publication in 1684 – to represent the dominant model for the genre of the *grand motet* (it seems that the masterly contributions of Du Mont, though of uncertain chronology, do not pre-date those of Lully, but are roughly contemporary with them). These are double-choir motets, though – in line with a peculiarly French usage originating in the reign of Louis XIII – quite different in kind to those of the Italian and German traditions: not two 'balanced' groups (similar in size and distribution of voices) which sing separately or together, but a large *grand choeur* (normally 5-part) and solo *petit choeur* (again 5-part) with orchestral accompaniment (winds, 5-part strings). In spatial terms, the acoustical result is not so much the symmetry or mirror effect of the Italian double-choir tradition, more a sonorous perspective (distance/nearness, crowd/individual). *Grand choeur*, *petit choeur*, individual soloists, groups of soloists: all are alternated, contrasted, isolated and brought together in compliance not with any formal design but rather with the needs (themselves largely arbitrary) of textual declamation; the result is a multiform sequence of numerous and highly differentiated sections (one per verse, though with the possibility for further division or, indeed, amalgamation). Nor have these sections any formally defined structure. Solo verses are treated in the manner of *récits*: musical declamation, oscillating between modest recitation, emphatic pleading, beseeching prayers of supplication and jubilant proclamations (if, on occasion, in the hands of de La Lande, these recitatives are treated as fully-fledged *airs* – with or without concerted solo instruments – this merely represents an extension of the declamatory nature of the vocal line to incorporate a kind of formalized melodiousness, and does not imply the adoption of any heterogeneous structural principle).

Declamation, indeed, pervades the compositional style as a whole: it would be wrong to speak of the *récits* for two or more voices as duos and trios, in so far as the individuality of each part is maintained through the application of highly differentiated rhythms and accentuations. The *grands choeurs* – at times fugally treated, more frequently given over to rhythmically excited declamation – are songs of the multitude, not of the anonymous mass. The accentuation of the vocal lines, obtained through a variety of harmonic and melodic devices (suspensions, appoggiaturas, *ports de voix*, mordents, etc.), is based not on the principle of metre (itself rather fluctuating and amorphous) but on oratorical necessity. The martial rhythm and military 'blaze' of the various *Te Deum* settings – which, performed on the occasion of military victories or the birth of male heirs to the throne, do homage to the policy of national expansion or the prosperity of the dynasty (not by chance has the introductory *symphonie* to the *Te Deum* of Charpentier become famous as the Eurovision signature tune) – is symptomatic of a conception which is more symbolic than formal, 'lived' and not abstracted through rhythm and sound. At most, in these *grands motets*, the role of Gregorian chant is limited to that of theatrical 'prop' for the evocation of the musical *mise en scène*: the trembling motto which opens the *Dies irae* of Lully, the *cantus firmus* of de La Lande's setting of the hymn *Sacris solemniis* (where, for a few bars, the effect is that of 'sacramental' polyphony).

Astonishing, in the *grands motets* of Lully, Du Mont, de La Lande and Charpentier, is the enormity of emotional range, liable to sudden transformation from penitence to joy, aggressiveness to tenderness, contemplative ecstasy to military fervour. In the long run, however, the continuous constraints of a language dominated by the needs of sustained expression and emphatic incitement becomes tedious. Exalting in tone are the pleading exhortations of the imperatives in Lully's *Miserere*: 'Miserere . . . dele . . . lava me . . . munda me . . .asperge me . . . averte faciem . . . crea . . . innova . . . redde . . . confirma . . . libera . . . benigne fac, Domine . . . '; monotonous the fixedness of the unvarying C minor tonality. In the sacred music of the French Chapel Royal, rhetoric is less a question of verbal images than an expression of the tone of the discourse; spurning the symbolic musical *figurae* of Monteverdi and Schütz, Lully and his contemporaries declaim the sacred Latin text with every possible *pathos* in the manner of a sermon or oration by Bossuet (himself responsible for the drafting of the Gallican *Declaration* quoted above). Personal pronouns, verbal forms and conjunctions are accentuated in preference to adjectives and nouns. In the phrases '*tu* . . . *non* horruisti virginis uterum' and '*non* confundar in aeternum', particular musical emphasis is reserved for the words in italics; here, in contrast, the Italian composer might dwell rather more heavily on words such as 'virginis' and 'aeternum' (with decorative melismas or long held notes) or 'horruisti' and 'confundar' (with dissonances and chromaticism). Finally, it should be noted how the *grand motet*, more than any other genre, exploits the particular harmonic resources of French music as a means of rhetorical emphasis; this, indeed, further accentuates the effect of extraneousness experienced by the foreigner on hearing this music. Here it will be sufficient to cite a single example: the use of fleeting – yet pungent – overlappings of dissonant anticipations and suspensions as a means of emphasis. At times, in the approach to a minor cadence, this can lead to the apparently irregular juxtaposition of augmented fifth, major seventh and ninth on the mediant of the scale (in C minor: E♭–G–B–D–F); the designation 'ninth chord on the third degree' is not, however, appropriate, in so far as it does not correspond to the real harmonic function of the chord (which, if anything, might be described as an anticipation of the minor third of the tonic below a chord of the dominant seventh, itself regularly prepared and resolved; this anticipation gains further in significance in view of the subsequent elimination of the 'minor' effect by means of the customary insertion of a major third in the final chord).

As also in France, the music of the English Chapel Royal undergoes institutional and stylistic reform in the seventh decade of the century (with the end of Cromwell's Commonwealth and the restoration of the monarchy); the model chosen by Charles II (1660–85) for the music of the re-established English court was, in fact, of unequivocal French descent (Charles, following the beheading of his father in 1649, had fled into exile at the court of his cousin Louis XIV of France). Significant in this respect was the immediate institution of a modern ensemble of twenty-four 'violins' (in reality, a string orchestra), modelled closely on the 'grande bande des vingt-quatre violons de la Chambre du roi' and quite alien to the indigenous – and glorious – tradition of instrumental polyphony for consort of viols which, cultivated from before the time of Elizabeth I, had evolved through the highly elaborate 'fancies' of three generations of English composers. The last of these composers, John Jenkins (1592–1678), is perhaps to be identified as a teacher of the young Henry Purcell, himself the author of some twelve unpublished fancies for viols. Characteristic of these pieces by Purcell is their exuberance of melodic and contrapuntal invention; one, in five parts, proceeds in lively imitation against the backcloth of a single long-held note (F), heard continuously in the tenor viol from beginning to end. Purcell's appointment in 1677 as Master of the Twenty-Four Violins might almost be seen as providing symbolic confirmation of a definitive break in the ancient English viol tradition (just two years earlier, in fact, Thomas Mace erects a sorrowfully nostalgic *Musick's monument* to this very repertory: a retrospective 'remembrancer of the best practical musick, both divine, and civil, that has ever been known, to have been in the world').

In sacred music, too, Charles II was responsible for imposing a new compositional genre: namely, the concerted anthem for solo voices, *basso continuo* and, not infrequently, *concertato* instruments. This is the true English equivalent of the contemporary French *grand motet*. 'Anthem', indeed, means 'motet': like the continental motet, the English anthem ranged in style from *a cappella* polyphony (as in the anthems of the pre-Commonwealth period) to solo and concerted motets of a type more akin to those of seventeenth-century Italy (it should, however, be noted that the use of the term 'anthem' in connection with liturgical compositions is a relatively late development which appears only with the issue of Charles II's Restoration prayer-book in 1662). Unlike France, however, the situation in England is rendered notably more complex – in music as in politics – by the chronic instability engendered by a history of antagonism and conflict: the albeit copious production of concerted anthems under the patronage of Charles II and James II is interrupted in 1689 with the accession of

William of Orange, and thus never acquires the longevity and stylistic stability more typical of the *grand motet* under the absolute monarchy of France. Significant, in this respect, is the almost exclusively manuscript tradition which marks the transmission of the Restoration anthem.

The Puritan revolution, while boosting the domestic – bourgeois – consumption of instrumental and vocal music, had nonetheless resulted in the total banishment of art music from divine worship (where only the community singing of the psalms was now tolerated). It thus marked a radical break in the Elizabethan and Jacobean tradition of sacred polyphony as represented in the anthems and services of William Byrd, Orlando Gibbons, Thomas Tomkins and Thomas Tallis. Truth to tell, this repertory had never been cultivated in any but a handful of privileged centres – i.e., by the small choirs of the great English cathedrals – where, however, it came to be venerated with a fervour matched only by that of the Catholic predilection for the music of Palestrina. After the Commonwealth, this music was fully reinstated by the Restoration Church; the Cathedral choirs of St Paul's, Salisbury, York, Lincoln, Chichester, Wells, Canterbury, Durham, Winchester, Gloucester, Oxford (Christ Church) and other such centres – not to mention the Chapel Royal itself – turned once again to the cultivation of the sacred 'services' and anthems of the reigns of Elizabeth I and James I. A collection of anthems in current use both at court and in the various cathedrals, published in 1663, faithfully reproduces the texts of dozens of polyphonic anthems by Byrd, Gibbons, Tallis and Tomkins: all date from the first three decades of the century and, in several cases, earlier still. The second (enlarged) edition of this collection (1664), however, already incorporates a number of newly-composed solo anthems for the court of Charles II; composers represented are Matthew Locke, Pelham Humfrey, Henry Lawes, John Blow – in short, that generation of musicians which straddles the years between Commonwealth and Restoration, and which embraces those very same genres for which the newly-crowned sovereign, recently returned from the court of Louis XIV, expressed a predilection. The contrast between the renewed vigour of the glorious 'Anglican' polyphonic tradition and the royally-backed introduction of a modern – and alien – style of sacred music acquires, in its very simultaneity, the character of a conflict. This contradiction was felt by theologians and musicians alike; the quarrel, however, over the alleged 'profanity' of the new musical style (in particular, as regards the use of *concertato* instruments in church) serves only to hide the fundamental problem of the historical legitimization of monarchy and cult. Concerted solo anthems were not totally unknown in the years prior to the Commonwealth; only after the Restoration, however, does the contrast between the two opposing styles come to be regarded as symbolic – in musical terms – of the rivalry between two opposing political positions. Paradoxically, it is the parliamentarian Whigs (inclined to the Puritan faith) who lend greatest support to the Anglican tradition, while the Tories (conservative royalists, faithful to the Church of England) are identified, if anything, with all things sovereign – musical fashion included.

The concerted anthem of the Restoration period – 'public', regal, generally sung only on occasions when the King himself attended divine service in the Chapel Royal (i.e., Sundays and feast days), thus without prejudice to the traditional polyphonic repertory in everyday use at this latter institution – lends itself well to the politically and ideologically tendentious interpretation of sacred music as practised at court; this is further enhanced by the existence, in Anglican use, of a certain margin for 'editorial' discretion in the choice of psalm verses, thus facilitating the allusive – allegorical – use of the Biblical text for purposes of propaganda or polemics. The following example can be described as neither neutral nor naive: Psalm 18 contains the dual image of an imploringly sorrowful King David, persecuted by his enemies, and a warlike, triumphant king, recipient of divine protection; these two figures are represented respectively in Purcell's anthems *I will love thee, O Lord* (sung, apparently, in 1679, at a moment of grave political crisis for the ruling dynasty) and *The way of God is an undefiled way* (performed in 1694 in celebration of one of the victorious battles of William III against the French).

Some seventy anthems by Henry Purcell (1659–95) are known to have survived, almost all scored for voices and instruments: of these, approximately eighty per cent were composed in the reign of Charles II. Their declamatory technique is similar to that of the French *grand motet*: in the succession of psalm verses, variously entrusted to the chorus or a solo ensemble of three male voices (generally countertenor, tenor, bass), the recitation of the text assumes a variety of melodic contours reminiscent of sorrow or acclaim, loaded with rhetorical *pathos* by means of such vocal and harmonic affectations as appoggiaturas, suspensions and transitory dissonances. Like the *grand motet*, the concerted anthem consists of a series of distinct yet interlocking sections (one for each verse of the text), without ever assuming a 'closed' formal configuration. The almost total rejection of cyclic or periodic structures – strophic bass or *da capo* arias, ritornellos, 'grounds' (ostinato basses), dance movements, etc. – is in line with the prosaic (non-poetic, non-metrical, non-strophic) layout of the text, itself declaimed musically from beginning to end in the manner of an oration. Significant, in the anthems of Purcell, is the composer's refusal to apply to the Biblical texts what is otherwise his favourite formal principle: the ground. This procedure, elsewhere developed by Purcell to insuperable heights of complexity and representational force (above all in his theatrical music, discussed below at chapter 26), inevitably gives rise to 'closed' formal patterns. In cases where Purcell's anthems do make use of ground procedures, this is restricted exclusively to the instrumental episodes; examples are the opening sinfonias of the anthems *Rejoice in the Lord alway* and *In thee, O Lord, do I put my trust* (both constructed on the basis of multiples of five: the innate asymmetry of the 2½- and 5-bar ostinato artfully unbalances the periodic and tonal regularity implicit in the very basis of the ground-bass technique).

Like the *grand motet*, the anthems of Purcell are saturated by the need to give moving and eloquent musical expression to the Scriptural text: in fact, it is in this very context of 'moving eloquence' that one notes the very majesty of a sacred repertory which, eschewing the reverential demeanour and codified stylistic compunction of traditional sacred music, addresses itself directly – without need for mediation – to the King of heaven. Like the *grand motet*, so also do the anthems of Purcell invoke the aid of a number of peculiar harmonic resources (of which the composer proves an imaginative and ingenious manipulator) for the purposes of this 'address'. The originality of Purcell's harmony – rich and succulent in sonority and dissonance – frequently derives from his exploitation of certain residual traces of sixteenth-century modal polyphony (with its now decidedly archaic connotations in terms of colour) within the overall context of a periodic and syntactic organization of the musical phrase (itself now fully tonal). Frequent in this respect, in the approach to a final cadence, is the co-existence (in two different voices) of the flattened and leading seventh, both sung in the course of a single bar: here, however, the effect is more coloristic than structural (thus, in the final page of the aforementioned anthem *Rejoice in the Lord alway*, the modal archaism of B♭ in the immediate run-up to a picturesquely chromatic cadence in C major is added only in the echo repetition, almost as though to enhance its affirmative, evocative effect). The monumental 8-part chorus *Hear my prayer, O Lord* (itself a fragment of an anthem) encompasses, in the course of just thirty-four bars, approximately 100 dissonances (some simultaneous) of the most varied shapes and sizes (suspensions, appoggiaturas, passing and auxiliary notes, augmented and diminished intervals); these, however, exalt rather than undermine the tonal compactness of the composition in question (C minor). Though the purpose of this plethora of dissonances is essentially figurative – the musical representation of the desperate invocation at the beginning of Psalm 102 (101) – the dissonances themselves have their roots in the very structure of the two musical subjects which form the basis of the piece:

Hear	my	pray -	er,	O	Lord
C	C	C	C	E♭	C

and	let	my	cry -	ing	come	un -	to	Thee
G	G	A	B♭–C–B♮	B♮	C	D	E♭	C

In the polyphonic elaboration, the E♭ of the first subject most frequently occurs in cadential position (where, normally, a D might seem 'necessary'): in functional terms, this harmonic anomaly leads to a heightening of cadential tension and consequent strengthening of tonality; in expressive terms, it serves to accentuate the vocative emphasis on the particle 'O'. The winding three-note chromatic inflexion on the first syllable of 'crying' intensively exploits the modal/tonal ambiguity of the seventh degree, as also the dissonant friction sometimes inevitably produced between the second note of the syllable and the other voices; harmonically, the continuous oscillation between major and minor third (B♭/B♮, for example) leads not to any sense of tonal disorientation but rather to the perception of the obsessive – thus affirmative – reverberation of a rhetorically motivated chromatic perturbation.

With the loss of its original ceremonial function, little of the concerted anthem was destined to survive in the historical consciousness of the nation. In the constitutional monarchy which followed the bloodless 'revolution' of 1688, the anthem persists only as a commemorative, representational genre, reserved for performance on a few rare occasions of exceptional importance (this reduction in frequency of performance was compensated, at most, by a corresponding increase in pomp and magnificence). On the contrary, immediate and lasting was the success of the *Te Deum* of 1694, in commemoration of the feast of St Cecilia, patron saint of musicians; beginning, in fact, in the penultimate decade of the seventeenth century, the performance of such pieces becomes something of a custom at the Musical Society of London). Conspicuous among Purcell's Odes for St Cecilia's Day (the same composer is also the author of numerous birthday and funeral odes for the court, while his colleague, John Blow, was traditionally responsible for the Ode for New Year's Day) is the enormously vast and ambitious *Hail, bright Cecilia* of 1692, whose thirteen numbers (for chorus, fourteen soloists and an orchestra replete with trumpets, drums, recorders and oboes), in their enthusiastic celebration of the power of music, draw on the now somewhat threadbare *topoi* of the *effectus musices* and praise the specific qualities of each individual instrument. The most exalting moments in this piece are reserved for the chorus (one such number provides a visionary representation of the harmony instilled in the macrocosm, microcosm, atoms and celestial spheres by the virtues of music). The most celebrated passage of all, however, is the countertenor recitative *'Tis Nature's voice*, in which the voice was heard to proclaim – amid *gorgheggi*, languid sighs, erotic joy, voluptuous dissonance, anguished modulation and simple declamation – the magic dominion of harmony over the affections and 'animal spirits' (see chapter 9). *'Tis Nature's voice* is indicative of the intense civil and social – if not liturgical or religious – veneration for the art of music on the part of a 'new' English society which, in the aftermath of no less than two different revolutions, now found itself in the forefront of European social and political developments. Music, indeed, provides the perfect tool for edification of the soul – individual and collective alike:

> 'Tis Nature's Voice; by all the moving Wood
> Of Creatures understood
> The Universal Tongue to none
> Of all her num'rous Race unknown!
> From her it learned the mighty Art
> To court the Ear and strike the Heart:
> At once the Passions to express and move;
> We hear, and straight we grieve or hate, rejoice or love:
> In unseen chains it does the Fancy bind;
> At once it charms the Sense and captivates the Mind.

IV

OPERA

19 The historiography of opera

For Italy, as for Europe as a whole, the most remarkable innovation of the entire seventeenth century was without doubt the introduction of opera. The sheer enormity of this 'invention' may be gauged in relation to the complexity of its constituent parts: no other form of contemporary artistic expression brings together such numerous, varied and costly means of organization and production. Moreover, the history and fortunes of opera are at all times deeply rooted in historical and social events: conditioned as it is by the various prevailing economic and political situations, opera has been and continues to be exploited as a not insignificant tool of ideological persuasion and mobilization, a public demonstration of sovereign power, a means of collective entertainment, a vehicle for the community celebration of civic events.

Down the centuries, the introduction of opera has had enormous repercussions: in Italy, France, England and German-speaking lands, modern operatic life is nothing but the continuation of an institutional tradition which, despite constant transformation (not least in the emergence of many non-European operatic capitals – New York, San Francisco, Buenos Aires, Sydney, etc. – in the course of the twentieth century), can be traced without interruption through three centuries of history. The very existence of the phenomenon and the tenacity of its tradition – a tenacity which fully reflects the dynamism of the operatic system and its capacity for change, evolution and incorporation of new social and cultural functions without ever renouncing its intrinsic structure and constitution – would themselves be sufficient to justify the extraordinary interest of musical, literary and theatre historians in the origins or 'dawn' of opera: an interest, indeed, whose own beginnings date back to the seventeenth century. How, when, where and why should such an apparently abnormal yet lastingly attractive form have been born? More than the subsequent journey of opera (a journey fraught with quagmires and dangerous passes), attention was focussed on the distant point of departure as something of a yardstick against which to measure the arduousness, glory, delusions and unfulfilled hopes and ambitions of later developments.

In order to avoid confusion – and at the risk of appearing over-schematic – one can give two distinct replies to the question of the origins of opera: either one says that opera began in Florence in 1600; or one says that operatic theatre began in Venice in 1637. To opt for one or other of these 'alternatives' – each, in its own way, perfectly legitimate – implies certain decisive critical consequences. To opt for both together – the two replies, though each formulated in accordance with significantly different criteria, are by no means mutually exclusive – requires the careful maintenance of certain conceptual distinctions if disastrous critical misunderstandings are to be avoided. It is true that the first entirely sung drama of which the score (or, more precisely, the scores: one for each of the two composers – Jacopo Peri and Giulio Caccini – involved in the production) has survived (both scores were published in 1600) is Ottavio Rinuccini's *Euridice*, first performed in Florence in 1600–01. It is also true that this first operatic production was shortly followed by others: some twenty-five operas performed at the courts of Florence, Mantua and Rome during the first forty years of the century. Equally, however, it may be said that only with the advent of public, commercially-based theatre, first introduced in Venice in 1637, did the new genre finally acquire that degree of stability, continuity, regularity and frequency of performance – in short, that economic and artistic 'solidity' – which would make it the dominant form of theatrical entertainment in Italy (as in Europe as a whole) for centuries to come. Paradoxically, it could be argued that only with the opening of these first public theatres was opera transformed from its original condition as a curious and somewhat ephemeral episode in the life of a handful of early seventeenth-century Italian courts to its subsequent position as an enduring and historically relevant 'institution'. (Note, however, that the converse is equally true: without the stimulus to reproduce in a Republican city like Venice that sort of entertainment which had been exclusive to courtly domains, this 'institutionalization' of opera would hardly have been possible.)

The process of institutionalizaition begun in Venice in the fourth decade of the century – a process which, some twenty years later, had already expanded to cover the length and breadth of the Italian peninsula (from Milan to Palermo) and even spilled across the Alps to northern Europe – exerted a radical influence on the artistic structure of opera itself: 1637, in fact, is less to be regarded as a point of demarcation between two different organizational structures (court opera and public opera) as between two radically different approaches to the performance, perception and, indeed, conception of musical theatre. To such an extent is this true that the difference in 'genre' between any two operas of 1640 and 1700 (or, for that matter, 1750 and 1800) is less, for example, than the difference between *Orfeo* (1607) and *L'incoronazione di Poppea* (1643): two operas which, though set by a single composer (Claudio Monteverdi), seem light years apart.

Court opera, by very definition, is designed to accompany and embellish a particular, one-off festive event – a unique and unrepeatable celebration of dynasty or diplomacy – the 'extraordinary' nature of which it attempts to display before both court and world at large; it is offered for the consumption of – or imposed upon – a wide yet select audience of invited guests, for whom it furnishes a sumptuous demonstration of the munificence of the sovereign and the unrivalled skill of the artists in his service; costs are high (and seen to be high), but the result is admiration, stupefied envy and consensus of opinion; music, scenography and written descriptions are published with the aim of providing those unable to attend with a fascinating account of the proceedings. Public opera, on the contrary, is innately 'numerous' and repeatable (costs can thus be absorbed). 'Amazement' becomes the order of the day; spectacle is made an end in itself (or, at most, exalts the myth of good civilian government or the illusion of a civic life which wisely combines idle pleasantries and profitable trade) and is aimed only at the entertainment of those present (without the various 'souvenir' publications which customarily accompanied performances at court). Public opera, for its promoters, is a risky and somewhat uncertain financial investment. Spectators, however, contribute to its economic welfare through their purchase of entrance tickets, seats and boxes; the entertainment, as purchased, is 'consumed' and shared by persons of varying social standing. Luxurious, but not incapable of mass production, public opera generates little documentation but the tiny twelvemo-format librettos sold at the entrance to the theatre and preserved only in the private collections of men of letters and habitual frequenters of such entertainments. The 'memory', so to speak, of public opera takes root in the habits and customs of its faithful supporters; a trip to the opera becomes more of a social tradition than a memorable event. Though it is undoubtedly true that court opera acts as a catalyst in respect of its public counterpart (which reproduces and markets the original features and pretensions of its aristocratic model), the latter is also notably influenced by organizational systems derived from the *commedia dell'arte* (see chapter 21). The process of commercialization, moreover, is by no means a superficial matter from which the original material emerges unscathed; on the contrary, the very structure of the dramatic entertainment is necessarily affected by changes in its reasons for production, means of 'consumption' and forms of transmission and tradition. By the late seventeenth century, public opera has supplanted its courtly equivalent to such a degree that the original roles are reversed: for many courts (large and small alike, in Italy as elsewhere in Europe), the prevailing model becomes that of public opera, which, under the financial and political patronage of a sovereign prince, shines with a light which is at most more intense than – but not substantially different in kind from – that of civic theatres; to a very considerable extent, the repertories are identical.

The significant differences between earlier seventeenth-century court and public opera do not pass unnoticed – not least at the very moment of transition – by discerning observers of contemporary public life. The Jesuit priest Giovan Domenico Ottonelli, in his treatise on the *Cristiana moderazione del teatro* (1652), distinguishes between three types of 'sung comedies' (or operas), each with its own particular promoters and organizational system: the first – and most sumptuous and estimable – is intended for performance 'in the palaces of magnificent princes and other great temporal and ecclesiastical rulers' (an example is the aforementioned *Euridice* of Peri and Caccini, staged at the Palazzo Pitti – at the expense of a group of Florentine nobles – for the royal wedding celebrations of 1600); the second, closely analogous, comprises those operas which are 'sometimes performed by groups of virtuous gentlemen or citizens, or by erudite academicians' (typical is Monteverdi's *Orfeo*, produced at Mantua in 1607 by the Accademia degli Invaghiti, which itself enjoyed the protection of the ruling Gonzaga family); the third regards 'commercial productions of a musical and dramatic nature' as staged by organized theatrical companies of singers and instrumentalists whose very business was that of performing such 'operas composed by worthy authors and diligently set to music act by act, scene by scene, word by word, from beginning to end'. It is this third species of opera which evokes particular moral concern in the Jesuit Ottonelli: court and academic operas might indeed be described as virtuous – if not beneficial – initiatives on the part of discerning politicians and liberal citizens, but public opera – promoted by and accessible to one and all – is dedicated to profit and, as such, attempts to seduce the public, if necessary through the most insidious means available (such as the public performances of female singers). Thirty years later, by which time the supremacy of public opera had been accepted by all, the first short treatise dedicated entirely to opera – the *Memorie teatrali di Venezia* of the canon Cristoforo Ivanovich (see Source reading 6) – can trace the history of the Venetian theatres without reference to their non-Venetian precursors, save for the remark that the pomp and splendour of Venetian public opera is by no means inferior 'to that practised in various places by the magnificence of princes, with the sole difference that the latter procure enjoyment for all through their 'generosity', i.e. at their own expense, 'while opera in Venice is business'. When, in 1708, the Hamburg librettist Barthold Feind publishes his *Gedanken von der Opera* (see Source reading 7), his remarks are obviously based on modern, 'public' practice. In short, it would appear that seventeenth-century 'critics' were already fully conscious of the discriminating value inherent in that 'institutionalization' of operatic theatre symbolized so concisely in the caption 'Venice 1637'. Court operas were memorable events, and as such are 'remembered' in the chronicles; 'everyday' – i.e., public – opera, on the contrary, was more ianteresting from the point of view of its history, meaning and structure (or so, indeed, it must have seemed to whomever showed even the slightest awareness of its enormous importance for contemporary life).

From the eighteenth century onwards, however, historiographers and critics alike have invariably opted for the first of the two possible views on the origins of opera ('Florence 1600'), without stopping to consider (or, worse still, considering from a purely negative standpoint) the importance of the changes brought about by the opening of the first public theatres. The consequences are not difficult to see. The humanist and classicist pretensions of the earliest protagonists in the history of opera (Rinuccini, Peri, Caccini), in their declared – though highly cautious – intentions of reviving and restoring the theatrical music of ancient Greece (or, at least, of emulating its effects), are raised *ipso facto* to the level of a general yardstick, with total disregard for the fact that all academic speculations on the role of music in Greek and Roman theatre had been thoroughly forgotten in the subsequent passage from court/academic to 'regular' public opera. That the 'dawn' of opera should have coincided with the final splendours of humanist culture – what is more, a Florentine culture – was a circumstance which, right from the early seventeenth century, could hardly fail to occasion feelings of pleasure (least of all to such theorists and antiquarian 'musicologists' as the Florentine Giovan Battista Doni, whose *Trattato della musica scenica*, written in the fourth decade of the century, reveals not the slightest suspicion of the direction soon to be taken by musical theatre). Modern operatic historiographers, too, for a variety of reasons, have preferred the unmaintained promise of the classical tradition to the allurements of the more 'routine' public theatre. For proof of this, the reader need look no further than the two principal sources (though admittedly not acknowledged as such) of modern operatic historiography: eighteenth-century Italian literary history and theory and the writings of Richard Wagner.

In its attempts to reconstruct a comprehensive history of Italian literature (and thus also of theatre), it is the erudite literary scholarship of eighteenth-century Italy – the *Istoria* (1698) and *Bellezza della volgar poesia* (1700) of Giovanni Mario Crescimbeni, the *Perfetta poesia italiana* (1706) of Ludovico Antonio Muratori, the dialogue *Della tragedia antica e moderna* (1714–15) of Pier Jacopo Martello, the *Storia e ragione d'ogni poesia* (1744) of Francesco Saverio Quadrio, the *Storia della letteratura italiana* (1772–93) of Girolamo Tiraboschi, etc. – which gives rise to the earliest reflections on the development of opera as an historical and artistic phenomenon. Scholars, though appalled at what they see, are nevertheless compelled to admit the overwhelming, almost daily success of this hybrid and, indeed, 'abnormal' form of entertainment – which, needless to say, they are unable to grasp. Nothing, in fact, can compensate aesthetically for this mixture of sublimity and outright vulgarity, the ignorance of or lack of respect for the rules of dramatic composition, the liberties taken with respect to the rules of probability, the abuse of the poetic text on the part of composers and singers, the sumptuousness of a scenography which seems to reflect the ethical 'dissoluteness' of opera in the period around 1700: all this, at least, in the eyes of those militant Italian intellectuals and men of letters who, for the first time in the history of Italian literature, find themselves involved in a nation-wide organization of culture (the Arcadian Academy, now present in every city and province of the Italian peninsula), together with the laborious construction of a moral and conceptual image of Italian literary history. In their dismay, these scholars turn back to the texts and other sources of early opera as a standard against which to measure the degradation subsequently inflicted upon dramatic literature by the Seicento – a century of which they thoroughly disapproved. They take no interest whatever in the music of seventeenth-century opera, and little more – not, moreover, without a certain irritation – in the operatic music of their day (whose irrational fascination is blamed for much of the perversity of contemporary Italian theatre). Pier Jacopo Martello, most shrewd and discerning of all contemporary literary scholars, entrusts the defence of theatrical music – a defence in part sincere, in part tongue-in-cheek –

to a make-believe Aristotle: 'Music alone . . . contains the all-important secret of the separation of the soul from all human concerns, at least for that period of time in which the soul is held enthralled by the notes in their artful handling of the consonance of voices and instruments . . . This art has been developed to the utmost perfection in Italy; it is thus only correct that Italy should adopt it as its favourite and most magnificent type of theatrical entertainment, one indeed which raises a smile even in the most severe of judges; likewise, it is only correct that foreign nations should consent to the importation of a model of entertainment so justly found pleasing in Italy.' The plea for the regeneration of Italian theatre is impelling. Extremists like Muratori even go so far as to advocate the reduction of the repertory to a few 'noble and expurgated tragedies and comedies, to be performed every year', preferably without music, 'for the honest and profitable recreation of the citizens'; these scholars look with not inconsiderable envy upon the great literary/theatrical tradition of seventeenth-century France. Others, more accommodating, are content to accept the relatively 'purified' style introduced first by Apostolo Zeno and then Metastasio. Francesco Algarotti, in his *Saggio sopra l'opera in musica* of 1755, returns to the heart of the matter: in his opinion, the (classical) regeneration of musical theatre is possible only at court, where the authority of the ruling prince is unconditioned by economic restraints; public opera, on the contrary, is easily affected by the hideous precepts of prevailing contemporary taste. With these comments, Algarotti provides something of a foretaste of the Viennese and Parisian classicism of Gluck and his contemporaries.

A century later, Richard Wagner – the Wagner of *Opera and drama* (1852), a Wagner whose self-publicity and self-propaganda reveal him as champion of those very aesthetic theories which will accompany the dissemination of his musical dramas throughout Europe – lends further weight to this 'classical' point of view with his extremely attractive (and no less polemical) notion that 'in modern opera the means of expression – that is, the music – is wrongly elevated to the level of a goal, while the expressive goal – that is, the drama, is degraded to the level of a means'. This assertion is further elaborated by the devotees of Wagner, in whose hands it becomes a tenacious historiographical preconception: the history of opera is seen as a history of the various attempts – invariably hindered by a variety of obstacles and never entirely successful – at the mutual reconciliation and integration of music and drama. Implicit in this history is the tendency towards the creation of a musical theatre which, like that of ancient Greece, is deeply rooted in the life and culture of a people or nation. The Wagnerian *Musikdrama* represents – or would seem to represent – the obvious culmination and 'crowning' of this history and design; of operatic history, in fact, only those episodes (Monteverdi, Gluck, Weber) which aimed – or appeared to aim – at a deliberate integration of music and drama were now admitted, while the remainder (Lully, Scarlatti, Handel, Metastasio, Mozart, Rossini, Italian Romantic opera, grand opera, etc.) was condemned to oblivion. Any attempt at mediation between musical form and the poetics of drama is invariably complex and fraught with difficulties: the musical and dramatic discontinuity inherent in the very structure of seventeenth- and eighteenth-century opera (in its subserviency to the dual régime of aria and recitative: recitative = action, aria = representation of affect) is, however, the total negation of such mediation. The division between aria and recitative is also deplored by eighteenth-century Italian literary scholars, though for very different – above all, literary – reasons: the aria, whose somewhat bizarre and changeable metrical structure is devoid of any illustrious counterpart in the history of Italian literature (and for this very reason immediately suspect), represents whatever is worst in contemporary poetic taste; in this, the music is its fully-fledged accomplice. For the *dramma per musica*, the standardizing and 'homogenizing' influence of Metastasio (arias in a single poetic metre, with clear preponderance of seven-syllable lines, themselves amply legitimized by the Petrarchan tradition) proves sufficient as a rectifying influence. For the Wagnerian tradition, however, any interruption whatever of the musical and dramatic continuity (arias without dramatic motivation, musically irrelevant recitatives) is regarded as sacrilege. The combination of two complementary, yet also contradictory, sets of principles – those of a Wagnerian operatic historiography (whose validity still meets with tacit, unconscious acceptance in wide areas of modern historical musicology) and those of eighteenth-century Italian literary scholarship – leads inevitably to a kind of critical stalemate whose paralysing force may be gauged in direct proportion to the lack of modern awareness of the origins of present-day critical criteria. The fact that this contradiction between eighteenth-century literary scholarship and 'Wagnerian' musicology is particularly flagrant in the case of Metastasian opera (in respect of which the two critical traditions cannot but arrive at diametrically opposing conclusions) leads to the conclusion that these two critical standpoints are, in reality, quite irreconcilable, even in cases (e.g., seventeenth-century opera) where their verdict is uniformly negative. 'Uniformly', indeed, but by no means unanimously so!

One further historiographical tradition – derived from the history of art – which frequently obscures any overall clarity of vision in the interpretation of seventeenth-century opera is the subdivision of the operatic tradition into a series of different 'schools', each dominant in a particular historical period. Thus, the 'Florentine' opera of the early Seicento is succeeded by 'Roman' opera (c. 1630–40), 'Venetian' opera and, finally, eighteenth-century 'Neapolitan' opera. The concept of 'school' – which implies the direct transmission of skills and abilities from master to apprentice – is undoubtedly valid in the context of painting, as, indeed, in the field of vocal polyphony or solo song (see chapter 10); not so, however, for architecture and opera – economically more complex, and based on the principle of the division of labour – where it proves both inadequate and misleading. Fundamental in the formation of the typical theatrical musician is his ability to adapt to market necessities and take his place as part of a particular productive organism and structure; less significant is his artistic training in the tradition of a particular 'school' (his absorption, that is, of a particular set of stylistic and formal techniques). On the other hand, there exists an ample circulation of musical man-power between the theatres of various cities, which facilitates the diffusion of the repertory on a national scale. It is thus legitimate – indeed, necessary – to speak of a variety of 'centres of operatic production', pointless and misleading to attempt to identify a series of 'schools', each with its own distinctive stylistic characteristics which correspond to different – non-simultaneous – stages in the development of the genre. Indeed, a necessary consequence of traditional 'scholastic' divisions is the adoption of certain emergency critical expedients: the 'invention', for example, of a 'second Roman school' to account for the fervid production of this important theatrical centre in a period – or periods – other than that with which it is generally associated.

All attempts at historiographical enquiry must necessarily be preceded by a number of basic questions. What are the available sources? Why these and not other sources? By whom, for whom and for what purpose were they produced? What was their significance for their original 'authors', and what is their significance for us? In what respects can they be regarded as useful and reliable? In what are they misleading or of lesser importance? The unwitting and unreasoned adoption of two illustrious – yet indirect and not totally disinterested – 'sources' (eighteenth-century Italian literary scholarship; Wagnerian and post-Wagnerian theories of operatic history) has led to a number of misunderstandings on the part of modern operatic historiography. The clarification of these ambiguities has formed a prelude to what will be a necessarily brief examination of the history of seventeenth-century opera and its 'primary' sources in Italy and beyond.

20 Opera before 1637

The path from 'Florence 1600' to 'Venice 1637' is by no means straight and narrow. The overall picture, in fact, is notably heterogeneous, and understandably so; court entertainments, by their very nature and function, demand treatment as special events and not as links in a chain. Within this context of enormous variety, however, a number of constants emerge.

Firstly, the sources. The music of a large proportion of the operas of this period has survived in printed editions; manuscript sources are few. This situation, practically unique in the history of Italian opera, will re-emerge only in the early years of the nineteenth century after almost two centuries of transmission through manuscript copies supplied on commission. Printed sources are known to have circulated among contemporaries: almost never, however, were they used 'unaccompanied' for the revival of an entertainment elsewhere; on the contrary, their principal function was that of propagating a particular subject or style or disseminating the very concept of opera (atypical in this respect is the score of Loreto Vittori's *Galatea* which, though never previously performed, was published in Rome in 1639; the opera was privately staged five years later in Naples). In such few operatic revivals as exist, moreover, the principles of courtly emulation require a substantial revision of the original text: thus, for example, the Mantuan revival of *Dafne* in 1608 (text by Ottavio Rinuccini, music by Marco da Gagliano) represents an improved version of the pioneering *Dafne* performed in Florence in 1598 with music by Jacopo Peri. Naturally, each authorized revival necessitates the presence of specialized technical and artistic personnel – singers, musicians, scenographers, stage engineers, the 'inventor' of the entertainment himself (still, at this stage, the poet) – preferably the same as those involved in the original production (thus, for example, the *sine qua non* for the Bolognese *Euridice* of 1616 is the direct intervention of Rinuccini and Peri).

Not always, however, has the music of these early operas been preserved; almost totally lost, moreover, is the music of the *intermedi* (after the famous Florentine *intermedi* of 1589). These latter were brief but extremely spectacular scenic 'actions' of dance and song, performed between the acts of the principal dramatic entertainment (itself recited or, less frequently, sung); in the sixteenth and throughout the first half of the seventeenth century, these *intermedi* represented the most spectacular form of entertainment to be had at the courts (above all, at the Florentine court), academies and public theatres of Italy. *Intermedi* lacked the continuous dramatic action of true operas: in theatrical practice, however, the two genres co-existed quite happily together in a kind of multicoloured promiscuity, to the point at which it is sometimes impossible to establish their 'debit and credit' relationship in terms of their musical, literary and 'spectacular' content.

Besides the musical scores and librettos, a third category of source material – of considerable importance in arriving at a correct understanding of the significance of these earliest operas (and *intermedi*) – is represented by contemporary descriptions: official descriptions written and published on behalf or by order of the promoters of the entertainment; private descriptions in the letters and diaries of spectators. These sources are generally somewhat laconic in their treatment of the specific merits of music and *mise en scène* (which, at best, attract enthusiastic but generic praise); normally, moreover, they refer not so much to the isolated theatrical event as to the complex of court festivities which surrounded a particular ceremonial occasion (a marriage, birth, triumph, visit of State, etc.) and which included the performance of the opera in question. In this sense, they show that the function of the earliest operas was closely related to exigencies of court ceremonial (the allegorical celebration of sovereign power, visual ostentation of sovereign splendour, etc., in the overall context of a series of collective manifestations: banquets, processions, religious ritual, tournaments, ballets): further corroboration of this ceremonial function – itself not radically dissimilar in meaning (though radically different in kind) to the ballets and theatrical festivities described in Source reading 2 – is provided by the mythological subjects (susceptible as these are to allegorical and eulogistic interpretation) commonly adopted for librettos.

A further category of source material, by no means rare in connection with early seventeenth-century opera, is represented by engravings of the sets. It is, indeed, to the wonders of stagecraft and the remarkable illusions of theatrical perspective that spectators attribute much of the memorable effect of these earlier operas and *intermedi*. Technical expedients and other devices for the simulation of fires, floods, flights through the heavens, magic happenings and appearances of monsters and gods, or geared to the accomplishment of sudden and awe-inspiring changes of scene: all are jealously guarded by inventors and promoters alike. Secrets do, however, circulate from court to court (and are codified in a number of contemporary treatises, e.g., the *pratica di fabricar scene e machine ne' teatri*, 1637–38, of Niccolò Sabbatini); in this way, they eventually enter the stock-in-trade of theatrical practice and come to be accepted by playwrights in general for use in their libretti.

In the early decades of the century, the place of performance is still somewhat variable and undefined: sometimes 'occasional' (a hall pro-variable and undefined: sometimes 'occasional' (a hall provisionally converted to theatrical use, as for the *Orfeo* in Mantua, 1607 of Alessandro Striggio the younger and Monteverdi), sometimes permanent (the Uffizi theatre of the Medici in Florence, first used for the *intermedi* of 1586), sometimes 'super-permanent' (as in the immense – and quite extraordinary – Teatro Farnese of Parma, built in 1618 to house a performance which never took place and subsequently utilized once only – in 1628 – for an entertainment which, despite notable differences, was nevertheless contrived in such a way as to exploit the original scenic apparatus of ten years before). Equally variable is the position of the instruments with respect to the stage. Ideal, in the opinion of the earliest composers (e.g. Emilio de' Cavalieri), was a location behind the backdrop of the set; this, however, had a muffling effect on the sound on its passage to the auditorium, and no direct contact was possible between singers and instrumentalists. More suitable, then, was a location in the wings, to the side of the stage. For the 1628 performance at Parma, the instrumentalists were placed in front of the stage; this solution, however, was reluctantly received, in so far as the heads of the players, seen on a level with the feet of the actors, apparently interfered with the scenic illusion. Only in the permanent public theatres, where compromise of quite a different kind will govern the relationship between convention and probability, was this system uniformly imposed. Court opera, if anything, attempts to make something of a 'scenic' virtue of the necessity of locating the players in proximity to the stage yet out of sight of the audience: thus, in the colossal operatic spectacle *Le nozze degli dèi* (Florence, 1637), whose performance commemorates not only the marriage of Grand Duke Ferdinando II (himself little given to the promotion of theatrical displays) with the bigoted Vittoria della Rovere but also the definitive eclipse of Florentine operatic supremacy, the instruments, divided in two separate groups, appear to have been hidden behind two 'false' partitions to the sides of the stage (itself erected in the courtyard of the Palazzo Pitti); in the ballet finale of the opera, these two partitions fell away to reveal the densely populated clouds of a 'display of the whole of Heaven', in which the song of the deities was accompanied by two celestial choirs of instruments.

The 'stage' appearance of the instruments in the course of this final triumphal scene is nothing but the 'extreme' yet by no means incongruous outcome of a concept – itself clearly apparent in those very contemporary descriptions which otherwise yield such scanty information on the musical details of the production – which links instrumental sonorities more to spectacular than 'orchestral' concerns. This concept was derived from the *intermedi* of the sixteenth century. The various instruments – or instrumental colours – are used as the attributes in sound of particular characters or situations; the neutral support of the *basso continuo* can itself be made to adopt a variety of sonorous configurations through the discerning selection and combination of instruments (*violoni*, harpsichords, lutes, organs, harps, *chitarroni*, etc.; Cavalieri, for example, advises that 'the instruments be changed in accordance with the affection of the actor', though without specifying how). Particularly eloquent in this respect is the score of Monteverdi's *Orfeo*, where the instrumental distributions of 1607 are specified in a series of stage directions: pastoral scenes are represented by the merry sounds of treble and descant recorders, hell by the darker tones of regal and trombones, ballets by *violini piccoli alla francese*, etc.; in Act 3, the great invocation of Orpheus with his lyre is interspersed with virtuoso ritornellos for violins, cornetts and double harp. In short: a 'naturalistic' use of instrumental sonorities and techniques, which reflects there and then the scenes witnessed by the spectator on stage.

Subjects are predominantly mythological, mostly drawn from Ovid: Daphne (Florence 1598; Mantua 1608), Orpheus (the *Euridice* of Florence 1600 and *Orfeo* at Mantua 1607); the *Orfeo dolente* of Chiabrera and Belli, performed at Florence in 1616; the *Morte d'Orfeo*, set to music by Landi in 1619), Cephalus and Aurora (the *Rapimento di Cefalo* of Chiabrera and Caccini, Florence 1600; *Aurora ingannata* by Campeggi and Giacobbi, Bologna 1608), Narcissus (Rinuccini's drama of that name, never performed), Andromeda (Campeggi and Giacobbi, Bologna 1610; Cicognini and Belli, Florence 1608; Marigliani and Claudio Monteverdi, Mantua 1620), the rape of Proserpine (Marigliani and Giulio Cesare Monteverdi, Casale 1611; Campeggi and Giacobbi, Bologna 1613; Strozzi and Claudio Monteverdi, Venice 1630; Colonna and Virgilio Mazzocchi?, Rome 1645), Acis and Galatea (Chiabrera and Orlandi, Mantua, 1617), Arethusa (Corsini and Vitali, Rome 1620), Adonis (Tronsarelli and Domenico Mazzocchi, Rome 1626; the *Adone* of Cicognini and Peri, composed in 1611 but never performed), Flora (Salvadori and Gagliano, Florence 1628), Diana (Parisani and Cornacchioli, Rome 1629), Phaethon (Tronsarelli and Kapsberger, Rome 1630). These, in fact, account for almost all the early repertory. Truth to tell, there is a flagrant contradiction between the openly declared intention of a musical revival of ancient Greek tragedy and this prevalence of natural and metamorphic mythology of Ovidian descent. Wholly absent, in fact, are the heroic myths of ancient Greece (Aeschylus, Sophocles, Euripides) and Rome (Seneca) and their principal protagonists (Oedipus, Electra, Orestes, Alcestis, Antigone, Iphigenia, Medea, Hercules, etc.). The contradiction is particularly apparent in the Prologue to Rinuccini's *Euridice*, sung by a personification of Tragedy who, paradoxically, declares her renunciation of 'sad and tearful scenes' and resolves to kindle 'sweeter affections in the hearts' of the spectators (*Euridice*, indeed, represents a departure from classical models in its introduction of the *lieto fine* (happy ending) – a convention maintained almost without exception throughout the seventeenth century). By far the most common genre designation in these early operas is 'favola' (fable) (or 'favola pastorale', 'favola boschereccia'); note, however, that 'favola' and 'mito' (myth) are perfectly synonymous in contemporary usage. It is as though the foundation of the new musical and theatrical genre – based on a musical language that was capable of representing and moving the affections (a regeneration, so to speak, of the 'pathopoietic' properties of music) – was destined to take place less under the banner of the tragic catharsis of heroic and sacrificial mythology (the horror of which is sufficient to silence both music and text) than on the fertile – indeed, enchanted – terrain of a mythology of metamorphoses and origins. The very frequency of an Orpheus myth in which the hero, aided by the power of song, triumphs over the Furies and death is significant in this context, as also is the original importance of the Apollonian myth of Daphne (itself associated with the birth of the laurel, symbol of political and artistic glory). More specifically: the adoption of the Ovidian transformation myths and their pastoral setting complies with certain aesthetic requirements which, to the perpetrators of the earliest attempts to sustain an entire dramatic action through music, seemed inescapable.

In this respect, few more eloquent contemporary sources exist than the anonymous but skilful manuscript treatise *Il Corago* (i.e., he who 'is capable of prescribing all those ways and means required for the perfect staging of a dramatic action already composed by the poet'). Like Doni's *Trattato della musica scenica*, the *Corago* represents something of a summary of the experiences of the period 1600–30 (it was, indeed, written shortly after this latter date, probably by a Florentine): though its field of reference is theatre in general, it contains many pertinent observations on early opera. For our present purposes, discussion may be limited to a few of the artistic problems to which the author of the *Corago* (in contrast to Doni) addresses his attention with pragmatic expertise.

Principal defect in the theatre – in its every component – is the 'lack of naturalness'; on the contrary, 'the maximum achievement of the poet' lies in 'the invention of events, ordered and interwoven on the basis of some general truth, in accordance with the laws of probability'. Logical, then, is the choice of pastoral themes (which, as noted by Doni, 'represent deities, nymphs and shepherds in that far-off century in which music was natural and speech almost poetic') as most appropriate for wholly sung representation; only such figures as Daphne, Orpheus, Flora and Arethusa, deities of a mythical golden age, can realistically be expected to converse in song without overstepping the bounds of probability: 'musical speech is more to be associated with the concept of the superhuman than with the concept and manifest notion of ordinary man; harmonic reasoning is sweeter, more elevated, masterly and noble than ordinary speech, and is thus naturally to be attributed those characters which most embody the divine and sublime'. The same precept is equally valid in the case of personifications and allegories (the Virtues and Vices), the 'ancient fathers', angels and other inhabitants of Paradise, the astral and fluvial spirits. In short: the spatial, temporal or idealized detachment from the spectator reduces the incongruity of sung speech and confers upon the characters in question a greatly amplified nobility and magnificence. The same principle is unbecoming in the case of historical characters and contemporaries, where it incites to laughter. This, at least, is true of 'serious actions'; in 'comic' plots, the presence of 'characters of a silly or idiotic nature, endowed with a notable manner of reasoning with common or vulgar inflections', leads to situations in which 'the mirth and admiration excited by the imitation of their manners increases in relation to the closeness of the music to their manner of speech': in other words, a kind of musical caricature. The *Corago*, indeed, goes so far as to state that with time, if 'harmonic representations' continue to be cultivated, the public 'will learn to appreciate anything and everything represented in music': clearly implicit, in short, is the notion that the fundamental aesthetic requirement of opera – namely, the substitution of recitation by song – is destined to take root in the collective consciousness of the people, and that all apparent incongruities for the spectator of the early years of the century (e.g., the presence of 'historical' characters) would come to be accepted in the course of no more than a few decades. Already lurking in the wings is the chorus of railwaymen who, in Offenbach's *Vie parisienne*, sing through the various stations on the 'ligne de l'Ouest'.

The poet, in setting out his *dramma in musica*, must bear certain conventions in mind. The subject, 'from time to time if not always', must 'require or allow for the introduction of scenic machines or, at least, the appearance of caverns, gardens or other forms of variety such as choruses, ballets, *moresche* or *abbattimenti* [choreographed fights]'; these break up the 'musical soliloquy' (thus avoiding tedium) and also provide the sublime protagonists of the *opera in musica* with a series of suitably 'extraordinary appearances'. Lengthy narration must be avoided; this results in excessive uniformity of musical style. In so far, however, as narration is an essential ingredient of the drama, this should be interpolated with choral exclamations and interrogatives, or at least 'varied with different – indeed, opposing – affections and rhetorical figures'. Likewise, monodic laments (see chapter 23) are so much the better for the introduction of 'an aria (though necessarily of great beauty)', preferably of two or more strophes. Strophic arias are especially suited for use in the Prologue, which, 'right from the outset, most captivate the soul of the spectator' and must thus be particularly attractive (normally, in the earliest decades, the Prologue consists of nothing but a strophic aria: a series of quatrains of rhymed hendecasyllables – ABBA – sung by various idealized characters and personifications such as Music, Apollo, Ovid, etc.). Frequent use of the chorus (itself a 'particular feature' of opera) is to be advised. The libretto, in order to cater for the fancy of the composer and virtuosic skills of the singers (in supplying 'those passages and embellishments currently lacking in the *stile recitativo*'), should contain 'characters who sing without giving the appearance of reciting'; thus, canzonettas, *ariette* and *scherzi* – pieces, in short, which would also have been sung in the context of any normal, recited drama – should be inserted as such in the dialogue (this remarkably persistent convention is still present in the canzonetta of Cherubino and, later still, in Verdi's 'La donna è mobile'). 'In serious matters, the elocution . . . must be strong' and sustained; in music, however, it is best if 'the verses be easy and clear': thus, rhyme should abound and long convoluted periods be avoided.

Poetic metre, above all, should follow that of sixteenth-century tragedy and tragicomedy: in short, blank verse (free chains of hendecasyllables and seven-syllable lines, with no fixed rhyme scheme). The two principal literary models, the first of which is also noted by Doni, are (1) Sperone Speroni's mythological tragedy *Canace*, derived – significantly – from Ovid and, like the future *dramma in musica*, characterized by an abundance of rhymed seven-syllable lines; (2) the *favole pastorali* of Tasso and Guarini (specifically: *Aminta* and *Il pastor fido*), with their intersecting amorous plots and discursive structure, organized in a series of highly expressive little 'madrigals' which are easily isolated from their immediate context). Blank verse will remain a fundamental characteristic of all Italian recitative poetry. Quite apart from the force of literary tradition, there is also the fact – decisive in the present context – that, of all Italian metrical types, the hendecasyllable and seven-syllable line are alone in offering a relative freedom of accentuation – with the sole exception of the final stress, which (in both cases) falls regularly on the penultimate syllable – and thus a certain proximity to prose declamation. Already, however, for the author of the *Corago*, 'it is reasonable and praiseworthy . . . to introduce variety and eccentricity' of poetic metre; thus 'the composer will be able to avoid uniformity'. To this end, the poet may introduce 'a variety of canzonettas', i.e., arias and strophic *ariette* in measured verse (four-, five- and eight-syllable lines with their *tronco* and *sdrucciolo* variants; six-syllable lines are a regular feature of the 1630s, thanks largely to the work on Rospigliosi; the ten-syllable line begins a glorious operatic career towards the late 1660s) or couched in the more 'regular' literary forms: *ottava rima*, *terza rima* (*piano* and *sdrucciolo* versions), quatrain, *canzone* and – exceptionally – the sonnet, all of which enjoyed considerable popularity among the early seventeenth-century monodists (see chapter 3) but vanish entirely from the *dramma per musica* in the period after c. 1650. 'In our own time', says the author of the *Corago*, 'Gabriello Chiabrera has discovered and restored the beauty of many of these metres.' It would be difficult to overestimate the importance – albeit indirect – of Chiabrera's metrical innovations for the introduction of the aria in the *dramma per musica* (and, in general, for the development of a dynamic and accentual concept of musical rhythm). Chiabrera's librettos are notably sparing in their use of *ariette* – more so, indeed, than those of the 'father' of the libretto, Rinuccini, where (beginning with *Dafne*) four- and eight-syllable lines are a regular feature of the choruses, with *ottava* and *terza rima* reserved for the principal characters.

The 'motivated' integration of a formally heterogeneous and extraneous body – i.e., the aria – in an overall dramatic context which is dominated by dialogue and recitative: this represents an aesthetic and dramaturgical problem with which the conventions of probability – as codified in the *Corago* and subsequently modified and absorbed into everyday theatrical practice – must seek to come to terms. On the other hand, it is the aria – i.e., the variable and theatrically effective solution to a variable formal and/or dramaturgical problem – which provides both librettists and composers with their greatest opportunity for invention (to the obvious advantage of spectators). Clearly, the aria has innate limitations, as the author of the *Corago* is all too aware: while, in recitative, 'the meaning of the poetry is fully corroborated line by line, word by word', in the musical text, the aria 'is incapable of perfectly imitating the affections'; 'a cheerful aria, while communicating a cheerful overall affection, is nevertheless incapable of providing the appropriate expression required for each particular line or word'. The aria, if it is not to lose its very identity, is forced to maintain from beginning to end a certain tone and rhythmic and melodic 'personality'. (From a stylistic point of view, the strengthening and refinement of the imitative qualities of the aria is the central aesthetic question for which seventeenth- and eighteenth-century opera will attempt to provide a reply.) For obvious reasons, the *Corago* – in common with poets, musicians and spectators – is only too willing to tolerate the aesthetic inconsistencies of a type of aria which excels in 'grace and charm'; these characteristics are lacking from the *stile recitativo*, which 'generates tedium', 'is somewhat languid' and 'lacks those ornaments and graces which so embellish the art of song' (i.e., *passagi*, *trilli*, *gorgheggi*). The blending of an unmeasured *stile recitativo* (with which it is possible 'to imitate or give the impression of natural discourse') with the aria (accentual, periodic, strophic, melodically formalized) – in short, the apparently problematic co-existence of musical 'prose' and 'poetry' – is, however, perceived less as an obstacle than as a positive resource of which seventeenth- and eighteenth-century opera will attempt to take utmost advantage.

A number of cases reveal that at times when the function of mere entertainment prevails over that of allegorical celebration, the pastoral and mythological aura considered so important in the context of the earliest court operas is gladly abandoned in favour of a notable variety of themes and subjects – themes, it would appear, in which the aesthetic justification for the principle of *recitar cantando* poses less of a constraint, and in which the introduction of arias is less inhibited. Of particular significance in this context – not least from an institutional point of view – are the theatrical productions promoted by two great Tuscan intellectuals then resident in Rome: the reigning Pope Urban VIII (*alias* Maffeo Barberini) and the prelate (and future Pope Clement IX) Giulio Rospigliosi. Beginning in the early 1630s, the

Papal nephews – themselves installed in the key positions of Roman public life – foster a series of operatic productions (of which the first is *Sant'Alessio*) with Rospigliosi as librettist and overall director. Catalyst for the entire series was undoubtedly the enormous success of the first of these ventures (the music, published in 1634, is by Stefano Landi). The protagonist, Alessio, abandons his family and worldly comforts on the day of his marriage to dedicate himself to prayer; disguised as a beggar he subsequently returns to Rome, where he witnesses the grief of his relations and unwavering faith of his bride in her hope of one day re-uniting with her beloved. Urged in opposing directions by a Demon and an Angel, he oscillates distressed between conjugal love and devotion to God. His religious perseverance, however, continues undiminished and he dies in a blessed state of grace, mourned by his relatives (by whom he is recognized only after his death). The dramatic economy of this religious plot touches all the various registers of the pathetic in its representation of the differing emotions of the characters; the dialogue, in recitative style (a plain recitative, though not without a degree of rhetorical agitation at salient points in the drama), is interspersed with picturesquely elaborated choruses of demons, angels and servants, as also by comic episodes (played by pageboys and the Devil himself). *Sant'Alessio*, rightly termed by its author a 'dramma musicale' (as opposed to 'favola' or 'favola in musica'), was first performed in 1631 and revived for three consecutive years; its plot also took advantage of the vast popularity of the life of St Alexis in the realms of popular and devotional literature. Subsequent Barberini–Rospigliosi productions for the Roman Carnival are varied in kind; all, however, draw upon celebrated literary sources or the lives of the saints: in 1633, *Erminia sul Giordano*, taken from Tasso's *Gerusalemme liberata* (music, by Michelangelo Rossi, published in 1637); in 1635 and 1636, *SS. Didimo e Teodora* (music anonymous); in 1637, the 'musical comedy' *Chi soffre speri*, based on Boccaccio (music by Virgilio Mazzocchi and Marco Marazzoli), revived in 1639 in a memorable production which included the *intermedio* of *La fiera di Farfa* (Bernini's out-and-out scenic representation of a country fair); in 1638 and 1639, *San Bonifacio* (music by Virgilio Mazzocchi), with child performers; in 1641, *Santa Genoinda, ovvero L'innocenza difesa* (Mazzocchi); in 1642, *Lealtà con valore ossia Il palazzo d'Atlante* (music by Luigi Rossi), based on Ariosto; finally, in 1643, *Santo Eustachio* (music again by Mazzocchi). Rospigliosi is subsequently appointed as Papal Nuncio to Spain; in any case, the operatic activities of the Barberini family are officially brought to a close by the death of Pope Urban VIII in 1644.

The wide range of subjects to be observed in this first seasonally-based series of operatic productions would suggest a deliberate policy of variety on the part of its promoters. The Barberini operas are quite devoid of all 'occasional', festive connotations; absent, then, is the stimulus to allegory, as also to the ceremonial tendencies of Florentine and Mantuan court opera. Instead, Roman and non-Roman aristocracy alike receive an annual Carnival-tide invitation to savour the operatic 'spectacles' of Rospigliosi's highly-skilled team of experts. Performances take place in various parts of the city; the preferred location, however, is a kind of shed (capacity, 3,500) adjoining the Palazzo Barberini at the Quattro Fontane (benches for the spectators are temporarily requisitioned from a number of the city's churches). The wide range of subject matter, although enshrined within the regularity of the Roman Carnival season (which, under Urban VIII, assumes a certain prominence in the public life of Rome), still keeps alive something of the courtly tradition with its appearance of 'singularity'. Rospigliosi's use of the aria is basically consistent with the conventions as described in the *Corago*. Obviously, the *stile recitativo* loses somewhat in 'sublimity' through its application to heroic, comic and historical plots; this, however, has the effect of further bringing out the aria-like passages, as also the laments of the various protagonists and the comic *ariette* of the lower-class characters. The canzonetta (sung as such) prevails; in this genre, the Barberini composers prove themselves thoroughly at ease, with the adoption of dance-like formulas (both vocal and instrumental) including those of popular extraction. Gone is the all-pervading pastoral aura of earlier court opera; each character is now totally free to perform in accordance with his or her station or rank – affectionately, expressively, freely, jokingly or any other way. The sole 'condition': his acceptance, so to speak, of full responsibility for his song.

21 The Venetian theatres

The enormous financial burden of Rospigliosi's productions fell entirely on the shoulders of the powerful Barberini family. And, indeed, besides functioning as a public demonstration of generosity and splendour, these productions – like all such events – had the not unbeneficial effect of providing employment for a vast array of craftsmen and suppliers (carpenters, painters, stage-managers, tailors, hairdressers, second-hand dealers, chandlers, copyists, etc.), who depended for their very livelihood upon the patronage of the wealthy Roman aristocracy (typically, the choruses of traders and sellers in Bernini's *intermedio La fiera di Farfa* – performed, as noted in chapter 20, in conjunction with the 1639 production of Rospigliosi's *Chi soffre speri* – are made up entirely of cries such as 'over here with your money', 'come on, gents, money, money', 'cheap and no credit'). The artists themselves (singers, composers and set-designers) were all in the direct employ of the Roman institutions and aristocracy, and were paid in a variety of gifts: gloves, jewellery, silverware, etc.

At Venice, for Carnival 1637, a company of musicians rented the Teatro S. Caissiano (traditionally used for performances of the *commedia dell'arte*) and produced the first public opera: *Andromeda* (words and music respectively by Benedetto Ferrari and Francesco Manelli, themselves the two leaders of the company). The group was comprised of a number of singers from Rome (performers, in 1636, in a kind of scenic tournament, *Ermiona*, devised by the nobleman Pio Enea degli Obizzi and produced in the nearby city of Padua) and others from the choir of St Mark's, Venice. The libretto offers a tribute 'to the glory of the six musicians (collaborators with the author), who have performed the opera of *Andromeda* with great magnificence and refinement; this they have done entirely at their own expense, which was not inconspicuous'. The following year, 1638, *La maga fulminata* is produced by the identical company: the author, 'with his money, aided by five companion musicians and with an outlay of no more than 2,000 *scudi*, has succeeded in stealing the hearts of the listeners'; 'such operations, patronized by princes, cost infinitely greater sums of money'. The musicians (Ferrari himself was also a composer and theorbo player) pool their resources and produce the opera themselves. In 1639, Ferrari and Manelli transfer their activities to the Teatro SS. Giovanni e Paolo, an ex-comedy theatre hurriedly renovated by the Grimani family and converted for operatic productions. Meanwhile, the Teatro S. Cassiano continues to provide competition in the shape of a new and largely indigenous company of musicians led by Francesco Cavalli: though the opening production of this company, *Le nozze di Teti*, was something of an economic disaster, it also marks the beginning of what for Cavalli was to prove an enormously successful career, continuing practically uninterrupted until 1666. From the very earliest years, the economic history of opera is one of bankruptcy and insolvency; artistically, however, the story is one of unfailing success.

Underlying this paradox is the unique structure of the operatic production, which, roughly speaking, can be summarized in terms of three different levels of operator and operation. First, there are the theatre proprietors: the great noble families of Venice (Tron, Grimani, Capello, Giustinian, etc.), who, in their search for secure property and investment, purchase or renovate the buildings in question but avoid all direct involvement in the actual business of production (secret intervention, however, is by no means infrequent; at times, the politics of theatrical competition is seen to reflect the ever-fluctuating alliances and competition between different economic and ideological factions within the ruling class). Second, there is the figure of the impresario (or 'company' of impresarios), entrusted with the management of the theatre for one season (customarily, beginning on St Stephen's Day and ending on Shrove Tuesday) or several such seasons. The impresario invests his capital in certain unavoidable expenses, some (theatre rental, scenic production, artists' fees) fixed for the season as a whole, others (theatre illumination, orchestral players, stage hands) variable in accordance with the number of performances; likewise, he also benefits from certain guaranteed sources of profit, some calculable in advance (annual rental of boxes), others variable in accordance with the success of individual productions (nightly fees for benches in the stalls; entrance tickets, charged to all spectators – box-holders included – at the door). Third, there are the artists: composers, singers, dancers, set and costume designers. They, too, are sometimes directly involved in the financial venture as such; quickly, however, they come to prefer the position of hired professionals, paid according to contract (and thus on the debit side of the theatrical budget). The librettist – rightly or wrongly considered the true 'author' of the *dramma per musica* – enjoys a special status: he personally sustains the costs involved in printing the libretto and reaps the benefits from sales. In reality, this separate treatment results in his much increased interest in the financial success of the opera; while musician-impresarios are an extremely rare breed indeed (exceptional are the 'experiments' of the earliest years, from which the musician protagonists invariably emerge with not inconsiderable debts), cases of direct involvement of librettists in theatre management are by no means infrequent. This disparity also reflects the differing social status of librettists and musicians: while the former are generally members of the lawyer or even patrician class, the composers of opera are at most organist or *vicemaestro di capella* at St Marks, if they are not hired from outside Venice. A kind of tacitly-recognized incompatibility appears to exist between the role of *maestro di cappella* at the Ducal Basilica (i.e., the supreme musical functionary of State) and that of theatrical composer: the exceptions – notably, Monteverdi – are few and far between.

Of these three operative levels, that of impresario is crucial. Whatever the financial backing (declared or undeclared) of proprietors, whatever the professional interest of the artists, the economic risk is his. Normally one factor of relative stability – namely, the social custom of an evening at the opera – contains this risk within reasonable bounds. The operatic phenomenon immediately acquires an unshakeable position in civic life, dominating the Venetian Carnival with its veritable 'industry' of collective entertainment. Unforeseen events, however, can cause the total loss of theatrical investments (such a case occurs in 1645 with the State-imposed closure – *in tempore belli* – of all Venetian theatres); one or more artistic failures, moreover, can discredit the theatre, reduce box-office takings and thus compromise long-term financial security. One element of compensation is represented by the boxes (themselves a bastion of social custom): advance letting of boxes for the entire season provides a sizeable portion of the liquid capital required for investment in the operatic productions themselves. Theatres without boxes (such as, apparently, the Teatro Novissimo, host to the most extraordinary scenic spectacles of the 1640s) must rely on sales of tickets at the door, and thus inevitably succumb at a single artistic failure (the Novissimo, indeed, survives for five seasons only). The boxes and their occupants (i.e., the wealthy, opera-going citizens and nobles, essentially of the same social standing as the proprietor himself) are thus decisive for the survival of the theatre: impresarios may come and go, but proprietors remain, and perpetuation of the system is thus guaranteed. In reality, the Venetian-type theatre (stalls, with evening-to-evening rental of seats; two, three, four or more tiers of boxes, leased for the season as a whole; admittance tickets for all) comes to represent something of an economic and architectural prototype for Italy and Europe as a whole. At least architecturally, this prototype still survives essentially unchanged: examples (though admittedly eighteenth-century) are La Scala, Milan; the Teatro Comunale, Bologna; La Fenice, Venice; the San Carlo, Naples; etc.

The 'invention' of this prototype clearly pre-dates the introduction of opera itself: in fact, a large proportion of Venetian theatres are nothing but adaptations of pre-existing structures originally employed for the *commedia dell'arte* (itself, so to speak, the first 'modern' form of professional theatre). Undoubtedly significant is the fact that the earlier courtly tradition, on its arrival in republican Venice (where the model of a princely court is replaced by a State administration involving all branches of the aristocracy), links hands with a 'low' organizational system such as that of the professional comics, with its combination of financial precariousness and mercantile agility (evident, above all, in the competition between theatres). The financial precariousness of opera – burdened as it is with enormous costs of production – is certainly greater than that of the much poorer *commedia dell'arte*; greater too, however, is its luxuriousness and attractiveness. In 1683, a French traveller observes that 'the great public theatres of Venice are dedicated to the performance of operas commissioned by the nobility at their own expense, more for self-amusement than for profit, since only with difficulty do proceeds exceed fifty per cent of costs' (the widespread idea of the 'popularity' of Venetian opera as opposed to the aristocratic pretensions of court opera can no longer be sustained; available documentation on audience composition clearly shows the irrelevance of lower-class opera-goers for the economic structure of the theatre). Competition is fierce: new speculative ventures follow each other with the same easy rapidity as outright failures. More than one theatre (a full list is given by Ivanovich in Source reading 6) collapses after a few seasons only. Examples exist of able impresarios who 'graduate' from a small to a larger theatre, repaying the debts of the former with the fruits of the latter. Long-term contracts with the most 'popular' musicians, librettists and set designers ensure the continuing stake of these artists in the affairs of the theatre. Francesco Cavalli, for example, works uninterruptedly at the Teatro S. Cassiano from 1639 to 1650 (in 1642, he is also momentarily involved in the Teatro S. Moisè). From 1642, his standard librettist is the lawyer Giovanni Faustini, whom he follows when the latter sets up on his own at S. Apollinare (four Cavalli operas were composed for this theatre); on Faustini's death in 1651 Cavalli first moves to the Teatro SS. Giovanni e Paolo (1653), before returning to the Teatro S. Cassiano (1659), where he collaborates with the impresario Marco Faustini (brother of Giovanni) who had meanwhile procured the services of the librettist Nicolò Minato. After a further season at SS. Giovanni e Paolo (again with Faustini as impresario), he moves briefly with Minato to the Teatro S. Salvatore (for which he composes two operas), before returning to SS. Giovanni e Paolo (1668), where he produces one final score. This, however, is never staged (for presumably ideological motives not unconnected with the subject and tragic finale), thus contributing indirectly to the financial collapse of Faustini himself.

The quality, quantity and regularity of Cavalli's operatic output confirm him as the dominant artistic personality in the first three decades of public opera in Venice. Decisive, too, though for obviously different reasons, is the role of the architect Giacomo Torelli, moving spirit behind the amazing scenic effects of the Teatro Novissimo. Torelli is the inventor of a system of sliding wings which, coupled together, inserted on 'channels' (tracks) at the sides of the stage and connected by a brace to a central winch located under the stage, could be changed with a single turn of the winch itself. Instantaneous transformations of scenic perspective, performed in full view of spectators (with truly astounding effects, unsurpassed even by the marvels of twentieth-century stagecraft), are of fundamental importance for the success and development of seventeenth-century public opera (where they reproduce in miniature the production principle of maximum effect with minimum energy and expense). The musical and dramatic structure of the opera also reaps advantages from Torelli's agile changes of perspective (an extremely brief instrumental ritornello is now sufficient to divide and connect any two consecutive sequences of scenes); the new system is infinitely more versatile and practical than the complicated and ephemeral stage machinery and other expedients of court opera. As regards ownership: the scenes of a public opera, once used, revert to the impresario or come to form part of the regular props of the theatre concerned; after the necessary adjustments, they can subsequently be re-used.

As a whole, then, the 'productive structures' of Venetian theatres are fragile only in appearance; in reality they are solidly based and capable of expansion. These 'structures' lead to radical change both in artistic conventions and the expectations of the public. The seasonal continuity and regularity of opera, for example, not only comes to be seen on a level of social custom and collective need, but also represents a vital co-efficient for the recuperation of initial expenditure. Long-term contracts with composers and librettists ensure reasonable constancy of standards. Singers, on the contrary, are engaged on a season-to-season basis, and this leads to fierce competition among theatres in their efforts to assemble the most prestigious cast (virtuosi are engaged from throughout the Italian peninsula, and at times even abroad); in this sector, the free market conditions and resulting cost inflation leaves theatres in grave financial straits. Half of the budget for a typical Venetian *dramma per musica* of the 1650s is absorbed by the musical expenses alone; a leading singer earns double the fee of Cavalli (himself the best-paid composer on the market). As the century wears on, the balance shifts even further to the advantage of the virtuoso performers. Over and above the costs of contracts and production, however, management and orchestral expenses are minimal (the orchestra, indeed, consists of less than ten instrumentalists), and every extra performance of the opera – even if played before half-empty houses – represents a 'plus' for the budget. Thus, in contrast to the limited number of performances (frequently one, and generally no more than three) of a typical court opera, a Venetian *dramma per musica* may run for ten, twenty or even thirty nights (some spectators are known to have been present at up to fifteen performances of a single opera). Particularly successful productions (Cavalli's *Giasone*, Cesti's *La Dori*) may subsequently be revived in an attempt to improve the standing of some financially precarious impresario. This, however, is the exception. Each theatre, in general, produces two new operas per season. In each, the cast is identical. The new operas presented in the course of a single Carnival season can number up to twelve! The inevitable result: market saturation, 'stylistic' levelling through overproduction, an increasingly sophisticated and – inevitably – ever less differentiated pattern of competition.

Rapidly changing taste necessitates a not inconsiderable adaptation of both music and text for all subsequent revivals; the 'life' of any one opera in the collective memory is in any case limited. Given such conditions of market abundance, the operatic tradition becomes one of substitution and rotation (not accumulation): in the public consciousness, the *drammi per musica* of any given season are literally replaced by the following season's new productions (whose salient characteristics are in any case fully analogous), which in turn are obliterated from memory by the *drammi* of the following year. In this series of fundamentally homologous products, the rate of innovation and obsolescence (in terms of the form of the arias, outlines of plots, uniqueness of subjects, etc.) does not alter what is an essentially stable horizon of experience and expectation: saturation is 'neutralized' by habituation. In short, the demand is for constant innovation – an innovation, however, which satisfies the same expectations as those of earlier *drammi* (the parallel with the modern film industry is not inappropriate). These conditions inevitably lead to productions of highly conventional hue (see chapter 23); equally wide, however, is the margin of choice in the application of these conventions (significantly, no *Corago* exists for the Venetian-style *dramma per musica*). Of notable importance is the choice of subject for the libretto; this is an area of great sensitivity to changing tastes and trends in public life. Roughly speaking, the salient tendencies are as follows.

In its earliest stages, public opera continues in its exploitation of the same mythological themes also popular at court: self-evident in this respect are such titles as *Andromeda* (Ferrari and Manelli, 1637), *Delia*

(Strozzi and Manelli, 1639), *Le nozze di Teti e di Peleo* (Persiani and Cavalli, 1639), *Adone* (Vendramin and Manelli, 1639), *Gli amori d'Apollo e di Dafne* (Busenello and Cavalli, 1640), *Amore innamorato* (Michiel – Fusconi and Cavalli, 1642), *La virtù de' strali d'Amore* (Faustini and Cavalli, 1642), *Bellerofonte* (Nolfi and Sacrati, 1642), *Narciso ed Eco immortalati* (Persiani and Vitali – Marazzoli, 1642), *Venere gelosa* (Bartolini and Sacrati, 1643). In Venice, however, still more than in Rome (whence comes a part of the artistic personnel), the Ovidian tradition no longer holds sway. It would be interesting to see just how much of the mythological tendencies of the early Venetian librettists is inspired by the poetry of Marino. The heroic and romantic world of Tasso and Ariosto is equally important as a source for the representation of those 'changes of affections' so loved by composers, as also for those marvels of seventeenth-century stagecraft which so enchant contemporary audiences: examples are *Armida* (Ferrari and Ferrari, 1639), *Bradamante* (Bissari and ?, 1650), *Medoro* (Aureli and Lucio, 1658). A local innovation concerns derivations from Homer, Virgil, Trojan mythology and the various stories and legends surrounding the origins and foundation of Rome. Scenic motives, too, are at work behind the choice of such plots: the very title of *Ulisse errante* (Badoaro and Sacrati: Teatro SS. Giovanni e Paolo, 1644) provides Giacomo Torelli with the perfect excuse for ostentation of a wide range of scenic panoramas – in flagrant violation of the Aristotelian unities of time and place. (In this respect, Italian librettists could appeal to no less an authority than Lope de Vega who, in a letter to the Florentine dramatist Jacopo Cicognini– published in 1633 – recommends the ordering of 'actions' in such a way as 'to cover the space not just of a day, but also of many months and even years; in this way, the various happenings of the story need not be narrated as earlier actions but can be enjoyed in their own right as temporally distinct': the dramaturgy of opera is based on the immediate, direct portrayal of events, not – as in classical drama – on their narrative evocation.) 'Trojan' interest, however, is fuelled above all by republican ideology: in this way, Venice can be portrayed as the modern reincarnation of the ancient republic of Rome, itself the direct descendant of Troy. Right from the apparently incongruous insertion of a 'Judgment of Paris' in the *Nozze di Teti* of 1639, Trojan references abound; this is true of *Il ritorno di Ulisse in patria* (Badoaro and Monteverdi, 1640), *Le nozze d'Enea con Lavinia* (? and Monteverdi, 1641) and *Didone* (Busenello and Cavalli, 1641). In *Didone*, the entire first act is given over to an account of the fall of Troy; only in Act 2 (which ideally takes place many decades later) do we find the protagonist on the shores of Carthage. *La finta pazza (*Strozzi and Sacrati, 1641) is quite explicit: 'The Venetian and the Roman / not from Greek Achilles must be born, / but of good Trojan blood'; the plot, interwoven as it is with a veritable host of ironic gestures, is that of Achilles in Scyros (one of the various antecedents of the Trojan war). The door is now open for the free creative use of the entire range of mythological and historical (classical) plots; this repertory, however, is now invariably poised on the edge of a carnival-like transfiguration to a kind of entertainment whose salient features are shrewdness and discernment. Little of Jason, Alcestis and Hercules remains behind their respective seventeenth-century adaptations: *Giasone* (Cicognini and Cavalli, 1649), *Antigona delusa da Alceste* (Aureli and Ziani, 1660), *Le fatiche d'Ercole per Deianira* (Aureli and Ziani, 1662); at most, the operatic versions conserve nothing but the generally epic flavour of their classical sources, in an effort to legitimize the most unlikely among the various 'likely events' artfully introduced by their librettists; forty years after the first performance of Rinuccini's *Euridice*, Tragedy is replaced as the protagonist of the Prologue by a personification of Caprice: 'Caprice am I, and you my / op'ra on this stage shall see, / of happ'nings full, / of actions sad then gay'.

This unconstrained use of classical models is not without ideological significance. The most brilliant librettists of the fifth decade of the century – Giulio Strozzi (adoptive father of the celebrated singer and composer Barbara Strozzi), Giovan Battista Fusconi, Maiolino Bisaccioni, Scipione Errico, Giacomo Badoaro, Giacinto Andrea Cicognini – are all members or regular frequenters of the Accademia degli Incogniti, a club of libertine intellectuals whose apparent praise of deceit in reality cloaks nothing but an underlying attitude of bitter philosophical scepticism, intolerant of all preconstituted authority (political, moral, rational, religious; in literary terms, the Incogniti profess themselves followers of Marino). The Incogniti would appear to have grasped more than anyone else the intellectual significance of the new, somewhat irregular and highly fashionable form of dramatic entertainment. Another celebrated member of the Academy is Gianfrancesco Busenello, himself librettist of *L'incoronazione di Poppea* (1643), set to music – according to certain later testimonies (contemporary sources make no mention whatever of the composer's name) – by Claudio Monteverdi. Only the pessimistic scepticism and subtle immoralism of the Incogniti can explain the fanciful yet disenchanted mockery of certain scenes of this opera: the imprecations of the two sentinels, who curse Nerone and his nocturnal conquests (the scene in question, which follows immediately upon the opening monologue of the secondary character Ottone, provides a realistically sinister commentary on what reveals itself to be a story of corruption and immorality; the two soldiers, moreover, have the extra function of informing the spectators of certain circumstances of importance in understanding the plot); the quarrel of Nerone and Seneca, who reproach each other in rapid line-by-line dialogue with excited syllabic declamation (precepts of an all-too-degraded political law); the empty solemnity of the dying philosopher Seneca, ridiculed by his disciples in a funeral ballet which is at once both joyful and grotesque; the far from flattering representation of the Empress Ottavia, who resorts to blackmail and other abuses of power in her efforts to induce Ottone to eliminate Poppea; the protagonists' second love duet, where the 'fervours of the burning soul, / in loving ecstasy transhumanized' (a 'loving ecstasy' enshrined with flagrant sensual truthfulness in the accompanying music), are revealed as a means of persuasion to homicide; and so on.

The reign of the fervid and caustic Incogniti is, however, short-lived in intellectual and operatic circles alike. For the remainder of the century, Venice is engaged in a long and exhausting war of defence against the Turkish foe. Beginning in the early 1650s, certain common objectives and shared strategic interests with the Empire are reflected in the heroic and 'imperial' themes of the *drammi per musica*: *Alessandro vincitor di se stesso* (Sbarra and Cesti, 1651), *Gli amori di Alessandro Magno e di Rosanne* (Cicognini and Lucio, 1651), *Scipione Africano*, *Muzio Scevola* and *Pompeo Magno* (Minato and Cavalli, respectively 1664, 1665 and 1666) are all early examples of a veritable flood of ancient histories and bellicose heroes which follow each other virtually without interruption for the remainder of the century. Despite a wide margin for epic freedom, the dominant themes in Venetian public theatre are now the venerable spirit of ancient Rome, the military glories of Persia and Babylon, the nobility of soul of the barbarian commanders, the thoroughly tameable ferocity of tyrants – not, however, without ample excursions into the tempting realms of the 'vice of Venus', at least at those times when this is tolerated by the policy of 'free reign to all those things which the State do not offend'.

22 The diffusion of opera in Italy

Not many years will pass before the economic and artistic structure of Venetian opera has spread throughout the Italian peninsula, firmly – and lastingly – establishing the *dramma per musica* as the dominant contemporary form of theatrical entertainment. Opera, in fact, soon comes to represent the only form of entertainment (and, for that matter, of literary production) both cultivated on a national scale and accessible to a public that is not exclusively intellectual. (This is not to say however, that the seventeenth-century *dramma per musica* possesses the national and popular characteristics ascribed by Antonio Gramsci in his prison notebooks to nineteenth-century opera, itself the true Italian 'market' equivalent of the French and English popular novel. This is demonstrated by the exclusiveness of seventeenth-century audiences. Yet the distant origins of the phenomenon observed by Gramsci lie precisely in the exportation and establishment of mid-seventeenth-century 'Venetian' opera in the various cities of Italy). The 'structure' of commercial and public opera must and/or authority) and 'public-ness'. The extent of this 'publicity' may classes; yet, in contrast to all other forms of production of contemporary musical theatre, this 'structure' is intrinsically capable of adaptation to social and political conditions of radically differing complexion (by the end of the century, in fact, court theatres in general have come to adopt the impresarial model, with the sole addition of a sovereign power disposed to make good all financial loss) and tolerates – indeed, invites – the participation of the middle classes (all the more willingly in view of the relatively minor economic significance of the latter). Having, then, banished once and for all the highly improbable idea of the out-and-out 'popularity' of seventeenth-century opera, the salient ideological and social function of the latter emerges more clearly: namely, that of active, dynamic 'publicity' (see chapter 11), in its dual conception of propaganda (the public manifestation of power and/or authority) and 'public-ness'. The extent of this 'publicity' may vary from one case to another; the nature of the operation involved, however, is the same.

The phenomenon of a public form of cultural production and consumption, valid both geographically and (potentially, at least) socially for the nation as a whole, might today seem of little significance when compared with the 'unified' cultural history of modern Italy. Significant, however, it becomes if one stops to consider the prevailing political conditions of seventeenth-century Italy and the disparity of social structure between its various component States. A list of those States which in some way or other are involved in the operatic life of the day will suffice to give some idea of the unfavourable nature of socio-political conditions for the development of a truly national theatrical network such as that of the *dramma per musica*. These, from north to south (with their administrative and cultural capitals), are as follows: the duchy of Savoy (Turin), the Spanish dominion of Milan, the republics of Genoa and Venice (Venetian territories extend from Bergamo as far eastwards as Dalmatia), the duchies of Mantua, Parma and Piacenza, Modena and Reggio Emilia, the Grand Duchy of Tuscany (Florence, Pisa, Livorno, Siena), the principality of Massa, the republic of Lucca, the Papal States (Rome, Bologna, Ancona, Ferrara, Ravenna, Pesaro, Macerata) and, finally, the kingdoms of Naples and Sicily (Palermo, Messina), ruled by two Spanish viceroys.

The mechanics behind the creation of a nationally-based operatic 'system' may be best understood through consideration of the various types of compromise to which 'Venetian-style' opera is subjected in its contacts with pre-existing local traditions (themselves very largely – though not uniformly – eliminated and replaced: in Parma, Modena and Turin, a pre-existing court 'theatrical' tradition offers tenacious resistance until 1670 and beyond), and, still more, through examination of the various uses to which the 'original' model is bent. The unification of the operatic market does not imply *ipso facto* the unification of the various meanings which the same entertainment may assume. Any given opera – a good example is *Giustino* (Beregan and Legrenzi, 1683: the story of a peasant made warrior, prefect and, finally, emperor of Byzantium), performed with identical music and text first at Venice, then Naples – can assume a number of quite different meanings: the exaltation of the heroic ideals of defence of the fatherland (Venice), the glorification of the institution of the monarchy (Naples). The additional Prologue for the Neapolitan production, itself staged in honour of the sovereign Charles II, is such as would have induced even the most insensitive of spectators to a pro-monarchical interpretation of the text: Nino (King of Assyria), Cyrus (King of Persia), Alexander (King of Macedonia) and Caesar Augustus contend with each other for primacy in stateliness and majesty, but finally fall prostrate before an apparition of the King of Spain, himself seated upon the four continents and observed from above by a personification of Monarchy. It is, moreover, legitimate to suspect that market unification was aided at times by a certain degree of 'indifference' in the reception of opera, a selective mental perception more heedful of vocal and scenic allurements than of the cultural and ideological meanings embedded in the drama itself; with the consequent vagueness of the average spectator's horizon of expectations, the political and social heterogeneity of seventeenth-century Italy can have acted as little obstacle indeed to the diffusion of the *dramma per musica*.

It is not always easy to establish the precise meaning – itself, as noted, variable from occasion to occasion – of the numerous adaptations, alterations and 'modernizations' imposed on the music and text of certain *drammi per musica* in their wanderings from one city to another. Changes are frequently justified only vaguely in the prefaces to the librettos as the necessary adjustments 'for the use of our theatre', 'for current use' or in accordance with the custom of some particular town. Sometimes, these declarations are nothing but pretexts for changes of wholly fortuitous nature (the substitution of one singer for another, the reduction or extension of a role, the insertion or removal of comic scenes, the addition or suspension of scenes in accordance with difficulties or other necessities of staging and production, etc.); on other occasions, they must undoubtedly be seen as reflections of local theatrical practices and traditions which crystallize in a 'taste' that is shared by the entire public of any given city. Significant in this latter context are the Venetian revivals of works originally conceived and produced in cities other than Venice; in certain cases, the so-called 'adaptation' can literally involve the complete rewriting of the *dramma*. An excellent example is the 'festa teatrale' *Ercole in Tebe* (an old-style court opera in every sense of the word), first staged in Florence for the Medici wedding festivities of 1661 and revived ten years later at Venice as a straightforward *dramma per musica*: alterations include a reduction from five acts to three, the abolition of the *intermedi*, elimination of the stage machinery and divinities, the reduction of the recitatives and a corresponding increase in the number of arias, the levelling out of the original mythological plot in accordance with a 'civic realism' more in keeping with Venetian tradition (though inevitably incompatible at times with the original text). Whatever the case, the history of the diffusion of opera – intact or revised – as an artistic phenomenon is a story of singular versatility and a notable capacity for the satisfaction of a wide range of different expectations. Roughly speaking, three different – though overlapping – phases may be discerned. The first is dominated by the activities of the itinerant troupes, the second by the permanent institution of regular city theatres, the third (late on in the century) by the rule of the great virtuoso performers.

The 'seasonal' organization of opera at Venice leaves the singers unoccupied for some nine months of the year. During the two months of Carnival, however, Venice is more than ever a cosmopolitan city: among the enormous influx of persons who visit the city for business and pleasure are the foreign princes, themselves potential promoters of parallel theatrical initiatives elsewhere. In 1641, for example, Mattias de' Medici (brother of the Grand Duke of Tuscany) witnesses for himself 'all these sung comedies, five in all', with music by Cavalli, Ferrari, Monteverdi and Sacrati; five years later, as governor of Siena, he launches a first attempt at opera in the Tuscan city; ten years later, he initiates a period of intense 'trading' of singers and composers between Florence and Venice. Likewise, the network of literary scholars in some way connected with the Accademia degli Incogniti extends outwards from Venice and leads during the fifth decade of the century to an all-pervading dissemination of interest in the dramatic art of the Venetian librettists (the *dramma per musica* is fully represented in the first systematic bibliography of Italian theatre, the *Drammaturgia*, 1666, of the Vatican librarian Leone Allacci, himself a member of the Accademia degli Incogniti). In short, all the necessary conditions exist for the out-of-season departure of groups of singers from Venice for the various cities of northern Italy, and the revival here of the same entertainments already given in Venice. At Bologna, *Delia* and *Il ritorno di Ulisse* are restaged in 1640 by the Ferrari–Manelli consortium; the following year, the same company produces *La maga fulminata* and *Il pastor regio*. Ferrari, again, would appear to have been responsible for the earliest documented productions at Genoa, *Delia* and *Egisto* (Faustini and Cavalli, 1645); he also appears at Milan in 1646 for performances of *Delia* and *Il pastor regio*. Though company personnel may vary, the repertory itself is stable. One other frequent guest on the operatic circuit is *La finta pazza* (1641) of Strozzi and Sacrati, revived at Piacenza in 1644 by the 'Accademici Febiarmonici' and at Bologna three years later by the 'Accademici Discordati'. These same somewhat curious denominations subsequently appear at the head of a variety of groupings which, in the years immediately ahead, produce Venetian-style operas in a large number of different centres; components of one or other of these groupings can be found at Genoa in 1644, Florence (*La finta pazza*) and Lucca in 1645, Genoa and Florence (*Egisto*) in 1646, Genoa (*La finta pazza*), Bologna (*Egisto*, *La finta pazza*, *Gli amori d'Apollo e di*

Dafne) and Milan in 1647, Bologna (*La virtù de' strali d'Amore*), Turin, Reggio Emilia (*La finta pazza*), Ferrara (*Egisto*) and Rimini (*Egisto*) in 1648, Milan (*Giasone*) in 1649, Lucca (*Giasone* and other productions) in 1650, Naples (*Didone*) in 1650, 1651 (*Egisto*, *Giasone* and *L'incoronazione di Poppea*, the latter under the alternative title of *Nerone*) and 1652 (*La finta pazza*), Genoa (*Didone*) in 1652 – the list is undoubtedly incomplete. Meanwhile, Manelli accepts a permanent position at the court of Parma and produces there a series of festive court operas. Ferrari, on the contrary, perseveres in his wanderings, with productions of his works old and new at Piacenza, Bologna, Vienna and Modena; only at Modena does he finally cast anchor. The 'Febiarmonici' phenomenon – itself a perfect carbon-copy of the itinerant *commedia dell'arte* tradition – is of notable dimensions. Indicative of the profound and lasting effect of these productions is the very use of the term 'Febiarmonici', which in several cities – in particular, Naples, Genoa, Turin and Milan – long continues in local usage as a synonym for 'the singers'. This remains true even after the institution of permanent theatres.

The circulation of Venetian *drammi per musica* in the 'baggage' of itinerant singers and theatrical architects is a phenomenon of considerable importance. It is in this context of continual use, re-use and constant interaction with the differing requirements of stage and public that the *dramma in musica* and its various theatrical conventions develop and mature. Particularly instructive is the case of *L'incoronazione di Poppea*. Two scores of this opera have survived (one in Venice, the other in Naples), both somewhat removed from the text of the original production (Venice, 1643); both, in fact, exhibit much closer correspondence to the text of the 'Febiarmonici' revival in Naples in 1651. One of the two manuscripts formed part of the private library of Cavalli and shows clear signs of alterations in his hand: it is thus quite within the bounds of possibility that Cavalli was employed by one or other of the itinerant companies of singers as reviser of the original score. Conversely, the surviving score of Sacrati's *La finta pazza* (in its 'Febiarmonici' version of 1644 and following) opens with two *sinfonie* identical to those in the third finale of *Poppea*. These circumstances, however, are of little assistance in resolving the even more awkward problems of attribution regarding what is perhaps the most distinctive and unusual scene of the entire opera (and today justly famous): the love duet of Nerone and Poppea. While both scores conclude with this duet, it is nevertheless absent from the Venetian performance of 1643, where 'Nerone solemnly looks on at the coronation of Poppea who, in the name of the people and Senate of Rome, is crowned by consuls and tribunes; Cupid, in similar fashion, descends from the skies (accompanied by Venus, the Graces and cupids) and crowns Poppea as goddess of beauty on earth; and the opera ends.' The dual coronation, then, heavenly and earthly, of the protagonist. Both scores, on the contrary, replace the concluding chorus of cupids and the celestial coronation of Poppea with the pure, infectious, highly sensual and erotic ecstasy of the love duet: 'Pur ti miro / Pur ti godo / Pur ti stringo / Pur t'annodo / . . . '. The musical authorship of this explicit, disquieting yet captivating triumph of sensual love – a love which, right from the beginning of the *dramma*, victoriously prevails over moral and political decorum and which, in the closing duet, finds a passionate musical counterpart and symbol – is contested by no fewer than four different composers. Though apparently absent from the Venetian production of 1643, the 'Poppea' duet had already appeared as the final number in Benedetto Ferrari's *Il pastor regio* – not, however, in the original Venetian production of 1640, but in a Bolognese revival of 1641 (and subsequent revivals). The same ubiquitous duet appears upon the 'musical chariot' *Il trionfo della fatica*, staged during the Roman Carnival of 1647 with music by Filiberto Laurenzi. A native of the region of Romagna (east of Bologna), but Roman by training, Laurenzi had already been accompanied in his travels from Rome to Venice (1640) by his pupil Anna Renzi, greatest virtuoso soprano of her day; in the *Incoronazione di Poppea* of 1643, Renzi sings the supporting role of Ottavia. Laurenzi himself produces a number of theatrical compositions for Venice, with performances in the same theatre and season as the première of *Poppea*. The possibility of some direct involvement in *Poppea* itself cannot thus be excluded. Perhaps, moreover, he was acquainted with Benedetto Ferrari or with the Venetian singers in the Bolognese *Pastor regio* of 1641. To which (if any) of these composers, then, can be attributed the addition of the celebrated duet to the final scene of the opera? And when? At Venice, or at the time of the Neapolitan performances of 1651 (the latter, perhaps, produced by Cavalli)? Or, indeed, on the occasion of some intervening 'Febiarmonici' production of which all trace is now lost? Who, in short, is the author of this enchanting, seductive yet mysterious duet: Monteverdi (the most likely composer of the 1643 *Poppea*), or – more probably – Ferrari, Laurenzi or Cavalli? Or Francesco Sacrati, who in his *Finta pazza* sets a trio on the very same ground bass? In the present state of research, definitive replies are impossible: the modern listener has no certainties beyond those of the pervasive vocal and erotic delights of the music itself. It is, indeed, instructive to reflect on the somewhat modest significance of questions of attribution in the context of a form of production (such as that of mid-seventeenth-century opera) which is by very nature 'collective'. Equally, we may observe how the effect of the duet in question, when placed at the end of a story of pastoral love (*Il pastor regio*) or moral allegory (*Il trionfo della fatica*), is quite different from its effect as the vocal 'apotheosis' to a love such as that of Poppea and Nerone with its ever-present themes of adultery, unfaithfulness, threatened suicide, disguise, attempted murder, repudiation and exile of opponents. The identity of the author, in fact, is of little importance; what really matters is that *this* piece at *this* very moment of *this* drama is nothing short of a true *coup de théâtre* – even if due, maybe, to the wayward whims of some anonymous 'Feboarmonico'.

This initial, 'itinerant' phase in the fortunes of seventeenth-century opera is followed after the middle of the century by the institution of permanent public theatres in the principal cities and towns of the Italian peninsula. Eloquent testimony of the magnitude of this phenomenon is provided by the extraordinarily long-lasting success of certain operas. A case in point is *Giasone* (Cicognini and Cavalli: Venice, 1649). Examination of the librettos (which, in the present context, constitute the principal source of documentation) show that performances of this opera frequently coincide with the opening or earliest years of regular theatrical activity in the centres concerned: Milan 1649, Florence 1650, Lucca 1650, Naples 1651 (revived in 1652 and 1653), Bologna 1651, Milan c. 1652, Piacenza 1655, Palermo 1655, Livorno 1656–57, Vicenza 1658, Ferrara 1659, Genoa 1661, Ancona 1665, Venice 1666, ?Siena 1666, ?Brescia 1667, Reggio Emilia 1668, Rome 1671, Naples 1672, Bologna 1673, Bergamo *ante* 1676, Rome 1678 (private performance with marionettes), Genoa 1681 (with the title *Il trionfo d'Amor nelle vendette*), ?Genoa 1685, Brescia 1690 (entitled *Medea in Colco*). Thirty years after the first performance of *Giasone* the basic pattern is still closely analogous; *Il Vespesiano* (1678), inaugural drama of the Teatro S. Giovanni Grisostomo and the first of a lengthy series of operas composed by Carlo Pallavicino for this very theatre, is subsequently revived at Genoa (1680 and 1692), Venice (1680), Ferrara (1682 and 1687), Milan (1685), Modena (1685), Parma (1689), Fabriano (1692, in a production partially imported from Parma), Livorno (1693), Rome (1693), Crema (1694), Bologna (1695) and Naples (1707).

By 1678 (date of the first performance of *Il Vespesiano*), the strictly binary organization of the *dramma per musica* into arias and recitatives permits the free substitution of the former (both music and text) without necessary alteration of the latter; in certain cases, the musical setting is subjected to thoroughgoing revision without prejudice to the dramatic action. This principle is already clearly present in mid-seventeenth-century opera (as, indeed, in *Giasone*), where, however, it is not yet 'exclusive': in a number of scenes, the aria–recitative relationship is still much more subtle and fluid and thus little susceptible to manipulation (a case in point – again from *Giasone*, where it forms the effective climax to the opera – is the enchantment scene of Medea, celebrated among contemporaries and frequently imitated and parodied in the comic scenes of other operas of the time); these scenes are designed for a permanent place in the opera in question. In any case, it is surely not an exaggeration to speak of the enormous contribution of these and similar *drammi* to the formation of a 'taste', a level of audience expectation which might be regarded as valid for the Italian peninsula as a whole.

Within this overall picture, however, certain local characteristics emerge. In Naples, for example, the institution of a permanent theatre has clearly political implications. Count d'Oñate, restoration viceroy after the Neapolitan revolt of 1647–48, introduces the Febiarmonici in a theatre which, though adjacent to the Royal Palace, is also open to the public; on his initiative, Naples celebrates the suppression of the anti-Spanish revolt of Barcelona (1652) with the performance of a new Venetian opera, *Veremonda l'amazzone d'Aragona* (Strozzi and Cavalli) – a light-hearted yet thoroughly transparent allegory on the supremacy of the Spanish crown over its various territories and provinces. From the very beginning, opera in Naples is exploited as a public demonstration of viceregal supremacy, consciously aimed at those very classes of society – i.e., city and court – on which the power of the Spanish viceroy, in his opposition to the feudal aristocracy, is effectively based (this, indeed, is true until the final years of the régime). This situation emerges all the more clearly in 1654, with the opening of the public theatre of S. Bartolomeo to operatic performances. Frequently, dual productions are held: at court for the viceroy, at S. Bartolomeo for the citizens; by the end of the century, the interest of the authorities in the health of public opera at Naples has reached such proportions that the Viceroy Medinaceli can assume personal control of the management of S. Bartolomeo and summon from Parma the theatrical architect Ferdinando Galli Bibiena with the aim of effecting a complete modernization of the now aging stage. The Medinaceli era sees the production at Naples of several operas subsequently destined to achieve enormous success: examples are *Il trionfo di Camilla regina de' Volsci* (Stampiglia and Bononcini, 1696), *La caduta de' decemviri* (Stampiglia and Alessandro Scarlatti, 1697), *La Partenope* (Stampiglia and Mancia, 1699). Prior to this date the repertory is largely dominated by imports from Venice; 'home-grown' Neapolitan *drammi* are few and far between and enjoy very limited success outside Naples itself. Not even the arrival in 1683 of the young Alessandro Scarlatti (1660–1725) with the retinue of the former Spanish ambassador to Rome – now Neapolitan viceroy – has any appreciable effect on the firmly Venetian orientation of operatic life in the southern capital – this despite the fact that Scarlatti already enjoyed a somewhat precocious reputation as a brilliant theatrical composer. His role, prior to the arrival of Medinaceli, is mainly that of supervising the musical aspects of imported productions and composing new arias and comic scenes.

In Florence, Cardinal Giovanni Carlo de' Medici (brother of the Grand Duke of Tuscany) personally supervises theatrical activities at court; Giovanni Carlo is also the promoter of the luxurious but short-lived and financially ruinous 'experiment' of the Teatro della Pergola (1657–61), a 'mixed' academic/impresarial type of theatre (under the management of the aristocratic Accademia degli Immobili) whose total productions amount to nothing but two grand mythological operas with stage machines (Cavalli's *Ipermestra*, commissioned for the inauguration of the theatre in 1654 but repeatedly postponed for technical reasons and finally performed only in 1658; and *Ercole in Tebe* of 1661, with music by Jacopo Melani) and a brief series of 'drammi civili rusticali', complete with comic characters whose language makes ample and picturesque use of the local Tuscan dialect (one such example is Melani's *Potestà di Colognole*); librettist of all these productions is the academician Giovanni Andrea Moniglia. It is perhaps not without significance that alongside this vain attempt to create a 'home-grown' theatre which would be capable of competing on a level with Venice, the Medici also patronize the more modest but efficient theatrical establishment of the bourgeois Accademia dei Sorgenti; this commercially-based theatre, with its productions of normal Venetian-style operas by Cavalli, Cesti, Ziani, etc., enjoys a certain economic success.

At Milan, wholly Venetian is the repertory of the local Teatro Ducale (one would-be 'first performance' – Cavalli's *Orione* of 1653 – is nothing but an earlier opera originally commissioned for Venice but never performed). The short-lived attempt of Count Vitaliano Borromeo to establish a summer theatre on Isola Bella c.1669–1673) gives rise to some of the most subtle and entertaining librettos of the entire seventeenth century. The author of these texts is Carlo Maria

Maggi, secretary to the Senate of Milan; Maggi is also the adapter of the 'imported' *drammi per musica* for the Teatro Ducale. His works, with their many allusions to real events in the everyday life of the capital (as also to the life of their author), were destined to enjoy no circulation whatever outside Milan. This was also the fate of Maggi's dialect comedies (without music), written in the 1690s for the Collegio dei Nobili; though Milanese dialect is not a feature of Maggi's *drammi per musica*, it does appear in one or two roles of the earlier *Farsa musicale*, written in 1664 by a comic singer whose declared models were the 'drammi rusticali' of Moniglia given at the Florentine Teatro della Pergola (where he himself had performed).

Besides the various differences between the cities of the 'Venetian' circuit, there are also some outright anomalies: many cities (above all, the ducal centres of Parma, Modena and Turin, and the university towns of Pisa, Padua, Pavia and Catania) adhere only belatedly to the Venetian-based system; in other cases, the very concept of a 'permanent' theatre finds little favour (this is true of Fabriano, Viterbo, Foligno and many other provincial centres; it is also evident at Mantua, a dukedom which, though in grave political crisis, is nevertheless rich in great virtuosi, themselves patronized by the duke and active in the principal theatres of Italy); lastly, there is the case of Rome, where the conditioning of Papal cultural policy – a policy which changes with every new Papal succession, frequently with detriment to theatrical life – long mitigates against the introduction of a form of production which, as noted above, survives only in conditions of guaranteed stability and continuity. The artistically successful Teatro Tordinona – a Venetian-style public theatre, patronized by Christina of Sweden and guided by a brilliant team which comprised the talented impresario Filippo Acciaiuoli, the elderly librettist Giovanni Filippo Apolloni (charged with the revision of 'imported' texts) and the young Bernardo Pasquini and Alessandro Stradella (with responsibility for the musical aspects of the production) – opens from 1671 to 1674, closes (in common with all Roman theatres) for Holy Year 1675, and subsequently fails to re-open on account of the stiff opposition of Innocent XI to theatre in general. With this one brief exception, Rome remains wholly (or largely) apart from the influence of the Venetian *dramma per musica* – at least, until 1683. In this year, the formation of the Holy anti-Ottoman League between Rome, Venice, Poland and the Austrian Empire connects the two great Italian capitals in an objective sharing of ideological interests. Beginning in 1683, 'Venetian-style' operas of Venetian or Viennese origin are regularly produced in the theatres of Rome; these operas, with their new-found 'martial' or 'imperial' ideology (typical, as already noted, of late seventeenth-century 'Venetian' opera), are well suited to the expression of ideas of sovereignty and authority.

Before this date (as, indeed, after 1683), the necessarily intermittent operatic life of Rome is characterized by a wide variety of subject types. Two categories, however, prevail: operas derived from contemporary Spanish comedy, and Arcadian themes. Contrary to the affirmations of certain scholars, the direct influence of Spanish theatre on the Italian *dramma per musica* in general can be regarded as negligible (beyond, that is, such generic affinities as the highly irregular use of the Aristotelian unities of time, place and action, the incorporation of elements of a picturesque or moralistic nature, the mixture of 'high-' and 'low-born' characters); it is for this very reason that the Roman exceptions stand out so clearly. Originator and driving force behind these developments was probably – once again – Giulio Rospigliosi, who, on his return from Spain, produces two cloak-and-dagger musical comedies (*Dal male il bene* and *L'armi e gli amori*), respectively 1654 and 1656), based word for word on (non-musical) Spanish originals by Antonio Sigler de Huerta and Calderón de la Barca. Even after his election as Pope – his brief reign (1667–69) as Clement IX provides an enormous incentive for theatrical activities in Rome – Rospigliosi promotes the performance of a third 'Spanish' comedy (once again, to his own libretto); this time, however, the theme is essentially 'religious': *La comica del cielo*, taken from the *Gran comedia de la Baltasara* of Luis Vélez de Guevara, recounts the real-life conversion of a celebrated Spanish comic actress to a life of religious piety and devotion. (The curtain rises to reveal the stage of a comedy theatre where the actors are about to appear; the realization of this scene within a scene, however, is prevented by the sudden mystic crisis of the protagonist.) In musical terms, the lengthy yet highly flowing dialogue recitative of the comedies of Rospigliosi (set by Marco Marazzoli and Antonio Maria Abbatini) – which, with its almost prose-like fluency, is almost to be imagined more recited than sung – is interrupted only infrequently by a limited number of picturesquely rhythmic canzonettas. Spanish models, in Rome, are by no means restricted to comedies. Allegorical and mythological dramas – as, for example, *Ni Amor se libra de amor* by Calderón, recited in Spanish (with incidental music) at the Spanish embassy in Rome (1682) and subsequently adapted as *La Psiche* (Naples, 1683) by the Romans Giuseppe De Totis and Alessandro Scarlatti; or the colossal 'festa teatrale' *La caduta del regno dell'Amazzoni* (De Totis and Bernardo Pasquini, 1690), adapted from Antonio de Solis y Ribadeneira's *Las*

Amazonas de Scitia, and notable also by virtue of the presence of female singers (normally prohibited in Rome) and the splendid set design – provide the material for a series of memorable musical entertainments at Spanish quarters in Rome (the Spanish embassy, the Colonna family circle).

The so-called 'Arcadian' operas – the designation, however, is one of pure convenience, reflecting the preference of authors for pastoral subjects and their affiliation (real or ideal) to the Accademia d'Arcadia (founded in 1690) – make use of a limited number of characters (four, five or six); plots are 'adventure-loving' and fictitious, frequently with rural settings. Scenically, these operas are quite unpretentious, produced as they are on a limited budget by one or other of the various Roman cardinals or other princes – frequently in some hall or even garden as an evening's entertainment during Carnival or for the summer vacation in their summer estates. The pastoral 'aura' of these operas – themselves laid out as veritable *drammi per musica* – is quite unlike the *favole pastorali* of the early seventeenth century (see chapter 20), and (if anything) takes as its point of departure the process of 'feudalization' by which the various Papal families, having moved to Rome on account of the advancement of their members in the ecclesiastical/State hierarchy, put down roots through a series of land acquisitions and expansions. Conspicuous in this respect is the case of the Chigi family of Sienese bankers who, under the papacy of Alexander VII, acquire a variety of suburban territories; one of these localities, Ariccia, is rebuilt in the course of a very few years by the Papal architect Bernini and subsequently houses a series of *drammi per musica* which make explicit reference to the *genius loci*. Among the 'few-voiced' Carnival operas, particular mention is due to such operas as *Gli equivoci nel sembiante* (1679) and *L'onestà negli amori* (1680), both set to music by the young Scarlatti and destined to achieve enormous popularity in private and other 'minor' theatres from the Mazarino estates in southern Sicily (maximum point of southwards expansion of seventeenth-century opera) to the garden of the Ca' Altieri in Venice (sole seventeenth-century example of a Venetian – and, significantly, private – performance of Scarlatti). The key: their simplicity of staging and unfailing artistic effect.

Here, a short digression will be necessary to dispose of one of the various legends which appear here and there among the annals of operatic historiography: namely, the existence of a seventeenth-century 'opera comica'. Operas with comic subjects (i.e., operas laid out as comedies, not as heroic dramas) do exist; unlike eighteenth-century opera, however, these never come to represent any kind of unified tradition. In the seventeenth century, the sole continuous operatic tradition is that of the Venetian-style *dramma per musica*. In relation to this nation-wide public tradition, 'comic' operas (public or private) must be seen as deliberate attempts at highly localized variants, contrasting sharply with the cosmopolitanism of the Venetian export market. No direct relationship can be said to exist between these different local variants, which rely for their very *raison d'être* upon performance in their respective cities of origin. This, as already observed, is the case with Moniglia's librettos for Florence, Rospigliosi's cloak-and-dagger production at Rome, Maggi's contributions at Milan, and a large proportion of the 'feudal' operas of the Roman aristocracy; it is equally true of the 'action-packed' operas of Francesco Provenzale (*maestro di cappella* of the City of Naples), performed not at the 'official' city theatre but rather in occasional productions staged under the patronage of the Neapolitan aristocracy. In matters comic, the case of Naples is instructive: the birth of Neapolitan comic opera in the first decade of the Settecento – itself one of the decisive events in the creation of the entire eighteenth-century comic opera tradition – occurs as a 'particularist' initiative of the Neapolitan aristocracy in opposition to the heroic opera in vogue at court.

In the final two decades of the century, the uniform expansion of the operatic 'network' over Italy as a whole permits – indeed, brings about – a further homogenization of the repertory. Salient characteristic of this phase is the total supremacy of the aria, itself symptomatic of the now predominant role of the singers. This transpires from the very structure of the sources: more and more frequently, the names of the singers (and their illustrious patrons) are given in the librettos (previously, they are mentioned only rarely); more and more frequently, musical manuscripts contain only the arias of operas (often reduced for voices with *basso continuo* accompaniment) and not the works as a whole. The musical content of the *dramma* is identified ever more strongly with the sum of its various arias. Manuscripts of this type are destined for the domestic 'reproduction' of theatrical music and its celebrated arias; in this respect, their use coincides with that of the contemporary *cantata da camera*, itself a small-scale genre (solo or few-voiced with *basso continuo* and, at times, an occasional *obbligato* instrument) which, like opera, is based on the alternation of aria and recitative in settings of newly-invented poetic texts (monologues and dialogues). This is not to deny the existence of notable stylistic differences between the two genres in question: by virtue of its very destination as entertainment for a choice, refined and somewhat restricted circle of connoisseurs, the *cantata da camera* reveals a greater interest in compositional subtlety than in the attainment of great emotional effect (a feature more typical of the *dramma per musica*). In the theatre, even cantatas by opera composers such as Cesti, Marazzoli, Stradella and Scarlatti would fail to reveal their subtleties of poetic, melodic and harmonic invention in the vastness of the operatic public and stage. This, however, is not to deny the essential affinity in function and form between an operatic aria and a cantata aria. There do, indeed, exist a number of 'intermediate' cases: one such example is Bononcini's *Trionfo di Camilla*, a *dramma per musica* of essentially heroic complexion which contains a dozen arias 'borrowed' from an earlier 4-voice Arcadian-style *serenata* originally composed by Bononcini for Rome in 1696.

'Vehicles', so to speak, for the aria are the virtuoso performers, themselves the greatest attraction of the operatic stage; even the introduction of 'angle' or 'multiple focus' perspective by such architectural geniuses as Ferdinando Galli Bibiena is ultimately harnessed to the focussing of visual attention on the singers, whose performance from the centre of the proscenium is transformed as a dazzling centre of attraction. Dazzling, indeed, are the careers of the most successful virtuosi. The tenor Giovanni Buzzoleni appears at Mantua (1682), Milan (1683, 1684, 1686, 1687), Reggio (1684, 1686), Modena (1685, 1690), Crema (1689), Piacenza (1690, 1700), Venice (1690, 1691, 1693, 1703), Naples (1697, 1698), Genoa (1701): the list is undoubtedly incomplete. This is despite the fact that the seventeenth-century tenor is never a 'protagonist'. The soprano Margherita Salicola – herself one of the most celebrated singers of the Bolognese school (by far the most prolific 'school' of the period in question) – sings at Modena (1677), Bologna and Reggio (1679), Venice (1680), Mantua (1682), Reggio (1683) and Venice (1682, 1683, 1684, 1685). In Venice, she is noticed – in more ways than one – by the Elector of Saxony, who illicitly abducts her from her patron the Duke of Mantua and offers her a permanent engagement at the court of Dresden; she subsequently sings at Munich (1688) and – on her return to Italy under the successive patronage of the Dukes of Parma and Modena – Milan (1696), Modena (1697, 1698), Reggio (1697, 1698, 1699, 1701), Turin (1699), Vienna (1699), Piacenza (1700), Venice (1703, 1704, 1705) and Florence (1710). Such is the European-based reputation of Salicola that she is even cited (along with two other stars of the operatic stage: the castrato Francesco Pistocchi and the composer Carlo Francesco Pollarolo) in the text of the opera *Der Carnaval von Venedig*, set to music by Reinhard Keiser and performed in Hamburg in 1707.

Her fame is not without its 'worldly' implications. Leaving aside her 'abduction' to Dresden, the German traveller Adam Ebert – who made her acquaintance in 1680 – remarks that 'she could be had for a ducat; a ducat, together with a little box of confectionery, was quite sufficient to satisfy mother, father and little brother'. This is but one of the scores of such cases, which together provide ample documentation of the 'worldly' condition of the *prima donna* – a condition which undoubtedly pre-dates the rise of public opera. Writing from Rome in 1633, Fulvio Testi (in a letter to the Duke of Modena) notes as follows: 'If Your Highness seeks perfect honesty in his female singers, he should not look in this direction. Here the female singers permit themselves the odd licentious pleasure; and, in this way, many other ladies who [in reality] are [quite] unable to sing nevertheless become singers.' The seductive qualities of contemporary opera are doubtless further enhanced by this particular aspect of contemporary social life.

23 Formal and dramatic convention; the lament

In the eyes of eighteenth-century literary scholars, joint perpetrators of the worst aesthetic atrocities are those very singers and arias which, for spectators, represent the greatest source of delight. During the period 1670–1700, as also (in general terms) for the entire eighteenth century, the individual aria – seen in isolation from the context of the surrounding recitative dialogue – represents what might conveniently be described as the minimum 'semantic unit' on which authors, composers and spectators may legitimately focus their attention. The text of the aria is comprised of a limited number of verbal – poetic – images (expressed in the course of some ten lines of verse) and communicates a single homogeneous concept or affection; each aria, moreover, is endowed with its own individual and clearly defined musical physiognomy. Subdivision of the aria into its various component parts is tantamount to the reduction of an originally organic whole to the level of an inert and unrecognizable sequence of verbal and musical 'matter'. In other words: the reader should beware of all anatomical 'descriptions' and 'categorizations' of arias in accordance with stereotyped formal schemes (ABA, ABB′), as also of all would-be histories of opera which limit themselves to mere questions of musical form and analysis. Equally vain, moreover, are all attempts to read any deliberate intention or perceptible character of musical unity into the internal plan of the typical *dramma per musica* (which, as noted, is comprised of the sum of its various individual arias and recitatives). Beyond all questions of the greater or lesser persistence – intentional or unintentional – of personal styles in the work of each individual composer (styles, however, necessarily valid for more than one work of the composer concerned), the overall musical layout of the average *dramma per musica* is based on the principle of maximum variety. The task of the librettist is that of endowing the inevitable succession of arias with the greatest possible variety of colour and form; responsibility then passes to the composer, who attempts to confer a specific and differentiated musical physiognomy – melodic, rhythmic, stylistic – on each of the arias concerned. On the other hand, it has already been noted how every single aria of every single *dramma per musica* is potentially capable of substitution by any other aria whose content and meaning are not incompatible with the text of the drama. In musical terms, the overall 'semantic unit' is thus represented less by the original score of the composer (at most, an entity of essentially bibliographical significance) than by the particular production of the opera in question, with its own particular variants, interpolations and outright alterations. In short: the 'unit' of the aria and the 'unit' of the *dramma per musica* co-exist as independent and 'incommensurable' categories. The 'unit' of the individual aria is the 'objective' unit of a poetic and musical text; that of the *dramma per musica* is the empirical unit of a scenic and dramatic event.

Not analogy but subtle contrast is the key to the varied and discontinuous succession of arias, for which any convincing justification must be sought in the drama alone. In the hierarchy of roles, each character of equal rank will normally be accorded an equal number of arias of equally varying affection and general character (or, from the point of view of the spectator: quantity and variety of arias provide a useful yardstick by which to gauge the relative importance of any given character). The 'typology' of the arias is described by a large number of eighteenth-century observers. Noticeable is what can only be described as an unwavering heterogeneity of criteria – indiscriminately technical ('aria presta), vocal ('di bravura'), affective ('patetica', 'di sdegno'), stylistic ('parlante') or simply generic ('d'espressione') – which can hardly be seen as reflecting any authentic or binding system (dramaturgical, poetic, musical or whatever). Taken, nevertheless, at their face value (as empirical attempts to describe the distribution, character by character, of the various types of arias), the eighteenth-century writings can be regarded as equally valid for the late seventeenth-century *dramma per musica*.

In compositional terms, the characterization of the aria derives less from the melody than from metre and rhythm: this, indeed, represents the true point of union between textual elocution and musical structure. Resources are virtually unlimited, ranging from a maximum of rhythmic and metric regularity to a maximum of irregularity. An aria such as that from Act 1 of *Giasone* (Cicognini and Cavalli), in which a lustfully lethargic Giasone has just emerged from the sweet bed of Medea, artfully exploits the hypnotic accentual regularity of the six-syllable lines of the text (mirrored in the music by a rocking ternary rhythm); the result is a kind of perversely construed lullaby, sung by a protagonist who, if left to his own free will, would never cease to taste the sweet delights of slumber:

×	′	×	×	′	×
De-	li-	zie,	con-	ten-	ti
che	l'al-	ma	be-	a-	te,
fer-	ma-	te,	fer-	ma-	te!
Su	que-	sto	mio	co-	re
deh	più	non	stil-	la-	te
le	gio-	ie	d'a-	mo-	re!
De-	li-	zie	mie	ca-	re,
fer-	ma-	te-	vi	qui!	
Non	so	più	bra-	ma-	re,
mi	ba-	sta	co-	sì!	

(This is followed by a second strophe, metrically and musically identical to the first.) In the context of this all-pervading rhythmic regularity (accents occur on the second and fifth syllables of each line, i.e., every third syllable of text; syllable/note 1 of each textual and musical phrase is invariably an upbeat), the vocal part – which literally 'stops' on a long-held note at the words 'fer*ma*te, fer*ma*te' ('halt, halt'), while the instruments observe a bar of silence – represents a musical gesture of grand yet simple effect. Obviously, the six-syllable line is capable of different interpretations: for Metastasio, the strong caesura between the third and fourth syllables can be used as a favourite vehicle for painful and troubled affections (as in the following aria from *L'Olimpiade*: 'Se cerca, se dice: / "L'amante dov'è?", / "L'amico infelice", / rispondi "morì" '; 'If she seeks, and says: / "My beloved, where is he?" / "Unhappy friend" / you reply "He is dead" '); for Da Ponte, the six-syllable line can have idyllic or playful connotations ('Soave sia il vento'; 'Soft blow the wind' or 'Se a caso madama'; 'If, by chance, Madame'). In short: while each type of verse has a relatively limited number of standard rhythmic applications, this does not imply the existence of any rigidly predetermined affective context or contexts. At the opposite extreme to the aria from *Giasone* quoted above is one such as the following, where no less than five different poetic metres (ternary, five-syllable, seven-syllable *tronco*, decasyllabic, quadrisyllabic, decasyllabic *tronco*) are brought together in the space of six lines of text; this is mirrored in the music by a nervous, excited, trembling elocution, perfectly in keeping with the affection of erotic trepidation experienced in that particular moment by the character (in *Flavio Cuniberto*, music by Domenico Gabrielli, 1688):

Vedrai	You will see
ne' suoi bei rai	in its beautiful rays
diviso il sol scherzar.	the sun divided play.
In quel seno, in quel labbro, in quel volto,	In that breast, that lip, that face
sta raccolto	is wrapp'd
tutt'il bello per farsi adorar.	the beauty all, that she may be adored.
Vedrai *etc.*	You will see, *etc.*

The rhythmic *volte-face* of line 4, which introduces the hammering sonority of decasyllables and quadrisyllabic verse (fixed accents on syllables 3, 6 and 9, with double 'upbeat') is 'balanced' by the *da capo* repeat of the entire opening section. The *da capo*, as a formal expedient, has the effect of sealing the unity of the aria, especially when – as here – the antithesis between sections 'A' and 'B' is nothing but the musical representation of a single, essentially composite and ambivalent affection. No full understanding of the affective implications of an aria, however, is possible without consideration of its more general dramatic context; in the present example, it is the Queen who explicitly exhorts her august consort to admiration of the same beautiful and virtuous lady with whom she herself is secretly in love: thus, the aria also contains an implicit declaration – before both herself and the public – of her own unavowable love. Only this subtle interplay of 'nods and winks' can provide any adequate explanation for the innate affective inconstancy of metrical structure in a poetic text which, on first sight, might appear to contain a single, unequivocal affection. This shows that the connection between dramatic action and aria is more than just a fragile 'pretext' for music, and that it represents an essential element for the correct – and reciprocal – understanding of the opera and its contents.

Not all seventeenth-century Italian opera is governed by this rigid distinction between recitative and aria: the contrast between a musically conveyed dialogue and the musically 'organized' portrayal of a momentary affection. Only from the eighth decade of the century is this binary system dominant to the exclusion of almost every other form; this situation, however, is nothing but the extreme application of earlier dramatic and theatrical convention. Convention, perfect antidote to all aesthetic systems based on premisses of expressive authenticity and originality, represents an essential ingredient of all theatrical communication: a tacit agreement, stipulated between author, actors and spectators, by means of certain commonly accepted signs and theatrical codes. For a full understanding of the active 'dynamic' role of dramatic convention, it is necessary to establish some general cultural terms of reference: the 'horizons of expectation', the preconceptions brought by the public to any given operatic entertainment (the ability of opera to produce a highly conventional and repetitive horizon of expectations has already been illustrated in chapter 21).

Prior to the point at which the aria gains total supremacy, the minimum 'semantic unit' of an opera – i.e., the smallest 'meaningful' segment on which the spectators may focus their attention – can be various in kind. One possibility, now as later, is the individual aria: the earliest operas already contain a number of 'detachable' arias, the use of which is actually recommended by the theorists under certain conditions (see, for example, the *Corago*, chapter 20). From the very beginning, the librettist is faced with the task of justifying and in some way providing motivation for the insertion of this somewhat 'extraneous' musical body in the midst of a continuous dialogue – in short, the momentary suspension of scenic events. In mid-seventeenth-century opera, however, the individual character or role may constitute an autonomous unit. This, above all, is true of comic roles, unfettered as they are by participation in decisive moments of the action or by limitations of a significant place in the hierarchy of the serious roles. These characters, indeed, remain somewhat apart; as 'comedians,', they enjoy something of an 'extra-territorial' status. In the hands of specialized singers they become truly ubiquitous: it is, perhaps, the theatrical talent of a single actor which leads to the fashion for stammering hunchbacks in Venetian operas of the period 1648–52 (*Giasone* included); Arnalta, in *Poppea*, is the first example of the shrewd and lustful elderly woman (ever-present for the remainder of the century), sung as a caricature role by specialized 'transvestite' tenors; even such high-standing theatres as the Teatro S. Giovanni Grisostomo allow themselves the attraction of a 'routine' comic actor – Tomaso Bovi, for example, is active uninterruptedly at S. Giovanni Grisostomo from 1678 to 1700 – for *buffo* roles (themselves standardized even so far as their names: Bleso, Lesbo, Zelto, Gildo, Leno, etc.). The conventional repertory of comic gags, the common morality of the gnomic *ariette*, the margin presumably allowed for clownish improvisation: all these factors would tend to locate the roles in question in the familiar tradition – familiar, at least, to every seventeenth-century spectator – of the *commedia dell'arte* with its professional yet invariably exhilarating effects. Professional specialization in individual roles, together with the interchangeability of comic scenes as a whole (freely transferable from one entertainment to another), will eventually lead – in the period around 1700 – to the detachment of comic episodes from the main body of the *dramma per musica*. (Untenable in this respect are the theories of eighteenth-century literary scholars, who – whether out of *esprit de corps* or by reason of a somewhat myopic critical stance – attribute the detachment of the comic scenes to motives of classical purgation and the deliberate initiative of one of their number, Apostolo Zeno.)

A significant unit may also be formed from a sequence of two or more scenes, united by a single scenography or set. A scenic characterization can be made to prevail over its various component units (musical or literary): on the appearance of a particular type of scene, certain conventional expectations (musical and dramatic) are conjured up in the minds of spectators, who can thus already look forward to the ballets of devils in hell, the vocal caresses of 'scenes of delight', the plaintive monologues which emanate from 'horrid prisons', etc. Finally, certain conventional dramatic situations may also be accorded the status of autonomous units: the lament of the male or (more frequently) female protagonist, the invocation of some 'other-world' spirit, the love scene with duet, the lullaby and slumber (with or without visualized dream), etc. Sufficient for present purposes will be a brief examination of one such stereotype: the lament, veritable 'tear-jerker' (to cite a term more appropriate in the context of nineteenth-century opera than for Monteverdi, Cavalli and their successors) of a not inconsiderable number of *drammi per musica*. It will be shown how the various intersections and juxtapositions of heterogeneous literary and cultural terms of reference and multiple forms of musical and dramatic perception contribute to the definition of a conventional scene.

A convenient point of departure is provided by two similar yet dissimilar works by Monteverdi: the *Lamento d'Arianna* and the *Lamento della Ninfa*. One is an original operatic scene (climax to the Mantuan *Arianna* of 1608) which also, however, goes on to enjoy an enormous success as a chamber cantata; the other might be described as a veritable cantata: an *aria da camera* which, though published as part of a collection of madrigals (Monteverdi's Book 8, 1638), is actually written 'in genere rappresentativo' ('in theatrical style': significant in this respect is the author's prescription that the *Lamento della Ninfa* 'be sung in time to the affections of the soul, not to those of the hand'). Both these laments, in their own different ways, are prototypes of what will subsequently become a veritable flood of seventeenth-century theatrical laments. Both are settings of texts by Ottavio Rinuccini; in origins, literary configuration and musical structure, however, both are totally different. Different, too, are the cultural traditions to which they belong and those which they are instrumental in creating.

The effect of the *Lamento d'Arianna* was indeed enduring (even towards the middle of the century, it can still be said that 'there has not been any house with theorbos or harpsichords which did not also possess the lament' of Arianna) and profound ('of the ladies', notes the chronicler of the first performance, 'not one did not shed some little tear at the lament'). Surviving musical sources provide ample testimony as to its fortunes. Originally published as a 5-part polyphonic madrigal (Book 6, 1614), it first appears as a monody only in 1623, in an edition which also includes the two 'lettere amorose in genere rappresentativo' of Book 7. The monodic version, however, must previously have circulated widely in manuscript form: this can be inferred from the fact that the music of the *Lamento d'Arianna* was also published anonymously in 1623, in an anthology of monodies by an obscure organist from Orvieto. The *Lamento d'Arianna* is also a frequent guest among the pages of manuscript collections of music for solo voice – often in the company of other chamber laments of similar complexion. Early examples are as follows: a Roman manuscript of c.1614 (now housed in Venice), which also contains a *Lamento d'Erminia* to words by Tasso; a Modenese manuscript of c.1623; a Florentine manuscript, which also contains music for a number of the lines immediately following the lament in Rinuccini's libretto (and which must thus be regarded as the closest of all extant manuscript sources to the original operatic version); a manuscript in the former possession of Luigi Rossi (now in London), which also contains a *Lamento d'Olimpia* (an imitation, in blank verse, of an episode from Ariosto) incautiously ascribed to Monteverdi in a contemporary hand. Later sources are as follows: a sacred Latin paraphrase (the *Pianto della Madonna sopra il lamento d'Arianna*), published by Monteverdi himself in his *Selva morale* of 1641; a further sacred parody, a vernacular *Lamento della Maddalena* contained in a Roman manuscript (compiled in the fifth decade of the century and now housed in Bologna) of music for performance during Holy Week (this paraphrase of Monteverdi's lament may well be identical to a 'complaint of St Mary Magdalene' whose famous performance by Loreto Vittori was celebrated by a Roman writer in 1645; Vittori included a further paraphrase of the lament in his *Dialoghi sacri e morali* of 1652); a second *Lamento della Maddalena sopra quel d'Arianna*, contained in a Neapolitan manuscript (today in Bologna) compiled sometime after 1646. This latter date can be established from the text of another lament in the same collection: the *Lamento del re di Tunisi*, an account of the real-life conversion of a Moslem prince to Christianity (itself magnificently celebrated by the Jesuits at Palermo, 1646); this same event is the subject of a further (and similar) *Lamento della principessa di Tunisi*, published in 1649 with words and music by Loreto Vittori. Towards mid-century, in fact, the 'political' *lamento da camera* begins to prosper: Luigi Rossi's *Lamento della regina di Svezia* (*ante* 1641) for the death of Gustavus Adolphus is based on one of the crucial events of the Thirty Years War; Giacomo Carissimi's *Lamento della regina Maria di Scozia*, to words by Giovanni Filippo Apolloni, was written after 1650 at a time when the bloody events of the English Civil War had once again focussed attention on the theme of regicide (likewise evoked in a contemporary *Lamento della regina d'Inghilterra*); a lament by Barbara Strozzi refers to the execution in 1642 by order of Louis XIII of a noble member of the Fronde; an anonymous *Lamento di Marinetta per la morte di Masaniello suo marito* is a lively caricature of the events of the Neapolitan revolt. This list, though incomplete, clearly illustrates the mid-century vogue by which the chamber lament becomes a 'model' *poesia per musica* for the treatment of topical – political – themes.

Two conclusions emerge from our listing of sources for the *Lamento d'Arianna*: first, that this originally operatic monologue actually circulates as a *cantata da camera*; second, that the *Lamento d'Arianna* shows a strong inclination for 'fraternization' with other similar *lamenti da camera*, for which it comes to represent something of a model. In fact, the monologue lament is quick to gain popularity among poets and musicians alike. We have already mentioned the laments of Sigismondo d'India, set to texts by the composer himself (see chapter 3); a *Proserpina gelosa* (1636), music by Giovanni Felice Sances, bears the title *Lamento*; in 1626, Rinuccini's own lament of Arianna was set to music by a certain Francesco Costa; it is also paraphrased in blank (seven-syllable) verse in Marino's idyll *Arianna*, itself set to music by Pellegrino Possenti in 1623. A comparison of the text of the original *Lamento d'Arianna* (Rinuccini and Monteverdi) with those of other contemporary laments reveals *Arianna* as something of a prototype for the genre as a whole. One obvious example is the *Lamento d'Olimpia*, itself so flagrantly derived (in music as in words!) from *Arianna* as to render quite unlikely any attribution to Monteverdi:

Arianna (Rinuccini and Monteverdi)
Lasciatemi morire,
lasciatemi morire!
E che volete voi che mi conforte
in così dura sorte,
in così gran martire?
Lasciatemi morire!

O Teseo, o Teseo mio,
sì che mio ti vo' dir, che mio pur sei
benché t'involi, ahi crudo, a gli occhi miei
. . .

Ahi, che non pur risponde!
Ahi, che più d'aspe è sordo a' miei lamenti!
O nembi, o turbi, o venti,
sommergetelo voi dentr'a quell'onde!
Correte, orche e balene,
e de le membra immonde
empiete le voragini profonde!
Che parlo, ahi! che vaneggio?
Misera, ohimè, che chieggio?
O Teseo, o Teseo mio,
non son, non son quell'io
non so quell'io che i feri detti sciolse:
parlò l'affanno mio, parlò il dolore,
parlò la lingua, sì, ma non gia 'l core.

Olimpia (? and ?)
Voglio, voglio morir, voglio morire!
Vano è il conforto tuo, vana ogni aita,
il martir con la vita
vedrai così finire.
Voglio, voglio morir, voglio morire!

O Bireno, o Bireno, ahi non poss'io
dirti Bireno mio,
se per non esser mio le vele sciogli
. . .

Ma perché, o ciel, invendicato lassi
il tradimento indegno,
e tu, del vasto e procelloso regno
superbo domator, ché no'l sommergi?
Eolo, ché non commovi i venti alteri,
perché non li sprigioni,
sì che s'affondi entr'al vorace seno
il disleale a me crudo Bireno?
Ma troppo, ohimè, dure querele spargo,
deh ritornate a me voci serene!
Bireno, o mio Bireno,
in virtute d'amor, se non il duolo,
le mie giust'ire affreno;
perdona, ohimè perdona,
perché altro il cor, altro la lingua suona!

Arianna (Rinuccini and Monteverdi)
Let me die, / let me die! / And do you wish that consolation I may find / in so hard a destiny, / so great a martyrdom? / Let me die!

Theseus, Theseus mine, / indeed I wish to call you mine, that mine you are, / though cruel you flee from my eyes . . .

Ah, nor e'en does he reply! / and more than an asp is he deaf to my laments!

O clouds, O throngs, O winds, / sumberge him within those waves! / Run, O whales and monsters of the sea, / and of limbs unclean / the deep abysses fill! / What do I say, ah, what do I rave? / Wretched that I am, alas, what do I ask? / Theseus, O Theseus mine, / I am not she, / I am not she who these savage things did say: / did speak my anguish and my fear, / did speak my tongue but not my heart.

Olimpia (? and ?)
I wish, to die I wish, I wish to die! / In vain your comforting, in vain all aid, / the martyr, you'll see, / with life will finish thus. / To die I wish, I wish to die.

O Bireno, O Bireno, ah nor can I / call you Bireno mine, / if the sails you loose that you be not with me . . .

But why, O heav'ns, unavenged you leave / this base betrayal, / and you, who reign supreme above / the vast and stormy kingdom, why do you submerge it not? / Aeolus, why do you not move the proud and haughty winds, / unleashing them, / that Bireno, cruel and unfaithful, be sunk in [my] voracious breast? / But, alas, too much my hard laments I spread, / ah, words serene, return to me! / Bireno, O Bireno mine, / for love, if not my grief / my wrath (though just) I'll curb; / forgive, alas, forgive: / the heart one thing, the tongue another sounds.

In musical terms, all the laments mentioned above are set as multisectional monologue recitatives. The original model, the *Lamento d'Arianna*, consists of four distinct sections, in which violently contrasting affections are juxtaposed: mortal desperation, self-pity, supplication of the unfaithful lover, nostalgic evocation of past joys, reproach for unmaintained promises, oath of vendetta in respect of the fugitive and – immediately, with an abrupt change of mood – shocked consternation for the wickedness of her words, literally pronounced 'out of her mind' ('I am not she . . . did speak my tongue but not my heart'). This identical succession of passions (or some analogous mixture thereof) provides both the literary and compositional material for subsequent laments. Yet, in the original operatic version, the four sections of the *Lamento d'Arianna* were interspersed (in the manner of classical tragedy) with the choruses of the sorrowful fishermen who witness the desperation of the beautiful queen on the beach of Naxos. No trace of the music for these choruses has survived; the sources, all evidently designed for *da camera* consumption, preserve not one note of the original operatic interjections. Significantly, the only surviving music for the choruses of fiserhmen is that of Severo Bonini, whose *Lamento d'Arianna* of 1613 (based, like that of Monteverdi, on Rinuccini's original text) post-dates the first performance of Monteverdi but precedes the first edition – an edition, indeed, whose very lack of choral interjections would appear to have obliterated their very memory from the minds of contemporaries.

Quite different is the history of the *Lamento della Ninfa*. Here, too, the author of the text is Rinuccini; unlike *Arianna*, however, the *Lamento della Ninfa* did not involve direct collaboration between poet and musician. The text appears without title in the posthumous edition of the works of Rinuccini (1622) – an edition used by Monteverdi for other compositions in Book 8. In the case of the *Lamento della Ninfa*, however, the composer might also have appropriated the text from one of the *Canzonette a voce sola* of Giovanni Battista Piazza (1633), or even from the *Scherzi, arie, canzonette e madrigali* for solo voice, published by Antonio Brunelli as early as 1614. Poetically, indeed, this piece is nothing but an innocent and playful strophic canzonetta: four rhymed seven-syllable lines (ABAB), with a fixed ritornello of a single rhymed octosyllabic couplet; this is clearly reflected in the smoothly syllabic settings of Brunelli and Piazza. The following strophe will serve by way of example:

'Amor', diceva e 'l piè,	'Love', she said, gazing at the heav'ns,
mirando il ciel, fermò,	and her foot stopped still,
'Dove, dov'è la fé	'Where, where is the faith
che 'l traditor giurò?'	the traitor swore to me?'
Miserella, ahi più, no no,	Wretched maid, ah, no, no,
tanto gel soffrir non può.	longer so much iciness can bear.

Yet, in the hands of Monteverdi, this originally trivial canzonetta becomes a musical scenography of notably tragic dimensions. The idea, in itself quite ingenious, is that of extrapolating from Rinuccini's strophic original the direct speech of the Nymph, which is thus rendered independent from the passages in indirect speech: the words of the Nymph are set as a long, sorrowful monologue for soprano (without strophic caesurae); the remainder becomes a 'chorus' of three male voices, whose compassionate interjections from the rear of the imaginary musical 'stage' reflect the desperation of the abandoned heroine. This operation is rendered possible by the ambivalence of the seven-syllable lines, themselves highly appropriate for use not only as strophic verse (as in Rinuccini's original text) but also as blank-verse recitative. The resulting musical structure is that of a formally organized aria, quite different from the recitative – a formal organization, however, which eschews all attempts at classification. The fixedly impassive melodic and harmonic scheme of an ostinato bass (four descending notes: A–G–F–E) is repeated for a total of thirty-four statements; against this rigid and somewhat rudimentary backcloth, the sinuous, erratic, 'bewildered' melody of the Nymph produces a series of dissonant collisions. Musically, then, this is a work of notable interest. There is, however, no lack of illustrious precedents. One particularly beautiful *Cantada a voce sola sopra il passacaglio* by Giovanni Felice Sances (1633) is based on the very same *basso ostinato*, an identical relationship of contradiction between the rigidity of the bass and mobility of the voice, an identical ambivalence of text. The airy strophes of alternating seven- and eleven-syllable lines are all highly compatible with the requirements of declamatory recitative; towards the end, indeed, the *basso ostinato* momentarily makes way for some bars of fully-fledged recitative (whence the denomination 'cantata' in preference to 'aria', a title reserved for compositions that are 'all of a piece'). Monteverdi, then, is to be credited less with the invention of a new – and fascinating – type of aria than with the application of the *basso ostinato* principle to an anomalous form of 'lament': a 'lament aria', we might say, in opposition to the 'lament scene' of *Arianna* (1608) and the 'lament cantata' of the subsequent *da camera* version of *Arianna*.

As with the *Lamento d'Arianna*, the effect of the *Lamento della Ninfa* was both immediate and profound. First published in 1638 (thus 'sandwiched' between the opening of the first Venetian public theatre in 1637 and the *début* of Francesco Cavalli in 1639), Monteverdi's composition subsequently becomes the archetype for dozens of theatrical lament arias over an ostinato bass. The bass in question – a repeated diatonic tetrachord in triple time – lends itself conveniently to a notable range of variants in general. Take, for example, the lament aria for Cassandra from Cavalli's *Didone*. This proceeds in common time. The chromatic bass (D–C♯–C♮–B–B♭–A) is stated on four different levels (one for each of the four seven-syllable lines): four tetrachords, covering a range of two full octaves (D→A, G→D, D→A, G→D); it is also prolonged (two hendecasyllables in *stile recitativo*, set to a descending chromatic tetrachord: A → E). Though every note of this lament aria is different from Monteverdi's prototype, the structural technique and ultimately sorrowful affection remain quite unimpaired. Elsewhere in *Didone*, Ecuba literally evokes her spirit out of herself:

'	×	×	'	×	×
Tre-	mu-	lo	spi-	ri-	to,
fle-	bi-	le e	lan-	gui-	do,
e-	sci-	mi	su-	bi-	to . . .

The ostinato bass (descending chromatic tetrachord, triple metre) is perfectly in keeping with the sustained dactylic rhythm of the five-syllable *sdrucciolo* verse (and, indeed, the words themselves) – a rhythm conventionally applied in scenes of 'other-world' deprecation and invocations of spirits; particularly famous are the *sdruccioli* of Medea's sorcery scene ('Dell'antro magico / Stridenti cardini / Il varco apritemi . . . ') in *Giasone*. The descending tetrachord (chromatic or diatonic, composite or simple, with or without ostinato repetitions) subsequently becomes something of a generalized musical symbol for affections of sorrow: this is plainly visible in such later masterpieces as the *Crucifixus* of Bach's Mass in B Minor, the beginning of Mozart's Quartet in D Minor (K.421) and some twenty *Lieder* by Schubert. In an attempt to illustrate the declamatory origins of musical phraseology,

Momigny (in his *Cours complet d'harmonie*) 'sets' the Mozart quartet to the words of a 'Dido's lament' of his own.

Yet almost none of the *basso ostinato* arias in the scores of Cavalli and his contemporaries bears the designation 'lament': sorrowful as these pieces may be, their status remains one of simple 'aria'. The denomination 'lament' occurs only exceptionally. In one of the manuscript copies of *Giasone*, for example, the great lament of Isifile in Act 3 (a lament of such power as to more even Giasone to acknowledge his faults, thus preparing for the denouement of the drama) is labelled as such: here, however, the passage in question is not a *basso ostinato* aria but a multisectional monologue in the manner of the *Lamento d'Arianna*. In the case of *basso ostinato* arias, the designation 'lament' is not incorrect (proof of this is Monteverdi's original *Lamento della Ninfa*); it is, however, necessary to distinguish clearly between the 'lament' as an aria and the 'lament' as a monologue (scene). This distinction may be best understood through reference to the different cultural orientations of the term itself: in the first case the inference is musical–morphological, in the second dramaturgical–literary–semantic.

In short: the lament scene (as exemplified by *Arianna* and its various descendants) is recognizable less on account of its musical physiognomy than by virtue of its literary and dramatic characteristics. The lament scene is a scene of desperation, imprecation and self-pity on the part of the heroine; a monologue, it comes at a critical point in the drama; for the protagonist, it represents the culmination of the various inner conflicts raised in the course of the preceding action. One of its principal structural features – already illustrated with reference to the *Lamento d'Arianna* – is the violent, abrupt alternation of opposite states of mind, the 'over-representation' of desperation by means of extreme states of consciousness and unconsciousness ('non amant sed insaniunt mulieres'). Like Arianna, Ottavia (in *Poppea*) gives free rein to her imprecations, then repents:

. . . Destin, se stai là sù,	Destiny, if in heav'n you be,
Giove, ascoltami tu:	Jove, give ear to me:
se per punir Nerone	if thunderbolt
fulmini tu non hai,	to punish Nero have you not,
d'impotenza t'accuso,	of impotence I charge you,
d'ingiustizia t'incolpo!	of injustice blame you!
Ahi, trapasso tropp'oltre, e me ne pento . . .	Ah, I go too far, and I repent . . .

and, with this, the music passes suddenly – without modulation – to an unrelated tonality. At this point, Ottavia ('che fo, ove son, che penso?') is no less bewildered – literally, 'out of her senses' – than

Arianna, Isifile ('... oh dio, / che vaneggio, a chi parlo, ove mi trovo?') and the host of other unfortunate heroines who give vent to their sorrows on the stages of Venice and the other theatres of Italy (as late as Verdi's *Don Carlos*, indeed, Eboli takes leave of the world with an agitated aria which oscillates between imprecation and faith, penitence and desperation). The agglomeration of invective, imprecation, recrimination and forbearance, moreover, can frequently act as a dramatically necessary exposition of actions which precede the beginning of the drama itself (and which are unknown to the spectator), thus contributing to a full understanding of the plot; above all, however, it comes to crystallize in a type of scenic and vocal behaviour whose main characteristics may be described as its 'prominence' and precipitous changes of affection. (Though perhaps anomalous, it is by no means illegitimate to define the literary and compositional configuration of a dramatic and musical form more in terms of its articulation – or, rather, its deliberate 'disarticulation' – than with reference to the verbal and musical conformation of its text.) It can, however, occur (as in the operas of Cavalli and his contemporaries) that one (and one only) of the many sections of a lament scene be composed as a lament aria, with or without *basso ostinato*. Indeed, the gradual increase in the importance of the operatic aria is accompanied by a parallel increase in the predominance of the 'aria' section with respect to the other (recitative-like) components of the lament scene (this process can be seen at its clearest in the variants progressively inflicted upon the laments of Isifile in the course of the various performances of *Giasone*, 1649–81: salient characteristic is the constant increase in the use of 'arioso', with corresponding reductions in the quantity of recitative), to the point at which this literary and musical genre is finally absorbed altogether as one of the many different species of aria. Yet something of the abrupt and fragmented alternation of contradictory affections (typical of the lament scene) survives in a number of later *da capo* arias, where a sorrowful opening (and closing) section exists side by side with an intervening passage of particular fury (a late example occurs in Handel's *Giulio Cesare*: Cleopatra's words 'Piangerò la sorte mia / sì crudele e tanto ria', sung above a semi-ostinato tetrachord, suddenly make way for a passage in which the protagonist unleashes her passion in a flood of fury and invective: 'Ma poi, morta, d'ogni intorno / il tiranno e notte e giorno / fatta spettro agiterò'; the *da capo* stamps a desolate seal on the futility of the imprecation).

The lament scene and the lament aria can thus be seen to derive from two different musical traditions, which co-exist on the cultural horizons of composer and public alike with no reciprocal loss of identity or specifity. The *Lamento d'Arianna*, however, with its diverse offspring of chamber and theatrical laments, permits a glimpse of one other aspect of the seventeenth-century spectator's horizon of expectations. In literary terms, the source for *Arianna* (as, indeed, for other operas of the earliest years: see chapter 20) is the *Metamorphoses* of Ovid. Though few lines only are devoted in the original version to the heroine of Rinuccini's operatic revision (Ariadne, at Book 8, stanzas 169–82, is transformed into a constellation by Bacchus), one Italian translation – an *ottava rima* version (itself something of a best-seller, with at least thirty-five separate editions in the period 1561–1677) by Giovan Andrea dell'Anguillara – interpolates a lament for Ariadne of no less than thirty-six stanzas (Book 8, stanzas 106–41). Anguillara's declared source is the lament of Olimpia from *Orlando furioso* (Book 10, stanzas 20–34): in his own commentary on the Italianized *Metamorphoses* he emphasizes those very 'antithetical digressions' and 'stunning transformations' – i.e., those abrupt deviations between opposing states of mind – which are peculiar to Ariosto's Olimpia and his own 'Ovidian' Arianna, and which will later typify the musical laments of Arianna *et al.* Ariosto, in turn, derives from Ovid his model for Olimpia's lament: not, however, from the *Metamorphoses*, but from the *Heroides* (a series of 'letters' in elegiac verse, written by the heroines of old to their unfaithful lovers). Thus, Anguillara's vernacular translation of Ovid for the 'average' Italian reader (couched as it is in the 'popular' metre of the *ottava rima*) also embraces the model of Ariosto (in a passage itself derived originally from Ovid) – a model of proven popularity. We might add that not only Olimpia but also a whole series of other heroes and heroines from *Orlando* and *Gerusalemme liberata* are provided with scenes of grand 'Ovidian' desperation. Tasso's Armida and Erminia, for example, like Olimpia (and with similar 'antithetical digressions' and 'stunning transformations'), fuel a not inconsiderable sequence of epic madrigals in the course of the sixteenth and seventeenth centuries. The lament of Rinuccini's *Arianna* – climax to the opera as a whole – thus builds upon the diffusion of a whole series of 'popular' literary models, ably re-proposing the same characteristic poetic images. That this was indeed the case, that it was indeed easy to make the mental connection between Arianna's lament, its various derivatives and its Ovidian source (in the translation by Anguillara), that there existed a tangible link between 'popular' literature and the cultural horizons of the opera-going public: all this is eloquently suggested in the *Lamento d'Ariana abandonata da Teseo* (Bologna, 1640), a small, inexpensive and 'popular' publication which reproduces the thirty-six stanzas of

Anguillara; the printer, finding himself with some little space at the end, adds by way of appendix the text of a certain *Ariana tradita*, itself none other than the text of Rinuccini's (Monteverdi's) lament.

The *Heroides*, too, enjoyed enormous success in Italian translation (above all, in the blank verse adaptation by Remigio Fiorentino, which runs to a total of some twenty editions in the period 1555–1630). In poetical and rhetorical terms, the letters of Penelope to Ulysses, Dido to Aeneas, Hypsipyle to Jason, Hypermnestra to Lynceus, Helen to Paris, etc. are as much 'laments' as that of Arianna herself: indeed, the theatrical laments of these same characters provide a nucleus for those very seventeenth-century operas which bear their names. The Ovidian 'heroic letter' was also fashionable as a literary genre in seventeenth-century Italy; examples are the 'lettere amorose' of Monteverdi, published together with the *Lamento d'Arianna* in 1623. Likewise, the *Epistole eroiche* of Antonio Bruni (these, too, frequently reprinted between 1627 and 1678) are nothing but 'laments' (in blank verse and *terza rima*), variously derived from *Orlando*, *Gerusalemme liberata*, *Adone* and ancient history. The *Scherzi geniali* (themselves in prose) of Giovan Francesco Loredano, 'prince' of the Incogniti, enjoyed some thirty editions between 1632 and 1676; these, too, consist of nothing but the invectives of heroes and heroines. The subjects – Radamisto and Zenobia, Sophonisba and Massinissa, Seneca and Nero, Semiramis and Nino, the wrathful Achilles, the implorations of Poppea, Sejanus disgraced, Hannibal the invincible, the tearful Helen, Germanicus betrayed, the modesty of Roxana, etc. – all find ample correspondence in the themes of Venetian libretti (beginning in the 1640s). It is difficult to avoid the suspicion that some kind of relationship exists between this 'popular' type of literary production, the propensity of librettists and composers for the construction of operas around the grand lament of the protagonist, and the tendency of the public to identify the climax of the opera in the invective or 'letter of accusation' of some mythical or historical character. Here, however, the nature of our enquiry broadens out into what might be termed the sociological history of culture. It is sufficient to note how our brief examination of the lament provides ample illustration of the complexity and fecundity of certain theatrical conventions – conventions which represent the effective basis of seventeenth-century opera.

24 Opera in German-speaking lands: Vienna and Hamburg

The diffusion of Italian opera north of the Alps and the establishment of more or less autonomous local and/or national operatic traditions is a phenomenon of eminent importance for the musical and cultural life of Europe during the second half of the seventeenth century. Its many different manifestations range from wholesale importation and/or imitation to outright rejection; common to all these forms, however, is a single point of reference: Italian opera. Whereas, in Italy, the enormously rapid yet organic growth and development of this new social and theatrical institution is deeply rooted in the cultural reality of the nation, elsewhere it is more legitimate to speak of the 'transplantation' – invariably problematic – of what is essentially an alien artistic and organizational model. A description – impossible in the present context – of all the various situations of importance would include a number of 'mere' episodes, some of very early date (for example, the series or operas produced between 1635 and 1648 at the Polish royal court, thanks essentially to the activities of the Italian literary scholar and royal secretary Virgilio Puccitelli) – episodes which, if at times for no other reason than dynastic succession, are destined never to assume the dimensions of continuous theatrical traditions. Significant, too, are the various unsuccessful theatrical initiatives (as, for example, in Amsterdam, where a limited number of French and Italian operas are produced in the penultimate decade of the century), themselves symptomatic of the cultural rejection of what is perceived as an essentially extraneous innovation. Sufficient, for present purposes, will be a brief examination of five representative yet highly differentiated cases: (1) the Imperial court of Vienna, where Italian-language operas based on a model virtually identical with that of Venetian operas but produced by a local theatrical structure which differs notably from that described by Ivanovich (imitation and re-production of original artistic model with different means of production and consumption); (2) the public theatre of Hamburg, where German-language operas of similar character to Venetian-style *drammi per musica* are produced in a way and for a type of public not dissimilar to those of contemporary Venetian theatres (reproduction of similar forms of consumption through adoption and adaptation – *mutatis mutandis* – of original artistic model and productive system); (3) Paris and the French court, where operatic entertainments of deliberately differing complexion from those of Venice, produced by an organizational system of equally differing structure, act as a local equivalent – culturally and ideologically specific – of the Italian *dramma per musica* (rejection of original artistic model and production of substitute model, different yet akin); (4) England, where the music of the Restoration theatre 'borrows' much from the style of contemporary French and Italian opera, yet without the formation of any local operatic tradition on the basis of imitation, substitution or direct importation, as subsequently occurs at the time of Bononcini and Handel (selective adoption of particular characteristics of artistic model, converted for use in connection with essentially alien theatrical tradition); (5) Spain, where outright rejection of the original Italian model is coupled with a reluctance to tolerate the very principles of operatic theatre, itself admitted only under certain circumstances and conditions (resistance to original artistic model, limited acceptance of its basic presuppositions, and replacement on a localized basis).

Clearly, not only the artistic and/or institutional constitution of opera varies widely from one country to another; different, too, are the various expressions of power, social structure, cultural conditions, literary, theatrical and musical traditions. A measure of these differences is provided by the alterations – radical or purely cosmetic – undergone by the Italian model in its 'transference' to the various countries concerned, as also by the reactions with which it is greeted. Without exception, however, the basic point of reference and comparison is provided by the Italian *dramma per musica* – so much so, in fact, as to cast serious doubt on all attempts to justify and explain the establishment and development of opera as the product of a relationship of continuity with pre-existing national or local theatrical forms and traditions. For example, the various modern attempts to perceive in the opera of Hamburg the 'origins' of a German national operatic 'school' (itself a cultural notion of late eighteenth-century descent, given concrete form only in the decades which followed) misrepresent what is essentially an isolated episode of limited geographical and historical dimensions and essentially alien cultural orientation (with little projection in the direction of other German-speaking centres). If anything, we might say that the Hamburg experience, with its associated moral, aesthetic and ideological debate, is of notable consequence for the establishment of the typically Germanic propensity for theatrical controversy and the parallel tradition of dramaturgical and critical consciousness (a tradition which, in the course of the eighteenth century, yields results of outstanding importance: see Source reading 7). If one omits to draw a distinction between opera as an artistic genre and operatic theatre as an artistic institution (see chapter 19), research on the various 'dawns' and 'precursors' of opera can be pushed back a decade, a century or more in terms of any given country. This, however, avoids the central issue (in the present context, the institutionalization of opera) and invests with overwhelming historical significance those episodes which only in the light of subsequent developments can have come to seem 'decisive'. Two such episodes – two 'German operas' of no 'real' historical importance – may be cited in this context. Neither can be said to represent an early stage in the development of German opera; on the contrary, both examples provide ample illustration of the enormous fascination exerted by the earliest Italian operatic productions on German literary (more, indeed, than musical) circles.

The first of these episodes is *Seelewig*, itself frequently – and somewhat inaccurately – described as the first German 'opera' (1644) of which the music (by Sigmund Gottlieb Staden) has been preserved. This 'spiritual *Waldgedicht* [woodland fable], sung in the Italian style', has indeed the appearance of a miniature *dramma* set throughout in *stile recitativo*; the source itself, however, explicitly discounts a definition of the composition in question as a theatrical entertainment in the true sense of the word. *Seelewig*, indeed, is only one of the many 'conversational games' – virtuous academic pastimes – contained in the *Frauenzimmergesprächspiele* of Georg Philipp Harsdörffer (Nuremberg, 1641–49): a collection, this, of society games, derived from a variety of Italian models (including, for example, the *Trattenimenti* of the Sienese Accademia degli Intronati, a publication with which Harsdörffer demonstrates a certain familiarity) and comprised of a somewhat eclectic mixture of literary genres and philosophical themes of the widest possible geographical origins (with derivations from Italy, France, England and Spain). Viewed in terms of this medley of conversational inventions, *Seelewig* can be understood in its true light of an 'academic' imitation of those now somewhat outdated *drammi musicali* which Harsdörffer himself, during his Italian sojourn of 1629, could have known only through the medium of printed editions: recognizable models, in fact, are the printed sources of Cavalieri's *Rappresentazione* of 1600 and Agostino Agazzari's *Eumelio* (this latter a *dramma pastorale* 'recitato in musica' in the Roman Seminary during Carnival 1606). Like its models, *Seelewig* may best be described as an edifying moral allegory; the name of the protagonist translates literally as 'immortal soul'. No less weighty are the names of the other characters: Hertzigild (Heart), Gwissulda (Conscience), Trügewalt (Deceit), etc. The imitation of the Italian originals gives a curiously hybrid effect – as, for example, when the nymph Sinnigunda (Sensuality) seduces Seelewig to *carpe diem* and frivolity with a fascinating vocal imitation of the nightingale (not unreminiscent, in literary terms, of the nightingale episode in Marino's *Adone*: see chapter 2), to which Seelewig responds with a *memento mori* performed to the sober, upright melody of a Lutheran chorale. Any attempt to interpret this somewhat eccentric academic exercise as a 'precursor' of German opera can hardly be said to do justice to the historical reality and circumstances under which it was born, nor indeed to the didactic and educational intentions of its versatile author. The *Frauenzimmergesprächspiele* also contains a detailed description and music for an 'imaginary' masque (*Tugendsterne*, or 'Stars of Virtue'), inserted in the midst of a German translation of an English allegorical comedy. Basis of this masque are the neoplatonic notions of *musica mundana*, coupled with a network of symbolic analogies between planetary divinities, Christian virtues, heraldic colours, musical modes, triumphal chariots and instrumental timbres (e.g., Saturn – Temperance – black – Hypoaeolian – tigers – *pifferi* and harp); like *Seelewig*, this too can be seen as an attempt to assimilate into German culture certain pre-existing themes and concepts. In short: rather than introducing a new theatrical genre into German cultural life, *Seelewig* aims at the building up of a complex pedagogical programme around the logical and sensory arts.

The primarily literary, non-musical nature of the earliest German 'experiments' with Italian opera is equally apparent in a second interesting episode not infrequently cited as the archetype of a would-be national operatic tradition: this is the German *Dafne*, performed during the 1627 wedding celebrations at the court of Saxony, with words (from Rinuccini) by Martin Opitz and music (lost) by Heinrich Schütz. In material terms, two 'original' Italian sources were available to both librettist and composer: the printed libretto for the Florentine production (the music, by Peri, never having been published) and the printed score of the music (by Marco da Gagliano) for the Mantuan 'revival' of 1608 (for which, despite the various additions by Rinuccini himself to the original text, no libretto was ever published). Comparison with the libretto of 1627 reveals the latter as nothing but a German translation of the original Florentine text: essentially, then, the source for both Opitz and Schütz was the literary – non-musical – text of the original Florentine version. The only significant variant occurs at the climax to the tale: the metamorphosis of Daphne into a laurel tree.

Rinuccini, mindful of the dramatic canons of classical literature, sets the entire episode offstage (it is subsequently reported by a Messenger to an awestruck Chorus); in the German version, the figure of the Messenger is eliminated and the metamorphosis is presented on stage in full view of the public. This difference is symptomatic of a general propensity on the part of seventeenth-century German tragic literature for the direct and open display of events (not least of violence and bloody strife): in short, a propensity for visual theatre. For the literary theorist Sigmund von Birken (1679), the open staging of such actions as the assassination, shooting or hanging of some scoundrel is fully justified by the terror and pity of tragedy. Beheading alone is unseemly for stage representation; it must thus be reported, though all such accounts of 'invisible' actions should be suitably corroborated by display of the head on a platter . . . Faced, then, with a choice between alternative draftings of any given *dramma per musica* – one with a *lieto fine*, the other with a 'true-to-life' portrayal of the death of the protagonist on stage (a good example is the Venetian *Ercole in Tebe* of 1671) – the German tradition will invariably opt for the tragic version (enhanced, if anything, by an extra dose of atrocity).

Opitz, then, can hardly be regarded as the founder of any German national tradition of opera. In one sense, however, his name must be credited with a certain importance for the subsequent development of German music – so much so as to merit a brief, 'non-theatrical' digression. The literary horizons of a politically shattered 'nation' – *scenario* and victim of a Thirty Years War which, in turn, can be seen as both outcome and source of an age-old tradition of social and religious strife – are, to say the least, highly eclectic. Characteristic of seventeenth-century Germany (in contrast to France, Italy and Spain) is the active circulation of itinerant theatrical companies with performances of Shakespeare and other works from the Elizabethan repertory (e.g., Marlowe's *Doctor Faustus*); contemporary German writers draw inspiration from the poetry of Marino (as also from the publications of Incogniti, not least by virtue of their political and ideological implications) and the preciosity of the Parisian authors; in Catholic regions, moreover, the Latin theatre of the Jesuits fulfils an important didactic function in promoting the cause of the ruling classes. This is the eclecticism of a country itself essentially devoid of any solid national literary tradition – a country, indeed, of only recent linguistic unification. In this context, Martin Opitz's treatise on poetics, the *Buch von der deutschen Poeterei* of 1624, is a veritable source of legislation for the future of German poetry and literature in general. Included in Opitz's classification of poetic genres is the *poesia per musica*:

> Lyric poetry, a genre highly suited to music, requires in the first place a free and happy mind; unlike the other genres, it must be adorned with many beautiful maxims and precepts . . . Concerning its themes: it is capable of describing anything that can be contained in a brief composition – gallantries, dances, ballets, beautiful women, gardens, vineyards, eulogies of modesty, the vanities of life, etc., but above all exhortation to joy.

The subsequent poetic and musical development of this light and gay variety of *poesia per musica* is due, above all, to the regulating principles introduced by Opitz for German versification. To Opitz, indeed, belongs the credit for the reduction of German versification to its 'standing' modern accentual form, in a way which regenerated the very face of vocal music in its treatment of vernacular texts (absent all trace of the earlier polyphonic tradition, as also of the prose and hymn-like manner of Biblical texts and chorales) and fuelled the fashion for strophic *ariette da camera* with *basso continuo* (with or without instruments). German metre is based essentially on the strict and regular alternation of strong and weak (accented and unaccented) syllables similar in style to the iambic (w/s) and trochaic (s/w) feet – or, more rarely, the dactyl (s/w/w) and anapaest (w/w/s) – of classical poetry. In contrast to the typically iambic trimeter of heroic, tragic and epic verse (which, with its obligatory caesura after syllable 6, is the effective equivalent of the French Alexandrine and as such little suited to melodic composition), the needs of lyric poetry are best served by iambic and trochaic dimeters. In a text such as the following (a malicious piece of advice by Paul Fleming – himself a follower of Opitz – on how to give the perfect kiss), the trochaic dimeters, coupled with the strictly isochronous, syllabic music – one crotchet per syllable – of Andreas Hammerschmidt (*Weltliche Oden*, 1642, for solo voice and *basso continuo*), assume *ipso facto* the wittily repetitive nature of some affected little canzonetta (not, indeed, unlike the many Italian solo aria settings of octosyllabic strophes):

′	×	′	×	′	×	′	×
Nicht	zu	har-	te,	nicht	zu	weich,	
bald	zu-	gleich,	bald	nicht	zu-	gleich,	
nicht	zu	lang-	sam,	nicht	zu	schnel-	le,
nicht	ohn'	Un-	ter-	scheid	der	Stel-	le.

In contrast, the iambic dimeter resembles more closely the seven-syllable line. This is true not only of its characteristic fluency and easiness but also of its themes and urbane and colloquial style: exemplary in this respect is the eulogy on brotherly friendship (itself a dominant theme in seventeenth-century German literature, not unrelated to the contemporary growth of academies within and without the universities, themselves the effective recipients and 'purchasers' of the flowering German repertory of *arie da camera*) of Simon Dach (like Fleming, another imitator of Opitz), set to music in the *Arien oder Melodeyen* (1640) of Heinrich Albert:

×	′	×	′	×	′	×
Der	Mensch	hat	nichts	so	ei-	gen,
so	wohl	steht	ihm	nichts	an,	
als	daß	er	Treu	er-	zei-	gen
und	Freund-	schaft	hal-	ten	kann.	

Of particular prominence in this mid-century chamber repertory are the names of the composer Adam Krieger (1634–66), the theologian, poet and *dilettante* musician Johann Rist (himself the most representative exponent of the academic and fraternalistic ideology which pervades the repertory as a whole), the trumpeter Gabriel Voigtländer (active as a musician in various cities and courts of the Baltic area). Voigtländer, with an anthology of (his own) German translations of Italian, French and English songs (1642), may be regarded as the 'popularizer' *par excellence* of the repertory. Characteristic of this music in general is what might be described as an almost obsessively syllabic style, naively designed – it might appear – to complement the new metrical clarity of Opitz's reformed German poetry. Particular – though indirect – beneficiaries of this reform are the various later exponents of the fully-developed German-language *dramma per musica*.

Passing from the civilized atmosphere surrounding mid-seventeenth-century German poets and musicians to the much more overtly political events which accompany the establishment of opera in the various German-speaking centres, the picture changes. The two cultural 'extremes' are represented by Vienna and Hamburg. Theatrical representations (with or without music) of a kind not unlike those in vogue at the various Italian courts were already a feature of Imperial circles in the first half of the seventeenth century. Indeed the various Imperial *Kapellmeister* and many court singers were Italian. In 1651, however, two thoroughly 'Venetian' theatrical personalities – the set designer Giovanni Burnacini and the ubiquitous Benedetto Ferrari – are summoned to Vienna, with the task of producing not *drammi per musica* but tournaments and ballets with music: ceremonial entertainments, salient moments in court etiquette and protocol. A first opera in the true sense of the word – albeit intended as a pompous display of Imperial power in the eyes of the world – is produced by the court musicians (text by Ferrari, music by the Imperial *Kapellmeister* Antonio Bertali) before the electoral princes at the Diet of Regensburg (1653). It would be difficult to overestimate the importance of this theatrical event: opera, indeed, quickly comes to be accepted in German court circles in general as the theatrical symbol of sovereign power. Later that year, the visit of the Emperor to the court of Bavaria is celebrated with the production of the first Munich opera: *L'arpa festante*, by Giovan Battista Maccioni; the manuscript score of this brief dramatic action of eulogistic hue was presented in homage to the illustrious guest, and is now in Vienna. In the same summer of 1653, the Archduke of Innsbruck – recently returned from a journey to a number of southern courts (where he witnesses a wide variety of musical and theatrical entertainments) – establishes his own opera house at Innsbruck; in this venture, he secures the permanent collaboration of a highly-qualified team of Italian operatic personalities: *Kapellmeister* Antonio Cesti, librettist Giovan Filippo Apolloni, a variety of Italian castrati, and *prima donna* Anna Renzi. It is, indeed, thanks to the 1655 Innsbruck production of *Argia* that the newly-abdicated Queen Christina of Sweden (herself officially converted to Catholicism on that very occasion on her journey through Innsbruck to the Holy See) makes her first acquaintance with the *dramma per musica*: that remarkable theatrical innovation of Catholic culture and society, which she herself will subsequently patronize in Rome. Returning to 1653, we note the presence in Germany of the celebrated Medici *castrato* Atto Melani. Melani will sing in the presence of the Emperor himself; at the same time, however, he also initiates a whole series of undercover diplomatic missions and espionage activities which will continue to occupy his interests until his death in 1714.

The image of sovereignty – in particular, the 'imperial' pretensions which in Germany remain indelibly associated with the notion of opera ('opera is more a matter for princes and kings than for shopkeepers and traders' is Johann Mattheson's icy sentence of 1728 on the decadence of opera in Hamburg) – is an element of both weakness and strength. While guaranteeing the rapid dissemination of the *dramma per musica* in even the smallest of courts, it is instrumental in binding the institutional continuity of opera even more than in Italy to the pleasure of sovereign princes and the unpredictable turns of events in dynastic fortunes and hierarchies. Symptomatic is the case of Innsbruck itself. On the extinction of the Tyrolean branch of the ruling family in 1665, the archduchy passes under direct Imperial administration, and the efficient Tyrolean theatrical enterprise is transferred lock, stock and barrel to Vienna (singers and operatic scores included). Here, in contrast, continuity is fully guaranteed by the rock-like stability of the productive system as perpetuated by the exceptionally long reign of Leopold I (1657–1705).

Leopold I, himself a composer of no small ability in all the various contemporary styles (theatrical, chamber, ecclesiastical), was only too aware of the ceremonial and demonstrative functions of court theatre as a symbol and instrument of strong social and political cohesion around the figure of the Emperor and Imperial institutions. The most glittering manifestation of his expansive and sumptuous theatrical policy (duly publicized on a European scale in the accounts and descriptions of the *Theatrum Europaeum* and other similar information sheets and gazettes) are the two-year-long celebrations of his marriage with Margarita, Infanta of Spain. The list of theatrical spectaculars speaks for itself. Already in July, 1666, five months before the arrival of the bride in Vienna, her birthday is commemorated in the Imperial capital with a performance of the allegorical 'operetta' *Nettuno e Flora festeggianti* (Francesco Sbarra and Antonio Cesti), which was in reality an introduction to the grand ballet composed, like all such entertainments at the Imperial court, by the court ballet composer, Johann Heinrich Schmelzer. This is followed in November by a second festive ballet, the *Concorso dell'allegrezza universale*; in November, too, the birthday of Eleonora Gonzaga, mother of the Emperor, is celebrated – as always – with a *dramma per musica* produced by her private *cappella* under its director, the Venetian composer Pietro Andrea Ziani. Most sensational of all the 'public' wedding entertainments is the 'festa a cavallo' *La contesa dell'aria e dell'acqua*, held in January 1667 in the courtyard of honour of the Imperial palace; participants in this cosmic glorification of the Caesarian myth (replete with heraldic symbols, martial ceremonies and other chivalrous motifs) are the librettist Sbarra, the composer Bertali, the ballet composer Schmelzer, the choreographer Alessandro Carducci of Florence, a one-hundred-strong band of strings, several dozen winds, some one thousand participants (on horseback and foot) and the illustrious figure of the Emperor himself. Carnival brings a new series of ballets and comedies, a *favola pastorale* (*Galatea*: Antonio Draghi and Ziani) and the 'dramma giocoso-morale' *Le disgrazie d'amore* (Sbarra and Cesti, with 'danceable' music by Schmelzer and Leopold I). In June, the Emperor's birthday provides the occasion for a production of Cesti's opera *La Semirami* (originally composed for Innsbruck but never performed); in July, the birthday of the Empress is marked by a further *balletto a cavallo* by the inevitable Schmelzer (*introduzione* by Sbarra and Cesti). November and December bring a further series of operas for the mother of the Emperor and Christmas-tide ballets. The supreme event of the entire sequence of entertainments, however, is the enormous 'festa teatrale' *Il pomo d'oro*, performed – not without some delay – in July 1668 after two years of preparations. Text and music (respectively by Sbarra and Cesti) were already complete by the winter of 1666–67; not so, however, the wooden theatre and the extraordinary stage especially prepared by Ludovico Ottavio Burnacini for the occasion. Meanwhile, the illustrious bride – herself, by express decree of Jove (who appears in the final scene of the opera) and contrary to all traditions of classical mythology, outright winner of the same bitterly contested golden apple once fought for by Juno, Minerva and Venus which has earlier provoked such tensions in the relationships between the various divinities and worldly heroes of the opera (itself, no less than the present description, literally brimming with secondary episodes and 'parallel' actions!) – gives birth to an heir to the throne (and Cesti to a 'birth-day' addition to the Prologue). The heir dies (return by Cesti to the earlier 'nuptial' Prologue) before the opera is finally produced on the occasion of the birthday of the Empress, herself newly pregnant. The entertainment – articulated in a Prologue, five acts and six ballets (themselves incorporated in the action), with a total of twenty-three changes of scene, thirty-eight singing characters and an unspecified number of 'extras' and dancers – was so long as to necessitate performance on two different days. The Emperor himself had a hand in the composition of the music, which incorporates all the various *loci communes* of Italian opera (laments, 'other-world' and/or pastoral invocations, infernal scenes, heroism in war, lullabies, etc.); the orchestration, in contrast to the modest sonorities of Venetian opera (two violins, two violas and a number of continuo instruments), recalls the 'figurative' instrumentation of early seventeenth-century Italian court opera (see chapter 20): trumpets for martial scenes, cornetts, trombones, bassoons and regals for evocations of spirits and the 'other world', *viole da gamba* and 'gravi-organo' for laments. All the incredible magnificence and splendour of *Il pomo d'oro* – which undoubtedly merits definition as the most ambitious production of the century, outdoing even its Parisian counterpart, *L'Ercole amante* for the wedding of Louis XIV in 1662 (see chapter 25) – is 'consumed' in the course of a single performance. The theatre itself, erected *ad hoc* for the occasion, subsequently remains almost unused; court theatrical life, after this one exceptional moment of folly, withdraws to the various halls of the Imperial palace – institutionally strengthened but necessarily more routine.

The institutional bases are two: a theatrical calendar strictly geared to the various commemorative festivities in the life of the court; a team of functionaries entrusted with the production of operas and other entertainments in accordance with specific requirements. Burnacini, perpetrator of the astonishing scenic wonders of *Il pomo d'oro*, oversees the staging of productions; Johann Heinrich and Andreas Anton Schmelzer are the composers of the dance music; resident choreographers are Santo and Domenico Ventura; new arrivals, on the death of Sbarra and departure of Cesti in 1668, are Nicolò Minato (who arrives from Venice in 1669, fresh from his collaboration with Cavalli) and Antonio Draghi (himself active at Vienna from 1658, first as librettist, then as composer and finally – beginning in 1674 – as 'superintendant' of theatrical music). Over a period of some three decades, Minato and Draghi are jointly responsible for some 120 productions. The Viennese theatrical calendar may be illustrated with reference to a single sample year (other years, with the appropriate changes of titles, are identical). For Carnival 1670, the 'trattenimento per musica' *Le risa di Democrito* (Minato–Draghi–Schmelzer–Burnacini–Ventura) is produced on a 'secret' stage, i.e. for the restricted circle of the court; Holy Week brings the production of an 'azione sepolcrale' and a 'rappresentazione sacra', *Li sette dolori* (Ferri and Draghi) and *Le sette consolazioni di Maria Vergine* (Minato and Sances); for the Emperor's birthday in June, the 'dramma per musica' *Leonida in Tegea* (Minato–Draghi and Leopold I–Schmelzer) is produced in the summer residence of Laxenburg; in July, the Empress's birthday provides the occasion for a further 'dramma per musica', *Ifide greca* (Minato-Draghi–Leopold I–Schmelzer-Burnacini –Ventura); in mid-November, the name-day of the Emperor's mother is celebrated in the 'dramma per musica' *Penelope* (Minato–Draghi –Schmelzer–Burnacini–Ventura); on 22 December, the 'dramma per musica' *Aristomene Messenio* (Minato–Sances–Leopold I–Schmelzer–Burnacini–Ventura) commemorates the birthday of the Queen of Spain. Empresses might come and go (with resulting changes in the dates of name-days and birthdays); Sances, too, dies in 1679. Continuing features, however, of Viennese court productions – which total some six to ten musical entertainments per year – are Minato (d. 1698), Draghi (d. 1700), Schmelzer sen. (d. 1680) and jun. (d. 1701), Burnacini (d. 1707) and the two Ventura brothers. The entertainments themselves, though invariably newly composed, are stylistically quite invariable, true to their very function as one-off symbols and focal points of court celebration and rejoicing (as such, indeed, destined to a permanent place on the shelves of the Imperial library). Formally, these are thoroughly Italian productions, similar in every respect to 'Venetian-style' opera: a handful of such 'drammi per musica' subsequently enter the Italian theatrical circuit. Yet the musical theatre of Leopold I – a sovereign whose strenuous defence of the European *status quo* stands out in clear opposition to the turbulent policies of the Roi Soleil – replaces the notions of continuity and progress (themselves implicit in the very concept of Venetian theatre: see chapter 21) with their opposite: maximum stability and persistent identity. The impresarial economic structure of 'Venetian-type' opera (capital investment, redemption of costs, full exploitation of products) now gives way to a feudal/absolutist principle of the ostentation of Imperial wealth through unrestricted 'squandering' of public funds and the continuous dissipation of artistic resources. The result is a fundamental shift in the underlying conditions of 'Italian-style' opera. Expectations are rigidly determined by questions of etiquette; a carefully pre-selected public is chosen on the basis of the only effective variable in the Viennese operatic calendar: the ceremonial event and its relationship to State protocol. At Carnival, a highly restricted court audience shows particular appreciation of plots of moral-political-satirical hue: a good example is the 'allegorical' comedy *La lanterna di Diogene* (1674), in which Leopold I is represented by Alexander the Great, Louis XIV by Darius, King of Persia, the 'sooth-saying poet' (Minato) by Diogenes, etc.; in contrast, 'public' occasions (commemorated in 'official' entertainments for the court and the Viennese aristocracy)a require a shift in emphasis to ancient Greek and Roman heroism (albeit with a not inconsiderable dose of political allusion: *Tullio Ostilio aprendo il tempio di Giano*, for example, explicitly alludes in 1684 to the anti-Ottoman military actions of the Emperor).

Fundamentally opposed to the functional and ceremonial orientation of opera at Vienna is the situation in Hamburg, itself the perfect example of the 'soft' adoption of an original Venetian model. The city-state of Hamburg, with some 70,000 inhabitants in 1675 (roughly half the population of Venice), is the second city of the Empire, and by far the most lively and open to cultural developments elsewhere in Europe. This, indeed, reflects its prosperous commercial and financial situation, as also its civic tradition of independence and neutrality. As merchant port and tourist centre, Hamburg accepts a wide range of political and religious refugees, including sovereigns in temporary or permanent leave. It reaps the various benefits of republican prosperity (its total of some 1,000 street lamps is something of a record for seventeenth-century Europe) and overseas commerce (the earliest tea and coffee houses can be traced to this very period), yet is also far from immune to the ideological and economic conflicts between the various interest groups and aristocratic oligarchies, conveniently disguised behind a veil of theological and moral diatribes (involving Pietists and orthodox Lutherans) from which opera, too, emerges by no means unscathed. There are many obvious affinities with 'Venetian-style' opera: the establishment, however, of a type of musical theatre which corresponds in more than one respect with Venice is less the result of any deliberate policy of imitation than the necessary consequence of a power structure which differs from that of other German cities. The construction and opening of the Gänsemarkt Theatre in 1678 takes place on the initiative not of any sovereign power but of a group of well-to-do citizens who, with the consent of the city council, invest their capital in this new theatrical venture. Characteristic of the Gänsemarkt is the same economic and architectural structure as its Italian models (see chapter 21), with annual letting of boxes, night-to-night rental of seats in the stalls, fixed-price admittance for all. The interest of its promoters lies less in the pure and simple imitation of any Italian original (as witnessed, for example, by the many German tourists in Italy) than in the re-production, in their own city-state, of a worthy – and agreeable – civic institution: this is indirectly confirmed by the fact that opera in Hamburg is sung in German and not (as in Vienna and all other theatres hitherto in existence in German-speaking climes) in Italian; though, beginning in 1703, a number of arias are indeed sung in Italian, these are mostly derived from *drammi per musica* of clearly Italian descent.

The variants undergone by the original Venetian model of production, while seemingly modest, are in reality of notable dimensions. For example, the distinction between theatre proprietor and theatre impresario, fundamental in Venice, is much less defined at the Gänsemarkt of Hamburg. Conspicuous among the group of promoters who guide the theatre in its development prior to 1685 is the high-ranking jurist and well-to-do senator Gerhard Schott. Schott, in 1685, purchases the proprietorship of the theatre, which he manages single-handed until 1693. In 1694–95, the theatre is leased out on contract, with disastrous results; Schott then resumes direct control, which he retains (with only one brief interruption in 1699) until his death in 1702. The property then passes to his widow, who continues to manage theatrical activities for a further year. Only beginning in 1703 does leasing become a regular practice in theatre organization, though the contract reserves for the owner a notable influence in matters of programming and management. Whereas, however, the era of Schott (who is also active in the field of stage effects and design) brings a certain financial and artistic prosperity to the affairs of the theatre, the same cannot be said of the activities of the other impresarios (both before and after Schott's death), who invariably finish in bankruptcy and failure. It is difficult to ascertain what monetary capital, political support and civil consensus were at Schott's disposition: it is, however, clear that the Gänsemarkt Theatre was effectively regarded as his – so much so that his death is commemorated in the theatre itself with a funeral ode (*Der Tod des großen Pans*) by the up-and-coming star of Hamburg music Johann Mattheson. In contrast, the various periods of management by outside businessmen-'contractors' – persons, perhaps, who are unable to count (like Schott) on the goodwill and support of the resident local and foreign nobility, and whose fundamental interests are geared towards reducing the costs of staging and production and economizing on singers' contracts, costumes, maintenance of props and maintenance of the theatre itself – are characterized by artistic and physical decline; empty stalls, indeed, lead inevitably to the closure of the theatre in 1738. The fault lies not with insufficient artistic talent or managerial ability: even such a talented theatrical musician as Reinhard Keiser (manager, 1703–07) is unable to secure economic results which do justice to the truly extraordinary quality of the music. (Keiser, indeed, is a musician of truly 'European' stature: only the discontinuous and eclectic nature of eighteenth-century German operatic life, as opposed to his own effective vocation as an operatic composer, have relegated him to a figure of merely local importance in the eyes of later generations; much more 'local', in reality, is Alessandro Scarlatti, whose success in Rome, Naples and Florence is rivalled only by his total failure at Venice, and whose posthumous fame rests largely on the persistent success of his chamber cantatas.) In short: only the direct interest of the proprietor himself in the maintenance of the 'business' is sufficient, in Hamburg, to guarantee the ongoing success of operatic life.

Further differences exist between the Gänsemarkt and its Italian models. In line with the somewhat blurred distinction between the figures of impresario and proprietor, Hamburg also lacks that powerful artistic and economic incentive which in Venice derived from the strong competition between the various individual theatres. In reality, Schott and 'company' are the owners of a kind of theatrical privilege, and even go so far as to petition the city council against the operation of itinerant companies of comedians in Hamburg – companies, they claim, whose effect on opera attendances is detrimental (typical of the essentially community-orientated conception of theatre in Hamburg are the reasons advanced by the widow of the former proprietor Schott in her petition of 1702: namely, that whereas 'operatic' wealth is both locally produced and consumed and thus necessarily benefits the local community, the profits of theatrical companies are inevitably destined to 'emigrate' with the companies themselves on their departure from Hamburg). In Venice, while competition between the various theatres leads to mounting inflation in singers' fees, the plurality of the entertainments on offer and the differentiation between individual theatres ensure both a 'competitive' level of performance and continued public interest. The existence of a single theatre at Hamburg brings about a certain reduction of costs (albeit thwarted by the economically competitive situation of singers at the various German court theatres): the danger of 'routine' performances, however, and 'habituation' of the public are a constant source of risk. There is one further – and still more notable – difference between the Gänsemarkt and its contemporary Italian equivalents: in Hamburg, the theatre operates not on a seasonal basis (as in Italy) but throughout the year as a whole. With the exception of Lent, Advent, religious feasts and the summer months, performances take place every Monday, Wednesday and Thursday from January to December: an average of some 100 performances of approximately five (though also as many as ten) new operas per year. This difference clearly anticipates the modern distinction between the permanent operatic companies of German theatres and the ephemeral 'cast' of *prime donne*, *primi uomini* and secondary actors more typical of the average Italian production – the difference, in short, between the hundreds of performances of any single opera in Berlin and the five or six in Milan. One difficulty, however, remains: whereas the limited Venetian season as described in chapter 22 permits the free circulation of singers and scores throughout the Italian peninsula, the continuous operation of the Gänsemarkt represents something of a 'blockage' in the circuit. German-language theatres, indeed, are rare: the Braunschweig theatre (1690–1749), impresarial in structure though established and patronized by the Duke of Braunschweig-Wolfenbüttel, produces operas for Carnival and the St Laurence fair (most eminent of the various *Kapellmeister* is Georg Caspar Schürmann); the 'public' theatre of Leipzig (1693–1720), founded by the composer Nikolaus Adam Strungk (who invests his every possession in the venture), and active during the three annual city fairs, is endowed with decidedly limited financial possibilities (five scenes only are available for productions: a 'forest', a 'garden of cypresses', a 'room', a 'royal court', an 'infernal scene'); and the court theatre of Weißenfels (1684–1736), directed by the local *Kapellmeister* Johann Philipp Krieger (himself previously associated with the elderly Cavalli at Venice). Politics, geography and 'seasonal' arrangements permit a more or less regular interchange of repertory and personnel between Braunschweig and Hamburg alone: active at both are the librettists Friedrich Christian Bressand and Johann Ulrich König, the composers Johann Sigismund Kusser and Reinhard Keiser and a number of celebrated singers: one famous performer was Mme Margaretha Susanna Kayser (herself involved as impresario in a vain attempt to better the waning fortunes of the Gänsemarkt Theatre), whose truly astonishing vocal abilities and expressive versatility were quite sufficient – to judge from her music in Keiser's *Tomyris* of 1717, with its furious, *saltato* high Ds and sudden moments of compassion and tenderness – to dispose of the earlier 'myth' by which the Hamburg cast were accused of popular and bourgeois dilettantism (a 'myth', indeed, consistent only with the equally unfounded idea of the 'popularity' of opera at Hamburg). In reality, however, the Hamburg–Braunschweig circuit is of insufficient dimensions to permit the capacity operation of a productive system based essentially on much more expansive market needs and conditions – conditions quite non-existent in Germany (in contrast, as noted, to the situation in Venice and elsewhere in Italy). Even between the two extremes of Hamburg and Vienna, too many and various are the ways in which the Italian *dramma per musica* is appropriated by the German tradition. Clearly, in this context of limited consistency of approach, the chances of survival of the autocratic Viennese system are much greater than those at the other end of the scale – not least since the room for manoeuvre left open for the 'capitalist' system of Hamburg is further reduced by adoption of the Imperial model at other important court operatic centres (Dresden, Hanover, Munich). Thus, the conditions essential for the very survival of the Gänsemarkt come under increasing attack, with consequent reduction of the theatre to an isolated position of economic and artistic 'autonomy'. In the 1730s, German-language opera gives way entirely to the Italian *dramma per musica*, performed by the Italian *cappelle musicali* of the various German courts or imported directly from Italy and briskly 'distributed' by itinerant troupes. In 1740, two years after the definitive closure of the Gänsemarkt to German-language opera, the theatre is successfully re-opened to performances of Italian *drammi per musica*; only now does it take a permanent place in an operatic circuit which stretches north from Graz to Copenhagen – a circuit dominated by the Italian company of the brothers Mingotti.

Yet despite its inherent economic and institutional weakness, Hamburg represents a truly extraordinary episode in seventeenth-century operatic history. No other city in Europe boasts a similar quantity of operas of such varying provenance and artistic tendency. Few in number (less than ten out of a total of some 250 operas) but culturally not insignificant are the Old Testament themes of the earliest years: a kind of *captatio benevolentiae* with respect to the clergy, and symptomatic of a certain diffidence towards the theatre; examples are *Adam und Eva* (Richter and Theile, 1678), *Michal und David* (Elmenhorst and Franck, 1679), *Esther* (Köler and Strungk, 1680). From the very beginning, however, Venetian *drammi per musica* of 'historical' complexion are translated and re-set to new music: examples are *La prosperità di Elio Seiano* and *La caduta di Elio Seiano* by Minato (re-set by Strungk). While there is an overall majority of Venetian libretti, importation is not always direct: after 1690, in fact, Braunschweig frequently represents an intermediate step. The Venetian preponderance, moreover, is by no means overwhelming. Certain subjects are derived from French literary drama or direct from mythological or literary-mythological sources: an example is *Adonis* (1697) by Christian Heinrich Postel and Reinhard Keiser, based on Marino ('most charming and gracious poet in the world'). Others revive original French or Italian scores, with performances in the original language or in translation: two cases in point are *Acis et Galatée* by Lully (first produced in 1689 and revived in German six years later) and the monumental *Gerusalemme liberata* of Giulio Cesare Corradi and Carlo Pallavicino. This latter, a Venice–Dresden co-production for Carnival 1687, might almost be described as a visible symbol and seal of the anti-Ottoman alliance between these two city-states; the opera is subsequently revived at Hamburg in 1694 and 1695 (respectively, in Italian and German). The years 1695–99 see the triumph – again in German translation – of the heroic operas of Agostino Steffani. Insufficient data is available on the operas composed by native Hamburg musicians before Reinhard Keiser to allow full evaluation of the impact (presumably strong) of the highly pathetic style, sublime eloquence and grandiose manner of Steffani on public and musicians at the Gänsemarkt. Certainly, the originality of orchestration, bold melodic invention and affective directness of Keiser seem somehow to draw on the earlier operas of Steffani (himself an Italian of largely German upbringing and training, destined to a career in the upper-middle bracket of the diplomatic and ecclesiastical hierarchy) for the court theatre of Hanover. This theatre was itself erected in the 1680s in emulation of the theatres of Venice (where the Dukes of Braunschweig and Hanover, suppliers of troops in support of the anti-Ottoman campaign, are also frequent visitors at Carnival, patronizing composers, librettists and singers) and as visible symbol of the pretensions of Hanover in terms of Imperial politics (with a view to the inclusion of the Duke of Hanover in the college of electoral princes, 1692).

Finally, the literary tradition of German political theatre, coupled with a strong propensity for the open dramatic representation of political violence and cruelty, favour the frequent performance in Hamburg of new operas based on political themes: examples are the *Cara Mustapha* (von Bostel and Franck) of 1686 (i.e., in the aftermath of the Turkish siege of Vienna), which sings the rise and fall of the Grand Vizier, and the *Masagniello furioso* of Feind and Keiser (1706). Present, too, are 'local' themes (not unlike the 'drammi civili rusticali' of the Teatro della Pergola in Florence), replete with dialect characters and salacious satires on local custom. Keiser's *Störtebecker und Jödge Michaels* (1701) recounts the bloody adventures of two corsairs brought to justice and executed in Hamburg; in 1725, two 'comic' operas – the *Hamburger Jahrmarkt* and *Hamburger Schlachtzeit* (respectively, the 'fair' and 'slaughter-time at Hamburg') – earn the censure of the local city council for indecency.

25 The *tragédie lyrique*: Jean-Baptiste Lully

In contrast to the essentially literary tendencies of the earliest German approaches to Italian opera (Opitz, Harsdörffer), the French attitude is decidedly authoritarian. A case in point is the policy of Cardinal Mazarin (successor of Richelieu as effective governor of the nation) in his introduction of Italian opera to the Parisian stage; this is symptomatic of a much wider programme of cultural 'Italianization' of court and capital alike. 'Italianization', indeed, which necessarily entails an alliance with 'francophile' groupings on the Italian peninsula itself: it is thus hardly surprising to note the presence of large numbers of Italian musicians in Paris during the fifth and sixth decades of the century – musicians supplied by the Medici, Este, Farnese and, above all, the Barberini descendants of Pope Urban VIII (who, having fallen into disfavour under the papacy of Urban's pro-Spanish successor Innocent X, pass something of a golden exile in France). The Barberini, in fact, are bearers of a brilliant operatic tradition (see chapter 20); practically 'Barberini' is the first opera composed specifically for the Parisian court: *Orfeo* (Francesco Buti and Luigi Rossi) of 1647.

This, however, is not the earliest production of an Italian opera in Paris. In 1645, the indefatigable Febiarmonici, following in the wake of a host of celebrated Italian comic actors (among them Tiberio Fiorilli, known as 'Scaramuccia'), had already produced a Parisian *Finta pazza*, in a performance which was half-sung, half-recited. Scenographer on this occasion was Giacomo Torelli, veritable wizard of Venetian stagecraft and scenic effects. As in the Prologue of *Bellerofonte*, performed at the Teatro Novissimo, Venice, against a back-cloth of the Piazzetta S. Marco, Torelli here provides for the sudden appearance – amidst a panoramic view of the port of Scyros – of the Île de la Cité, with views of the monument to Henri IV, Pont-Neuf and bells of Notre-Dame: a beautiful mirror effect of theatrical reflection in which the city becomes the unsuspecting object of extraordinary scenic illusions of self-admiration – an effect clearly calculated to win favour with the Parisian public. As such, it was not wholly unsuccessful. Torelli, indeed, remains in Paris for a further fifteen years. In general, however, Italian opera meets with a lukewarm reception in France. The extraordinary stage machinery of the no less extraordinarily expensive *Orfeo* was immediately re-used with much greater success in Pierre Corneille's expressly devised 'tragédie à machines', *Andromède*, itself somewhat limited in its utilization of music (which is in any case strictly excluded from dialogue sections).

Of particular repugnance for contemporary French observers is the sheer 'improbability' of singing a dialogue, together with the propensity of Italian composers for melodic expression (which interrupts the action), secondary episodes, comic digressions, the non-observance of the Aristotelian unities of time, place and action, floridity of style and the artificial voice of the *castrati* (savagely mocked by a Parisian public whose preference lies clearly with the high range of the French male contraltos or *haute-contres*). Not even the remarkable intuition of Mazarin – one of whose informants is the ubiquitous Atto Melani – in his choice of Cavalli (rather than some Roman musician) as composer of the music for the marriage of Louis XIV with the Infanta of Spain (itself the perfect seal to Mazarin's own diplomatic masterpiece of 1659: the Treaty of the Pyrenees, however, proves little more than ephemeral as guarantee of European peace) is sufficient to improve the fortunes of the Italian *drammi per musica* at Paris. The Venetian *Xerse* (Minato and Cavalli) of 1654 – with *Giasone*, perhaps the most lively and witty of all Cavalli's contributions to the operatic stage (as such, aided in no small degree by a libretto of such quality as to merit re-settings as late as Bononcini and Handel) – is, in fact, revived in 1660 on a makeshift stage at the Louvre, prior to the completion of the enormous Tuileries theatre (designer Gaspare Vigarani, successor to Torelli) for the 'official' celebrations. The Parisian version of *Xerse* makes three significant concessions to contemporary French taste: the role of the protagonist, originally contralto, is now transposed for baritone; the overall dramatic structure is re-organized from three acts to five (in accordance with then-current usage in French-language tragedies and comedies); inserted between the acts is a picturesque series of 'ridiculous' *entrées de ballet* (featuring Spaniards, Basques and French, Iberian peasants, Scaramouche and Trivellino, negro slaves and sailors, buffoons, satyrs and sylvans), set to music by Jean-Baptiste Lully (composer of ballet and instrumental music to the King of France). Its success, however, was far from assured. It was simply too long: eight hours of totally incomprehensible text! No more enthusiastic was the reception of the 'tragedia' *Ercole amante* (Buti and Cavalli), performed in February 1662 'for the wedding of Their Most Christian Majesties'. Here, too, a total of eighteen *entrées de ballet* (again set to music by Lully) are inserted between the five acts of the opera; the King himself appeared as Pluto, Mars and, inevitably, the Sun. To spectators, themselves victims of the somewhat unfortunate acoustic of the great theatre, the enormously protracted score (albeit of considerable beauty) inevitably created the impression of a 'royal ballet, intertwined with a tragic poem sung to music', with a note-worthy reversal of perspective and interest. Several decades will now pass before the next French production of an Italian *dramma per musica*.

Mazarin's authoritarian attempt to impose Italian opera in France – in common, indeed, with his entire cultural policy of Italianization, including an unrealized project by Bernini for the extension of the Louvre – was thus destined to failure. It did, however, act as catalyst for the formation of a new and proudly autonomous musical and theatrical genre: the *tragédie lyrique*. (In reality, this now current denomination is a later – eighteenth-century – invention: seventeenth-century terminology prefers the definition *tragédie en musique*, itself the perfect French homologue of the Italian *dramma per musica*.) The authoritarianism of Mazarin's original initiative, however, remains fully typical of later French developments. Authoritarian is the policy of Louis XIV in his institution of a permanent organism for the exclusive production of opera in French: the Académie royale de musique. Authoritarian (in terms of managerial ability, artistic talent and, inevitably, royal consent) is the role played in this organization by a single musician: Jean-Baptiste Lully. An early attempt – that of Pierre Perrin and Robert Cambert (1669) – to introduce French-language opera on the basis of royal privilege had foundered – amidst rampant economic intrigue and artistic jealousy – after two productions only. The patent granted Lully in 1672 makes interesting reading:

> In so far as the most beautiful ornaments of any State are the sciences and arts, no other type of amusement has been more to Our pleasure – having secured peace for Our peoples – than their revival, calling to Our service all those who are reputed to excel in their respective fields, not only within the confines of Our kingdom, but also from abroad. As inducement to further improvement, We have honoured them with tokens of Our goodwill and esteem. And, since music occupies one of the foremost positions among the liberal arts, with the aim of encouraging its favourable development We had granted permission (with patent letter of 28 June 1669) to M. Perrin for the establishment of musical academies in Our city of Paris and other cities of Our kingdom with a view to the public performance of theatrical dramas in the manner of Italy, Germany and England. This patent was to have the duration of twelve years. Having subsequently been informed, however, that the abundant efforts and care of M. Perrin in this venture were nevertheless insufficient in respect of Our intentions to raise the art of music to the levels desired, We have believed it appropriate to appoint a person of known experience and ability, capable of training future experts in singing and scenic action and establishing ensembles of violins, flutes and other instruments.
>
> To this end, well aware of the intelligence and great musical knowledge of Our dear and much-beloved Jean-Baptiste Lully (who, since entering Our service, has given, and continues to give, daily – and pleasurable – proof of his abilities, for which reason he has already been honoured with the post of *Surintendant et compositeur de la Musique de Notre Chambre*), We hereby grant and permit the said Lully (with the present letter, signed by Our hand) to establish a Royal Academy of Music in Our city of Paris, to consist of the quality and quantity of persons which he shall retain most appropriate and whom We ourselves shall select and register on the basis of his references and recommendations for the performance in Our presence (when We so desire) of *piéces de musique* in French verse and foreign tongues, in the manner of the Italian academies. And M. Lully shall be granted this privilege for life – as, after him, whichever of his sons shall inherit the aforesaid office of *Surintendant de la Musique de Notre Chambre* – with power to associate with whomsoever he deems most appropriate for the establishment of the aforesaid Academy.
>
> And as compensation for the notable expenses which M. Lully shall inevitably be required to sustain in connection with the aforesaid representations (with regard to the scenes, costumes, machines, theatre and all other necessities), We hereby grant him permission to give public performances of all his compositions, including those represented in Our presence, save that he shall not be permitted to make use of those musicians in Our personal employ for performances of the said dramas; he shall also be authorized to request such sums as he shall retain necessary and to station guards or other officials at the entrances of the venues where the aforesaid performances shall be given. At the same time, all persons of whatsoever quality or condition (including Our own court officials) are expressly forbidden to enter the venues in question without having paid; likewise, no person whatever may organize the performance of any wholly

> musical drama (in French or any other language) without the written consent of M. Lully, upon pain of a fine of ten thousand *livres* and confiscation of theatres, scenes, machines, costumes and other things – a third for Our own direct benefit, a third for the *hôpital-général*, and a third for M. Lully, who shall also be empowered to establish private schools of music in Our city of Paris and wherever else he deems necessary for the good and well-being of the aforesaid *Académie royale*. And since the said Academy shall be modelled upon those already in existence in Italy, where gentlemen may sing in public without contravening aristocratic decorum, We desire and hereby command that all gentlemen and *Mademoiselles* be permitted to sing in the aforesaid dramas and other entertainments in Our Royal Academy without prejudice to their titles of nobility, privileges, offices, rights and immunities.

Naturally, this latter clause is not to be regarded as representative of the situation in Italian public theatres (where, with the rare exception of those singers fortunate enough to merit elevation to knighthood by virtue of their vocal abilities, performers are exclusively professional) or as indicating any easy access on the part of aristocratic *dilettantes* to the stage of the Académie. Nevertheless, it certainly suited the aristocratic ambitions of the composer himself; Lully, having acquired by royal donation the hereditary position of *Surintendant* (a 'purchasable' office, the nominal value of which was the subject of an annual percentage tax to be paid by its incumbent), could legitimately claim consideration as a recently elevated member of the *noblesse de robe*. The royal privilege, moreover, conferred upon Lully and his descendants a literally absolute sovereignty over musical theatre in the nation as a whole. When, in 1685 and 1688, the towns of Marseilles and Lyons express a desire to open theatres of their own for performances of the *tragédies lyriques* of Lully (then on the crest of their Parisian success), they must first acquire the rights from the composer and his heirs; on his death, his wife and sons are given obligatory life pensions by the Académie royale. In contrast to the other academies established by Richelieu (the Académie française) and, subsequently, by the royal minister Colbert (the Académies des sciences, des inscriptions, medailles et belles-lettres, de peinture et sculpture, d'architecture), the Académie de musique has neither statute nor constitution; more than an influential forum of artists, literary scholars or men of learning, employed by the public exchequer for the moral and economic welfare and development of the kingdom, it is established as an essentially productive organization and is placed under the plenipotentiary control of a single individual: Jean-Baptiste Lully.

Lully's appropriation of French musical theatre, while undoubtedly the result of royal favour, was also the outcome of his already sufficiently prestigious theatrical experience. From 1663 to 1671, in fact, he is permanent musical collaborator with Molière. Fruits of their relationship are some twelve *comédies-ballets*: i.e., comedies interspersed with *entrées de ballet*, themselves more or less integrated in the dramatic action. Maximum integration is achieved in the thoroughly entertaining *Le bourgeois gentilhomme* (1670), in which the insertion of each individual *entrée* at the particular moment in question can be seen as a clearly justifiable dramatic decision; here, the 'interludes' of dance function as an integral part of the comedy itself. In Act 1, the Maître à danser and the Maître de musique try out the various pieces to be submitted for the perusal of the infatuated Gentilhomme: in particular, 'a little demonstration of the various passions which music is capable of expressing'. This piece, in reality a pastoral dialogue, fails to arouse the enthusiasm of monsieur Jourdain, who is thoroughly bored with the fashionable affections and preciosity of contemporary pastoral poetry; to no avail is the objection of the Maître à danser: 'When characters must recite in music, the laws of probability necessitate recourse to pastoral scenes; song has always been an attribute of shepherds, and it is hardly natural for princes or bourgeois characters to sing their passions in dialogue.' Act 2 concludes with an *entrée* of 'quatre garçons tailleurs', who help monsieur Jourdain try on his new fashionable suit. Act 3, likewise, concludes with a ballet of cooks, who prepare a banquet for the guests of monsieur Jourdain. Act 4 is centred entirely upon the exhilarating Turkish investiture ceremony inflicted upon an unsuspecting monsieur Jourdain (Lully himself, in the presence of the King, played the comic role of the Mufti). Finally, the denouement of Act 5 is commemorated in a joyful polyglot ballet performed by Italians, French and Spaniards, who vie with each other in song and dance; the choral conclusion, however, is a hymn in praise of the *théâtre* of Molière–Lully: 'Quels spectacles charmants, quels plaisirs goûtons-nous! / Les dieux mêmes, les dieux n'en ont point de plus doux'. Elsewhere, the interludes of song and dance form a series of individual episodes in a single, unified action which parallels the main action of the comedy without obvious – or even necessary – connections. This procedure can lead to a kind of mirror relationship between comedy and *entrées de ballet*. In *Georges Dandin* (1668), for example, the bitter-sweet comedy of a rich yet miserly peasant – betrayed and ridiculed by his young bourgeois wife – is alternated (in song) with the amorous adventures of four shepherds (Climène, Cloris, Tircis and Philène), in a relationship of contrast–analogy where the greater the stylistic gap, the greater the irony.

Quite different, however, from the supply of *intermèdes*, *entrées* and pastoral scenes for comedies and *ballets de cour* is the composition of an entire 'tragédie en musique'. French objections to the latter stem less from the differences between French and Italian music – differences already perceptible by the mid-seventeenth century (when they provide the material for the humorous bilingual dialogue in Lully's *Ballet de la raillerie*, 1659), but which only later (with the mature operas of Lully and their posthumous 'canonization') will assume the dimensions of mutually irreconcilable national styles – than from their different aesthetic bases and the enormous importance of French 'literary' theatre (to the point, indeed, at which the latter inevitably functions as aesthetic norm for the creation of the new 'tragédie en musique'). In Italy the *dramma per musica* may be seen as a sublimation and ennoblement of the then dominant theatrical form: the *commedia dell'arte*. In France, on the contrary, the classical moderation and sublime pathos of the tragedies of Corneille and Racine cast an all-pervading shadow on the operatic repertory; Lully, indeed, meets with not inconsiderable censure on the part of literary critics.

A clearer idea of the nature of the disputes in question may be gained from a reading of the *Critique de l'opera, ou Examen de la tragédie intitulée 'Alceste ou Le triomphe d'Alcide'*. *Alceste* (1674) is the second of the *tragédies lyriques* produced by Lully and his 'resident' librettist Philippe Quinault for the Académie royale de musique. (Quinault, indeed, is bound to the composer by contract; over the period 1673–86, he provides no less than eleven of the thirteen texts of Lully's 'tragédies en musique'.) The *Critique*, though published anonymously, is the work of Charles Perrault: future author of the celebrated 'Tales of Mother Goose' and the poem *Le siècle de Louis le Grand* of 1687, an unbridled exaltation of the prosperity of the arts under Louis XIV in the true *grand siècle* of the nation. He is also an unflinching supporter of 'modernity' in the *Querelle des anciens et des modernes* – a dispute between the advocates of ancient Greek and Latin literature (Boileau and his *Art poétique* to the fore) and the champions of contemporary French drama and its autonomy from strict observance of the ancient literary canons, which ravaged French literary circles throughout the second half of the seventeenth century. Perrault, indeed, can hardly be accused of any adverse preconceptions in the field of theatrical music: his *Critique* is entirely positive. In common with his various opponents (Boileau included), however, his attention is centred entirely on matters of text, to the total exclusion of music: this one-sided critical approach itself provides eloquent testimony to the overwhelming importance of literary theatre (in court and city alike) for the development of the *tragédie lyrique*. It is not accidental that *Alceste* was to remain the sole 'tragédie' by Quinault and Lully based upon an ancient drama, Euripides' *Alcestis*, which by itself provided a basis for a detailed literary comparison all too detrimental to the 'modern' dramatic form.

Protagonists of the *Critique* are Cléon (whose case in support of modern opera makes allusion to the apparent 'antagonism' between court and city tastes: part of the Parisian criticism of *Alceste* is attributed to the favour with which the opera has already been received at Versailles) and his opponent Aristippe (who immediately declares himself 'thoroughly pleased with both music and scenes' but no less disgusted by the poetry). Aristippe's objections touch upon questions of plot, versification, the presence of comic characters (whose *ariettes*, notes Cléon, are on the lips of every Parisian) and the elimination of certain episodes included in Euripides' original plot. Cléon, on the contrary, provides a point-by-point justification for every departure from Euripides. Eliminated is the dialogue between Apollo and Death, in so far as its anticipation of future events would reduce dramatic expectation; eliminated, too, is Alceste's tale of woe, since amorous laments are hardly appropriate for women of her particular maturity and wisdom (the inevitable result being laughter); other 'cuts' regard the dialogue scene in which Admète convinces his wife Alceste to sacrifice herself on his behalf (nowadays, says Cléon, such requests are quite intolerable), the dialogue between Phérès and the King (Admète's mistreatment of his elderly father is unseemly), the valet's mockery of Alcide *alias* Hercules (the modern image of Hercules is hardly compatible with his portrayal as drunkard and reveller), the restoration of the veiled Alceste to Admète (deceit is more appropriate to comedy than tragedy). On the contrary, the 'invention' of Alcide's love for Alceste binds the figure of Hercules more closely to the tragedy and 'marvellously exalts his glory' (in his triumph over his passions and Death). Further innovations regard Licomède's love for Alceste and his mortal wounding of Admète (a more 'noble' death for the latter as compared with his fatal illness in Euripides); the fickle love of Céphise for Lychas and Straton, themselves comic confidants of the protagonists (comic interplay between the followers of the heroes is quite acceptable, and has the added advantage of strengthening the contrast between the faithfulness of the heroes and the unfaithfulness of the others; the fifteen-year-old Céphise, moreover, provides suitable contrast and complement to the noble figure of the elderly Phérès who, like her, refuses to die in order that the King be saved); the appearance of Apollo in the heavens, and his order that a monument be erected to the memory of whomsoever gives his life for Admète (a scenically effective justification for the erecion of the catafalque on which Alceste will subsequently be sacrificed, as also for the elimination of long and tedious descriptive narrations); the horrified amazement of Admète on beholding the dead Alceste (accompanied in the music by a sudden and deeply moving shift from jubilation to grief and despair); and, finally, Alcide's victory over himself, which, with its addition of 'a kind of climactic episode and subsequent denouement, brings a redoubling of attention and pleasure' (this scene is nothing but the aforementioned dual victory of Hercules and his elevation from semi-god to a rank of heroic sublimity: a rank in which the image of the Roi Soleil is presumably never far away). Cléon (*alias* Perrault), while advocating the necessity for a certain adaptation of ancient themes to modern customs and usage, freely admits 'the superiority of the ancients over modern authors in their descriptions of nature, sentiments and the human heart, as also in everything concerned with expression'. 'In works of human intellect, however, certain other things must also be observed: as, for example, decorum, order, economy, distribution, the connection between the various parts and the whole'; these things are the product of experience, and are thus handled more satisfactorily by the modern dramatist. As for godly interventions: Horace's condemnation of the *deus ex machina* is valid for tragedy and comedy but not for opera (itself unknown at the time of Horace). The handling of 'probability' and/or the 'merveilleux', as prescribed by Aristotle, is graduated genre by genre: comedy is concerned only with the 'probable'; tragedy tolerates a certain level of the 'merveilleux'; opera, on the contrary, is principally concerned with this latter. In opera, then, sudden transformations of scene (earth/heaven/hell, etc.) have an excellent effect; indeed, the astonishing scenic effects of the so-called 'merveilleux' come to act almost as an alibi for the infractions inevitably committed against the laws of probability by music and *mise en scène*. Finally, observes Perrault, the true yardstick for the evaluation of all such entertainments is the 'good taste' of *honnêtes hommes*, of cultivated people: a criterion which embraces the idea of community consensus as the regulating force behind any collective cultural phenomenon.

The debate for and against opera – an essentially 'literary' debate, which assails (not to say 'persecutes') French opera for more than the first century of its existence, spilling over into eighteenth-century Germany and Italy – shows full awareness of the inherent irregularities and anomalies of the *tragédie lyrique* (judged, that is, from the point of view of classical drama). Seen, however, from the standpoint of Italian opera – the very 'model' whose imitation (or replacement) receives such hearty recommendation in the royal privilege of 1672 – the notable proximity of the *tragédie lyrique* to contemporary French 'dramatic' tragedy is all too apparent: a proximity rivalled only by the almost total contrast between seventeenth-century French and Italian opera. For the latter, we might add, no comparison with the ancient literary sources – such as that provided in the *Critique* – would be possible or, indeed, of any relevance.

The laws of probability are not without repercussions in the field of musical structure. Gone is the clear-cut Italian distinction between aria (*air*) and recitative (*récit*); the sole – and logical – exception is provided by certain *airs*, performed as independent pieces by some generally lower-class character who decides and openly declares his intention to pass the time in song. *Airs* and *récits* are characterized by similar melodic material: the only difference concerns the degree of density in the organization of the musical rhetoric. Typical of both is an almost exclusively syllabic declamation: in recitative, however, rhythm is subordinated to the tempo of the diction, to the point at which duple- and triple-time bars are seen (but not heard: the phenomenon in question is a matter of purely graphical convention; in metrical terms, the only perceptible means of organization is the accentual and emphatic rhythm of the textual declamation) to alternate freely in accordance with necessity. *Airs* differ from *récits* in their more or less consistent repetition of one or two lines of particular poetic expression and heightened melodic profile (mostly broad, emphatic phrases in cadential position): 'Terminez mes tourments, puissant maître du monde; / sans vous, sans votre amour, hélas! / je ne souffrirai pas' is Io's threefold invocation in her monologue of *Isis*; 'Le héros que j'attends ne reviendra-t-il pas?' (Louis XIV is still heavily involved in the Dutch military campaign) is the melodically tormented question of the Nymph of the Seine in the Prologue to *Alceste* (eight repetitions in an *air* of twenty-five lines). In short: the musical form of both *airs* and *récits* is fluid and rhetorically defined. Somewhat strange to Goldoni, on his first attendance as spectator at the Académie de musique, was the apparent lack of arias in Act 1: the Italian playwright had mistaken a total of no less than six *airs* for a continuous recitative!

Musically speaking, the *tragédie lyrique* is articulated in 'real time'. In Italian opera, the 'time' of the action proceeds arbitrarily and intermittently: 'fast' in recitative, momentarily suspended in the arias (with their long-drawn-out and 'closed' representation of affections which – in reality – are both instant and enduring), interrupted with every change of scene; the music, itself endowed with its own effective 'time', remains somewhat apart from all questions of temporal reality. In French opera, the 'time' of the action has its own regular flow of a kind which tends to coincide with that of the music: the time actually employed in the representation of events is virtually identical to that which would theoretically be necessary for their real-life enactment. The Aristotelian precept of the unity of time is rigorously observed within each individual act; strictly applied, too, are the so-called *liaison de scène* (the rule by which the simultaneous exit of all the characters at the end of a scene is prohibited) and the unity of place (with exceptions for spells, enchantments, divinities and other 'wondrous' apparitions). Symptomatic – almost symbolic – of this musical and dramatic *continuum* are the transition notes by which successive scenes are smoothly joined in the *basso continuo*; though each scene is endowed with its own basic tonality, the relationship between consecutive segments of text is thus characterized less by any marked interruption than by definite connection. Melodic expansiveness, necessarily accompanied by increasing density and decreasing speed in the musical and dramatic tempo, is notably restrained; when present, moreover, motivation for such expansiveness is also to be found in the text, its rhetorical configuration or the flagrancy of the dramatic events.

At points such as these, however, melodic expansiveness is sometimes lacking altogether and expression entrusted to the declamatory emphasis of recitative. A case in point is *Armide* (1686): in particular, the monologue of *Armide* herself, whose desire to kill her sleeping enemy Renaud is bettered only by her helpless love for him. This scene soon earned a reputation as the greatest, most powerful and 'truthful' moment in the entire history of the *tragédie lyrique*; Rameau, in his various theoretical writings (published both before and after his *début* as a theatrical composer), several times exalts its representative and expressive qualities. Precisely here, indeed, the conflict within the soul of the heroine is communicated less by any definite melodic or harmonic characterization than by a series of agonizing pauses, punctuated by distressed and disconnected exclamations. Lully's recitative, in such moments of great affective tension, is imbued with a sheer physical 'theatricality' quite absent from contemporary Italian recitative (or, at most, entrusted to the individual skills of the performer). The *air*, too, proceeds in full subordination to the dictates of dramatic declamation. The syntactic construction of the musical period and phrase of a 'Lully-style' melody is imbued with notable fluency and smoothness, further enhanced by the accentual indeterminacy of French metre and prose (Alexandrine verse, dominant to the point of exclusion in French literary theatre and basic to opera, assigns greater importance to caesuras than accents). The 'slumber' aria of Renaud, located shortly before the impassioned monologue of Armide (and thus, by virtue of a necessary dramatic contrast, characterized by sentiments of idyllic sweetness and peace), consists entirely of 'irregular' phrases (11, 6, 11, 8, 7 and 7 bars). Yet the outcome is certainly anything but 'crookedness' or asymmetry of diction, but on the contrary, a sustained naturalness and spontaneity of sound and expression: a 'normal' declamation of the text. The effect of pervasive, lulling regularity derives from the light and undulating *continuum* of quavers (3/4 time) in the accompaniment, together with the diffuse and voluptuous sound of muted violins.

The moderate use of musical resources for the purposes of dramatic dialogue (in other words: the traditional 'classical' reduction in the ostentation of expressive means), if uniformly applied, would deprive the *tragédie lyrique* of its very *raison d'être*. The action, however, is carried not only through dialogue but also by means of a series of visible and intrinsically spectacular events; it is, indeed, these events, with their recourse to the 'merveilleux', which safeguard the 'rights' of the music without prejudice to the laws of probability. One of the various dramatic rules of the *tragédie lyrique* prescribes the construction of each act around a particular incident or prominent event (mythological, magical, ceremonial, allegorical), itself capable of furnishing a suitable pretext for the creation of a scene-within-a-scene infused with ample quantities of music and dance. These so-called *divertissements* serve the dual function of momentary diversions from the action and entertainments for the senses. A good example is *Alceste*. The Prologue is itself a grand allegorical *divertissement*. The *divertissement* of Act 1 (fishermen and sailors, side by side with nymphs and tritons) is ostensibly a nautical festivity in honour of the newly-wed couple Admète and Alceste, but has in reality been offered by the jealous Licomède as a simple ploy (*coup de théâtre*) to kidnap Alceste and throw overboard Admète and Alcide – thus beginning the action of the drama. Act 1 concludes with the 'wondrous' interventions of Thétis (who unleashes a storm at sea) and Éole (who restores peace and calm); both are simple pretexts for the musical evocation of 'meteorological' effects. Act 2 brings the siege, assault and conquest of Scyros (the kingdom of Licomède) by Admète and Alcide at the head of an army of Thessalian soldiers: in this martial *divertissement*, an entire military action is described in the course of five exceptionally concentrated minutes of music and dance (obviously, in a highly accelerated temporal perspective), complete with opposing choruses of 'besiegers' and 'besieged', marches with trumpets and drums, and martial *entrées de ballet*. Now comes the *coup de théâtre*: the mortal wounding of Admète; the act concludes with the 'wondrous' appearance of Apollo and the Arts, who erect the catafalque destined to receive whomsoever be sacrificed for the King. Act 3 – veritable climax of the drama – is endowed with a 'ceremonial' structure of remarkable dimensions; its vastness and solemnity of theatrical invention are quite without equal in the history of seventeenth-century opera. First comes Alceste's austere and heart-broken lament for the dying Admète, echoed by the chorus of Thessalians with their sorrowful, threefold 'Hélas!' This is followed by a chorus of jubilation for the recovery of the King. Next comes the sudden revelation of the catafalque and corpse of Alceste (who has sacrificed herself to save her husband's life), with universal (choral) grief; the phrase 'Alceste est morte' – ritualistically proclaimed as a long, grave and mighty G minor cadence, thrice repeated by the choir – is destined to a certain longevity in the French collective memory: Rameau, sixty years later, provides almost identical music for his setting of the words 'Hippolyte n'est plus' (*Hippolyte et Aricie*, 1733); the 'opéra-comique' *Les funérailles de la Foire* (1718) is itself a perfect parody of Lully's original ('La foire est morte'). Finally, the funeral of Alceste brings a somewhat lugubrious march, dominated by the sonority of the two flutes (an attempted evocation of the tibias which customarily accompany funeral processions on the bas-reliefs of Roman sarcophagi) and punctuated by the desolate weeping of a mourner; Act 3 closes with the 'wondrous' apparition of Diana and Mercury, who themselves later accompany Alcide in his voyage through Hades in search of Alceste (whom he hopes to restore to the living). In Act 4, Charon (ferryman to the Shades, collector at the entrance to the Underworld and, so to speak, general 'dogsbody' of Hades) receives a joking characterization in the course of a comic *air*; on the contrary, the royal status of Pluto and Proserpine is reflected in the strongly marked rhythms – royal attribute *par excellence* – of the introductory 'largo' (similar in type to the opening of the typical French *ouverture*) of the 'infernal' *divertissement* for Alcide. Finally, Act 5 is articulated as a single, grand choral celebration of the deliverance of Alceste and magnanimity of Alcide; looking on are Apollo and the Muses, who descend from the skies amidst singing and dancing by Thessalian nobles and shepherds. There is thus no lack of opportunity for interpolations of music and dance between the various *récits* and *airs*; moreover, with the complicity of the 'merveilleux' and the introduction of artfully prepared *divertissements*, the laws of probability –

sacrosanct convention of French dramatic literature – emerge without unacceptable distortions. Epitome of the union of music and dance under the twin banner of ceremonial and the 'merveilleux' are certain colossally-structured *chaconnes* and *passacailles*, played and sung at the final apotheosis to a number of the *tragédies*. Most magnificent of all is the *passacaille* from Act 5 of *Armide* (*divertissement*): the Plaisirs, Amants fortunés and Amantes heureuses are summoned by the magic of Armide for the entertainment of Renaud during her absence. The basic four-bar scheme (the customary descending tetrachord: G–F–E♭–D) is reiterated and varied for a total of some one hundred statements: a veritable procession of violins, flutes, oboes, solo voices and choruses, articulated in a temporal dimension that is at once both magic and hypnotic, ceaselessly in motion yet eternally still.

For Lully, then, the 'merveilleux' of ancient mythological subjects (*Cadmus et Hermione*, *Alceste*, *Thésée*, *Atys*, *Isis*, *Psyché*, *Bellérophon*, *Proserpine*, *Persée*, *Phaëton*) and the magic world of Renaissance epic poetry (*Amadis*, *Roland*, *Armide*) provide numerous pretexts for musical 'additions'; these themes, however, are also construed as 'fairy-tale' allegories around the figure of a deified and idolized sovereign (whose personal approval is, in fact, required for every choice of plot): a latter-day Apollo, perpetrator of an aggressive European policy and acclaimed at home as peacemaker and conciliator of the world (a new Pericles or Augustus). In this respect, the Prologues are specific. The identification, indeed, of intentional or unintentional allusions to the life of the court at Versailles in the plots of the *tragédies lyriques* of Quinault and Lully becomes a favourite society game for Parisian intellectuals and aristocracy. Celebrated above all other themes, however, are the virtues of glory and love: noble and chivalrous ideals, proposed for the unanimous imitation of old and young aristocracy alike. The *tragédie lyrique* also benefits economically from royal favour; according to a letter of Madame de Sevigné (1673), 'a few days ago, the King observed that if he is in Paris during performances of the opera, he will go every day. This little word is worth 100,000 francs to Lully.' Normally, an opera is first given at Versailles before passing to the Académie. Costs are prohibitive in relation to the number of productions: the norm is one new *tragédie* per year. The Académie, however, has its own permanent company, and is regularly open on Tuesdays, Fridays and Sundays (with a pause for Easter and a few other brief periods of repose). Premières normally take place in the period immediately following the Easter break – after, that is, the definitive close of the play season (which is thus automatically eliminated from competition). Above all, successful works are retained in the repertory and immediately revived upon waning of interest in the season's new production: the Academy's theatre, situated in the Royal Palace in the heart of Paris, is thus invariably packed and long continues to prosper. *Thésée* (1675) for example, is revived in 1677, 1678, 1679, 1688, 1698, 1707–08, 1720, 1721, 1722, 1729, 1730, 1731, 1744, 1745, 1754–55, 1765, 1767, 1770, 1771 and 1779: 104 years (albeit with the various modifications undergone by the original score in the course of later eighteenth-century productions) are something of a record for any European opera in the period up to the mid-nineteenth century. Almost all the *tragédies lyriques* of Lully (in contrast to those of his successors) remain actively in the repertory until the time of Rameau; *Armide*, for example, was performed as late as 1764, just thirteen years before Gluck's new musical setting of the same libretto. The 'monumental' image of the scores of Lully is further – and lastingly – consolidated by the printing privilege granted the composer in 1672. First to be published (though, strangely, as a series of separate parts) is *Isis* (1677); beginning in 1679, scores are published in the same year as their premières; finally comes a series of retrospective publications of works composed prior to 1678.

In sharp contrast to contemporary Italian *drammi per musica* (themselves literally produced and consumed by the dozen), Lully's operas come to represent something of an 'unforgettable' experience: an ever-present creed and canon. For almost a century, their performance remains an integral part of Parisian cultural horizons. The frequency of musical, verbal and theatrical parodies provides further proof of their lasting popularity at every level of Parisian society. The grand *tragédies lyriques* form part – and as such, provide authoritative documentation – of a particular French taste and musical style, quickly elevated to the rank of aesthetic code and handed down from one generation to the next. Polemical treatises of a kind exemplified by the *Comparaison de la musique italienne et de la musique française* of Jean Le Cerf de la Viéville (1704) confirm the proud autonomy and superiority of French musical style – an autonomy fully reflected (both visually and in sound) in the scores themselves. Idiomatic melodic formulas, peculiarities of performance practice (both vocal and instrumental), voice leading and the handling of the parts, harmonic treatment, modulations, orchestration (five basic parts throughout, violin, three 'tenor violins' and 'basse de violon', with doublings and supplementary parts for flutes, oboes and bassoons) and the structure of the score: all are indicative of a peculiarly 'French' orientation. By this very token, however, the diffusion of Lully's *tragédies lyriques*, though not inconsiderable on the French provincial circuit, is necessarily limited abroad. Indeed, this grandiose musical and theatrical monument to a young, ambitious sovereign survives more as a splendid and isolated memorial to Lully himself (d. 1687) than as testimony to the subsequent decline – long and inexorable – of King (whose operatic interests in any case quickly wane) and kingdom.

26 Theatrical music in England and Spain

> Musick and poetry have ever been acknowledg'd sisters, which walking hand in hand, support each other; As poetry is the harmony of words, so musick is that of notes: and as poetry is a rise above prose and oratory, so is musick the exaltation of poetry. Both of them may excel apart, but sure they are most excellent when they are joyn'd, because nothing is then wanting to either of their perfections: for thus they appear like wit and beauty in the same person. Poetry and painting have arrived to their perfection in our own country: musick is yet but in its nonage, a forward child, which gives hope of what it may be hereafter in *England*, when the masters of it shall find more encouragement. 'Tis now learning *Italian*, which is its best master, and studying a little of the *French* air, to give it somewhat more of gayety and fashion. Thus being farther from the sun, we are of later growth than our neighbour countries, and must be content to shake off our barbarity by degrees. The present age seems already dispos'd to be refin'd, and to distinguish betwixt wild fancy, and a just, numerous composition.

With these words – or, rather, through the words of the poet John Dryden – Henry Purcell presents the published score (1691) of his incidental music for *The prophetess, or The history of Dioclesian*. In England, as elsewhere, it is quite normal for the dedications of musical scores to be penned by professional authors (on commission from composers): peculiar, however, to the English tradition is a deep and basic affinity between poetry and music – an affinity fully evident in the lines quoted above (Dryden himself is the author of various poems written expressly for the music of Purcell, as also of an ode on the death of the composer: see Source reading 5). The influence of Italy and France shines through on the first reading – and hearing – of every page of Purcell. It is futile to ask which of the two influences predominates: Purcell's style is voraciously heterogeneous and versatile, to the point at which the strength of the composer's own personal imprint of melodic and harmonic invention becomes the only truly recognizable factor. Direct sources are the *tragédies lyriques* of Lully (*Cadmus et*

Hermione, in the London production of 1686; at least some of the other scores were available in printed editions) and a limited number of Italian *drammi per musica* (a recently discovered manuscript score of Cavalli's *Erismena* contains a translation of the text in a contemporary English hand; a further, unidentified Italian opera is known to have been performed in London in 1674). A further characteristic of the music of Purcell is its definite orientation towards suggestive scenic evocation, rapid histrionic characterization and theatrical gesticulation – much more, indeed, than that of contemporary Italian composers. This albeit necessary orientation is, however, insufficient in itself for the creation of an operatic tradition of any real strength or endurance. In the absence of the requisite cultural and institutional conditions for the favourable reception and development of this essentially alien phenomenon (conditions which emerge only in the first decade of the eighteenth century), the theatrical music of Purcell necessarily finds expression in forms of production which, to the eyes of continental observers, may appear 'isolated', anomalous and (on the death of the thirty-six-year-old composer in 1695) devoid of any real historical continuity: almost, one might say, a kind of historical 'wastage' (were such teleological concepts of the history of music not meaningless by very definition).

The English stage can boast a rich tradition in the theatrical employment of music. An obvious example is the abundant use of vocal insertions in the works of Shakespeare and, indeed, Elizabethan theatre in general. The compositions in question are ballads or canzonets of narrative or aphoristic hue, and are generally sung by secondary characters. Sometimes, however, they are entrusted to the protagonists themselves in what, for them, are critical moments in the drama; examples are the song of the deranged Ophelia in *Hamlet* and the 'willow' song of Desdemona in *Othello* (of which the music, with lute accompaniment, still survives). There are also a number of examples of out-and-out musical dramas-within-a-drama: a case in point is the ballet of Ceres, evoked by Prospero in *The tempest* (1611) – a comedy, this, replete with sound effects and esoteric harmonies of truly 'magical' derivation. Neither in the open-air Globe Theatre nor in the covered theatre of Blackfriars is the position of the musicians (themselves, like lutenist and composer Robert Johnson, in the employment of the monarch) clearly defined in relation to the stage: a considerable amount of music, indeed, is performed directly on stage, though it frequently arrives 'invisibly' from behind or from the upper reaches of the set (almost as though part of the scenery itself). In Shakespeare, however, music is less to be defined as a vehicle for communication of the emotions (as in opera) than as a simple theatrical expedient (when not, indeed, mere decoration or accompaniment); at most, its function is that of arousing deep sentiments of feeling and poetic expression in the hearts (and words) of the characters (as, for example, Lorenzo at the beginning of Act 5 in *The merchant of Venice*).

The co-existence of scenic actions, ballet, collective dance, danceable music and sung declamation in an overall context of ceremonial and carnival-like ritual is a particular feature of the English masques of the first half of the seventeenth century. These masques, produced both at court and in the houses of the aristocracy, might best be defined as theatrical ballets; in their allegorical and spectacularly exuberant invention and formal complexity (developed, above all, in the course of a thirty-year-long collaboration between the playwright Ben Jonson and the architect Inigo Jones), they are, in fact, nothing but a somewhat sophisticated development from French and Italian court ballet (see Source reading 2). The music of the masques – to judge from the few fragments now surviving (a situation equally familiar in the contemporary French and Italian court ballet repertories) – is composite and somewhat 'casual' in style, and extremely slow to embrace the *stile recitativo* (*sine qua non* for the musical recitation of any dramatic action). Though the languid, tender chamber monodies of Caccini enjoyed an early success and diffusion in England (a situation, perhaps, not unrelated to a certain propensity on the part of English poets for the association of music with essentially melancholic affections), the first artistically significant attempt to apply the Italian *stile recitativo* to an English dialogue text appears to date only from the period around 1630: the lament of Hero and Leander, by the lutenist, singer and painter Nicholas Lanier, composed on his return from a voyage to Italy. In any case, masque (and related forms: see Source reading 2) and opera are characterized by a radical and irreconcilable diversity of function: on the one hand, the community celebration of a social rite and ceremonial of symbolic and affirmative significance; on the other, the scenically 'standardized' simulation/representation of some exemplary or admirable process or conflict. In its heterogeneous mixture of action, dance, ballet and music, the masque can hardly be described as a true forerunner of opera; on the contrary, it seems to represent something of an obstacle to the establishment of opera in England. The masque, indeed, meets with enormous success under James I and Charles I, who squander extravagant sums in productions of increasingly phantasmagoric complexion. It is proscribed during the Commonwealth (though a number of private performances continue to be given on diplomatic occasions of exceptional importance, as also in scholastic circles); nor is it reinstated under the Restoration monarchy, by which time it has come to be seen as politically discredited. The cultural horizons of the English aristocracy, however, remain somewhat nostalgically linked to this varied and versatile form of ceremonial entertainment – as though to an inalienable prerogative of caste. The result: the tenacious survival of a single – theatrical – variant of a now essentially altered and 'defunctionalized' genre. Even before the Civil War masques had occasionally been performed in the overall context of some theatrical drama (without direct involvement of the spectators in the central ballet): after the Restoration, the public theatre – now blossoming as never before – replaces the court and the other private masques of the earlier Stuarts in their role as community and social ritual and meeting place for the English aristocracy, with the incorporation of what can only be described as miniature masques in the dramatic action; of a total of some 500 comedies and tragedies produced between 1660 and and 1700, almost all are endowed with some kind of musical insertion. These masques, however, preserve nothing but the formal skeleton of their Jacobean and Caroline percursors (the mixture of *entrées de ballet*, sung exhortation to dance, community dance); in reality, they are simple 'images' projected on stage, segregated in terms of theatrical space, directly accessible to the characters of the drama but not to their 'true' protagonists: the nobility. Yet these formal projections are deeply rooted in long-standing collective theatrical tradition.

The use of music in Restoration theatre thus proceeds in full accordance with local English tradition: 'act music' (instrumental pieces inserted before the Prologue and prior to each of the five acts) and sound effects (for the action); vocal insertions (songs and airs sung within the action), wherever motivated (for merriment, melancholy or simple pastime); choreographical actions of ceremonial kind (miniature masque-like insertions in the scenic representation). These insertions are at times quite superb and theatrically effective; an excellent example occurs in Thomas Durfey's *Massaniello* (1699): note, in particular, the grotesque and savage irony which pervades the scene in which the obscenely fat Blowzabella, wife of the revolutionary fisherman, taste the joys of power as she gazes contentedly at the masque performed in her honour by the noblewomen of the kingdom, now her subjects; unknown to her, however, Massaniello has meanwhile been killed, and the masque – itself a thinly disguised allegory of the fisherman's fateful rise to power – concludes with the appearance of Rebellion, Death and Executioner, who compel Blowzabella to their dance: ''Tis part of the entertainment, Madam, you must go with him'; soon after, the corpse of Blowzabella is seen dangling from the gallows. The laws of probability, as reflected in the reluctance with which the musical recitation of dramatic dialogue is accepted in England, apparently rule supreme: in reality, however, this supremacy is illusory and paradoxical. Dramatic probability is literally thrown to the winds on those many occasions in Restoration theatre when any pretext whatever (including those of the most unlikely complexion) can serve for the insertion of music and dance in sufficient quantities to satisfy public demand. The extreme case of 'formal' probability observed to the total exclusion of any 'real' probability occurs precisely at the moment of transition from English- to Italian-style opera when, in 1705, the Drury Lane Theatre (itself in competition with its Haymarket rival) successfully stages the first English production of a truly all-sung musical: *Arsinoe*. This entertainment – a *pasticcio* of Italian operatic arias of various provenance, stitched together and transformed into English – is, however, preceded by the performance of a number of fragments of English dramatic prose (in the form of individual acts from earlier comedies), suitably chosen as pretexts – and, consequently, 'justifications' – for the scenic representation of some masque or other wholly musical entertainment. Thus, for the contemporary English stage, certain fragments of theatrical prose – meaningless in their own right – seem to have provided a sufficiently persuasive and rational excuse for the aesthetic legitimization of the operatic 'performance': a phenomenon now widely – and whole-heartedly – accepted in such centres as Naples, Hamburg and Paris, and which in less than five years would gain such unconditional approval in London as to identify the English capital as one of the great international centres of Italian-language opera.

The relatively late but nonetheless triumphant establishment of Italian opera in London – ultimate, if almost fortuitous, consequence of the gradual appropriation of English dramatic theatre on the part of vocal music and dance – was a source of initial disquiet among 'theatrical' actors; operatic competition, it was feared, would lead to reductions in audiences and takings. In the course of four critical years, however, a truly 'rational' re-organization of the productive system brings a clear-cut division of interests and concerns: English (musical and non-musical) drama at Drury Lane, Italian opera at the Haymarket. English-language theatre, too, reaps considerable benefit from this new arrangement, in so far as it is now free – as required – to rid itself of the various musical 'trimmings' which had earlier proliferated out of all proportion to dramatic needs. Whereas, in 1706, one Drury Lane actor can remark that 'Our stage is in a very indifferent condition. There has been a very fierce combat between the Haymarket and Drury Lane, and the two sisters, Music and Poetry, quarrel like two fishwives at Billingsgate . . .', in 1711 the theatre critic Joseph Addison will willingly lend his blessing to the new theatrical 'reality' with the following words:

> There is nothing that has more startled our *English* audience, than the *Italian recitativo* at its first entrance upon the stage. People were wonderfully surprized to hear generals singing the word of command, and ladies delivering messages in musick . . .
>
> But however this *Italian* method of acting in *recitativo* might appear at first hearing, I cannot but think it much more just than that which prevailed in our *English* opera before this innovation. The transition from air to recitative musick being more natural than the passing from a song to plain and ordinary speaking, which was the common method in *Purcell's* opera's.'
>
> (*The Spectator*, 3 April 1711)

'*Purcell's* opera's'/'our *English* opera' ('semi-operas' in modern terminology, 'dramatic operas' in the language of Dryden and his contemporaries) are in reality no more than a handful of dramas in which incidental music is accorded greatly expanded scope for manoeuvre. The works in question date from the final five years of the composer's life. All but one are based on pre-existing dramas, suitably adapted for the inclusion of copious episodes of music and dance. *Dioclesian* (1690) is arranged from an original Jacobean drama; *The fairy-queen* (1692) is a spectacular series of masques for Shakespeare's *Midsummer night's dream*; *The Indian queen* (1695) is an arrangement from Dryden; *The tempest* (1695?) is the remake of an earlier adaptation (1674) of Shakespeare's original. The sole exception – Dryden's *King Arthur* (1691) – is a heroic/patriotic drama on the mythical origins of the Britons; it was, in fact, conceived as the 'ideal' continuation of Dryden's own *Albion and Albanius* (music – of somewhat mediocre quality – by the French composer Louis Grabu) of 1685, itself one of a very limited number of invariably unsuccessful attempts to stage a true English opera in public. All these 'operas' provide clear illustration of the notion – as set out by Dryden – that only minor, marginal or supernatural characters (and not the protagonists themselves) are suitable as 'carriers' of vocal music, and that the best 'musical' situations are provided by magic, ceremonial and spectacle (not entirely unlike the *divertissements* of contemporary French opera).

Common, too, to all the 'operas' of Purcell are the borrowings from continental traditions. The 'frost scene' of *King Arthur* – a magic, allegorical and, indeed, comic scene, evoked by the magician Osmond as proof that the fire of love can overcome even the coldest of hearts – is comprised of the following sections: an instrumental prelude for the appearance of Cupid on the deserted plains of the kingdom of Ice (Yzeland); the recitative of Cupid, who awakens the Cold Genius; the song of the frost-bitten Cold Genius, who scarcely manages to articulate his words; the dance-like aria of Cupid, who derides the Cold Genius; the solemn recitative (with instrumental accompaniment) of the Cold Genius, who, having recognized Cupid, pays his respects; Cupid's exhortation to the Cold People to rouse themselves and make love; the *entrée* of the Cold People; the Chorus of the Cold People, who, stiff with cold, follow Cupid's advice and, together, dance (the music of the chorus and dance is essentially the same as that of the opening song of the Cold Genius; finally, Cupid's triumphant air, echoed (to identical music) by a jubilant chorus, itself interrupted momentarily by a 'warming' duet between Cupid and the Cold Genius. This scene is virtually a masque, and as such authentically 'English'. Yet the music of the Cold Genius, as also the chorus and dance of the Cold People, is based from beginning to end on a Lully original. *Isis*, Act 4, opens with a scenic representation of 'the coldest place in Scythia', in which the Peoples of the Glacial Climes – articulating their words with a kind of curious trembling of the voice – sing a thoroughly 'frost-bitten' chorus; this identical effect is applied by Purcell in the music of *King Arthur*, with 'shivering' tremolos in the violins. Common ground, however, which serves also to highlight the difference between the two composers: Lully's chorus is 'stiffened' by a rigidly diatonic framework, that of Purcell is traversed by a devastating chromatic 'shiver' (for seventeenth-century music, only the idea of ice can hold together the tonally destructive sonorities of two consecutive augmented fifth chords in first inversion). Italian in origin is the profusely emotive melody of a lament aria (see chapter 23) such as that in Act 5 of *The fairy-queen*, whose *basso ostinato* also provides a tortuous and somewhat ingenious variant (*D–C♯*–D–*C♮–B*–A–*B♭*–G–*A*–F–G–A[–D]) of the characteristic descending tetrachord (see chapter 23). The positioning of this enormously skilful (and movingly beautiful) composition at this particular point in the drama, however, is based also on sheer necessity: at this moment in the late seventeenth-century adaptation of Shakespeare's original, Oberon (the fairy king) expresses his desire to hear a 'noble lament'. It is also quite within the bounds of possibility that the aria in question served the practical function of gaining time for the preparation of an extraordinary change of scene (conjured up by Oberon immediately after the lament): a transformed stage now reveals an enchanted Chinese garden, scene of the final, phantasmagoric masque of the entertainment.

In this enchanted world of magic apparitions, no less than in the profoundly human world of such an exceptional little work as *Dido and Aeneas*, Purcell – with endless inventiveness and imagination – exploits a compositional procedure of which he himself may be described as the principal seventeenth-century exponent: the *basso ostinato* (*Dido and Aeneas* might itself be defined as a true opera in miniature: three acts, sung from beginning to end in an entertainment originally conceived in 1689 for performance at a school for young ladies in Chelsea and subsequently (in 1700) arranged for public performance as a scenic masque in conjunction with Shakespeare's *Measure for measure* – an entertainment which, despite its prohibitively minuscule dimensions, is today numbered among the few thoroughly enjoyable operatic masterpieces of the seventeenth century.) Besides the great festive chaconnes and *passacailles* (such as that of *King Arthur*, itself reminiscent of Lully's *Armide*) and lament arias (those of Dido in *Dido and Aeneas*: two airs of matchlessly tragic sublimity), Purcell's *bassi ostinati*, in all their innumerable variants (fast/slow, binary/ternary, diatonic/chromatic, major/minor, symmetrical/asymmetrical, skeletal/florid, varied/unvaried), lend themselves well to the representation of events, poetic discourses and affections of every kind (from jubilation to desperation). The inherently static structure of the *basso ostinato* – which itself effectively blocks all dynamic development of the action, enduring a single 'situation' and affection for the duration of the 'ostinato' repetitions (regardless of their number) – is compensated by the ample margins of harmonic and melodic freedom allowed to the other parts by the very inalterability (rhythmic, periodic, tonal) of the bass; even the boldest of contrapuntal licences are insufficient to impair the tonal and metrical orientation of the whole, which remains clearly perceptible at every moment. A dance-like, circular motion can be seen to underline more than one of Purcell's *bassi ostinati*, thus further legitimizing their insertion among the dances and *entrées de ballet* of Restoration 'operas'. Yet, just ten years after the death of Purcell, the *basso ostinato* has already been supplanted by the so-called '*da-capo*' aria – a clear reflection, this, of the new-found hegemony of the Italian *dramma per musica*. Supplanted, too, is another feature of the Purcellian 'heritage': that 'he was particularly admir'd for his vocal music, having a peculiar genius to express the energy of English words, whereby he mov'd the passions as well as caus'd admiration in all his auditors'. A genius, indeed, eloquently enshrined in the epitaph *Orpheus britannicus*, added by a publisher to a posthumous edition of the works of the composer.

As in England, the use of music (both 'operatic' and incidental) in mid-seventeenth-century Spanish theatre is governed by a whole series of prohibitions, particular associations and relationships – less, however, with regard to fundamental aesthetic precepts than in terms of the symbolic application of different styles of composition. The development of this practice is due, above all, to the work of the great dramatic playwright Pedro Calderón de la Barca. The arrival of the very notion of opera in Spain, however, must principally be attributed to the activities of the Florentine theatrical architects Cosimo Lotti and Baccio del Bianco at the court of Madrid, together with the presence in the Spanish capital of Giulio Rospigliosi as Papal Legate. All represent a pre-institutional, pre-'Venetian' phase of operatic history. The efforts of Calderón and his Italian collaborators, however, meet with no limited degree of resistance. In 1652, a *festa teatrale* – possibly *La fiera, el rayo y la piedra* – with *sinfonie*, vocal music, dancing, comic *intermedi*, stage machinery and allegories of planets and volcanos is described as follows by Baccio del Bianco (the organizer of the entertainment is Calderón):

> The music was composed by the most valiant D. Domingo Scherdo [?] of Toldeo, himself greatly desirous of introducing the *stile recitativo* – little by little, however, since these gentlemen will simply not accept the notion of *parlar cantando*; he, indeed, hopes that with patience he shall eventually win approval and procure the enjoyment of a type of entertainment that is presently the object of such strong condemnation from persons by whom it has been neither seen nor heard. For this reason, a *favola* has already been written by the Papal Nuncio Monsignor Rospigliosi, with the express intention of showing it to His Majesty and these valiant gentlemen.

(In Spain, adds Del Bianco, such is the novelty of this kind of entertainment with music and machines that he himself must act as everything from carpenter to painter, builder, engineer and tailor . . .) The fact remains that the seventeenth century gives rise to no lasting tradition of Spanish musical theatre, nor – in effect – does it witness the importation of any Italian operatic productions.

Calderón himself foresaw the quantitatively modest success – if not outright failure – of his attempts to create a native Spanish musical theatre: in the Prologue to his first entirely sung opera, *La púrpura de la rosa* (1659–60), Sorrow objects that the 'cólera española' – the irritable and intemperate character of the Spanish – will not tolerate an action based entirely on music ('toda música'). In fact, *La púrpura de la rosa* (the subject is that of Venus and Adonis) is not only the first but also the penultimate fully-sung theatrical production to be performed at the Spanish court (the other is the *Celos aun del aire matan* of 1660, itself based on the mythological story of Cephalus and Procris). If anything, it is the mixed form of theatrical recitation with musical insertions which – thanks, again, to Calderón (whose plots are always based on mythological themes) – enjoys a somewhat more acceptable degree of success. Such is the level of production of this theatrical genre that it finally comes to be known after one of the two royal residences where it was customarily performed; the term 'zarzuela' is still used in Spain to denote the Iberian variant of operetta.

One of the consequences of the somewhat ephemeral success of Spanish opera is the woeful lack of surviving musical sources; this is true even in the case of the *zarzuelas*. *Celos aun del aire matan*, set by court harpsichordist and harpist Juan Hidalgo (greatest of all seventeenth-century Spanish composers), has been preserved in manuscript score. Of the original *Púrpura de la rosa*, however, all trace is now lost; sole survivor in this sense is the score of Tomás de Torrejón y Velasco's setting of the opera (1701) for a performance in Lima! The music of a third 'Spanish' opera still awaits detailed investigation: *El robo de Proserpina*, a 'comedia armonica' (text *not* by Calderón), was produced and performed at the Spanish court of Naples in 1678 with music by the local composer Filippo Coppola (who admittedly encountered not inconsiderable difficulty in adapting his style to what was essentially an alien manner of singing). At Naples, 1682 brings a further production of *Celos aun del aire matan* (though with what music and success is unclear): in the Spanish province of the Two Sicilies, no less than on the Spanish 'mainland' itself, these few attempts to create a Spanish variant of opera are devoid of all significant effect. The situation, indeed, is further accentuated in the presence of a well-established and consolidated Italian operatic tradition. In short: two of the three (indirect) musical testimonies of Calderón's operatic initiatives and activities are to be found on the periphery (Naples, Peru) of what, in terms of seventeenth-century opera, is in any case a somewhat peripheral tradition. The albeit limited number of surviving fragments of *zarzuelas* all derive from contemporary manuscript *cancioneros*: collections of arias (or 'tonos') for solo voice and *basso continuo*, themselves destined for domestic consumption.

The intrinsic weakness – and great fascination – of Calderón's initiative resides in the series of prohibitions and associations which govern the distribution of the various musical styles among the characters of a dramatic action. This is true no less of the mythological *zarzuelas* than of the two out-and-out operas of 1659–60. To judge from what little information can be gleaned from the musical scores, the rules which govern these associations are essentially symbolic in nature and not incongruous with the Spanish terminological distinction between *tonos humanos* and *tonos divinos* (secular and spiritual airs). The voice of God – origin and fountain of all harmony – is represented by an off-stage chorus or voice. The Italian *stile recitativo*, itself somewhat 'stiff' in the hands of a musician such as Hidalgo, is reserved for pre-Christian deities; half sung (i.e., 'divine'), half spoken (i.e., 'human'), this style denotes the imperfect status of the pagan gods with regard to their Christian 'successors'. Melodic sweetness is above all associated with diabolic seductiveness and allurement. Rustic and other lesser characters sing *coplas*: stereotyped melodic formulas, repeated as often as required, which serve as vehicles (above all, however, when the underlying purpose is narrative and not recitation) for long sections of dialogue in quatrains; in *Celos aun del aire matan*, for example, one such *copla* runs to a total of some fifteen repetitions in the course of three consecutive scenes, thus establishing an effect of mechanical reiteration and indifference to textual elocution (the strongest possible antithesis, indeed, to Italian recitative). Dances, too are delegated (or relegated) to the humbler characters. The *zarzuelas* add further possibilities to this series of associations: in *Laurel de Apolo* (c.1657), for example, Apollo and Cupid sing when dialoguing with mortal characters (as, indeed, befits their status as divinities) yet recite among themselves; in *Estatua de Prometeo* (c.1672), it is the serious and totally human figure of the protagonist Prometheus who remains consistently apart from all musical expression (grotesque, sublime or of any other kind).

This symbolic, 'attributive' concept of theatrical song and recitation, antithesis of the functional/expressive (recitative/aria) concept of contemporary Italian opera, necessarily entails a plurality of forms – a plurality which, in the context of an aesthetic based primarily on the 'value' of stylistic unity, might nowadays seem nothing but sterile or insidious eclecticism, but which, in the eyes of contemporary Spanish playwrights, must have offered a notable strengthening of symbolic possibilities. The concept is itself an obvious and ideologically coherent manifestation of a vision of the 'divineness' of harmony – a sublime vision (readily apparent in the various categories of *tonos humanos* and *tonos divinos*) of Augustinian and neoplatonic descent which pervades the theatrical works of Calderón, ennobling (under the guise of mythological allegory) their Christian message. A vision destined not to take root on the Spanish peninsula (any more, indeed, than elsewhere in Europe), but one which nevertheless casts its own ecstatic light on the fruitfully contradictory and, indeed, 'critical' nature of the seventeenth century.

SOURCE READINGS

1 A musical banquet: Florence, 1608

Following a centuries-old tradition, music continued in the Seicento to represent an element of not inconsiderable importance as an adjunct to the greatest, most prestigious and memorable banquets. Reproduced by way of example (and not without a number of cuts in the enormous menu) in the following pages is the order of the banquet given by the Grand Duke of Tuscany on 19 October 1608 in the Salone dei Cinquecento of the Palazzo Vecchio, Florence, in celebration of the marriage of Crown Prince Cosimo II. The description – originally published by the celebrated cook Vittorio Lancellotti da Camerino in his no less authoritative treatise on banquets, *Lo scalco prattico* (Rome, 1627) – is interesting in several respects. As in the banquets of sixteenth-century Ferrara (see *Rivista italiana di musicologia*, X (1975), 216ff.), the musical interludes between the various courses function as true *entremets*: moments of relief and entertainment for the senses, which act as both pauses and links between the different phases of convivial pleasure. The exuberant sixteenth-century agglomeration of sundry musical offerings, however, is here replaced by the overall organization of homogeneous musical interludes which finally converge in the apotheosis of the concluding grand 'concerto' (over 150 performers, in the words of one eyewitness): allegorical characters appear and recede on a series of self-propelling machines in songful homage to bride, groom and dynasty. No longer merely a succession of musical and spectacular episodes, the banquet itself now undergoes transformation as a grand ceremonial representation in which the guests are both participants and onlookers: the role of 'astonishment' (quickly overcome) is secondary to that of self-representation. Astonishing, if anything, are the literally indescribable voices of the singers (see chapter 10), who are cited individually: Vittoria Archilei, Ippolita Recupito, Melchiorre Palantrotti, Francesca and Settimia Caccini (daughters of Giulio) – in short, the cream of virtuoso singing in Florence and Rome. Virtuoso music for solo voices is, indeed, a rare 'privilege', to be tasted only at court (see chapter 3); as a particular attribute of Florentine supremacy, it is here 'exhibited' in the context of a *mise en scène* which guarantees it suitably high-ranking publicity. In reality, this banquet might be described as a message of power and magnificence, addressed to the various courtly establishments of Europe; in this, it is little different from all the remaining festivities staged in connection with the wedding celebrations of 1608: two short *favole in musica* by Chiabrera; a game of football at S. Croce; a (danced) ball at the Palazzo Pitti; a *favola pastorale*, *Il giudizio di Paride* (*The judgment of Paris*), much favoured as a theme for marriage celebrations up to and including

Il pomo d'oro in Vienna, 1668: see chapter 24), performed at the Uffizi with six musical *intermedi*; a *balletto a cavallo*, again at S. Croce; a naval battle of the Argonauts, staged upon the Arno, etc. (see *Acta Musicologica*, LV (1983), 89ff.). It is, indeed, scarcely coincidence that the most detailed information of all on the subject of the Florentine festivities and their machinery is to be found in the dispatches of a Mantuan theatrical engineer sent specifically to Florence by his Gonzaga employers (see *Civiltà mantovana*, XII (1978), 14ff.); Mantua, at this time, is still the only court capable of successfully competing with Florence for the splendour of its festivities.

The reader, however, should note that this type of festivity, while providing ample opportunity for the ostentatious display of every conceivable scenic and musical resource, is firmly anchored to a repetitive and somewhat tenacious code of ceremonial practice. For example, the grand 'concerto' (in the widest sense of the term: see chapter 6) which concludes the banquet of 1608 is but one further example of an illustrious tradition which includes the famous 40-part motet composed by Alessandro Striggio of Mantua for a Medici reception of 1561, offered later that year to Guglielmo Gonzaga on the occasion of his own marriage celebrations, and revived in 1568 on the occasion of a further round of ducal marriage festivities at Munich (see *Early Music*, VIII (1980), 829ff.).

Finally, the reader should note that neither Lancellotti nor any of the other sources refer specifically to the texts, subjects and allegories/personifications of the various musical episodes. At most, then, it can only be surmised that Aurora, Venus, Cupid, a nymph and Apollo were included among the singing characters in the banquet of 1608. The indifference of readers and spectators to iconographical and mythological references, together with their imperviousness to the allegorical intentions of the 'inventors' of the entertainment, is destined to have enormous repercussions for the development of seventeenth-century culture (in a ratio which increases in direct proportion to the use, overuse and consequent 'emptiness' of a now threadbare repertory of symbols and emblems). The phenomenon, however, still awaits systematic investigation and definition.

Banquet of thirty-four dishes, given at Florence on the occasion of the marriage of His Serene Highness Cosimo II Grand Duke of Tuscany with the Most Serene Archduchess Maria Maddalena of Austria, served in the Sala Reale of the Palazzo Vecchio in the evening of Sunday 19 October 1608.

Prepared at the head of the room was the royal table; this was crescent-shaped, approached by a flight of steps and crowned by a canopy of white damask. The said table was adorned with gold lace. The white tablecloth of light silk was embroidered in gold with various mottoes and devices of great beauty. On the tablecloth was the cutlery. At the centre of the table, to the right, was the Most Serene Bride, flanked by Her Serenity the Grand Duchess; on the left was the Most Serene Bridegroom, followed, in order, by the Most Illustrious Cardinals del

Monte, Sforza, Farnese, Montalto and Este, the most Serene Arch-duke of Austria and the Grand Duke Ferdinand, all on one side. A further fifteen tables were laid out around the room. Underneath these tables was the fruit, thus placed in order to avoid confusion; above each table was a kind of platform, utilized during dinner by various unknown princes and cavaliers. Under each platform was a collection of wines – one for each table. Four dishes were served at the royal table, two at each of the other fifteen tables – around which were the ladies, served by their husbands and brothers. At the end of the room, opposite the royal table, was a sideboard of great beauty; this was decked with bowls, imperial and royal dishes, bread-baskets and cups of various kinds, all wrought out of sugar but so true to life that many of those present were deceived. Never, in fact, was a more beautiful sight to be seen.

First service (cold)

Pies of suckling calf, in the form of rosettes . . . encircled by six balls of marzipan paste, with three lilies on the face of the blue ball . . .
Sliced salami . . . topped by an imperial crown of sugar paste . . .
Sugar peacocks, with raised heads, wings and tails . . . the breasts meticulously larded with pumpkin lardoons . . .
Beaten eggs, heaped in the manner of a mountain . . . with three lilies decorated with gold, interspersed with the arms of the Most Serene Bride wrought in pistachio paste . . . with various devices of the houses of Austria and Florence . . .
Pigs' heads, decked with sour cherries . . .
Blancmange, in the form of lilies, in half-relief . . .
Roast turkeys, larded with candied citron-peel lardoons . . .
Jelly, in half-relief, over turkeys in the manner of golden eagles . . .
Lilies, stuffed with candies of marzipan paste . . .
Hams iced with sugar, served upon six lions' busts . . .
Candied tarts, decked with *cannellone* sweetmeats . . .
A golden chariot, laden with candied citron-peel, drawn by four white sugar doves, with a sugar Cupid with reins in hand . . .
Another chariot, drawn by two white sugar capons . . . laden with marzipan . . .
Another chariot, drawn by two white rabbits with coachman . . . laden with little pistachio pastries . . .
Another chariot, drawn by two white guinea-chicks . . . laden with large Genoa pumpkins . . .

A lion, a horse with armed rider, an eagle, a bear, all in butter . . .
The Queen of France on horseback, made in sugar paste . . .
The King of France at war, likewise on horseback . . .

At either end of the royal table was a large sugar tree with sugar cages; these cages contained live birds which sang without interruption.

Armida in a chariot, drawn by two dragons, with Rinaldo asleep and in chains, the whole cast in sugar . . .

Jupiter on a lofty throne, with lightning in hand . . .

Clorinda, languishing, with Tancredi nearby, armed, in the act of wanting to bathe his head with the water in his morion . . .

Pluto, chain in hand, bearing Proserpine in his arms . . .

These, together with other sugar representations, were removed immediately upon arrival at the table; in this way, the view of the theatre was not impeded . . .

First service (cooked)

Boiled capons with soup underneath, covered in tiny slices of cardoon, pieces of sweetbread, slices of ham, chopped salami and saveloys . . .
Fried veal sweetbread, served with slices of sponge-cake . . .
Stuffed pies, with veal chops, truffles, pieces of sweetbread, fat and marrow of beef . . .
Roast ortolans, served with fried bread done in the dripping pan, garnished with fried greens . . .
Roast quails, served with fried sausage . . .
Medlar tarts and slices of pumpkin . . .
Sliced Seville oranges on napkins; blancmange . . .

On the appearance of this first service Signora Vittoria appeared in a cloud at one end of the table, with Signora Ippolita in another cloud at the other end of the table. Both were ceremoniously dressed, and both sang most beautifully. The words were in praise of the Most Serene Bride. These two ladies sang and paraded around for some fifteen minutes until the arrival of the second course, at which point the clouds receded in the same way as they had appeared.

Second service

Boiled suckling calf, served with borage flowers in syrup . . .
Roast turtle-doves, served with slices of sponge-cake . . .
Pigeons stuffed under the skin with sweetbread, fat of beef, marrow,

thin slices of truffle, crumbled salami, egg yolks done in the oven . . .
Royal soups of breast and skin of capon, slices of fresh buffalo-milk cheese fried in butter, kid's eyes and ears . . .
Roast partridge, served with lilies of puff-pastry . . .
English-style pies with suckling calf, pieces of sweetbread, calves' brains, marrow . . .
Sliced limes, with sugar; jelly, with strips of capon breast . . .

On the arrival of this second service a triumphal chariot appeared in the air; in this chariot was Sig. Melchiorre, bass, singer in the choir of His Holiness. The words of his music were in praise of the Most Serene Bride and Bridegroom. The singing continued until the arrival of the third service, at which point the chariot withdrew.

Third service

Boiled partridge, covered with a stuffing of cardoons and truffles, slices of pig's head and ham . . .
Loaves stuffed with quince in syrup, beaten egg, candied citron-peel and pistachio, done in the oven . . .
Roast pheasants, well hung, removed from the paper and served in marzipan pastry . . .
Puff-pastry pies of veal, pieces of sweetbread, slices of ham, pine-nuts, thin slices of truffle, egg yolks and their sauce . . .
Royal meat-loaves, round, as big as the inner section of a royal plate, made from suckling calf, sweetbread, marrow . . .
Cakes made from chopped blanched almonds, roast breast of capon, roast chicken livers . . .
Olives in porcelain; *pergolese* grapes on napkins . . .

On the arrival of this service a triumphal chariot appeared from the same direction as the clouds of the first service; in this were the two daughters of Sig. Giulio Romano, who sang in concert with every delicacy and refinement. These then remained still, while Signora Vittoria and Signora Ippolita reappeared on triumphal chariots, dressed beautifully as nymphs. Finally, having vied with each other both singly and together, all four united in a sound of such sweetness that words cannot describe. Thus they continued until the appearance of the remaining course, at which point all the chariots returned whence they came.

Fourth service

Calves' heads, boned . . . served over an imperial soup . . .
Roast turkeys, served with marzipan festoons . . .
Fried pigeons with dressing, served with slices of sponge-cake . . .
Rosettes of puff-pastry, stuffed with quince jam . . .
Roast suckling calf, served with blancmange-filled tartlets . . .
Rennet apple tarts with pumpkin slices . . .

On the appearance of this service a recess suddenly opened above the aforementioned sideboard and table at the foot of the room, revealing a representation of the glory of Paradise, with lights, musicians and instruments, which filled the sights of the onlookers; and, above all, being in such numbers and in such variegated costumes, as of angels and saints, that they appeared quite infinite; these combined together with sounds and songs in various kinds of *concerti* of music and sounds, in such a way that those present had occasion to convince themselves of the enormity of the glory of heaven (judging, that is, from the sweetness of the melody which emanated from this mortal representation). This continued until the end of the meal, with ever new *concerti* of music.

Second sideboard service

Scented napkins for all . . .
White cakes of blancmange . . .
Green cakes, made with fresh buffalo-milk cheese, cottage cheese, grated Parmesan cheese and spinach juice . . .
Pies made with truffles, slices of cardoon and prunes . . .
Whole quince pies . . .
Parmesan cheese, sheep's and buffalo-milk cheese, on napkins.
Florentine pears, rose apples, rennet apples, cardoons with salt and pepper . . .
Blancmange fried in butter, in slices . . .
Olives, grapes, chestnuts, with salt and pepper, fennel . . .
Roman-style fried puff-pastry cakes in royal bowls . . .
Portuguese and Bolognese quince jams and jellies . . .

At the end, water was brought for the hands, with tooth-picks and beautiful flowers; and, the tablecloths having been removed, a most beautiful barrier was formed by the Most Serene Princes. After this, the Most Serene Grand Duke Ferdinand commanded that the populace be permitted to loot everything that remained in the hall; he then retired towards the private rooms, accompanied by the Most Serene Bride and Bridegroom, the Grand Duchess and the other Most Serene Princes and Cardinals, with all the ladies in the service of the Most Serene Bride. Passing by way of the gallery, the company came upon an enormous table, laden with fine confectionery and extremely well made Genoese cakes in such quantities as seem almost impossible to describe; these were magnificently presented by His Highness to the ladies one and all.

2 A court ballet: Turin, 1620

The marriage of Christine of France with Crown Prince Vittorio Amedeo of Savoy (1619) gave rise to a whole series of festivities, of which numerous musical and literary testimonies (albeit fragmentary and scattered) have survived. Principal designer of the celebrations was the marchese and poet Lodovico d'Agliè who, for the music, availed himself of the assistance of Sigismondo d'India (see chapter 3): these two men are undoubtedly to be attributed with the composition of a ballet personified by the Po, the Stura and the Dora (the three rivers of Turin), given in honour of the bride, prior to her public entry into Turin, in a villa in the outskirts belonging to Cardinal Maurizio of Savoy; the ballet, held at the beginning of Carnival 1620, is described in M.-T. Bouquet, *Storia del Teatro Regio di Torino* (Turin, 1976), vol. I, Appendix 2. Carlo Emanuele I took a personal hand in the preparations for the tournament *Il giudizio di Flora*, fought in the Piazza Castello, Turin on 18 February 1620 and preceded, at court, by a performance of the ballet *Le accoglienze* (invented, in all probability, by d'Agliè). The printed description of this ballet, here reproduced in its entirety from a copy now held in the Biblioteca Oliveriana of Pesaro (where, perhaps, its presence derives from the activities of a contemporary nobleman and collector of descriptions of festivals and displays: see *Giornale storico della letteratura italiana*, XLI (1903), 42–77), is both tedious and instructive. More than the specific characteristics of the ballets produced at the court of Savoy (for an excellent account of which see M. Viale Ferrero, *Feste delle Madame Reali di Savoia* (Turin, 1965)), it is important to illustrate how typical are certain of the ingredients of *Le accoglienze* and its structure and how the entertainment of 1620 is related to many other Italian (above all, Florentine) court ballets and masquerades of the early seventeenth century, as also to the French *ballet de cour* (in accordance with the very nationality of Madame, dedicatee of *Le accoglienze* and future promoter of a large number of ballets at the court of Savoy; the description of 1620, moreover, is permeated with Gallicisms) and English court masque under the early Stuarts. The relationships in question, however, are less governed by any 'historical' system of mutual influence and derivation as by a deep functional, structural and, in the final analysis, symbolic affinity.

This affinity is perhaps most suitably illustrated by means of the following summary comparison (see below, pp. 274–8) of *Le accoglienze* with a further two stage ballets, roughly contemporary and selected at random from the dozens of such entertainments produced in Paris and London: the *ballet royal* of *La délivrance de Renaud*, given in Paris on 29 January 1617 (for a summary of the text by Estienne Durand, together with the music of Gabriel Bataille, Pierre Guédron and Antoine Boësset, see the appendix to H. Prunières, *Le ballet de cour en France avant Benserade et Lully* (Paris, 1914); for scenery and commentary see chapter 6 of M. M. McGowan, *L'art du ballet de cour en France 1581–1643* (Paris, 1963)) and the court masque of *Oberon*, produced at London on New Year's Day, 1611 (for a reproduction and commentary on the text by Ben Jonson, as also on the scenes and costume-sketches by Inigo Jones, see *A book of masques*, ed. T. J. B. Spencer and S. W. Wells (Cambridge, 1970); for the surviving music by Alfonso Ferrabosco and Robert Johnson see *Four hundred songs and dances from the Stuart masque*, ed. A. J. Sabol (Providence, R.I., 1978), index and Appendix A).

The three ballets, for all their differences, have certain features in common. The admittance of the audience to the place of performance is tantamount to its immersion in the 'tempo' of the festival, itself the idealized self-representation or self-portrayal of the court. The curtain opens on a suggestively horrifying scene (rocky landscape, caves, crags), gradually modified in the course of a somewhat lengthy series of scene changes to form the final scenic apotheosis. In all three, the opening actions and ballets are unmistakably grotesque, comically 'discordant' (Sins, Demons, Satyrs) with 'low' sonorities (winds). In the masque, this burlesque and somewhat unsettling opening is developed into a full-blooded antimasque (a 'false masque', conceived as a 'spectacle of strangeness' and artfully calculated to heighten the effect of the masque itself) before the appearance of the masquers (Oberon with retinue): antimasquers, indeed, are generally comic and grotesque, for the most part recited without song by professional actors (as opposed to the *dilettante* courtiers who impersonate the masquers) with strange and outlandish dances. In all three cases, however, the more aristocratic characters and dancers gradually come to dominate the stage; at a certain point, the protagonists of the respective ballets (the two Infantas, Louis XIII, Prince Henry), all present on stage right from the beginning of the entertainment (or, in the case of *Oberon*, from the beginning of the 'real' entertainment at the conclusion of the antimasque), give rise to the principal dance. Then, descending from the stage to a position in front of the august spectators, they introduce the concluding general dance, which represents the climax and true culmination of the contemporary court ballet.

In all three cases, moreover, the role of solo song is ancillary, exhorting the courtiers or *ballerini* to the dance or announcing scenic apparitions. In all three cases, the ballet provides visible and audible affirmation of the triumph of Harmony over Discord, Virtue over Sin, Order over Chaos (see P. Walls, 'The music of the King's peace' in *La chanson à la renaissance*, ed. J.-M. Vaccaro (Tours, 1981), 190–208. In all three cases, the triumph reaches its climax at the point in which the tangible world of the court (the spectators) and the imaginary world of the dancers are juxtaposed and identified with each other in the concluding general ballet. In all three cases, the *mise en scène* revolves around the glorification – eulogistic, allegorical, symbolic – of the sovereign and ruling dynasty, a glorification which 'builds' a public image of the sovereign as trustee and bestower of political and internal harmony. The collective festivity thus undergoes transformation as a ceremonial rite of affirmation; each and every carnival-like transgression and disguise is sublimated (in accordance with a tacitly-recognized precept which holds good throughout the seventeenth century) in the ritual celebration of an inalienable code of honour, nobility of blood and divine right. The costumes of the dancers, each minutely described, are the visual symbol of this ceremonial etiquette.

It would, however, be misleading to seek historical connections and cross-influences where none exist and attempt to identify the precursors and, indeed, beginnings of opera in the court ballets, masques and masquerades of the early seventeenth century. For all their various affinities in terms of staging, singing styles and mythological derivations and sources, court ballet and opera are radically different genres, incompatible in function (ceremonial versus representative), temporal structure (festival versus action), spatial organization (communicating stage and stalls versus non-communicating), relative importance of music (accessory versus essential), social context (court versus city or State), intent (allegory and symbolism versus motion and entertainment of feelings and emotions). If anything, it may be said that court ballet is superseded by opera – in cases, that is, where the latter is invested with permanent institutional status and forms. On the contrary, a deeply-rooted tradition of court ballet or similar types of entertainment could constitute a lasting obstacle to the introduction and establishment of opera. This is the case in seventeenth-century England (see chapter 26); it can also be said of the court of Savoy, with its truly lasting and voracious appetite for the *balletto di corte*. In Turin, even such shrewd scholars and observers as Emanuele Tesauro (whose treatise on poetics, the *Cannocchiale aristotelico* of 1670, praises those 'figurative ballets which, with truly astonishing stagecraft and machinery, strangeness of costumes, liveliness of actions, peculiarities of metre and step and sweetly echoing accompaniment of musical instruments', allude 'to some salutary or politic text'), in writing a *tragedia musicale* (in the case of Tesauro, his five-act *Alcesti o sia L'amor sincero*, anonymously printed in 1665), leave practically no possibility whatever for the musical representation of the affections (in arias). The result is a hybrid form of entertainment whose every aspect reveals the peripheral nature of Turin with respect to the generally blossoming market in contemporary operatic production.

Le accoglienze (Turin, 1620)	*La délivrance de Renaud* (Paris, 1617)	*Oberon* (London, 1611)
The infantas rehearse a ballet with their ladies and invite the noble ladies of the city	the sixteen-year-old Louis XIII celebrates his accession to power and the end of the regency of the Queen Mother and her advisers with a *ballet de cour*; he personally chooses the theme (from Tasso): the liberation of Renaud from the evil spells of Armide.	sovereigns, with ambassadors of Spain and Venice, enter banqueting hall in procession (fifes); the hall itself has already been prepared for the entertainment
toilettes of the ladies displayed on parade through the city		
ducal banquet: food and music of more modest dimensions than at Florence, 1608 (see Source reading 1); those nobles not admitted to ducal banquet pass time in dancing	the scene is prepared in the Great Hall of the Louvre	
lords and ladies enter hall, followed by ruling family (sound of trumpets)		[ANTIMASQUE:]
curtain: the temple of Glory, the garden of Virtues, Parnassus	*curtain: view of palace and, in the distance, a landscape*	*curtain: dim, rocky scene, moonlit*
the Infantas with twelve Ladies; Toil fights the wild beasts; the indolent Sins; the industrious Virtues; eight poet laureates and the nine Muses	INVISIBLE CHORUS: invitation to the pleasures of love (grand 'concerto' of 64 voices, 28 viols, 14 lutes)	a Satyr (horn sounds thrice), then ten Satyrs who converse confusedly with strange movements; finally their leader Silenus, who announces the arrival of Oberon, Prince of the Fairies [= the sixteen-year-old Prince Henry, eldest son of James I]
MADRIGAL OF TOIL: exhorts to virtue and banishes the Sins GROTESQUE BALLET OF FUGITIVE SINS (cornetts and trombones)	*scene changes: a rocky mountain, a bizarrely horrible cave* Renaud [= Duke of Luynes, confidant of King] asleep; above him, the Demon of fire [= the King, who burns with love for his faithful subjects and wrath for his	*the rocks open to reveal the splendid palace of Oberon*

enemies] with a further twelve Demons [= gentlemen] left by Armide to guard Renaud; Renaud advances towards the proscenium, the King descends a number of steps to the sound of 24 Spirits (24 violins)

ENTRÉE DE BALLET: RENAUD WITH DEMONS OF FIRE, WATER AND AIR

BIZARRE AND FANTASTIC ENTRÉES OF SPIRITS AND DEMONS

BALLET OF 14 CHARACTERS
Renaud and the 13 Demons

the Demons disappear; two Knights with ancient-style armour appear (trumpets); Armide casts a spell and the scene is transformed to reveal

a delightful garden with three gushing fountains

a Nymph appears, nude and dishevelled

AIR OF NYMPH, who calls upon Knights to leave Renaud to Armide

six Monsters appear (two jurist-owls, two peasant-dogs, two damsel-monkeys); the Monsters attack the Knights

two sleeping Sylvans guarding the palace; the Satyrs sing a burlesque canon, taunting and making fun of them; Silenus interrogates them

SONG OF SATYRS TO THE MOON

GROTESQUE BALLET OF SATYRS (BRANLE)

Le accoglienze (Turin, 1620)	*La délivrance de Renaus* (Paris, 1617)	*Oberon* (London, 1611)
	COMIC/SERIOUS ENTRÉE OF MONSTERS AND KNIGHTS	
	the Monsters flee, and Renaud is caught sight of by the Knights	
	AIR OF RENAUD, who sings of his happiness in love [?ENTRÉE OF KNIGHTS WITH RENAUD]: the Knights free Renaud from his golden captivity	
	Armide hastens to the scene, looks desperately at the desolation of the enchanted garden and summons her fiendish Ministers (three as prawns, two as turtles, two as snails)	
	AIR OF ARMIDE, who reproves the Monsters ENTRÉE OF MONSTERS AND THEIR TRANSFORMATION INTO MONSTROUS OLD WOMEN	at the crow of a cock: [MASQUE:]
Heroic Virtue appears with halberd and cornucopia (symbols of dominion and riches)	*earthquake: the garden of Armide is transformed into a bare cavern; a thick wood enters stage on a machine; background of ancient ruins*	*the palace opens: the Fairy People appear, surrounding the Knights [= the 13 gentlemen masquers] who, in turn, surround Oberon*

QUATRAINS OF HEROIC VIRTUE (music by S. d'India, see chapter 3), who exhorts the Virtues to assist the Royal Madame in her arrival BALLET OF VIRTUES ('sinfonia' of '100 voices' and instruments)	in the wood, Peter the Hermit (who, in his wisdom, had planned the liberation of Renaud) and 16 soldiers from the army of Godfrey	Oberon's triumphal chariot, drawn by white bears and driven by the Sylvans, advances towards the proscenium (fanfares)
enter Apollo	CHORUS OF THE SOLDIERS OF GODFREY in search of Renaud SUNG DIALOGUE BETWEEN HERMIT AND SOLDIERS: announcement of the liberation of Renaud CHORUS [AND BALLET?] OF JUBILATION (92 voices and over 45 instruments)	SONG, addressed to King Arthur [= James I, seated in the hall]
MADRIGAL OF APOLLO, who invites the Poets to sing the praises of the bride BALLET OF MUSES AND POETS ('grave and dramatic harmony')		eulogistic addresses by a Sylvan and Silenus
enter Glory		SONG OF TWO FAIRIES (two boys, to the sound of ten lutes) BALLET OF LESSER FAIRIES: ten pages
MADRIGAL OF GLORY, who announces a change of scene		
the temple of Glory opens: Honour, Victory and Fame appear on a triumphal arch	*the wood vanishes, and the golden pavilion of Godfrey appears with palms and trophies of victory*	SONG FOR FULL CHORUS: exhortation to dance of the masquers ENTRANCE BALLET OF MASQUERS, danced by Oberon and Knights
MADRIGAL OF HONOUR, who exhorts the Infantas to afford the Royal Madame a fitting reception	apotheosis of Godfrey [= King] and his Knights [= the same gentlemen who initially played the part of the Demons] in splendid array; the King, having descended from his throne, gives the signal for the beginning of the	SONG: invitation to continue the dance of the masquers

Le accoglienze (Turin, 1620)	*La délivrance de Renaus* (Paris, 1617)	*Oberon* (London, 1611)
GRAND BALLET OF INFANTAS WITH THEIR LADIES (violins)	GRAND TRIUMPHAL DANCE (violins) followed by the	GRAND BALLET OF MASQUERS: Oberon and Knights dance at considerable length
reverence of Infantas to Royal Madame ('sweetest melody', choral and instrumental)		SONG: exhortation for general dancing to begin
BRANLE, DANCED BY THE ENTIRE ROYAL FAMILY, AND GENERAL BALLET (violins)	GRAND GENERAL BALLET	REVELS (GENERAL DANCES) OF MASQUES WITH LADIES FROM AUDIENCE: descending from the stage, Prince Henry [= Oberon] with the queen and the other masquers with other ladies dance a pavane, *coranto*, galliard, *branle de Poitou*, etc.
publication of tournament cartel		on a discreet signal from the king, the morning star Phosphorus appears
		SONG OF A SYLVAN, who announces the end of the night and ballets Phosphorus exhorts those present to retire LEAVE-TAKING BALLET, DANCED BY THE MASQUERS AND SATYRS
		SONG FOR FULL CHORUS: masquers' reverences, addressed to Their Majesties
		the sovereigns with their retinue and the ambassadors set off in the direction of the place where the banquet has been prepared

***Le accoglienze*, ballet performed on 30 January 1620 by the Most Serene Infantas of Savoy, in honour of Madame of France.**

The harshness of winter having prevented the displays and constructions prepared for the arrival of Madame from being staged, it was deemed necessary to defer her solemn entry to the city until the beginning of March *prox*. Meanwhile, however, Madame being desirous of joining His Highness and the Most Serene Infantas and of spending Carnival in Turin, she resolved to enter the city privately in mask and costume, which she did on 14 January, accompanied by His Highness, the Most Serene Infantas, the princes, the ladies of court and a considerable number of gentlemen, all in masks and costume, with strange and most beautiful inventions.

It would be difficult to describe the delight of Their Most Serene Highnesses and, indeed, of the city as a whole on the unexpected sight of Madame; among others, however, the Most Serene Infantas resolved to celebrate this so happy and much-awaited occasion with all those particular signs of jubilation, observance and affection which sprang from the depths of the heart. With this in mind, they and their ladies rehearsed a ballet, to which all the ladies of the town were invited, each vying with the other by virtue of the richness of their garments and precious gems. Thus, on the appointed day, they appeared in their carriages on the Strada di Po, which avenue is customarily adopted on such occasions; also present, in accordance with tradition, were the knights of the court, more numerous than usual and conspicuous for the splendour of their garments, the inestimable quantity of their jewels and the variegated and magnificent harnesses of their ferocious horses.

His Highness decided to receive Madame and the Most Serene Infantas in his rooms, as these were closest to the hall where the festivities were to be staged.

To this effect, he was pleased to prepare a sumptuous dinner for their benefit, with trout of enormous dimensions, tunny and various other kinds of salt-water fish, together with those animals of earth and air which are wont to appear on the worthiest of tables.

The whole was presented with most orderly grace and with a variety of floral decorations, whose perfumes mingled with those of the ambergris and the many other scents with results of incomparable sweetness. These dishes were followed by a selection of strange fruits, uncommon for this season of the year. Next came a selection of the finest confectionery and cakes, with artful representations of everything that is to be admired as most beautiful, charming and novel in nature. These gastronomic pleasures were further enhanced by the sweetness of the music, which gave nourishment to the ears and filled the souls of those present with contentment. Prior to this, the ladies of the city and almost all the remaining nobility had withdrawn to the lower apartments, where they passed the time in dancing until it was learned, shortly before midnight, that dinner was over. At this point, the guests returned to the upper level, each to his appointed seat, the hall having been set out as follows: towards the north end was a great staircase of ten steps, covered in Syrian tapestries; at the top was a platform with the chairs of Their Highnesses, under a rich canopy, with sufficient space to accommodate the ladies of court. From the four corners, that is, running along the sides of this platform, was a cloth covered in velvets and brocades. This ended in a cloth, itself bordered in clouds made in excellent imitation of nature; the said cloth was painted with beautiful landscapes and provided a most agreeable lateral view from the opposite side to the staircase. The space under the stands was reserved for the gentlemen (upon another staircase) and the other spectators (between this latter staircase and the columns sustaining the said stands). The scenes thus having been set, and after the arrival of the Most Serene Madame and Infanta Margarita, accompanied by His Highness and the Most Serene princes, the spectators were enjoined to silence at the sound of the trumpets and the entire cloth was seen to disappear in a flash behind the clouds, revealing all at once such a quantity of wonderful and admirable things that many of those present were lost in amazement. In the first place, the scene depicted a parched Alpine mountain, with crags vegetated by nothing but a few nettles and briars among the cracks and stiff, unyielding and discoloured grass. At the top of this mountain, the Temple of Glory shone out with brightest rays; this was made in crystal with columns of gold. In the middle, the Most Serene Infantas Maria and Caterina could be seen with twelve of their ladies dressed as queens, as will be described below. At the foot, in the middle, Toil – practically, one might say, a second Hercules – wielded his bludgeon, striking down lions, serpents, wild boars and sundry other beasts; at the base of the mountain, Love, Indolence, Oblivion, Sloth, Slumber, Gluttony, Sin and Pleasure sleepily and lazily kept watch. To the right, on a slightly lower level than the mountain, was a delightful garden, representing the garden of the Virtues. This was overflowing with plants and flowers, with a number of charming paths, ornamented and enriched at the sides by strange and outlandish vases; here, the Virtues themselves could be seen continuously wreathing and braiding garlands of flowers. On the left, surrounded by a thick laurel wood, was Mount Parnassus, its summit raised almost to the sky, from whence a representation of Pegasus seemed to leap into flight, supporting himself on his hind legs and cleaving the clouds with his wings. There, by a burbling spring of crystal-clear water, eight poets could be seen writing in the company of the nine Muses, the latter splendidly adorned and holding in their hands the various instruments denoting the sciences and liberal arts to which each is inclined. All thoughts, however, on the varied appearance of the aforementioned characters and machinery were immediately dispelled by the harmony of Toil, who sang the following madrigal:

> He who treads the flowery path
> of tyrant pleasure
> finally will wretched fall,
> deceived, in the bottomless pit of everlasting loss.
> He alone, who by virtue crosses
> with you, royal bride,
> the stony mount, can brighten and prolong
> his hours and days, and gloriously
> take from such divinity
> breath for the course, aid for the flight, plumes for the wings.

After which, while Toil struck out against the aforementioned Sins with his knotted bludgeon, driving them thence from that agreeable abode onto the floor of the hall, where they now appeared in short green tunics with silver arabesques, each bearing the hieroglyphic attributed him by the Ancients; the cornetts and trombones took up a broken melody with artfully contrived retardations, to which rhythm the Sins recommenced their ballet, occasionally stopping with an air of bewilderment and then resuming their figures in imitation of the faltering and swaying of the sleepy, but in perfect measure and in such perfect time as to leave an indelible impression on the minds of those present. After their ballet, the Sins took refuge in the caves and hovels at the foot of the mountain. Following this, Heroic Virtue made her graceful appearance in the garden of Virtue, near a spring of delectable fountains which watered the grass and the flowers. Heroic Virtue was herself adorned with garlands of flowers and wore a highly decorated skirt of silk cloth woven with gold thread. Around her shoulders was an undulating mantle of similar cloth with a deep border of gold lace at the hem; from her belt, a gold-ornamented bodice spread out above her skirt. In her right hand was a halberd, in her left the horn of plenty overflowing with fruit and flowers. Advancing one step forward, she sang the following words:

I, who in the eternal fields of heaven
stretch out my flight on great wings of gold
and, decked with garlands, glow brilliantly
with Virtuous beauty among shining beams,

immortal daughter of Jove, now the earth do tread
with celestial footsteps in these venerable parts
in which the royal bride, daughter of Mars,
overcomes my unworthy enemy Sin.

Already, fearless, to the temple of Honour and Glory
does she ascend by mountain way,
and, now far from mortal thought,
with my magnificence adorns her locks and heart.

Thus, noble sisters, be you escorts
of the great goddess in her pilgrim path;
behold how, with fated destiny, she
shines upon the choirs on earth, the stars in heaven.

During this, the Virtues descended to the floor, dressed in green calf-length dresses with gold and silver arabesques and other decorations, argent buskins, their long hair interwoven with gold threat; each held in her hands an insignia made of papier-mâché, which distinguished her from the others. These Virtues, to a *sinfonia* of no less than one hundred voices and a similar number of instruments, then danced an extremely long ballet; this they did with incredible agility and with extremely graceful turns and capers. At the end of which Apollo, decked with a crown of rays, lyre in hand and dressed in a mantle and red costume decorated with gold embroidery – this, too, in sunburst formation – was heard from Mount Parnassus to sing the following words:

You, skilful archers
of the ivory lyre,
who with flattering tones
immortalize the deeds of warring heroes;
now that the golden lily of the Franks,
decked in laurels, is by you admired,
let your silver bows redouble their harmony
on the golden citharas, silver strings.

To this the Muses then added their full chorus of voices. Meanwhile, the Poets, bearing wreaths of gold laurel leaves, with gold leaf shining in their hair, were lowered into the theatre; they were dressed in mantles of gold silk, with a deep gold lace border, and thigh-length amaranth coats adorned with silver arabesques (these, too, in the form of crowns and laurel tree trunks) and open down the front to reveal white hose with wide slashes of gold braid. To the sound of a grave and dramatic harmony they formed a most graceful ballet with unsurpassable elegance and design. When the Poets had withdrawn, Glory then raised her song from the uppermost reaches of the temple. On her head was a gold crown decked with the most precious jewels; in her hand she held a trumpet. She wore a gown of cloth of silver with gold designs around the edge and a mantle of gold silk embroidered in silk flowers with gold and silver. These were her words:

> Great and celebrated spirits,
> whose works and sublime thoughts
> gave sustenance to the heights of my heaven:
> glorious souls,
> come forth, come forth,
> here to gaze upon the light
> brought by the goddess of the great golden lilies.
> Welcome her: may the temple of Glory,
> open wide, keep watch over such virtue.

At this, the temple of Glory was opened; in an instant, little by little, a rock from the middle of the mountain disappeared and a triumphal arch was suddenly seen to rise. This arch was dedicated to Honour. Seated upon it were Victory, Fame and, in between, Honour herself, decked in garlands of flowers, with a dress in cloth of gold, gold-embroidered bodice and a mantle of gold silk, itself worked with true-to-life floral designs. Shaking her sceptre in her right hand, she sang the following madrigal:

> Go forth, ye who earned,
> on the path of toil,
> the laurels of Glory;
> go forth and welcome her
> who will the Alps adorn with semi-gods.
> Go forth, while to the great eternal goddess
> is raised an arch of honour which will live for ever.

On hearing this song, the Most Serene Infantas with their twelve ladies immediately set out from the temple of Glory to welcome Madame and accompany her to the spot where, together with the other wise and valorous queens, she might enjoy the prize of immortality. Having passed under the arch, they divided themselves into two groups, seven on each side of the mountain, leading off sideways to the ballet, where they came together again and lined up in pairs. On their heads were gleaming crowns entwined with plaster flowers and cascades of fine pearls, themselves interposed with huge diamonds and rubies and topped with great bunches of heron feathers, the colours of which complemented nicely the colours of the dresses below. The dresses themselves were all identical in every respect and of unusual richness. No less remarkable was their novelty of style, further enhanced by their grace of carriage: each, in fact, was made in cloth of gold and silver, adorned, pleat upon pleat, with six rows of embroidery, each two finger-breadths wide and slightly elevated by means of alder-berries worked in gold; each dress, moreover, was closed up around the bodice like a coat of armour, widening out around the skirts, which skimmed the floor. Likewise reaching the floor were the tips of the open rose-coloured sleeves, lined in cloth of gold; these were shaped as leaves, receding in the form of palms, and were of similar length to the body of the dress. The mantle of fine silver blades glittered at the shoulders, spreading out as it fell with great splendour to the level of the belt, where it was joined to a bodice 2½ palms high, itself embroidered entirely in alder-berries over a base of gold plate. But of truly admirable beauty and almost inestimable value was the ruff, which divided at the breast, disclosing in the intervening space a great jewel; both collar and jewel were composed of diamonds and other gems, of such quality and quantity as to outshine even the candelabra positioned around the hall, dazzling the eyes of the onlookers. Having advanced further, at the sound of the violins they commenced a most beautiful ballet of forty figures, which they danced with a combination of charming majesty and majestic charm, passing from one figure to another in various courantes and galliards with such justness and in such perfect time that it seemed almost by habit and not specially contrived. This ballet continued without interruption for an hour, at which point it finally ended close to the great staircase. After a general curtsey, the Infantas with their ladies were conducted by His Highness and the Most Serene brothers to take their seats with the Most Serene sister-in-law and sister, by whom they were received with great joy, while all the instruments and voices, previously heard in their various separate groups, united together in a melody of extraordinary sweetness. After this they fell silent, and the solo violins took up a branle danced by Their Most Serene Highnesses and other favourite dances for the pleasure of the ladies and gentlemen present. This continued for some time, and the revelries were thus concluded.

[At this point, a herald with trumpets 'proclaims' the tournament cartel of Prince Filiberto, masquerading under the name of Prince Fiammidoro.]

3 The social and intellectual condition of the musician: Antonio Maria Abbatini

Sometime around 1667, Antonio Maria bbatini (Città di Castello, c.1609–c. 1679) addresses a short poetic autobiography to the poet and literary scholar Sebastiano Baldini – himself the author of numerous burlesque cantatas set to music by Antonio Cesti, Atto Melani, Alessandro Stradella, Marco Marazzoli, etc., secretary to the University of Rome and personal friend of the family of Pope Alexander VII Chigi – with a request that he intercede with the 'master' (as he light-heartedly and irreverently refers to the Holy Father) for a number of unspecified favours. The literary quality of Abbatini's doggerel is low, and more than one allusion is obscure (as, for example, the theoretical confutation of the work of an unidentified 'German': lines 193ff.). Nevertheless, some significant facts do emerge in connection not only with the life of the composer himself but also, in general, as regards the condition of contemporary musicians: the eternal wanderings between the various principal *cappelle musicali* of Rome (the Gesù, St John Lateran, S. Maria Maggiore and St Louis, national church of the French community in Rome, cited respectively at lines 80, 85, 109ff., 114ff.); the Papal commission (lines 100 ff.) of an appropriate musical setting for the hymns as revised by the humanist pope Urban VIII (Abbatini, in fact, adapts the new texts to the music of Palestrina's hymns: as noted in chapter 12, the new musical edition – sumptuously prepared – was published in Antwerp in 1644); Abbatini's endless activities as a teacher of singers and composers (activities whose influence was destined to be felt as far afield as South America, on the tide of missionary expeditions: lines 133ff. and chapter 10); the modest economic and social conditions – as compared, even, to singers and instrumentalists (see lines 163–8) – of the *maestro di cappella*, compelled to eke out his living from the meagre income of an ecclesiastical benefice (lines 10ff.) and modest chapel allowance (lines 247ff.), and to petition for pensions and other subsidies (lines 25ff.) in an attempt to allow himself the occasional luxury of a coachman (lines 260ff.); Abbatini's fame as a theorist (lines 148ff.), seem in the general context of the decline of seventeenth-century musical theory (lines 178–92 contain a rich listing of fifteenth- and sixteenth-century musical theorists), itself intrinsic cause of the corresponding decline in prestige of the *maestro di cappella* (see chapter 10); the musical academies (lines 206–46) held at the house of Abbatini in the years after 1663, with performances of madrigals (see chapter 1) and other vocal and instrumental pieces at the keyboard, theoretical lessons and debates (printed in G. Ciliberti, *Antonio Maria Abbatini e la musica del suo tempo* (Perugia, 1986), chapter 19). On the other hand, there is no mention whatever of theatrical music (see chapter 22), which, for Abbatini, can thus have represented no more than one of his many tasks in the service of 'various princes' (lines 151–3). The text, here reproduced in its entirety, is preserved among the papers of Baldini at the Biblioteca Vaticana (ms. Chigi L.VI.191).

To Sig. Bastiano Baldini

More than once have I desired, Baldini mine,
my condition to relate to you in full
and analyse my fortunes,
since the master gives you ear
5 and holds you highly in esteem, as indeed do I
and every man, and rightly so,
for you are learned, pious, just,
willingly you give a helping hand to all,
you, in short, are just the man I need.
10 Benefice from the Palace seek I not,
since this I have these thirty years with ministry,
though never do I celebrate the holy office.
From this obtain I neither bread nor wine
(as renders every other benefice in kind),
15 but loss and detriment alone.
Here, another Padre [Luigi] Albrizzi should I need,
to recount the damage which it brings,
the torment and the agony I endure.
Not only every nourishment is squandered,
20 but also does it press and overwhelm my breast,
that only *à la grecque* [at a distance?] do I succeed in saying Mass.
Thus am I compelled to do without
all blessings which from the Datary derive,
a mouthful which I swallow to my scorn.
25 In faith, Baldini, I do swear,
that but the other day, in desperation sheer,
did I resolve to throw myself upon the road.
Boldly, I resolved to seek a certain pension,
to which I had rescript with gratefully received reply.
30 But listen to what happened in the end.
Immediately, the *Perobitum* objects
that I, since bound in married state,
require for this a special dispensation.
Still as a statue was I struck; yet my heart resolves
35 to do everything in its resource
to guarantee my daily bread.
I find out more about the cost and (true indeed)
discover it impedes my will;
disappointment thus rewards my thoughts.

40 Of fate and destiny, wicked and perverse,
to very Heaven I complain, and in one I grieve
that every hope already is forgotten.
What, say you, is my distress
on failing in my life to win
45 a place in the Capitol?
And yet I have not failed to toil, and jealousy
has caused the best in my profession,
seeking always to ascertain the *quia*.
With your aid I do believe
50 that I will manage to achieve my end;
thus, I beg you, lend me your attention.
Now shall I explain to you my every thought,
my birth, my native land, and everything
that in this life and world I've made and done,
55 that, acquainted with my every work,
the master you may openly petition
for an end to my misfortune.
Forgive me if my speech is bold,
since if I hold my tongue the truth you will elude
60 and you will never be of aid to me.
Now open you your ears and hear
that my native land is Città di Castello
and, as you know, my family name is Abbatini.
To me, as noble citizen, were giv'n,
65 as to all my peers, the privileges
of this gracious, charming town,
rich in palms, in wreaths, adornments,
famous men at every street and corner:
my glories, too, resound among these worthy deeds.
70 In my more youthful days, the Jesuits
to science opened up the ways; music
I in every age did eagerly await.
At the age of fourteen years declined I not,
with the best of votes, the post
75 of *maestro di cappella* of my native town.
In little time at all my name
was cited here and there with wonderment;
Josquin, Palestrina they called me.
With celerity my fame arrived in Rome,
80 where I was called upon to govern music at the Gesù,
more than one eyebrow there to raise.

Such a thing, you may believe, cannot be true,
that a lad of merely sixteen years of age
reached such a rank, indeed more too,
85 since I did follow Cifra at the Lateran,
chief and mother of all the other churches,
where ne'er one goes before a certain age?
By virtue of my many toils,
weary and enfeebled did I finally become;
90 half dead to my native town did I return.
Still very much alive, nursed back to health,
there with Dorotea Giustini did I set up house;
with goodness and nobility was she highly blessed.
While in the company of these my fellow citizens,
95 passing time in hunting, songs and sounds,
jumps, jousts, tournaments and feasting,
am I by the master called to Rome;
oh what sobs, what anguished tears were shed
by my beloved wife and brothers there!
100 Arrived in Rome, the master graciously commands
that I to music set the hymns
by great Pope Urban re-arranged.
Never did I drink a better cup,
and home did I return with joy,
105 thanking heaven for the blessing sent.
To serve that lord, with greatest warmth,
I set myself to giving them the greatest sound I knew,
which, indeed, I promptly did, within a year.
Then, on Mount Esquiline itself, where Maggiore
110 is the mother great of God, I had the charge
of being of the music *maestro di cappella*.
Continuous labours made me fear
my health again, for which reason did I run
to serve St Louis, within its yearned-for walls.
115 Here I go no further, since it is said:
the papacy of the *maestri* is St Louis.
Here, indeed, I wish to live and die.
Here never does one sing in Phrygian modes,
since nowhere is there argument and din,
120 but only in the Lydian, as in Paris used.
Here I draw a line and here I stop,
for I am tired and, weary as I am,
I cannot pass beyond.

Only shall I add 'tis now full forty years
125 that I have served my masters like a slave,
boiled for the ones, and for the others roast.
Almost, now, for half-score years and one
have I remained to serve the French,
and twenty years served I the Esquiline.
130 Seven years and some months too the Lateran,
two years incomplete the Church of the Gesù:
in all some forty years spent none too well.
In all my various employments have I taught
some five score followers and more, and principally *castrati*:
135 throughout the world are they dispersed, e'en in Peru;
neither is there parish nor monastic church
in Rome not brimming with the same;
in the Papal Chapel too are they the first.
With this thought do I regain my strength,
140 get back my breath, o my dear friend,
what I have said to date is but two-thirds.
Ten works have I had printed; mark well
what I do say, and you will be amazed,
for everything I e'er did now I curse and damn.
145 For money ne'er did I have greed,
since certainly for wrath should I have died,
as you yourself will presently conclude.
On doubtful cases sent to Rome
from Naples, B'logna, Portugal,
150 I only did reply, I only did cast lightness on the dark.
A thousand time, if err I not,
the various princes have I served in their encumbrances;
as still I serve, since I do find myself involved.
For all that hereto I have said in my unworthy verse,
155 ne'er did I receive a farthing as a gift,
but only of my riches made I quick dispatch.
More than bread and wine alone one needs,
which is, Baldini mine, the most
that [musical] *cappelle* do provide, yet err I not!
160 The perfect music, instrumental,
comes from *maestri*, voices, instruments,
which more is worth than any other kind.
The players have a mouthful for to chew,
since a twofold market they do have:
165 Capitol and Castle (and thus are they content).

The singers, then, the noble banderole
perpetually enjoy, in the palace of the Pontifex;
vassalage have I ne'er seen better.
Marvel you at these my words, yet madness strikes me not:
170 music is created by the *maestri*,
yet in the pack the *maestri* are they not.
The pie without the cream: thus might one describe
the lot of who to be *maestro di cappella* does decide,
with bread on earth denied him but in hospital.
175 Wherever is that age, so beautiful,
when lectures in [the art of] music
were in use (and this is not a tale)?
Bologna is the proof of this,
which offered such a rich array that [Ramos de] Pareia
180 left Spain and other duties for her sake.
He, while at the University, did print
at tender age a noble treatise,
and more would he have printed had he longer lived.
Thus, the science of composing well
185 was truly lit from every side; [compare]
our own confusion and unhappy state!
Boethius and Guido are today abhorred by all,
as indeed are Aron, Franco, Fogliano and Zarlino,
Guglielmo, Torre, Ponzio and Glarean,
190 Lusitano, Tigrini, Psello and Bonini,
and all the rest, that I would never end,
were I to give a list of every author here.
Thus, o [dear] Baldini, it's no surprise
if, when came that German to sustain
195 the logics of every harmony,
no-one, by God, would let himself be seen
e'en to translate his words into our tongue;
I alone, for sheer scarcity of others, did speak out,
since, in Germany, like Portugal
200 and England, public lectures
teach the laws of composition.
In defence of this there was a quite enormous crowd
of men from every other erudite profession:
he, amazed, returned home to his fatherland.
205 Now see you the state to which we are reduced!
However, many years ago,
an academy did I open at my home; and, Your Lordship,

be not you offended if I point out to you,
that you alone of all the citizens of Rome
210 have never come: what great discourtesy!
Though no-one gives you formal invitation, I myself
have begged you time and time again, invariably in vain:
of us, I know not who is rascal greater.
I, indeed, am cross with you, and gradually
215 I feel my bile increasing: but here I'll hold my tongue,
for I would speak in madness like an insane man.
I'll thus return to tell you what I do
in the afore-described academy; I'll thus
remove from me all fraud or trick, from you all awkwardness.
220 First, the now-lost madrigals of once upon a time
are, at table, sung with great delight:
the reason, for respect, I will not tell.
There follows my address: I spread my wings
to raise myself to the harmonious skies;
225 but they [the wings] are just like those of Icarus.
Every liberty the virtuosi are allowed
to contradict whatever I have said,
though this role with reluctance do they play.
Kircher has, however, always argued,
230 as, too, Orlandi, general of the Carmelites,
Dal Pane has his doubts, beloved Lelio too.
Discussion over, as, by grace of God,
invariably occurs without ill-will,
due praise is then accorded he who most deserves.
235 Here the unveiled truth is seen,
since almost all are in the fore-front row
and everything is discerned minutely.
Then to the harpsichord the company transfers,
and each man takes upon himself to show, with song
240 and sound, his virtue, which binds the heart and soul.
In all are set aside three hours of time,
from nine o' clock (p.m.) for the remainder of the day,
and never without wonder do those present go away.
It's now five years that I these evenings hold,
245 and not without some small expense (the truth to tell),
that more to think of it does stir the mind.
At Rome, I find myself with only that allowance
which is left me by the Church; as I have said,
from persons have I ne'er a penny had.

250 For all this seek I not to cheat nor take up arms,
to live how I believe is fitting;
no debts shall I incur, for I am not so silly.
Because a certain quota comes my way each year,
and this makes good whate'er the mouth does lack,
255 enabling me to dress well and to keep good house.
This, too, is true: my foot, my leg, my hip
in part my gait impede;
my growing years, indeed, [begin to] weigh and tire me down;
it will be best if I to my fatherland go home,
260 my income being insufficient here
for e'en a single horse to pull me on my way.
Oh I would that ancient custom did return;
still should I desire to run my lance
and strike these lines at that same point
265 where you are placed [i.e., the University]! And, though all this is jest and idle talk
(or, more precisely, great impertinence),
my belly and my tale provide a good excuse.
Whatever I have said remains in confidence,
because, through you, I know that means of consolation
270 are not lacking. And thus I pay you my regards,
bound as I am to you a thousand times and more.

4 Historical and stylistic awareness: Heinrich Schütz

Heinrich Schütz (see chapter 17), *Kapellmeister* – and, as such, a fully-fledged official – at the court of Dresden, submitted a large number of memoranda and petitions regarding the maintenance of the ducal chapel to his patron Duke Johann Georg I. Particularly sorrowful are the memoranda of the 1630s and 40s, in which the composer puts forward a series of emergency solutions aimed at the very survival of the choir in a period of serious economic crisis during the Thirty Years War. In the memorandum of 1651, which accompanied the presentation to the Duke of Schütz's newly published Op. 12, the sixty-six-year-old composer asks permission to retire, or at least to be relieved of a significant part of his duties in the choir. In support of his request, Schütz cites not only the fickleness of musical fashion (tailors and musicians alike, he observes, are quickly rendered out of date!) but also the unremitting arduousness of his exceptionally lengthy career of artistic and institutional commitment – a commitment which, from his earliest youth, had cost the composer great study, sacrifice and travels (conveniently, however, Schütz omits every mention of his repeated wartime visits to Copenhagen as *Kapellmeister* at the royal court).

A true miniature autobiography, then, which describes: the humanistic education of the composer (prior, still, to his musical training); his apprenticeship and the publication of his madrigals in Venice under the guidance of Giovanni Gabrieli (himself, in youthful days, a visitor to the Bavarian court, and never to relinquish his close ties with Germany: his publications, for example, are dedicated to the Fuggers of Augsburg; as noted, moreover, in chapter 1, Gabrieli was also the teacher and something of a father-figure for a numerous group of young northern musicians); the solemn gesture of the dying Gabrieli who, *in memoriam*, bequeaths to his pupil a ring (appointing, for the purpose, his father confessor Fra Taddeo da Venezia; the latter, in 1615, himself dedicates a posthumous collection of instrumental music by Giovanni – the *Canzoni e sonate* – to the Duke of Bavaria); Schütz's exceptional awareness of his own personal role and historical position; the seriousness of the composer's approach to his institutional commitments and his unswerving dedication to the protection of what he terms a certain 'German gravity' (the words are those of a further memorandum) in the management of the choir. In reality, Schütz – who here requests that he be granted the assistance of a *castrato* from the 'Italian' *cappella* of the Crown Prince – is well aware of the looming Italianization and secularization of music at the Dresden court.

Despite the composer's thorough expertise in the music of the Italians, his non-adherence to the rampant yet facile applications of the fashionable Italian style – a style, indeed, without doctrine (see chapter 10) – is clearly apparent in his preface to the *Geistliche Chor-Music* (Op. 11) of 1648 (in which his use of vocal polyphony without *basso continuo* reaches unsurpassable heights of representative and elocutionary force). Schütz's declaration is emblematic of the seventeenth-century plurality of styles – modern styles, styles based on long-established tradition – and their co-existence in the compositional and performance practice of the age: without mentioning names, the composer alludes to a treatise (still in preparation) in which Marco Scacchi – an Italian musician then active at the Polish Chapel Royal – discusses precisely this question (see chapter 8). Scacchi's volume, the *Breve discorso sopra la musica moderna*, was published shortly after in 1649.

Memorandum to the Duke of Saxony

In most humbly offering this little work of mine, which now appears under the name of Your Most Serene Highness, I take the opportunity to touch upon the events in a life which, from my youth to this very day, has been marked by no small degree of affliction and torment – not, however, without entreating (with deepest devotion) the forgiveness and benevolent attention of Your Most Serene Highness. Born on the feast of St Burkhard, [14 October] 1585, at the tender age of thirteen I left the house of my parents (of blessed memory) at Weißenfels and, since that time, have always lived abroad. At first, as *puer cantor* in the court chapel of the Landgrave Moritz of Hesse, I underwent several years of instruction in music, as also in Latin and other languages. My parents, however, were unremittingly against the idea that I should one day make music my profession; thus, my voice having broken, I continued my studies at the University of Marburg, with the aim of choosing a suitable profession and obtaining some honourable degree. These plans, however, were soon overturned (undoubtedly by the will of God): the Landgrave Moritz – who, perhaps, had become aware of my notable inclination for music during my service at his chapel – passing through Marburg, caused me to be offered a scholarship of 200 thalers *per annum*, that without hesitation I might journey to Italy, to study at the school of a famous – though now aged – musician and composer. Young as I was, and desirous of seeing the world, I willingly accepted this proposal; thus, in 1609, and almost against my parents' will, I left Marburg for Venice. When, then, on arrival (and having studied some little time with my master), I became aware of the importance and difficulty of compositional studies and the limitations of my earlier preparation, and thus had begun to regret having rashly left aside my university studies (in which I had already made some progress), I was nevertheless unable to avoid looking on the brighter side of things and resolving to fulfil the aims of my journey to Venice – to such an extent that I fully abandoned my other studies and dedicated myself as conscientiously as possible to the study of music. In which, by the grace of God, I met with such success as to enable me to publish in Venice (three years after my arrival, and a year before leaving Italy) my first musical work, in Italian, dedicated with every gratitude to the Landgrave Moritz. This publication earned me the particular praise of the best musicians in Venice. And, having published this first little work of mine, I was encouraged and, indeed, exhorted not only by my teacher, Giovanni Gabrieli, but also by the *maestro di cappella* [of St Mark's] and other illustrious musicians to persevere in the study of music, in which, it was said, I was destined to enjoy the greatest success. After a further year, during which time I completed my studies in Venice (this time at my parents' expense), my teacher died: on his death-bed, he gave instructions and ordered his confessor, an Augustinian monk, that, in perpetual memory, I should inherit a certain ring. The Landgrave Moritz, then, was right to sustain that anyone who wished to benefit from the teachings of this most talented man should not hesitate for a moment to make the journey to his school.

Having, then, returned to Germany in 1613 after my first Italian sojourn, I secretly planned to continue my musical studies (in which I had now built a solid foundation) for a few years unobserved and to present myself at some suitable moment with a work truly worthy. Nor did my relations fail to provide constant stimulus and advice to the effect that, with my nevertheless modest qualities, I should procure for myself due reward and esteem in some other field and regard music as a pastime: as, in the end, I allowed myself to be convinced. Thus, after many years of neglect, I was on the point of taking up my books again when, in 1614, it pleased Almighty God – by whom, while still in my mother's womb, I had undoubtedly been predestined for the profession of music – to ordain that I be called to Dresden for the baptism service of Duke Augustus, now administrator of the arch-chapter of Magdeburg, and – I having given proof of my abilities – to offer me, in the name of Your Most Serene Highness, the direction of your choir. At which point my preants decided to remove all further resistance to the will of God and I was induced to accept with devoted gratitude the honourable condition offered, determined to fulfil my obligations with the greatest of zeal. What from 1615 (year of my nomination to this position, in which I shall continue till it please Almighty God or Your Highness to the contrary) to the present day (for a total of over thirty-five years of service) have been my duties – themselves of little worth, though of no little effort and toil – is certainly something that Your Most Serene Highness will in some way remember. May I here give thanks for the divine providence and goodness which for so many years – leaving aside my own private study and the publication of various musical works – have enabled me to serve Your Most Serene Highness with devotion on the occasion of a multitude of solemnities (the visits of emperors, monarchs, electors and princes, not only in the States belonging to Your Most Serene Highness but also elsewhere), provide for the musical education of the most beloved children of Your Highness, be present at their baptisms one and all and unceasingly do everything in my power – from the very beginning of my directorship – to render the court chapel of Your Most Serene Highness the most famous in Germany, maintaining it with respect to this day. Great would be my desire to continue directing the court chapel of Your Most Serene Highness, as I have until now. Not only, however, by reason of the continuous study, travel and writing which the exercise of my profession has cost me from my earliest days (and which the burden of my profession and employment has rendered indispensable, though, I believe, few of even the most erudite scholars are fully aware of this fact, since no similar type of study exists in our universities) but also by virtue of my age, failing sight and physical strength, I can no longer be fully certain of my ability to serve the choir with due honour and to maintain, in my old age, the good name earned in my younger days: it is, indeed, the opinion of the doctors that I must now interrupt my continuous work, writing and meditation if I am to avoid ruining my health. For this reason, I entreat the benevolence of Your Most Serene Highness to understand how I, your humble and devoted servant, am inevitably compelled to communicate the above, imploring you – not only for the aforementioned reasons, but also in view of the fact that the beloved children of Your Most Serene Highness have all now concluded their training – to grant that I be graciously accorded a less onerous position, that I be exonerated from the regular service of the choir (in order that, for the honour of my name, I may dedicate myself to collecting, completing and printing the musical works begun in my youth) and that I henceforth be considered (in whatever way shall most please Your Most Serene Highness) a pensioner: in which case, needless to say, I should willingly accept some small reduction in my remuneration. Should, however, Your Most Serene Highness desire that I not be released from the choir, or, for the present, prefer to make do with the modest services which, in view of my progressively failing strength, I am able to afford (rather, that is, than engaging another *Kapellmeister*), may it please Your Most Serene Highness to consider me willing, with humble gratitude, to lend my every assistance and to merit the title of *Kapellmeister* to Your Most Serene Highness and the Most Serene House of Saxony to my dying day – on condition that I be granted the collaboration of some qualified person to lighten my duties, give daily assistance to the young musicians newly engaged in the choir of Your Most Serene Highness, take care of the necessary drills and rehearsals, be able to co-ordinate the music and beat time: since otherwise, with the further deterioration of my strength (if, by the grace of God, I be granted still many days to come), I might easily suffer the same fate as befell an aged singer from one celebrated town (himself by no means lacking in merit), who, some time ago, wrote to me complaining that the younger senators of the town, displeased with his antiquated style of composition, and willingly disposed to liberate themselves from his services, told him quite frankly that a *Kapellmeister*, like a tailor, has no further use after thirty years' service; and it is undoubtedly true that the ways of the world tend quickly to tire of ancient manners and customs and move on to other things. And though I cannot expect treatment of this kind from any of the children of Your Most Serene Highness (always graciously benevolent in my regard), it could not nevertheless be ruled out with respect to one of those new musicians whose tendency – albeit unjust – is to favour their new manner of song at the expense of the old.

And since [Giovanni] Andrea Bontempi [Angelini], Italian *castrato* in the service of the heir apparent Duke Johann Georg, has on several occasions let it be known that his training – right from the days of his youth – is still more in the field of composition than in song, and since the said Bontempi, of his own free will, has offered to lend his services and take my place in directing the choir on all such occasions as I might desire, I have deemed it appropriate, in concluding this memorandum, to make mention of this fact to Your Most Serene Highness, in order that I might have your most gracious opinion and ask whether, with Your Most Serene consent, I be permitted to accept the offer of the said Andrea Bontempi and leave him, on occasion, to direct the music in my stead. To which, from what little I understand, Your Most Serene Highness would do well to assent the more quickly, since the said Bontempi, for the service in question, desires no increase whatever in salary nor any change in his role, being satisfied with his remuneration from the Most Serene heir apparent. This young man is highly qualified to carry out the task in question; I have, indeed, received favourable information from Venice (where he lived for some eight years) regarding his unquestionable merits, demonstrated on the occasion of various solemnities for which he acted as substitute for the *maestro di cappella* and publicly directed the music in the various churches. He is, moreover, discreet, and courteous and conciliatory in manner. I thus entreat Your Most Serene Highness to let me know your opinion, the more so since I should not wish to take regular advantage of the good services of this person without previously having informed Your Most Serene Highness . . .

Dresden, 14 January 1651

Heinrich Schütz, Kapellmeister
and most humble and devoted servant
of Your Most Serene Highness

Preface to the Geistliche Chor-Music

Benevolent reader,

It is well known that the *concertato* style of composition with *basso continuo*, a practice which originated in Italy but which has since come to the attention and been taken up by us Germans, has so pleased us as to find a larger number of followers than any other previous style: ample proof of this may be found in the various musical works that are published and sold by our music dealers. For my part, I by no means disapprove of these tendencies, in which, on the contrary, I recognize in our own German nation a large number of talents, able and gifted for the practice of music, to whom I certainly do not begrudge their justly earned praise – willingly, indeed, adding my own. It is, however, beyond all reason of doubt – as every well-trained composer will agree – that, in the exceptionally difficult study of counterpoint, no musician can correctly engage in or satisfactorily handle any other type of composition if he is not already sufficiently versed in the style without *basso continuo* and, in this way, in possession of the necessary prerequisites for composition in the well-ordered manner. These prerequisites, among others, are as follows: the disposition of the modes; simple, mixed and inverted fugue; double counterpoint; the differences between the various musical styles; the melodic handling of the individual voices; the connection of subjects; etc. They are treated at length by erudite theorists and taught *viva voce* to students of counterpoint in *schola practica*; without them, for an expert composer, there exists no composition whatsoever (even when, to the untrained ear, such a composition sets out to create an impression of celestial harmony), or, rather, it will be worth little more than an empty nut-shell.

It is thus that I have been persuaded to undertake a little work such as the present – without *basso continuo* – as a means, indeed, of admonishing many composers (in particular, the younger generation of Germans) of the need to crack this tough nut with their own teeth and to seek out the sweet kernel and foundations of a just counterpoint before progressing to the *stile concertante* – wishing, in this way, to stand up to their first test. In Italy (true and honest school of all music), when, in my youth, I laid the foundations of my profession, it was normal practice for beginners to start by devising and publishing some little work, sacred or secular, without *basso continuo*: as, probably, is still the custom in these southern climes. I have wished to give this account of my personal experience in the study of music (and for the greater fame of our nation) that it be used by each man as he sees fit, and without wishing to discredit anyone.

Nor, however, can it be forgotten that not even this style of sacred music without *basso continuo* (which, indeed, is the reason for my choice of the title *Geistliche Chor-Music*) is without differentiation in type. Many of these compositions, in fact, are intended for performance by full choir with instrumental doubling of the vocal parts, while others, on the contrary, are conceived in such a way as their effect will be best if the parts are not doubled or tripled but assigned some to voices and others to instruments: the effect will also be good if they be performed on the organ, as, indeed, if they be divided into two or three choirs (in the case of compositions *a 8*, *a 12* or for even larger combinations). This little work of mine – composed, on this occasion, for few voices only – contains examples of both these different types of composition; in particular, among the final pieces in the volume are some in which I have omitted to print the text in the instrumental parts (where suitable, in certain of the preceding compositions, the competent musician will be capable of proceeding in similar fashion).

With all this, I wish nevertheless to protest and implore that no reader be led to interpret whatever I have said as though it were my intention to propose or recommend this or any other work of mine as a model or for the information of others (I myself would be the first to admit their inadequacy). On the contrary, for the example of all, I should like to point to those Italian musicians whose names, so to speak, have been canonized by the opinion of the very best composers, as also to the other *classici autores*, both ancient and modern, [all of] whom, with their excellent – not to say incomparable – works, shine clearly forth as exponents of both styles of composition for whomever wishes to study and examine them with diligence and let himself be guided down the straight and narrow path of contrapuntal studies. I also nourish the not unfounded hope that a musician well known to me, himself highly versed in both theory and practice, will quickly publish a treatise on the aforementioned things; this will be of great use and benefit, particularly for us Germans. I myself shall do everything in my power to urge its completion, to the enormous benefit of musical studies.

In conclusion: since some organists may like to provide a discreet and accurate accompaniment in performing this work of mine (though this, properly speaking, has been conceived without *basso continuo*), the said organists should have no displeasure in arranging it in tablature or score. On the contrary, I might confide that not only will the effort and pains invested in this operation give him no cause for regret, but also that this type of performance will further assist in producing the desired effect.

The grace of God be with us all!

THE AUTHOR

5 Celestial music and poetic *topoi*: Ode on the Death of Henry Purcell

In the course of his brief thirty-six years of life, Purcell accumulated many important positions at the English court: composer in ordinary for the Twenty-Four Violins, organist at Westminster Abbey, singer and organist at the Chapel Royal, keeper of the King's instruments. An intensely active existence outside the court, moreover, as teacher, publisher and composer of theatrical music not only supplemented his somewhat meagre royal salary but also won him the universal acclaim of the metropolis. His death, in 1695, occurred on the eve of the feast of St Cecilia (patron saint of musicians), which occasion he himself had frequently celebrated and ennobled with his odes in praise of music (see chapter 18). Unanimous was the grief of men of letters and musicians: preserved, indeed, are a total of some twelve poetic tributes, all published on the occasion of his death. In these, the composer is compared with such figures as David, Amphion, Orpheus (*Orpheus britannicus* is, in fact, the title of two posthumous volumes of vocal music by Purcell), Virgil, Michelangelo and Titian, great gods of the artistic world: gratifying, too, is the comparison with two other great contemporary musicians – Lully and Corelli – whose works, in the artistic consciousness of Europe, had come even before 1700 to represent the height of 'classical' perfection in the two dominant musical traditions (Italian and French: Purcell, indeed, as noted in chapter 26, draws avidly and inventively from both). Above all, however, in their various tributes to Purcell (as, indeed, in their poetic handling of any other theme of essentially musical orientation), the English poets avail themselves of a well-stocked arsenal of images which illustrate the power of music and its effects: a repertory of poetic *topoi*: accumulated in the course of the sixteenth and seventeenth centuries, which brings together a range of Christian and neoplatonic concepts (the harmony of the spheres, the 'accord' between macro- and microcosmos, the ethical function of music, the choirs of angels, music in praise of the Deity, etc.).

A succulent concentrate of these very types of theme, motif, image is provided by the *Ode on the Death of Purcell* by the composer's friend and collaborator John Dryden. The opening stanza contains a variety of ornithological similes with sounds from the world of nature; this is followed by the pagan myth of Orpheus in the underworld and, in the third and final stanza, the Christian image of the 'heavenly choirs', coupled with that of a 'scale of music' lowered from heaven to earth: a kind of *gradus ad Parnassum* made Christian! The music of Purcell – who, in song, towers above his rivals as the nightingale over every other bird – must truly be omnipotent, if this alone would suffice to rectify the discordant harmonies of hell (and thus destroy the underworld itself), and even to instruct the angels in matters of heavenly song! In other words: the myths and motifs of celestial music, the harmony of the spheres, the ethical effects of music – threadbare and trivialized as they are, reduced to the level of non-essential poetic schemes – come less and less to be seen in terms of their intrinsic significance and increasingly as a kind of evocative poetic game which, though indeed paradoxical, is also mournful and suggestive in its charm. (The history of this progressive demythologization and poeticization of the concept of music is traced by J. Hollander, in *The untuning of the sky. Ideas of music in English poetry, 1500–1700* (Princeton, 1961).)

John Blow, presumed teacher of Purcell and his colleague in the Chapel Royal (though ten years his senior, Blow survived his pupil until well into the first decade of the eighteenth century), supplied the music for this ode. The setting, for two countertenors, two recorders and *basso continuo*, is of great tenderness, overflowing with songful voluptuousness, mournful dissonances and soft melismatic efflorescences on the words of greatest emotional significance ('. . . sing . . . warbling . . . heav'nly . . . music . . . godlike . . . alas! . . . harmony . . . tuneful . . . lament . . . rejoice'); conversely, the diabolical dissonance of hell – the 'jarring sphere' – is conveyed by one harsh dissonance, percussively repeated. In general, the musical art of Blow (*Amphion anglicus*) is largely comparable to that of Purcell himself, though – unlike Purcell – he never composed for the stage. With, however, one notable exception. Blow's musical and theatrical entertainment *Venus and Adonis* – privately performed at the court of Charles II around 1682, with a mistress of the King in the role of Venus and her daughter as Cupid! – was no more influential than Purcell's *Dido and Aeneas* of 1689: like *Dido*, however, it is a true miniature opera, in which the languishing melodies of Blow's recitative enhance notably the bitter-sweet eroticism with which the tragic loves of Venus and Adonis are portrayed. A Lully-style overture is followed by a Prologue in which Cupid gaily criticizes the unfaithfulness of amorous life at court; in Act 1, after the seduction of Venus (whose enchanting voice is here consistently doubled at the third by the dulcet tones of a recorder), there follows a *divertissement* of huntsmen who seduce Adonis to the pleasures of their pastime. Act 2 features the lesson of Venus to Cupid and the little Cupids who, to the sound of a dance, learn to spell; this is followed by the dance of the Graces to an ostinato passacaglia. In Act 3, a desolate Venus – no longer accompanied by recorder! – looks on as Adonis, fatally injured by a wild boar, dies; their pathetic and passionate dialogue is set in highly emotional recitative and sealed by the funeral lament of the little Cupids over the body of Adonis.

I

Mark how the lark and linnet sing,
with rival notes
they strain their warbling throats,
to welcome in the Spring.
But in the close of night,
when Philomel begins her heav'nly lay,
they cease their mutual spite,
drink in her music with delight,
and list'ning and silent, and silent and list'ning, and list'ning
and silent obey.

II

So ceas'd the rival crew when Purcell came,
they sung no more, or only sung his fame.

Struck dumb, they all admir'd the godlike man:
  the godlike man
  alas! too soon retir'd,
  as he too late began.
We beg not hell our Orpheus to restore;
  had he been there,
  their sov'reign's fear
  had sent him back before.
The pow'r of harmony too well they knew,
He long e'er this had tun'd their jarring sphere,
  and left no hell below.

III
The heav'nly choir, who heard his notes from high,
let down the scale of music from the sky:
  they handed him along,
and all the way he taught, and all the way they sung.
Ye brethren of the lyre, and tuneful voice,
lament his lot, but at your own rejoice.
Now live secure and linger out your days,
the gods are pleas'd alone with Purcell's lays,
  nor know to mend their choice.

6 The impresarial organization of Venetian theatres: Cristoforo Ivanovich

In 1680, no less than seven opera houses are simultaneously in business in Venice. Competition – both artistic and commercial – is intense; market conditions are no less at work in deciding criteria for planning and programming than in establishing the price of the ticket at the door; 1677 had seen the opening of a 'poor man's' theatre – the Teatro S. Angelo – with prices accessible not only to the 'merchants and nobility' but also to the city-dwellers as a whole; 1678 brought the opening of the largest, most sumptuous and luxurious of ali Venetian theatres, the Teatro S. Giovanni Grisostomo (its noble proprietors, the Grimani brothers, were themselves old hands in the sphere of theatrical enterprise and initiative), where the greatest court virtuosi of Europe appeared to the accompaniment of a theatre orchestra of previously unheard-of dimensions. Meanwhile, at his villa of Piazzola sul Brenta, the Procurator Marco Contarini – 'with heroic generosity and magnificence' – inaugurated a splendid new theatre, designed for use during the annual vacation (and consequent exodus) from Venice: a private court theatre in every sense of the word, though established in those very years which mark the greatest period of expansion of impresarial theatre at Venice. The dukes of Braunschweig – suppliers of troops to the Republic – sojourn for lengthy periods in Venice, where they add their own patronage of opera singers and composers. At Carnival, various other sovereigns (in particular, the Dukes of Modena and Mantua) can be seen at the opera. The Parisian *Mercure galant* records the theatrical impressions of high-ranking tourists to Venice.

It is in this climate of theatrical euphoria that Cristoforo Ivanovich (native of Dalmatia, canon of St Mark's, resident in Venice since 1657) dedicates his *Memorie teatrali di Venezia* (1681) – an 'historical glance' at the origins, functions and organization of opera and operatic theatre in Venice – to the brothers Grimani. Indeed, the *Memorie teatrali*, at less than half a century from the introduction of public opera in Venice, provide what might be described as a first 'ratification' of its already illustrious history. Himself a librettist, Ivanovich nonetheless seems more interested in the impresarial structure of the theatres and their civil and ideological significance (with frequent references to their political importance as a means of authority and social control) than in their artistic organization. Theatres, he notes, are a source of pride for the republic of Venice (which considers itself the legitimate descendant of the ancient republic of Rome: this theme, carried back to the Trojan origins of Rome, appears frequently in the subjects of Venetian operas of the earliest decades – see chapter 21): equally, however, they provide an example of that thoroughly Venetian combination of business and art, financial investment and aesthetic profit, which Ivanovich here illustrates point by point (acquisition of initial capital and annual income guaranteed by means of the assignment and renting of bozes; fixed costs and management expenses for the production and performance of operas; night-by-night income conditioned by success).

Besides the various chapters reproduced in the following pages, other sections of the *Memorie teatrali* discuss: the events leading up to the coming of the first public opera house in 1637 (chapter V), the history of Venetian theatres before 1637 (chapter VIII), the diplomatically delicate procedures for the assignment of boxes to the various ambassadors (chapter XI), the magistratures responsible for the theatres (chapter XII), the profit of the librettist (chapter XVI), the great Teatro Contarini at Piazzola (chapter XVII), the usefulness of a chronology of productions (chapters XIX–XX). The *Memorie teatrali* then conclude with a chronological table of the *drammi per musica* performed in Venice between 1637 and 1681 – a total little short of 200 different productions.

Chapter I: The republic of Venice, imitating the greatness of the ancient republic of Rome, restored the magnificence of the theatres.

Of all the republics in the world, none was more perfect than the ancient republic of Rome; nor, indeed, was there ever a better imitation of this than the republic of Venice . . . And, in fact, it was out of the ruins of the former that the latter was born, succeeding no less to the heritage of a great republic than to that of the genius unfailingly present in every aspect of its magnificence . . . Here, however, it is not my intention to write histories or panegyrics in praise of the republic of Venice, whose excellence speaks for itself. Only in passing, as supporting material for my present undertaking in the *Memorie teatrali*, shall I mention how Time, in the everlasting succession of human events, saw the passing of theatrical displays from the banks of the Tiber to the shores of the Adriatic Sea, so that not even in this should Venice have come second to ancient Rome.

As every expert in history will own, the entertainments produced during Carnival-tide in Venice are as curious as the Bacchanalia of ancient Rome used to be, for which reason – today as in ancient times – the world converges in pilgrimage to watch the aforesaid displays.

Abundance and display are the tools of delicate political operation, on which can depend the good fortunes of the government itself; through these, if used in honest measure, a prince can acquire the love of his people, by whom the yoke is never more easily forgotten than when they are sated or constrained by the pleasures. The common people, when they have nothing better to gnaw, turn to gnawing the reputation of princes; deprived of entertainment their idleness can easily degenerate, with the most dreadful of consequences.

Chapter II: Brief description of Venice and of the pleasant entertainments to be enjoyed in the city before the introduction of the theatres: which entertainments are still to be enjoyed in every season of the year and, in particular, during Carnival.

. . . Spring. Sometimes, at the beginning of this youthful season, the observer has occasion to enjoy some equestrian drill and entertainments at the riding school. This is situated near the Mendicanti and has a capacity of over seventy horses . . . It is run by a patrician academy . . . Other common pastimes are for ladies and gentlemen with the pleasure of the town, since the game of football begins at the outset of Lent, practised only by gentlemen at the place of the goal at S. Bonaventura, with great crowds of noblemen and other persons . . . The so-called 'freschi' then begin on the second day of Easter; each feast-day, in the evening, there is a continuous parade of gondolas from the Palazzo Pesaro to the Ponte della Croce, all full of ladies and gentlemen, ministers of princes and other visitors to the city . . . Generally, the end of this joyful season coincides with the entertainments of Ascension, notable, in the first place, for the famous appearance of the Bucintoro . . . as also for the fair in the Piazza S. Marco; this lasts a fortnight and it patronized morning and evening by countless ladies, gentlemen and masquers, enticed by the magnificence of the goods on display, particularly those on the Listone, which, with their gold, silver and precious stones, give the impression of a hanging Peru. In the Piazza itself, the many booths with dancing marionettes provide continuous entertainment for visitors and common folk alike.

Summer. During the hot summer season the 'freschi' continue along their customary route . . . Frequently, the [Grand] Canal echoes to the sound of most beautiful serenades performed by harmonious boatloads of musicians, the beauty of whose voices attracts countless numbers of gondolas . . . Every feast day is marked by the so-called *guerre de' pugni* [= fist-fights] between the Castellani and Nicolotti; these are held upon the various bridges, particularly famous among which is the Ponte di S. Barnaba . . .

Autumn. This temperate season, though customarily marked by the emigration of the nobility and citizens to the villas, there to enjoy the countryside, also sees the opening of a few comedy theatres where curious and pleasant evening entertainments are performed . . . Opera rehearsals are first held in the houses of the gentlemen partners or patrons of the various theatres; they then transfer to the theatres themselves, with eager interest in the new voices, which can then be enjoyed at pleasure during the public performances, etc.

Winter. This brings the Carnival season, for which outsiders flock to the city, and which sees the citizens themselves in continuous activity, after the year's employment in political or domestic affairs. The opera houses are first to begin; this they do with incredible magnificence and splendour, by no means inferior to that practised in various places by the magnificence of princes, with the sole difference that the latter procure the enjoyment of all through their own generosity, while opera in Venice is business and thus lacks that decorum with which marriages and births are frequently celebrated by princes with a view to the greater display of their magnificence and power. The performance of these *drammi*, as also of comedies, continues without interruption until the final day of Carnival; in this way, each evening brings a variety of entertainments of several hours' length, held in a number of different theatres (each of which traditionally offers two different productions per season as a means of drawing the crowds) . . . Carnival begins on 26 December, feast of St Stephen, with masks and fancy dress – when these are not expressly prohibited by decree.

[There follows a long description of the entertainments available during Carnival.]

Chapter IV: Of the theatres of ancient Rome and the differences between these and the theatres of Venice.

. . . Though it is undoubtedly true that the most magnificent theatres already existed in many parts of Italy before their arrival in Venice, it is equally true that these theatres were used only on the occasion of such outstanding events as the marriages or births of princes. This, for example, was the case in both Parma and Florence. Public performances, since their introduction in Venice, have continued to take place every year during Carnival, thus setting an example which has come to be followed in many other parts of Europe. In order to define the differences between the theatres of Venice and those of Ancient Rome, it will be necessary to examine their various circumstances and situations.

. . . The principal difference is that the theatres of today, in comparison with those of the ancients, have room for only a limited number of persons; moreover, instead of stepwise tiers of seats, they are constructed with several tiers of boxes, mostly reserved for the convenience of the nobles, where the ladies can also remain in total liberty without masks. In the middle section [i.e., the stalls], the benches are rented out on a day-to-day basis without social distinction, since the use of masks obviates the necessity of former times for the observance of respect in the presence of the grandiose matrons and senators of Rome (the free-born republic of Venice embracing, as it does, a desire to preserve the freedom of all). Nor is the magnificence of one to be compared with the other, since Rome lavished great fortunes on its theatrical productions – once considered among its greatest splendours – and its machines were the wonder of the world. The headlong fall of Phaethon would be represented by some wretched convict, whose plunge from the chariot would be accompanied by the applause of the people. Likewise, the burning of the hand of Mucius Scaevola and other similar representations, it having been desired that the people be accustomed to horrors and destruction. Today, however, musical theatre exists more as relief for the soul and as virtuous recreation. The appearance of ingenious machines, as suggested by the drama, combines with the costumes and scenic displays in a way which proves extremely attractive and which fully satisfies the universal curiosity aroused. In this way, lifelike elephants and real-life camels have been seen to walk the stage, as also grandiose chariots drawn by horses or other wild beasts; other sights include flying horses, dancing horses, the most magnificent machines represented by air, earth and sea with fantastic contrivances and laudable invention, to the point at which royal apartments, illuminated as for night, have been seen to descent from the air with the entire company of actors and instrumentalists, and then to return whence they came, with the great admiration of all – but one of thousands of possible forms . . .

Chapter VII: Public attendances at plays have fallen with the introduction of the *dramma in musica* to such a degree that the former have been reduced to nothing.

Before the introduction of the *dramma in musica*, plays were much appreciated in Venice. The companies of actors enjoyed the greatest renown; their purpose was the virtuous amusement of a high-born gathering of spectators, otherwise devoid of theatrical entertainments. Their efforts were rewarded with both profit and honour . . . But the said actors, mindful of the reduced approbation of their virtuous toils with the triumphant introduction of the *poesia per musica* in the theatres, now avoid as much as possible the exercise of their profession in Venice, where, in the absence of their noble audiences of former days, they lack those circumstances of decorum, honour and benefit which once served as an incitement to study and to such delightful and profitable application. For this reason, and by virtue of the expenses necessarily incurred in maintaining themselves in their place of performance, the said actors risk rather to lose than to gain. Unless, with the passage of time, some change of direction occurs in the fortunes of opera, the spoken theatre will continue to decline, with obvious danger . . . of total eclipse . . .

Chapter IX: Of the numbers of theatres, past and present, in Venice, and the time of their appearance.

[This chapter contains a concise history of the twelve opera houses active continuously or intermittently at Venice over the period 1637–81: S. Cassiano (opened to operatic productions in 1637), S. Salvatore (1661), SS. Giovanni e Paolo (1639), S. Moisè (1640), Novissimo (1641), SS. Apostoli (1649), S. Apollinare (1651), the Teatro ai Saloni (1670), S. Samuele (1656: in reality, however, dedicated exclusively to plays), S. Angelo (1677), S. Giovanni Grisostomo (1678), the Teatro a Cannaregio (1679).]

Chapter X: The rental of boxes and the rights acquired by their renters.

The most secure income of every theatre is provided by the leasing of boxes. There are at least one hundred of these, besides the various orders of galleries; not all are equal in price, the latter being calculated on the basis of the order and number (i.e., the excellence of position) of each box . . . From the very beginning, theatre proprietors have customarily practised two types of charges: first, a cash payment for each box (this serves largely to cover construction costs, and is the principal reason for the ease and rapidity with which the construction of a number of theatres has been possible); second, an agreed annual rent, paid every year in which there is an opera season (only in this way does the said payment correspond both to the expenses incurred by the theatre and the comfort and convenience enjoyed by the occupants of the box). The right acquired by the possessor of the box is that of retaining it on his own account, without the option of reletting it to others; he may make use of it for his own purposes and lend it out as he likes . . . There are also various boxes at ground and gallery level, which, by virtue of their inferior or inconvenient position, are not all rented out from the beginning, but rather on a nightly or annual basis at the free discretion of the theatre proprietor, who thus attempts to procure for himself the greatest possible advantage.

Chapter XIII: Of the expenses which a theatre is obliged to sustain.

A theatre, before enjoying any profit whatever, has many expenses to sustain, all of which regard the performance of the dramas (without which every interest of the theatre would cease). The first and greatest of these expenses concerns the remuneration of the singers, the pretensions of these men and women having reached excessive levels (where earlier they were happy to perform irrespective of gain, or at most for honest recognition). It is also necessary to pay the composer of the *dramma per musica*. There follow the expenses for the costumes, *mutazioni di scena* and construction of the machines; an agreement must be reached with the *maestro de' balli*, and the various instrumentalists and theatrical hands must be paid on a nightly basis. A further expense regards the lighting of the theatre . . . Sufficient, at the beginning, were two delightful voices with a few arias to bring pleasure and a limited number of *mutazioni di scena* to satisfy the curiosity; today, more attention is paid to a voice that does not live up to expectations than to many of the greatest singers in Europe. Modern practice would require that every scene of the *dramma per musica* was replete with its own *mutazione*, and that the inventiveness of the machines was literally out of this world. These are the reasons for which expenses increase year by year, though prices at the door have actually fallen. The very continuation of opera could well be placed in jeopardy if this current state of affairs is not regulated more carefully.

Chapter XIV: Of the profits enjoyed by those theatres where *drammi per musica* are performed.

In my opinion, three were the principal motivations for the introduction of theatres in the world, corresponding to the same three goals as assigned by rhetoricians: honesty, pleasure and profit. And, indeed, what entertainment can aspire to greater honesty than that which is suggested by Virtue itself? . . . No pleasure, moreover, can be greater than that which is born from the harmonies taught by the very motion of the spheres: these qualities, together with the other particular circumstances of theatrical entertainments, render the latter enjoyable thrice over: pomp and display for the eye, music for the ear, poetry for the intellect . . . Profit, finally, is a necessary means of sustaining the very concept of the theatre (in view of the expenses described in the preceding chapter) and of inspiring the will to virtuous undertakings (for which profit represents an excellent incitement). Profits of various kinds are to be had from the theatre: the first regards the tickets (which allow admission on the evening concerned); the second derives from the leasing of benches (this, too, on a nightly basis); the third regards the agreed contributions for the refreshment stalls. All these profits reach considerable dimensions when the opera meets with success. Success or failure depends on a thousand different factors, mostly originating in a whimsical and ridiculous game of chance which is wont to harmonize well with the judgment of the common people. One final kind of profit derives from the rents of boxes; since the latter are almost one hundred in number, the sum involved is considerable. This profit, regardless of the success or failure of the opera, is always the same; nor, indeed, does it fall short in any year in which there is an opera season. In contrast, the profits to be had by a playhouse consist exclusively of the rents of the boxes. All other profits go to the actors; the theatre proprietor, moreover, is required to present the actors with a gift from the profits of the said boxes.

Chapter XV: The prices, both past (from the beginning) and present, charged at the theatre door.

The expenses incurred by the theatre are more than predictable; the profits, however, depend (as mentioned above) on the whim of fortune and are thus quite unpredictable. Though the theatre is always looking for ways of increasing its expenses, takings at the door (which represent the essential basis of profits) are presently decreasing, with obvious detriment and risk to the continuity of this most notable entertainment. The low price charged at the entrance reduces the means available to meet the considerable cost of the pomp and display, facilitates access on the part of the ignorant and tumultuous masses and lowers the dignity of that very virtue which exists no less for delight than for profit. The year of the introduction of the *dramma in musica* to Venice (an event which occurred in 1637), the cost of the entrance ticket was limited to an honest contribution of 4 *lire*. This practice continued unchanged until 1674, regardless of whatever misfortune might befall the performances; and it would have continued unabated to this day had not Francesco Santurini – on the basis of an advantageous rent negotiated for the use of the Teatro S. Moisè, and further aided by the use of the same scenes and materials which had served in the previous year for an academic entertainment, together with the engagement of a mediocre company of singers – broken with tradition with ¼ ducat [i.e., less than 2 *lire*] at the door. This innovation met with universal approval; thus, tempted by gain, and meeting with opposition in his continued management of the aforesaid Teatro S. Moisè, he, Santurini, with the aid of the initial donation for the boxes, decided to build the new Teatro S. Angelo, which he opened in 1677 with the very same price at the door . . . This drop of over half in the price of the said ticket attracted the crowds, to the detriment of those theatres which customarily charged an admission of 4 *lire*. Thus, in 1679, the celebrated Teatro SS. Giovanni e Paolo reduced the price to the aforesaid ¼ ducat, after forty years of seemly and honest contributions; this example was followed in 1680 by the theatres of S. Salvatore and S. Cassiano, leaving only the Teatro Novissimo at S. Giovanni Grisostomo at the original price. Here, however, the greatest possible magnificence is employed by its proprietors, the brothers Grimani.

Chapter XVIII: If the introduction of theatres in the world be for better or worse.

Were this problem to be posed within the precincts of an Academy, it would certainly provide ample scope for two great minds to argue the *pro* and *contra* . . . It would finally be concluded that the theatre has been of great benefit – and thus would still remain – had the honour and propriety of its origins been preserved without abuse and had genius been strengthened with better sentiment. Yet this problem, in my opinion, is more political than academic, and as such more appropriately to be solved by the ruling authorities than by the author's pen.

7 Dramaturgy of opera: Barthold Feind

Never, in seventeenth-century Italy, is opera the subject of critical reflection: this is as true of the attitudes of men of culture in general as of those actively involved in the life of the stage (the sole exceptions are two Neapolitan writers, the literary scholar Giuseppe Gaetano Salvadori and the comedian and librettist Andrea Perruccio, each of whose treatises – respectively, the *Poetica toscana all'uso* of 1691 and *Dell'arte rappresentativa premeditata ed all'improvviso* of 1699 – dedicate some few lines to the specific requirements of opera). In France, on the contrary, the *grand siècle* of tragedy and comedy is marked – in the operatic sector, too – by the persistent intervention of a shrewd and highly competent theatrical criticism. Almost invariably, however, the criteria adopted are of exclusively literary and strictly classical orientation; the result is a generally negative judgment of a form of entertainment which – in the theatrical life of court and metropolis alike – enjoyed levels of enormous prestige. Similarly, the defenders of opera – charged with transgressing the laws of decorum, probability and the Aristotelian unities of time, place and action – retaliate with what are clearly literary arguments, and thus never truly do justice to the peculiar dramaturgical structure of the *tragédie lyrique* (see chapter 25). The same critical perspective, with all its innate inconsistencies, is subsequently adopted by those Italian intellectuals who, beginning in the years around 1700, add their own contributions to the debate on opera (see chapter 19).

Deprived of any glorious literary tradition such as that of the Italians or French, but compensated by the presence of an ethical and religious preoccupation that was all the more acute, the Germans – for whom Italy had provided the source of this new theatrical and musical genre (see chapter 24), France the surrounding controversy – created a critical tradition conspicuous for its emphasis on problems of a moral, aesthetic and dramaturgical nature. This tradition is strongly present in all eighteenth-century German theatrical and literary criticism (see G. Flaherty, *Opera in the development of German critical thought*,

(Princeton, 1978)). The Hamburg librettist Barthold Feind (1678–1721) gives a sceptical view – both caustic and amused – of the Protestant contentions regarding the moral lawfulness of opera, as also of the classical controversies of the French. On several occasions in his *Gedanken von der Opera* of 1708, he cites and refutes the classical code as set out in the essay *Sur les opéras* of the French intellectual Saint-Evremond (a work which, though published in 1683 and several times reprinted, actually dates to the previous decade). As a man of the theatre, Feind's experience is direct (his, indeed, are the librettos of the most highly acclaimed of the operas of Reinhard Keiser, among them *Masagniello furioso* of 1706); extraordinarily vast, moreover, is his experience as a spectator (the *Gedanken von der Opera* reveals his thorough – and personal – knowledge of the theatres of Italy, France and Germany): all the more pragmatic and disenchanted are thus his precepts of musical drama. First and foremost, Feind speaks from a literary point of view; his interpretation of the doctrine of the affections (see chapter 9) – the mutual importance of temperament, passion and action in the various characters – is, however, tempered by his knowledge of the scenic and histrionic requirements of opera. More important, for Feind, than the canons of the Aristotelian tradition are the theatrical customs of each individual nation. Central, as also for the French classicists, is the question of probability: Feind, however, is aware that this has to do with convention. Theatrical convention – which might almost be described as a kind of tacit agreement between author and spectator, between stage and stalls (see chapter 23) – is dynamic in scope, subject as it is to the effects of 'wear', regeneration, revision and innovation. In this sense, Feind's *Gedanken von der Opera* gives a rare early glimpse and outline of the dramaturgical aspects of opera – the only such outline, indeed, legitimately attributable to the seventeenth-century field of experience.

No-one can accuse me of misanthropy if I say that opera is that unnatural yet splendid deception in which poetry and music (both sung and played) combine to the highest perfection. Everyone, however, will accept that this statement applies only to those operas of particular excellence in terms of their music, poetry, theatre, actors and scenes. In this, each nation boasts its pre-eminence over every other: Italians over French, French over Italians, Germans over French (but not over Italians), French over Germans. The *folie* of the French is second to none as regards the unnatural; the same may be said of the silliness of the Italians in all matters natural and the grotesqueness of the Germans in everything simple: thus, the former arrive at levels of highest perfection through an excess of stupidity and foolishness, while the latter, through weakness, are not at all far behind (though lacking *beaux esprits*). The French, however, have the extenuating circumstance of having been seduced and led astray in their particular weakness for display by the Italians and Germans, in so far as French opera is a much more recent phenomenon than the Italian or German, as is amply demonstrated – as though the matter were not thoroughly known to all and sundry – by the privilege granted by the present King of France to the Académie de musique (as the operatic establishment of Paris is called). To the best of my knowledge, in fact, no opera ever walked the stage in France before 1671; since then, some eighty productions have been given, all based on themes regarding pagan divinities, Greek myths, the bold knights of Amadis, ballets or other inventions, to the greater glory of their monarch: they have a particular *penchant* for the most mournful and plaintive *tragédies*, in which their heroic spirits excel. The *vertu* of the French virtuosi – as far as I have seen or heard – is of such mediocre quality that the difference between ordinary and 'cultivated' singing is barely perceptible; in this, they differ considerably from the Italians and (an albeit limited number of) Germans, in whose hands the art of singing has reached incomparable heights . . .

On the part of many judicious persons, I have heard severe criticism – if not total rejection – of the opera, on account of its continuous use of song. As Saint-Evremond remarks in his *Discours sur les opéras*: 'One other feature of opera is so contrary to nature as to offend my imagination: that is, that the drama is sung from beginning to end, as though the characters represented therein had for some ridiculous reason agreed to discuss the various questions of their lives – greatest and most trivial alike – in music. Is it not quite unthinkable that a master, singing, call his servant and assign him his task; that a friend, singing, confide in another friend; that a council, singing, make decisions; that orders be given in song; that warring soldiers be slain – melodiously – to strokes of the javelin and sword?' It seems to me that any child, on first hearing or reading an opera, would immediately arrive at this conclusion, if one were to persuade him that the matters in question were true and that the poet (through the actors) had attempted to convince his audience of the reality of what was actually fiction. The truth, in plays, is in any case represented through fiction: otherwise, it would surely be no less legitimate to recite in verse than to sing. One simply tries to imitate, to some extent, nature, and whoever wishes to see an example of the totally natural can avail himself of the daily performances – invariably different – on the great stage of the world (and certainly not the notably more limited world of the opera and comedy). A play, so to speak, is nothing but a play of shadows in which things may be clearly observed without contact with body or flesh; and if hundreds of lamps be lit up in the middle of the day and the spectator at the opera remain in darkness, who will undertake to convince him that the actors require him to believe it is night, when the sun is still on the horizon? Artificial waterfalls, fountains, statues, etc. are and continue to be natural objects, even if they have not been inspired by nature herself; never, however, has it been said that our idea of these objects be petrified along with the objects themselves. Operatic recitative of any kind is quite clearly distinguishable from the melody of ordinary arias and songs. The actions of narrating, asking, ordering, reading are all regulated by notes and harmonies which continually change. A semi-colon, full stop, question mark, exclamation mark, comma, colon: each of these has its own rules and inflexions, as different from each other as is fire from water; and when, in the operas of such a fine composer as Reinhard Keiser, a letter is read – or rather, sung – by an actor, one notes what is almost a *tertium quid* between singing and speaking which is proper for every recitative (unless, that is, the said recitative is not to be provided throughout with a fuller accompaniment of the type found in the arias, as at The Hague, where this somewhat eccentric fashion cannot fail to annoy on account of the resulting lack of variety and the continuously deafening throng of the instruments). I am well aware that now and then an 'arioso' or 'obbligato' recitative is composed – provided, however, that this has been versified as 'arioso' by the poet himself or that it expresses a particular affection such as frenzy, or a sudden change of mood, etc. Nor do I believe that anyone can reasonably doubt the assertion that song is capable of imbuing a discourse with ten times more energy than any declamation or simple speech. What, indeed, is song if not a means of sustaining the discourse and voice with maximum energy and force? A sustained discourse, however, is still, for all that, a discourse (albeit recited with a different tone), and by no means unnatural . . . In the poetry of operas, kings, emperors and empresses are heard to address each other informally [i.e., using the informal subject pronoun 'Du'], in exactly the same way as they address their messengers and servants, without poetic distinction between 'Du' and the more polite 'Er', 'Ihr' or 'Sie': though it is quite true that princes, *in vita civili*, refrain from addressing each other informally, in poetry and plays this is normal practice and thus not unnatural. Similarly, everyday conversation eschews versification (no master waxes poetic when ordering his servant to clean his shoes), yet never have I heard any critic of opera complain of this fact. Were opera written in prose, this would no longer be opera, which by very definition is a poem containing a large number of dialogues and set to music in accordance with the requirements of the verse – not *vice versa*, since it is the poet whose verses provide the musician with the opportunity to display his invention and who thus leads the way . . .

Nor, on the other hand, am I convinced that Saint-Evremond is not contradicting himself in recommending a 'revival of the manner of comedies, where dances and other pieces of music might easily be inserted with no detriment whatever to the performance concerned. A Prologue might thus be sung to an agreeable musical accompaniment; in *intermèdes*, song could be used to animate certain words which would thus function as the spirit or allegory of the subject represented. The performance would conclude with a sung epilogue or some other reflection on the excellent qualities on the work concerned, etc.' If, however, both Prologue and Epilogue can be sung without overstepping the bounds of probability, why should this not be extended to cover the play as a whole? The type of dialogue found in the Prologue and Epilogue is identical to that of the play itself: orders are given, discussions take place with regard to the unexpected arrival of some fabled divinity (as, indeed, is attested by the Prologue of every French opera). Had, alternatively, Saint-Evremond intended to reserve for the Prologue some other kind of invention, I would willingly have entertained his example. In any case, the notion that acting while singing is necessarily unnatural implies certain consequences which would have earned Saint-Evremond the severe criticism of his co-religionists in the Papal clergy: how many prayers and other formulas are not sung in church which ought rather to be declaimed? – the practice in question, however, is so ancient as to lack every trace of the unnatural . . .

It is, however, pointless to dwell further on such futile criticism. Much more serious are those defects of opera which regard the subjects, actors, poetry, theatre and machines. In the first place, all reasonably-minded persons will disapprove of the representation of Biblical stories in the theatre and the desecration of the holy on the altar of the most eminent and opulent vanity. No-one can object when I say that, under present-day conditions (in which the practices of Christianity differ notably from those of primitive times), many excellent stories of Biblical derivation could be exploited as top-class material for theatrical productions; this would have the added advantage of removing the sinister figures of the pagan deities and replacing them by angels or (as practised by Dr Postel at Hamburg) tutelary spirits. Truth to tell, however, the choice of an 'indifferent' subject [i.e., one which is neither moral nor immoral] invariably meets with the criticism of some pious soul who is only too willing to take offence (unless, that is, his own faith is not itself 'indifferent' to such a degree that the vivid scenic representation of the *faiblesses* of the *heroes Scripturae* will not cause him annoyance). With this, the reader might well be led to suspect that my aim is that of detracting from the reputation and merits of those who, with the best of intentions, have chosen Biblical themes for their plays. I should like to dispel all such doubt by recourse to the thoroughly respectable opinion of Saint-Evremond: 'Theatre loses every attractiveness in the representation of the sacred, and the latter too loses greatly in religious content through performance on stage.' Saint-Evremond, however, goes further, and asserts that the passage through the Red Sea, the jawbone of Samson's ass, the story of Joshua who commands the sun to stop still in its tracks, etc., represented on stage, would simply not be taken as true: thus, one would quickly reach the point of doubting the very truth of the Bible (though this latter argument seems to me far from convincing).

The Italians, inspired by a love for their country, are mostly attracted by Greek and Roman themes, of which they are superlative masters (as witness, for example, the libretti of the incomparable Matteo Noris). The French, on the contrary, show a particular predilection for the myths of Ovid, as also for stories invented to the glory of their great sovereign; in the latter category of opera, however, greater interest is paid to the quality and distinction of those individuals cast in the role of *personnages dansants* (frequently gentlemen of high birth) than to the subject and character of the material to be represented by the actors – not to mention the unprecedented adulations and allegories with which the French allude to the wondrous deeds of their King (as witness, without exception, their ballets, Prologues, panegyrics, etc.), though their excellent talents for the invention and realization of Prologues (in which, however, the Italians, though not the Germans, also excel) cannot be denied . . . In Hamburg, the public is characterized by a notable aversion to the fabulous myths of the pagan deities; I would, indeed, be unable to cite a single example of this kind which had met with success – convinced, however, as I am that Hamburg can boast not twenty persons with the ability to pass adequate judgment on the delicacy or virtue of an opera, and that frequently, of these twenty persons, not one can be seen at performances. Venice and Paris are endowed with more discerning observers, from which circumstance the poets derive considerable encouragement; they can, indeed, earn up to 400 thalers or, in London, 800 guineas (i.e., over 2,600 Hamburg marks in heavy coin) per libretto, in so far as every second or third performance is given for their benefit (with higher prices at the door).

The subject, then, may be taken from wherever one desires; it will, at all events, be necessary for the characters to be clearly differentiated from each other and carefully studied with regard to their temperament. For example: in presenting a great sovereign and king, the wisest monarch on earth, it will be necessary to take care that he pay no attention to what any jesting errand-boy tells him, founding his judgments upon him (should I so wish, I would have no difficulty in citing some very recent examples). A philosopher, a noble and high-minded person, a man in love, in despair, in frenzy, a suspicious, jealous, faltering or irresolute man, etc.: each must be presented in accordance with his own particular temperament and manner of speech (clearly differentiated from that of the others). This, however, requires enormous ability and skill, in so far as hundreds – indeed, thousands – of possibilities exist, variable in accordance with epoch, nation and traditions . . .

Today, observance of the *spatium XXIV horarum* [i.e., the unity of time] is no longer current: it is not even clear (and many have racked their brains over this question) whether Aristotle, in prescribing the duration of a day, intended the natural twenty-four-hour cycle or the conventional twelve-hour day. In this context, we may cite the celebrated French tragedian Pierre Corneille: 'I myself find it highly inconvenient to confine certain subjects within such a limited space of time. Not only would I grant the full twenty-four hours but also allow myself the liberty (admitted by the philosopher) of exceeding a little; I should, indeed, have no qualms about reaching thirty hours.' After which he goes on to cite examples of how Euripides and Aeschylus fail to comply with the point in question. It is not, however, necessary, to inconvenience the latter: *methodus* is and always will be *arbitraria*, and anyone, if he sees fit, is free to recognize an equally great authority in other men. Truth to tell, in the spoken tragedies described by Aristotle and Corneille, freedom in this respect was wont to be very restricted, and the Romans, Greeks and even modern German authors have closely adhered to these rules: in opera, however, there is a greater reluctance to accept the imposition of such strict regulations. The time-span of my own *Masagniello furioso* is some six to seven days; nor should I be offended were some colleague to allow himself the luxury of half as much again. Certainly, stories lasting seven or eight months or even years, represented in the course of a three-hour production, would constitute a sign of excessive foolishness, improbable to such a degree as even I find improper. If the sun rises on stage, and if after fifteen minutes it reaches its zenith, the full day will last some half an hour; a subject of six days duration will thus be legitimate. In *Masagniello*, in order to avoid the improbability surrounding the departure of Don Pedro from Naples to Venice, and his return to Naples, I resolved to feign that he had never left Naples but had simulated the journey to trick Don Velasco and Aloysia . . . Since, in the opera in question, three different and exceedingly complicated plots are interwoven, it was not easy to unravel them without some degree of deceit – mostly, however, effected through changes of scene. In fact, while unwilling to jump from the apartment of scene 3 to the hall of scene 4 and the gallery of scene 5, I am equally reluctant to introduce three different views in three consecutive scenes until prompted by absolute necessity or in coincidence with some scene of sorcery. In any case, procedures of this kind earn the poet an extremely poor reputation with the stage-hands. The poet must be thoroughly *au fait* with the stage: he must know how many times the wings may be changed in the course of an opera, how many may be withdrawn or made to appear at any given time, and the time required by the stage-hands (in this way, gaps will not occur between consecutive scenes, as frequently happens at Hamburg and Leipzig when new operas are performed). He must also be aware of the scenic and mechanical devices (flying chariots, machines for the deities and for lowering the actors from on high) available in the theatre and the points from which these are suspended, how the floor of the stage has been devised and what can be made to appear from below. In short, it is necessary that the poet be thoroughly acquainted with all the resources of the stage; this will enable him to choose suitable subjects for stage representation. Thus, on the basis of a single subject, he will be required to devise a variety of operas for the theatres of Braunschweig (the most perfect), Hanover (the most beautiful), Hamburg (the largest), Leipzig (the poorest) or Weißenfels.

The best theatre in Europe, the largest and most 'agile' as regards its scenic apparatus, is undoubtedly the incomparable royal court theatre at the Tuileries, Paris: it would be impossible to imagine a more majestic or sumptuous theatre. Architectural credit, however, belongs not to the French but to the genius of the Italian architect Gaspare Vigarani. Of greatest artifice of all, perhaps, is the Teatro [Farnese] of Parma, where a gondola can be taken between amphitheatre and stalls. The longest is the theatre at Fano; Venice can boast the most charming (S. Angelo), the smallest (S. Cassiano) and most precious (S. Marco [= S. Luca?, S. Moisè?]). I have not seen the theatre in Turin, and the Roman theatres have been closed since the last great earthquake. Though the Brussels theatre (erected by the Elector of Bavaria) cannot be compared with the greatest, it is, nevertheless, among the most beautiful; the stalls, moreover, are well laid out and of remarkable height; changes of scene, though less magnificent than at Paris, receive no less attention, and, in compensation, the orchestra is better. The regular Parisian theatre – located at the Palais-Royal – would make a meagre showing in comparison to others were it not for the magnificence of the scene and the painstaking care given to the *mise en scène*; in this way, the mediocrity of the architecture is forgotten: quite astonishing, however, are the choirs, where upwards of thirty young ladies, splendidly attired, are sometimes seen to appear, accompanied by an even larger number of men. Here, sixteen spirits can be seen in combat among the clouds; scene changes are seen to take place in a flash without need to lower the curtain; it is normal to see twelve, sixteen or even twenty dancers who vie with each other. This explains the preponderance of choruses and ballets in the operas produced at this theatre. Here, the amorous exploits and events in the lives of the protagonists are replaced, in each and every scene, by *tendresses* and *douceurs*; thus, these operas are clearly differentiated from their Italian and German counterparts. Highly unnatural, then, are the frequent appearances of divinities and personifications of fountains, trees, hills and rivers, represented as human beings; in order to show off the machines, these deities are dragged down by the feet in each act; the French dramas (or tragedies), whether sung or recited, invariably conclude in such lugubrious fashion that frequently no more than one or two actors remain on the stage (this, in Italy or Germany, would be considered ridiculous). Besides, their operas consist mostly of recitative. The arias, perhaps, will number no more than three or four, and, during their performance, the entire audience (which, apart from the occasional damsel, consists mostly of *abbés*) hums along, with the result that the actress involuntarily ends up in the shoes of the Lutheran cantor who leads the congregation in song; this occasionally seems strange to the Germans and offers a chance for derision (though I don't understand why: when in Rome, do as the Romans do!). Their machines are so hastily lowered from ceiling to stage that one might easily be led to believe that the clouds were cascading from heaven to earth, wars and sieges are treated more as tomfoolery than as serious events, to such a degree that the soldiers (all dressed in princely attire) seem more to resemble magnificent acrobats and tightrope walkers than anything else. Perhaps, indeed, the French are correct to distinguish between real and theatrical wars; in real life, the theatrically absurd often merits approval, and *vice versa*.

The art of arranging the entries and scenes resides chiefly in the ability to link them effortlessly, in such a way that the passage from one to the other is barely perceptible and the spectator does not remain with the impression that the actor leaves the stage for no other reason than that he has nothing else to say. On the contrary, the aforesaid arrangement should ensure that the reasons for the entry and exit of the actor be clear, explicitly (through his express declaration) or tacitly (by means of his behaviour and action). For example: if an uprising occurs, if a character faints or swoons, if a lad is surprised by his father while making love, if two lovers argue, etc., the reason can be found in the action itself. If, however, a single character, or two or three, appear one after the other, and every scene is endowed with some peculiarity of its own, unrelated to whatever comes after or before, the result is confusing and inartistic . . . Sometimes, however, such practices are necessary, in part through the lack of resources of a theatre, in part to gain time: the more so if you have a threefold plot . . . In any case, rules are rules and not laws, and while, indeed, their observance ensures that the poet is not of the worst, it will not *ipso facto* ensure that he be one of the most excellent. While, moreover, the actors are off-stage, the characters will continue to see to their affairs, and it will thus be necessary to take account of these invisible actions when the characters reappear . . .

Act 1 must end in total discord and confusion, and the characters be so thoroughly enveloped in intrigue that neither spectator nor reader can guess the poet's intention. This confusion, moreover, must be maintained not only for the whole of Act 2 but also right up to the very last scene; in this way, the spectator must remain both attentive and alert (naturally, I refer only to those spectators whose aim is to savour the opera itself and not to pass the time in conversation . . .) . . . On the contrary, things will go badly if, at the end of Acts 1 or 2, the reader or spectator is already in a position to predict the poet's design and the outcome of the drama: such a situation arises from the poet's poor application – or downright ignorance – of the rhetorical figures, in so far as a good orator will invariably take the utmost care to hide his figures and his art.

As regards the beginning of the opera, it must be said that it is not at all a bad effect if the curtain go up to reveal a large number of characters on stage, who together sing the opening *coro*; in the final analysis, however, things would appear disagreeable and lean were every single opera to begin in this way and were the spectators thus able to predict, even before the curtain was raised, that ten or twelve actors would be seen to sing through an aria all together . . .

The arias – spirit and soul of the entertainment – function almost as explanatory notes for the recitative and represent whatever is most charming and artistic in the poetry. I have already noted on other occasions that arias differ from recitative not only by virtue of their poetic metre or their bold type [on the page of the libretto] but also – and in particular – by reason of a moral, allegory, aphorism or similitude (enunciated in the first strophe, and with its applications in the ensuing second strophe), which refers to the contents of the preceding recitative, teaches some precept or contains some suggestion or other information. Failing this, the aria must consist of a prayer (tender, however, in expression, and clearly distinct from the expression of the recitative), an outburst of fury or the like. As regards the number of characters by whom it is sung, an aria may be simple, or sung as a duet, trio, quartet – at times, even, a sextet, etc. . . . The aria, as a genre, is subject to no other rule than that Alexandrine verse [i.e., tragic verse, blank verse] should be avoided as much as possible. This will help the singer; similarly, excessive length should be avoided in arias: never more than eight lines. This aside, the poet is perfectly free to write two, three or four *tronco* or *piano* lines in succession, mixing trochaic, Anacreontic, dactylic, anapaestic or any other kind of verse at will, adopting or eschewing the *da capo*, with rhyme throughout or merely in part: no one allows others to lay down the law. It may, however, be noted in the present context that dactylic and Anacreontic verse is well suited for the affections of fury and violence, while joyful affections are most aptly conveyed by flowing and sonorous words with many vowels (above all, *a* and *o*) . . .

Short lines are best for the recitative, [which is thus] rendered more graceful and comely; Alexandrine [i.e., blank] verse is both laborious for the composer and renders the opera tiresomely lengthy . . . In recitative, the distribution of the rhymes is not very important; here, indeed, the Italians excel, in so far as a good half of their recitative is often totally lacking in rhyme. In recitative, however, no-one is more able, gifted and meticulous than the French, who thus make good for all the defects of their arias.

Much would remain to be said on the subject of operatic style. Here, I need only remark that, in the same way as the words must interpret the heart of whoever is speaking and allow his temperament to shine through, the temperament of a character must correspond to his 'nature' and reflect the influence of the passion by which he is moved. The haughty will be boastful and arrogant, the magnanimous generous, a lover tender and charming, an old hand of the world sober and temperate, the historical tale of a messenger extended, etc. These are the essential elements; two or three scenes are sufficient to form an impression of the spirit and taste of a good poet. And since various characters appear in an opera, each different in passion and nature; since, moreover, each character must express his own will and actions in accordance with his nature and the laws of decorum: this is the principal reason why the opera has come to be seen as the highest yet also the most difficult of all poetic genres . . . To understand this, it will be necessary to look at the traditional subjects and themes of the art of poetry . . . If an emperor or monarch appears on stage, it is up to the poet to make sure that he speak sometimes in *plurale majestatis* (as when giving orders), sometimes in the singular (as is more plausible for a declaration of love, since in private council such shows of respect are unnecessary). Declarations of love can be made explicitly, or adorned with strange allusions, hyperboles or enigmas in accordance with the nature and temperament of the characters in question: in general, however, quality increases with tenderness, ornateness and discretion (though such refinements are rarely appreciated by audiences). It is timely, when many characters converge simultaneously on stage, that choruses and *entrées* also be provided, in particular on the occasion of important announcements, triumphs, victories, sacrifices, battles, enchantments, funerals, joyful banquets, etc. The aim of the *entrées de ballet* is that of providing – by means of particular figures and bodily gestures – a theatrical simulation of those actions (good or evil) which form part of normal life: funeral lamentations, the sacrificial ceremonies of the Jews, Orientals or pagans, the behaviour of the master pedants, the guzzling of banquets, etc.

These considerations lead me to speak of mime, or of the clown. Truth to tell, this does not pertain to opera at all, and the theatre is debased by its presence, since it seems that the intention – at every cost! – is that of pushing the public into laughter. This is unseemly and contrary to true enjoyment: if, in fact, something pleases me I do not show derision (if true it be that laughter speaks only disdain) but rejoice. At Hamburg, it is now well-established tradition that no opera be staged without its Harlequin: this is symptomatic of a widespread *mauvais goût* and bad *esprit* on the part of the public. Here, whatever seems vulgar and ridiculous to refined tastes now finds maximum approval – as occurred only last year on the occasion of *Le carnaval de Venise*, an opera of such absurdity and so full of nauseating and scornful gestures as to look like buffoonery. Yet this subject met with such applause as can hardly be believed: even the brewer boys went to spend their money on the opera, from which we may surmise that the Hamburg *Carnaval* was quite different from that staged at Paris in 1699. I have always been explicitly requested to insert a comic part in my operas for the pleasure of the public; I, however, would willingly have left it to the wandering charlatans and street Harlequins, rather than insert them, contrary to nature, in such an honest and civilized entertainment as the opera . . . If the introduction of a comic character proves quite unavoidable, I suggest that this part be assigned to a satirist, who derides the vices of the time.

The remaining actions of the characters are less dictated by the laws of rhetoric than, if anything, by the nature of the passion expressed and by the skill of the virtuosi (in this, the Italians excel). The poet must be thoroughly aware of the particular qualities of each virtuoso and reflect upon which of the characters is most suitable for the singer in question – without which appropriate expression of the desired affection would be impossible. When, indeed, the poet limits himself to simple *déclarations d'amour* or other passions devoid of movement or change, without providing occasion for the actor to flaunt his virtuosity, the result is extremely tedious . . . The affections of greatest effect – which, however, require both a consummate art and experience – are not manifested through speech but revealed more through the heroic behaviour of the characters: more acted, in short, than enunciated. The effect on the spectator is thus tacit and secret, without the intermediary of the words . . . In any case, whenever the affections are lacking so too is the action, and whenever the action is lacking the theatrical effect is like ice. The portrayal of an affection improves in proportion to the naturalness with which the idea of the object or affection to be represented is imagined by the poet and the precision with which he reflects both on the *mouvement d'esprit* required by the said affection and the circumstances in which it occurs (inventing suitable situations where none exists). For this reason, I cannot agree with the French tragedians when – in imitation of the ancient Greeks and Romans – they limit themselves to reporting the most important actions through stories and messages, with the result that the actor's principal action is reduced to nothing but a thoroughly melancholic narration (especially when the subject in question is the death of some character): and in this, as in many other things, they differ notably from the English. To compassionate souls it appears cruel to watch as a character is stabbed on the stage, yet whenever there are capital executions of the most atrocious kind, the streets and squares are full. And what is so cruel if a character (for example, Lucrezia) be seen, on stage, to run herself through and fall into her chair? Perhaps, in such cases, low and vile persons might desire that a river of red blood be seen to gush from the mouth of the victim, colouring the entire stage: such *naturalia* are certainly not stylish in opera and at most are appropriate for the theatres of clowns and marionettes. On the other hand, narration gives not half the idea as conveyed by the direct representation of events (not always, moreover, is one prepared to believe the descriptions of others); in any case, while large numbers of lengthy narrations are appropriate for spoken comedy, never – but never – are they suitable for operas, where not only would the spectator lack patience to hear them sung through to the very last syllable, the singer himself would be hard-pushed to sustain them. In French opera, the conclusion normally involves the death of one or more characters: yet I am quite convinced that the Parisian public is no less delicate in its tastes than the rest of the world. On the other hand, it is quite horrible that a man be hanged on stage, that he be thrust into a burning oven or transformed into a bear or some other monster (that his song become grumbling or roaring): all these things contravene operatic decorum.

I recall having heard that it is unseemly if a character be seen to lie in bed: illicit love affairs, however, are one thing, rest or illness another . . . I am, however, certain that the effect of Lucrezia's death would not have been the same had the action been narrated (and not presented on stage): this, indeed, is the most important action and greatest affection which the episode of Lucrezia – an episode which, deprived of the death of the protagonist, would appear incomplete – presents to the stage. The good poet will never fail to take advantage of such occasions to influence the emotions of his audience. In the fall of Turnus, from the same opera, the spectator is caught in a long-drawn-out suspense between fear, desire and attention. The poet will always obtain the appropriate effect if his representation of the affection is natural: this he can claim to have achieved when the reader or spectator is moved, when the thing in question appears true and provokes sentiments of wrath, terror, hope, fury or pity in the beholder. In poetics, this is known as *divinum quid* . . . According to Sir William Temple, in his treatise *Of poetry*, it frequently happens that many listeners, on hearing the tragedies of the celebrated English tragedian Shakespeare, cry bitterly and shout out at the tops of their voices. At the Comédie of Paris, when Mme Dancourt appears as the protagonist in *Andromaque* [by Racine] or *Médée* [by Corneille], not only are the ladies seen to weep, but also the most gallant and charming of war heroes recently returned from the front . . .

Returning briefly to the sets: the poet will demonstrate poor invention indeed if he limits himself to nothing but the customary woods, gallery, councils, hall, antechamber, garden, street, etc.; these things are to be seen in every opera. Some frequent the opera for the music, others for the scenes, others still for the subjects and dramatic actions, the clowning or costumes: all demand value for money. One theatre can be distinguished from another (and, in particular, from the comedy theatre) by means of the beauty of its sets: here, too, the poet will do well to demonstrate his experience, and will thus need some notion of architecture and mechanics . . . Hamburg is perhaps the theatre which allows the greatest number of changes of scene: the wings, in fact, can be changed thirty-nine times and the back-cloth, perhaps, a hundred times and more. It is, however, a shame that beautiful aquatic scenes or tempests at sea (to take but two examples) cannot be shown in this theatre (where the latter, at least, would appear somewhat ridiculous): these things, in the time of the late Mr Gerhard Schott, founder of the theatre, had positively astonishing effects. The portrayal of a swamp, slaughter-house, furnace or dung-heap is unseemly and would induce the spectators to resort to the use of their handkerchiefs, perfume bottles and snuff-boxes (as though, in reality, their noses were not sufficiently irritated by the smoke from the lamps). Prisons lend themselves well to beautiful scenic effects, but these have now become so common as to occur in almost every opera. The success of the scenes, too, can be measured in proportion to their naturalness; on the contrary, the effect is both miserable and mediocre if the Rialto Bridge is represented as any other, or the Porta Flaminia as the Brocksbrücke of Hamburg. The late Mr Schott took considerable care with the scenes: proof of this may be found in his representations of the Kalkberg of Lüneburg, the Capitol and the Temple of Solomon (which alone cost something like 15,000 thalers). Of great inconvenience is the necessity to bring down the curtain at each and every step in the course of the opera, or to sit through a series of half-successful changes of scene in a badly ordered theatre. Nothing could be more offensive to the spectator, particularly in those scenes in which some magical effect occurs and where it is thus a question of a second: the French and Italians are great masters of such scenes, which are also effected to perfection at the theatre of Braunschweig, though neglected at Hamburg. It is undoubtedly acceptable to choose as the subject for an opera an event which occurs in a single city or palace, but this is not totally regular and by no means necessary. Limitations of this kind would deprive the entertainment of a part of its lustre and reputation; were the poet always so strict, this would divest the opera of many beautiful sets which might otherwise have attracted the spectator for whose very benefit the opera is performed. To be sure, the shrewd poet will avoid all sudden passages from heaven to earth and *vice versa*; nor would it prove any less ridiculous – not even in a comedy like Doctor Faust – were one scene located at Nuremberg and the next at Augsburg.

In Italy and Germany, operas generally conclude with a *coro* in which all or almost all the characters are involved. The aim of this practice is excellent, since it is of great effect and produces a feeling of collective elation which rightly accompanies the spectator as he leaves the theatre. In French opera, conclusions of this kind are not considered essential (which, in themselves, they are not); I myself would not hesitate to do without them, since I consider them banal: every spectator, even without reading the libretto, knows perfectly well that when all the characters reappear on stage, lining up in a crescent shape on the proscenium, this signifies the beginning of the final *coro*. In tragedies, anyway, this usage will never be adopted; poets, if anything, prefer to follow the practice as suggested by the rules of the ancients, disregarding the existence of many of the characters and closing the action with the dismay of two or three principals. The spectator who dislikes such procedures is advised to save himself the price of the ticket and spend his money on the next comedy production . . .

In conclusion, I should like to observe that despite the expense, pomp and display, despite the best of musical scores and the most splendid of sets, an opera will always be boring and tedious if the poetry is poor. Though it is perfectly true that composers can set even the worst of damp squibs, experience shows that they do so without great pleasure and that their imagination is not fired nearly as much by such poetry as it is by a strong affection. It remains only to be noted that opera was invented for performance in well-to-do countries for the amusement of an idle and voluptuous public, but also to exercise the talents of the many artists and connoisseurs, as also to be watched by the innocent eyes of innocent spectators, no more and no less than a firework display, tournament, merry-go-round or any other manifestation of collective mirth and jubilation: as something, in short, not only indifferent from a moral point of view but positively decent and legitimate. Protestations against opera are as vain as they are useless; if such persons as are incompetent in poetry, music and painting will insist on numbering the opera among those follies unworthy of a Christian, this concerns me not: morally speaking, perhaps, our principles differ, and it would thus be necessary for me to enter into a lengthy dispute with the critics in question. Half the world – the most discerning half, I should almost like to add – approves or at least willingly accepts the existence of opera as a thing that neither edifies nor can be described as reprehensible. In the words of the Holy Scripture, the sons of the world are more shrewd in their business than the sons of the light.

Bibliography

In the German and Anglo-Saxon traditions, the history of seventeenth-century music is considered generically as part of the somewhat elastic category of 'baroque music': R. Haas, *Die Musik des Barocks* (Wildpark–Potsdam, 1928); M. F. Bukofzer, *Music in the baroque era from Monteverdi to Bach* (London, 1948); C. V. Palisca, *Baroque music* (Englewood Cliffs, N.J., 1968); W. Braun, *Die Musik des 17. Jahrhunderts* (Wiesbaden, 1981). A competent contribution to the discussion on the artistic 'baroque' – of wide-ranging cultural orientation and sober critical stance – is A. Blunt, *Some uses and misuses of the terms Baroque and Rococo as applied to architecture* (London, 1973).

I. The early decades

Chapters 1 and 2

Fundamental as a tool of research on the madrigal is E. Vogel, A. Einstein, F. Lesure, C. Sartori, *Bibliografia della musica italiana vocale profana pubblicata dal 1500 al 1700* (n.p., 1977); this recent edition, however, has not supplanted the original bibliography: E. Vogel, *Bibliothek der gedruckten weltlichen Vocalmusik Italiens aus den Jahren 1500–1700* (reprint: Hildesheim, 1962). Little discussion of the seventeenth-century madrigal is to be found in the otherwise monumental contribution of A. Einstein, *The Italian madrigal* (Princeton, N.J., 1949); important for an understanding of the theoretical and artistic criteria underlying the seventeenth-century repertory (much more, indeed, than its title suggests) is S. Schmalzriedt, *Heinrich Schütz und andere zeitgenössische Musiker in der Lehre Giovanni Gabrielis. Studien zu ihren Madrigalen* (Neuhausen–Stuttgart, 1972). For the English madrigalists see J. Kerman, *The Elizabethan madrigal. A comparative study* (New York, American Musicological Society, 1962). Most exhaustive of the various literary studies of the madrigal is U. Schulz-Buschhaus, *Das Madrigal. Zur Stilgeschichte der italienischen Lyrik zwischen Renaissance und Barock* (Bad Homburg, 1969). Access to the rich bibliography on Marino may be gained through G. Pozzi's exemplary edition of *Adone* (Milan, 1976). An outline of the history of Italian 'poesia per musica' may be found in L. Bianconi, 'Il Cinquecento e il Seicento', in *Letteratura italiana*, ed. A. Asor Rosa, VI: *Teatro, musica, tradizione dei classici* (Turin, 1986), pp. 319–63.

Chapter 3

For Adriana Basile, Leonora Baroni and the Caccini family, the reader is referred to the relevant entries in *Dizionario biografico degli italiani*; important, too, for Giulio Caccini and his style of singing are the studies of H. W. Hitchcock (see *The Musical Quarterly*, LVI (1970), and the *Journal of the American Musicological Society*, XXVIII (1974)), who has also edited the *Nuove musiche* of 1602 and 1614 (Madison, Wi., 1970 and 1978), and H. M. Brown, 'The geography of Florentine monody', in *Early Music*, IX (1981). On Sigismondo d'India see J. J. Joyce, *The monodies of Sigismondo d'India* (Ann Arbor, Mi., 1981). On the relationship between poetry and music see S. Leopold, 'Chiabrera und die Monodie: die Entwicklung der Arie', in *Studi musicali*, X (1981). The researches of N. Fortune on seventeenth-century vocal monody are summarized in his contribution to *The New Oxford History of Music*, IV, chapter 4 (London, 1968), also interesting by virtue of its comparison with contemporary English monodic practice; for John Dowland, greatest exponent of the English monodic style, see the biography by D. Poulton, *John Dowland* (London, 1982); a useful supplement is contained in vol. X (1977) of the *Journal of the Lute Society of America*, dedicated entirely to the music of Dowland.

Chapters 4 and 7

The standard monograph on Monteverdi: P. Fabbri, *Monteverdi* (Turin, 1985). See also D. Arnold, *Monteverdi* (London, 1963); *The New Monteverdi Companion*, ed. D. Arnold and N. Fortune (London, 1985); *The Letters of Claudio Monteverdi*, ed. D. Stevens (London and New York, 1980); *Claudio Monteverdi. Festschrift Reinhold Hammerstein zum 70. Geburtstag*, ed. L. Finscher (Wiesbaden, 1986); G. Tomlinson, *Monteverdi and the end of the renaissance* (Berkeley and Oxford, 1987). The chapter on Monteverdi in C. Dahlhaus, *Untersuchungen über die Entstehung der harmonischen Tonalität* (Kassel–Basel, 1968), and N. Pirrotta, 'Scelte poetiche di Monteverdi' in *Nuova rivista musicale italiana*, II (1968) (reprinted as 'Monteverdi's poetic choices', in *Music and culture in Italy from the Middle Ages to the Baroque* (Cambridge, Mass., 1984)), still make very profitable reading.

Chapter 5

Still fundamental is the study of R. Romano, 'Tra XVI e XVII secolo. Una crisi economica: 1619–1622', in *Rivista storica italiana*, LXXIV (1962), also available in R. Romano, *L'Europa tra due crisi. XIV e XVII secolo* (Turin, 1980). For the European context, the volume *Crisis in Europe, 1560–1660*, ed. T. Aston (London, 1965) represents the state of research at the time of publication; for a more recent study, see *The general crisis of the seventeenth century*, ed. G. Parker and L. M. Smith (London, 1978). The 'crisis' of the seventeenth century is re-examined in conceptual – and somewhat controversial – terms in T. K. Rabb, *The struggle for stability in early modern Europe* (New York, 1975); J. de Vries, *The economy of Europe in an age of crisis, 1600–1750* (Cambridge, 1976); I. Wallerstein, *Mercantilism and the consolidation of European world economy, 1600–1750* (London, 1980); V. G. Kiernan, *State and Society in Europe, 1550–1650* (Oxford, 1980). Four studies of particular importance for the history of culture in general are those of M. Foucault, *Les mots et les choses* (Paris, 1966), translated as *The order of things* (New York, 1977); P. Rossi, *I filosofi e le macchine (1400–1700)* (Milan, 1976); F. A. Yates, *The Rosicrucian enlightenment* (London, 1972); J. A. Maravall, *La cultura del Barroco. Análisis de una estructura histórica* (Barcelona, 1975).

Chapter 6

For the history of the term 'concerto', see the contribution by E. Reimer (1973) to the *Handwörterbuch der musikalischen Terminologie* (Wiesbaden, 1972ff.); its broader ideological and literary context is examined in chapter 5 of L. Spitzer, *Classical and Christian ideas of world harmony* (Baltimore, Md., 1963). On the origins of the *concerto grosso* see O. Jander, 'Concerto grosso instrumentation in Rome in the 1660s and 1670s', in *Journal of the American Musicological Society*, XXI (1968).

II. Problems of seventeenth-century music

Chapters 8, 9 and 10

On seventeenth-century musical theory, see the report on the round table 'National predilections in seventeenth-century music theory', in *Journal of Music Theory*, XVI (1972); D. P. Walker, *Studies in musical science in the late Renaissance* (London–Leiden, 1978); H. F. Cohen, *Quantifying music. The science of music at the first stage of the scientific revolution, 1580–1650* (Dordrecht–Boston–Lancaster, 1984); the relevant volumes in *Geschichte der Musiktheorie* (Darmstadt, 1984ff.). See also the following monographical studies: C. V. Palisca, 'Marco Scacchi's defense of modern music (1649)', in *Words and music: the scholar's view . . . in honor of A. Tillman Merritt*, ed. L. Berman (Cambridge, Ma., 1972); J. Müller-Blattau, *Die Kompositionslehre Heinrich Schützens in der Fassung seines Schülers Christoph Bernhard*, 2nd edn (Kassel–Basel, 1963), English translation of the treatises of Bernhard in *Music Forum*, III (1973); U. Scharlau, *Athanasius Kircher (1601–1680) als Musikschriftsteller. Ein Beitrag zur Musikanschauung des Barock* (Marburg, 1969); W. Seidel, 'Descartes' Bemerkungen zur musikalischen Zeit', in *Archiv für Musikwissenschaft*, XXVII (1970); M. Dickreiter, *Der Musiktheoretiker Johannes Kepler* (Berne–Munich, 1973). For the texts of Pietro Della Valle and Vincenzo Giustiniani, see A. Solerti, *Le origini del melodramma. Testimonianze dei contemporanei* (Turin, 1903), English translation of Giustiniani by C. MacClintock, *Musicological Studies and Documents*, IX (Rome, 1962).

On the *basso continuo* and its precepts, see F. T. Arnold, *The art of accompaniment from a thorough-bass as practised in the XVIIth and XVIIIth centuries* (Oxford, 1931) and P. Williams, *Figured bass accompaniment* (Edinburgh, 1970). In the absence of any exhaustive studies of seventeenth-century musical instruction, the reader is referred (for the Italian peninsula) to E. Surian, 'L'esordio teatrale del giovane Gasparini. Alcune considerazioni sull'apprendimento e tirocinio musicale nel Seicento', in *Francesco Gasparini (1661–1727). Atti del primo convegno internazionale*, ed. F. Della Seta and F. Piperno (Florence, 1981). See, too, the excellent documentary study of one musical and pedagogical institution in T. D. Culley, *Jesuits and music, I: A study of the musicians connected with the German College in Rome during the seventeenth century and of their activities in Northern Europe* (Rome–St Louis, Mo., 1970).

Chapters 11, 12 and 13

On the use of music for ideological purposes, with particular reference to the truly spectacular example of seventeenth-century France, see the excellent study of R. M. Isherwood, *Music in the service of the king. France in the seventeenth century* (Ithaca, N.Y.–London, 1973). For Italy, see too the fundamental contribution of G. Stefani, *Musica barocca. Poetica e ideologia* (Milan, 1974). For the various national and local institutions, the reader is referred to the relevant articles in *The new Grove dictionary of music and musicians* (London, 1980).

Music publishing still remains a largely uncharted territory. For Italy, see the excellent studies of C. Sartori, *Dizionario degli editori musicali italiani* (Florence, 1958), O. Mischiati, *Indici, cataloghi e avvisi degli editori e librai musicali italiani dal 1591 al 1798* (Florence, 1984), and A. Pompilio, 'Editoria musicale a Napoli e in Italia nel Cinque-Seicento', in *Musica e cultura a Napoli dal XV al XIX secolo*, ed. L. Bianconi and R. Bossa (Florence, 1983); for England, see D. W. Krummel, *English music printing, 1553–1700* (London, 1975).

Rare, too, are studies of the social history of seventeenth-century music. For a panoramic view, see H. Raynor, *A social history of music from the Middle Ages to Beethoven* (London, 1972). For England and France, worthy of mention are D. C. Price, *Patrons and musicians of the English Renaissance* (Cambridge, 1981); M. Benoit, *Versailles et les musiciens du roi. Étude institutionnelle et sociale. 1661–1733* (Paris, 1971) and C. Massip, *La vie des musiciens de Paris au temps de Mazarin (1643–1661). Essai d'étude sociale* (Paris, 1976), both published in the series La vie musicale en France sous les rois Bourbons. For Italy, documentary and 'topographically' limited studies abound (see, in particular, the periodicals *Note d'archivio per la storia musicale*, 1924–1943 (reprint Bologna 1970–71), and again new series, 1983ff. and *Rivista italiana di musicologia* (1966ff.); as yet, however, there are no syntheses of the kind attempted – with worthy results – in F. Haskell, *Patrons and painters. A study in the relations between Italian art and society in the age of the Baroque* (London, 1963).

Chapter 14

Fundamental for the study of Italian instrumental music is C. Sartori, *Bibliografia della musica strumentale italiana stampata in Italia fino al 1700* (Florence, 2 vols., 1952, 1968). For keyboard music, see the series Corpus of Early Keyboard Music (American Institute of Musicology, 1963ff.), itself promoted by the author of a monumental study of the repertory, W. A. Apel, *The history of keyboard music to 1700* (Bloomington, In., 1972). Apel is also responsible for a parallel series of 'Studien über die frühe Violinmusik', in *Archiv für Musikwissenschaft*, XXX–XXXVIII (1973–81). On Frescobaldi, see the introductory comments on the various volumes of the critical edition undertaken by the Società italiana di musicologia, published in the series Monumenti musicali italiani (Milan, 1975ff.); see, too, the excellent monograph of F. Hammond, *Girolamo Frescobaldi* (Cambridge, Ma. – London, 1983). For the north European keyboard repertory, see A. Curtis, *Sweelinck's keyboard music. A study of English elements in seventeenth-century Dutch composition* (London, 1972); most stimulating of all Sweelinck studies, however, is that of F. Noske, 'Forma formans', in *International Review of the Aesthetics and Sociology of Music*, VII (1976). For instrumental ensemble music, see the general study of W. S. Newman, *The sonata in the Baroque era* (Chapel Hill, N.C., 1959, 1966²) and (with particular reference to Venice) E. Selfridge-Field, *Venetian instrumental music from Gabrieli to Vivaldi* (Oxford, 1975).

Dance music is discussed in the relevant articles of *The new Grove dictionary*; see, too, such miscellaneous studies as T. Walker, 'Ciaccona and passacaglia: remarks on their origins and early history', in *Journal of the American Musicological Society*, XXI (1968), W. Kirkendale, *L'Aria di Fiorenza id est il Ballo del Gran Duca* (Florence, 1972) and R. Hudson, *The Allemande, the Balletto, and the Tanz* (Cambridge, 1986).

III. Sacred and vocal music

Chapters 15 and 16

Die Geschichte der katholischen Kirchenmusik, II, ed. K. G. Fellerer (Kassel–Basel, 1976), is less promising than its title might suggest. Excellent is G. Stefani, *Musica e religione nell'Italia barocca* (Palermo, 1975). See also J. Roche, *North Italian church music in the age of Monteverdi* (Oxford, 1984). A selection of the works of Grandi is available in the dissertation of M. Seelkopf, 'Das geistliche Schaffen von Alessandro Grandi' (Würzburg, 1973). For the use of instrumental music in the liturgy, see S. Bonta, 'The uses of the sonata da chiesa', in *Journal of the American Musicological Society*, XXII (1969). For a summary of ecclesiastical legislation on sacred music, see F. Romita, *Ius musicae liturgicae. Dissertatio historico-juridica* (Turin, 1936) and R. F. Hayburn, *Papal legislation on sacred music, 95 A.D. to 1977 A.D.* (Collegeville, Minnesota, 1979). On French sacred music, see the relevant chapters of J. R. Anthony's excellent *French Baroque music from Beaujoyeulx to Rameau* (London, 1973, 1978²); for a discussion of organ music, see G. Morche, *Muster und Nachahmung. Eine Untersuchung der klassischen französischen Orgelmusik* (Berne–Munich, 1979).

For an up-to-date history of the oratorio (Protestant and Catholic, Italian and in Europe as a whole), see the two-volume contribution of H. E. Smither, *A history of the oratorio. The oratorio in the Baroque era* (Chapel Hill, N.C., 1977); supplementary material appears in recent studies of the oratorio at such centres as Bologna, Florence, Perugia: see C. Vitali (in *Rivista italiana di musicologia*, XIV, 1979), J. W. Hill (in *Acta musicologica*, LI, 1979 and LVIII, 1986), B. Brumana (in *Esercizi. Arte, musica, spettacolo*, III, 1980), as well as D. and E. Arnold, *The oratorio in Venice* (London, 1986). A monograph on one of the protagonists of Latin oratorio: G. Dixon, *Carissimi* (Oxford, 1986). A large anthology of historically relevant works is now available: *Oratorios of the Italian baroque*, ed. H. E. Smither (Laaber, 1985ff.).

Chapters 17 and 18

Fundamental is the *Geschichte der evangelischen Kirchenmusik*, ed. F. Blume (Kassel–Basel, 1965), English translation as *Protestant church music. A history* (London, 1975), with an excellent addition on Anglican church music by

H. Watkins Shaw. Of the few monographical studies of Henry Purcell, most important are J. A. Westrup, *Purcell* (7th edn, London, 1975) and F. B. Zimmermann, *Henry Purcell, 1659–1695. His life and time* (London, 1967), as well as the same author's *Henry Purcell 1659–1695: an analytical catalogue of his music* (New York, 1963). Schütz, on the contrary, is the subject of a rich bibliography, accessible through A. B. Skei, *Heinrich Schütz: a guide to research* (New York, 1981). A critical revision of our image of Schütz is now given in J. Rifkin's entry in *The new Grove dictionary*; still fundamental, however, are the monographs of H. J. Moser, *Heinrich Schütz. Sein Leben und Werk* (Kassel, 1936), English translation as *Heinrich Schütz. His life and work* (St Louis, Mo., 1959), and H. H. Eggebrecht, *Heinrich Schütz. Musicus poeticus* (Göttingen, 1959). For the letters and other writings of Schütz, see the *Gesammelte Briefe und Schriften*, ed. E. H. Müller (Regensburg, 1931). On the so-called 'musical rhetoric' (codified, above all, in the treatises of Bernhard: cf. Müller-Blattau, *Die Kompositionslehre Heinrich Schützens*, see the relevant contribution in *The new Grove dictionary*, and C. Dahlhaus, 'Die figurae superficiales in den Traktaten Christoph Bernhards', in *Bericht über den internationalen musikwissenschaftlichen Kongress Bamberg 1953* (Kassel–Basel, 1954).

IV. Opera

Chapters 19 and 20

For the history of Italian opera, from its beginnings onwards, see *Storia dell'opera italiana*, ed. L. Bianconi and G. Pestelli (Turin, 1987ff.). The texts of the Florentine *favole pastorali* can be found in A. Solerti, *Gli albori del melodramma*, 3 vols. (Milan, 1904). A selection of seventeenth-century librettos appears in A. Della Corte, *Drammi per musica dal Rinuccini allo Zeno*, 2 vols. (Turin, 1958). The series Italian Opera 1640–1770, ed. H. M. Brown (New York, 1977ff.), contains the facsimiles of twenty-four seventeenth-century scores (with librettos), the series Drammaturgia musicale veneta, ed. G. Morelli, R. Strohm, T. Walker (Milan, 1983ff.), another nine. For the early seventeenth-century theoretical texts, see Solerti, *Le origini del melodramma*; more in general, see the recently published collection of Italian, French and German documentary sources on opera, covering the entire seventeenth century: *Quellentexte zur Konzeption der europäischen Oper im 17. Jahrhundert*, ed. H. Becker (Kassel, 1981). One important theoretical work on the writing and staging of early *favole pastorali* and the like has been published since: *Il Corago o vero Alcune osservazioni per metter bene in scena le composizioni drammatiche*, ed. P. Fabbri and A. Pompilio (Florence, 1983). Late seventeenth-century documentary sources are examined in R. Freeman, 'Apostolo Zeno's reform of the libretto', in *Journal of the American Musicological Society*, XXI (1968) and in his *Opera without drama. Currents of change in Italian opera, 1675–1725* (Ann Arbor, Mi., 1981). For a brilliant exposition of the aesthetic and artistic problems surrounding the origins of opera, see chapter 6 of N. Pirrotta, *Li due Orfei. Da Poliziano a Monteverdi* (Turin, 1975), translated as *Music and theatre from Poliziano to Monteverdi* (Cambridge, 1982), as well as the articles on early opera in Pirrotta, *Music and culture in Italy from the Middle Ages to the Baroque*.

Particularly prominent among the many studies of seventeenth-century set-design are those of P. Bjurström, *Giacomo Torelli and Baroque stage design* (Stockholm, 1962); C. Molinari, *Le nozze degli dèi. Un saggio sul grande spettacolo italiano nel Seicento* (Rome, 1968); *Illusione e pratica teatrale. Proposte per una lettura dello spazio scenico dagli intermedi fiorentini all'opera comica veneziana*, exhibition catalogue ed. F. Mancini, M. T. Muraro and E. Povoledo (Vicenza, 1975). On the contrary, there exists no satisfactory general study of the musical aspects of Italian opera during the first half of the seventeenth century: available literature includes the articles reprinted in *The Garland library of the history of Western music*, vol. XI (New York–London, 1985); R. Donington, *The rise of opera* (London–Boston, 1981); the unavoidably summary indications of the article 'Opera' in *The new Grove dictionary*, and such specific studies as S. Leopold, '"Quelle bazzicature, poetiche, appellate ariette". Dichtungsformen in der frühen italienischen Oper (1600–1660)', in *Hamburger Jahrbuch für Musikwissenschaft*, III (1978). On the Barberini–Rospigliosi operas, see M. Murata, *Operas for the Papal court 1631–1668* (Ann Arbor, 1981); for other Roman theatrical productions with music, the same author's article in *Early Music History*, IV (1984).

Chapters 21, 22 and 23

The studies of S. T. Worsthorne, *Venetian opera in the seventeenth century* (Oxford, 1954) and N. Mangini, *I teatri di Venezia* (Milan, 1974) are usefully supplemented by the interesting (though strongly ideological) ideas in the Venetian chapter of L. Zorzi's *Il teatro e la città. Saggi sulla scena italiana* (Turin, 1977) and the interdisciplinary studies of *Venezia e il melodramma nel Seicento*, ed. M. T. Muraro (Florence, 1976). Impresarial models and productive 'conditioning' are discussed in L. Bianconi and T. Walker, 'Production, consumption and political function of seventeenth-century opera', in *Early Music History*, IV (1984); for a summary of the same enquiry, together with the report on a round table (co-ordinated by P. Petrobelli) on *Seventeenth-century music drama* (which examines the question on a European scale), see the *Report of the twelfth congress, Berkeley 1977* (Kassel, 1981). More strictly musical in scope are a number of excellent monographs on important Venetian musicians: see, in particular, W. Osthoff, *Das dramatische Spätwerk Claudio Monteverdis* (Tutzing, 1960), and E. Rosand, 'Seneca and the interpretation of "L'incoronazione di Poppea"', in *Journal of the American Musicological Society*, XXXVIII (1985); J. Glover, *Cavalli* (London, 1978); E. Rosand, 'Barbara Strozzi, virtuosissima cantatrice: the composer's voice', in *Journal of the American Musicological Society*, XXXI (1978).

On the diffusion of Venetian opera in Italy, see L. Bianconi and T. Walker, 'Dalla "Finta pazza" alla "Veremonda": storie di Febiarmonici', in *Rivista italiana di musicologia*, X (1975) (English translation in *Drammaturgia musicale veneta*, vol. I). Of the rich bibliography on the local institution and development of operatic theatres in the various cities of the Italian peninsula, a few recent studies may be mentioned: P. Bjurström, *Feast and theatre in Queen Christina's Rome* (Stockholm, 1966); R. L. Weaver and N. W. Weaver, *A chronology of music in the Florentine theater, 1590–1750* (Detroit, Mi., 1978); L. Bianconi, 'Funktionen des Operntheaters in Neapel bis 1700 und die Rolle Alessandro Scarlattis', in *Colloquium Alessandro Scarlatti, Würzburg 1975*, ed.

W. Osthoff and J. Ruile-Dronke (Tutzing, 1979) (reprinted in *The Garland library*). For two of the ever-increasing numbers of studies of the fortunes of individual *drammi per musica* in the various theatres of Italy, see C. B. Schmidt, 'Antonio Cesti's "La Dori": A study of sources, performance traditions and musical style', in *Rivista Italiana di Musicologia*, X (1975), and L. Lindgren, 'I trionfi di Camilla', in *Studi musicali*, VI (1977).

On the chamber and operatic laments, see M. Murata, 'The recitative soliloquy', in *Journal of the American Musicological Society*, XXXII (1979) and E. Rosand, 'The descending tetrachord: an emblem of lament', in *The Musical Quarterly*, LXV (1979). The cantata repertory (prevalently Roman) is closely examined in *The Wellesley edition cantata index series*, ed. O. Jander *et al.* (Wellesley, Ma., 1964ff.); for a summary investigation, see G. Rose, 'The Italian cantata of the Baroque period', in *Gattungen der Musik in Einzeldarstellungen. Gedenkschrift Leo Schrade*, I (Berne–Munich, 1973). A series of facsimiles is published by Garland Publishing: *The Italian Cantata in the Seventeenth Century*, vols. 1–16 (New York).

Chapters 24, 25, 26

R. Strohm's chapter in *Storia dell'opera italiana*, vol. I, outlines the dissemination of Italian opera in late seventeenth-century Europe; see also his 'Italienische Barockoper in Deutschland: Eine Forschungsaufgabe', in *Festschrift Martin Ruhnke zum 65. Geburtstag* (Stuttgart–Neuhausen, 1985). For an introduction to the copious bibliography on opera in German-seaking lands, see R. Brockpähler, *Handbuch zur Geschichte der Barockoper in Deutschland* (Emsdetten, 1964). On opera at the Viennese court, see F. Hadamowsky, 'Barocktheater am Wiener Kaiserhof', in *Jahrbuch der Gesellschaft für Wiener Theaterforschung 1951/52* (Vienna, 1955); M. Dietrich, *Goldene Vlies-Opern der Barockzeit. Ihre politische Bedeutung und ihr Publikum* (Vienna, 1975); H. Seifert, *Die Oper am Wiener Kaiserhof im 17. Jahrhundert* (Tutzing, 1985). For opera in Hamburg, see the general study of H. C. Wolff, *Die Barockoper in Hamburg (1678–1738)*, 2 vols. (Wolfenbüttel, 1957); see also, in particular, vols. III (1978) and V (1980) of the *Hamburger Jahrbuch für Musikwissenschaft* and K. Zelm, *Die Opern Reinhard Keisers* (Munich–Salzburg, 1975).

On French opera in general, see the relevant chapters of the abovementioned studies by R. M. Isherwood and J. R. Anthony. For specialized investigations, see H. Prunières, *L'opéra italien en France avant Lulli* (Paris, 1913); C. Girdlestone, *La tragédie en musique (1673–1750) considérée comme genre littéraire* (Geneva–Paris, 1972); L. Newman, *Jean-Baptiste Lully and his tragédies lyriques* (Ann Arbor, Mi., 1979) as well as the two Lullian contributions by H. Schneider, *Chronologisch-thematisches Verzeichnis sämtlicher Werke von Jean-Baptiste Lully* (Tutzing, 1981) and *Die Rezeption der Opern Lullys im Frankreich des Ancien régime* (Tutzing, 1982). On the stylistic conflict between Italy and France, see G. Morche, 'Corelli und Lully. Über den Nationalstil', in *Nuovi studi corelliani*, ed. G. Giachin (Florence, 1978).

For theatrical music in England, the Purcell bibliography cited above is now supplemented by C. A. Price, *Henry Purcell and the London stage* (Cambridge, 1984). Other studies are *La musique de scène de la troupe de Shakespeare*, ed. J. P. Cutts (Paris, 1959); the fundamental E. J. Dent, *Foundations of English opera. A study of musical drama in England during the seventeenth century* (Cambridge, 1928); and two recent studies on Restoration theatre: E. Haun, *But hark! more harmony. The libretti of Restoration opera in English* (Ypsilanti, Mi., 1971) and C. A. Price, *Music in the Restoration theatre: with a catalogue of instrumental music in the plays 1665–1713* (Ann Arbor, Mi., 1979).

Particularly noteworthy among the vast but scattered literature on Spanish theatrical music are the modern editions (illuminating as critical and documentary studies and rich in bibliographical references) of J. Vélez de Guevara, *Los celos hacen estrellas*, ed. J. E. Varey, N. D. Shergold and J. Sage (London, 1970), and of P. Calderón de la Barca, *La estatua de Prometeo*, ed. M. Rich Greer and L. K. Stein (Kassel, 1986).

Index